D0212686

Divorce Reform at the Crossroads

About the Authors

David L. Chambers is professor of law at the University of Michigan.

Marsha Garrison is professor of law at Brooklyn Law School.

Herma Hill Kay is the Richard W. Jennings Professor of Law at the University of California, Berkeley.

Harry D. Krause is the Max L. Rowe Professor of Law at the University of Illinois at Urbana-Champaign.

Martha Minow is professor of law at Harvard University.

Robert H. Mnookin is the Adelbert H. Sweet Professor of Law at Stanford University.

Deborah L. Rhode is professor of law at Stanford University and director of the Institute for Research on Women and Gender.

Stephen D. Sugarman is professor of law at the University of California, Berkeley, and director of the Program in Family Law of the Earl Warren Legal Institute.

Franklin E. Zimring is professor of law at the University of California, Berkeley, and director of the Earl Warren Legal Institute.

Divorce

Reform

at the Crossroads

STEPHEN D. SUGARMAN

HERMA HILL KAY, Editors

With a Foreword by Franklin E. Zimring

Yale University Press   New Haven and London

Published with assistance from the
Louis Stern Memorial Fund.

Copyright © 1990 by Yale University.
All rights reserved.
This book may not be reproduced, in whole or in
part, including illustrations, in any form
(beyond that copying permitted by Sections 107
and 108 of the U.S. Copyright Law and except by
reviewers for the public press), without written
permission from the publishers.

Designed by Sonia L. Scanlon
Set in Galliard type by
The Composing Room of Michigan, Inc.
Printed in the United States of America by
Vail-Ballou Press, Binghamton, New York.

Library of Congress Cataloging-in-Publication
Data

Divorce reform at the crossroads / edited by
    Stephen D. Sugarman and Herma Hill Kay ;
    with a foreword by Franklin E. Zimring.
        p.   cm.
    Includes bibliographical references and index.
    ISBN 0-300-04831-9 (alk. paper)
    1. Divorce—Law and legislation—United
States. I. Sugarman, Stephen D. II. Kay,
Herma Hill.
KF535.A2D54   1991
346.7301'66—dc20
[347.306166]   90-33950
                    CIP

The paper in this book meets the guidelines for
permanence and durability of the Committee on
Production Guidelines for Book Longevity of the
Council on Library Resources.

10   9   8   7   6   5   4   3   2   1

Contents

Foreword

The class on domestic relations is the premier "consumer course" in the law schools of the United States. The divorce courts will be the most significant contact that many of our students will have with the legal system—but not as advocates. Since divorce rates run close to 50 percent in most states, there is about that chance that an aspiring attorney will someday be a party to divorce. When it occurs, divorce is a high-impact experience: its economic effects are more substantial than those of any other legal event in the life of the average citizen, and child custody matters are of surpassing importance to the adult litigants and their children.

The significance of divorce in the lives of individuals sums up to aggregate social impacts of substantial proportions. More property is held within the institution of marriage in the United States than by all forms of corporations. The millions of children subject to postdivorce custody orders in this nation constitute a significant fraction of the American future.

Thus, no area of state law is more important than the rules surrounding marriage and divorce, and no area of law in the United States has changed more rapidly. What has been called the no-fault revolution in divorce law and practice was launched in California in the late 1960s after several decades of pressure for change. Nationally, the shift from fault grounds to no-fault as a basis for divorce happened quickly. Within five years after the California law went into effect, most states adopted at least one no-fault ground, and no other regime had articulate defense in legislative halls or in the academy. The transition from reform proposal to statutory orthodoxy was shorter for no-fault divorce than for any of the other law reform proposals of its era.

From the standard of legislative acceptance, the no-fault reforms were a brilliant success. Whether these changes have also operated to the benefit of the individuals and families at risk of divorce is a separate question. Twenty years after the advent of no-fault, a chronically high rate of divorce is connected to precarious economic status for many women and children. The phrase "feminization of poverty" entered the American language in the 1980s, and there is widespread suspicion that the changes in divorce law either have placed the interests of women and children in jeopardy or have failed to provide safeguards that domestic relations law can and should establish.

Changes in the grounds for divorce were only one part of the legal experiment of the past two decades. Child custody law underwent multiple changes, and child support law became subject to the dramatic intervention of the federal government. Traditional legal norms governing property distribution and spousal support obligations on divorce were overturned. Even stepparents, long outside the law's view, have begun, here and there, to be recognized.

These experiments in legal change have not so far been accompanied by sufficient attention to the evaluation of reforms. Empirical studies of the impact of the shift from fault to no-fault divorce regimes have been rare events, with Lenore Weitzman's work for many years standing alone. In the area of child custody, California pioneered in the legal recognition and encouragement of joint custody in 1980 and then shifted back somewhat in 1988. Both generations of change took place with no public commitment or private initiative for the systematic assessment of the legal changes on patterns of custody or on child welfare. As fashions change and new interest groups emerge, family law is at risk of becoming a series of experiments that never report results in ways that can help inform the legislative process.

This book reexamines the impact of new directions in the law of domestic relations. The scholars who contribute to the venture are among the small group in academic American law who have been documenting and questioning the recent changes in family law. The empirical studies reported here are among the very few conducted in what should become a growth area of American legal studies.

The conference on divorce at the University of California at Berkeley that led to this volume was sponsored by the Program in Family Law and Policy Studies of the Earl Warren Legal Institute at Boalt Hall and the Institute for the Study of Women and Gender at Stanford University. This volume is the first book-length product of the Program in Family Law, currently under the direction of Stephen Sugarman. The program was established to conduct and encourage research on the effects of law on families and children. Reflecting the value of cooperative scholarly attention to the problems of family law, this volume also shows that significant problems in the field demand further scrutiny.

Franklin E. Zimring

Introduction

STEPHEN D. SUGARMAN

Divorce is an especially critical issue today. Divorce rates have climbed so rapidly that half of all marriages and the children of them will be touched directly. This means more families being supported by single parents, more child custody arrangements to be worked out, more remarriages and stepparent interests to be concerned about, more children who spend a portion of their youth living apart from their biologic parents, and so on. For all too many Americans, primarily women and children, divorce means being plunged into poverty.

This is a book about divorce law and policy written by legal scholars. Several chapters describe and appraise two decades of change in various aspects of domestic relations law. Several others feature divorce law's impact, both reporting for the first time the results of large-scale empirical studies and reassessing the past work of others. Some of the chapters are centrally about future reform—what divorce law should become or is likely to become.

Broadly speaking, the book has two themes: what has happened so far since the no-fault divorce revolution began in the 1960s, and how future reforms should be shaped. In general, the first four chapters are about the last twenty years, and the last three are about the next twenty. Chapter 1 tells the history of divorce reform from the 1960s to the present, including very recent legislative responses to several of no-fault's critics. Chapters 2 and 3 introduce new findings on child custody arrangements and the economic outcomes of divorce. Chapter 4 sets the barely begun legal recognition of stepparents in the context of our equivocal feelings about the roles stepparents should and do play. Chapters 5 and 6 explore the financial obligations that former spouses ought to have toward each other and that noncustodial parents ought to have toward their children. Chapter 7 completes the volume by providing feminist perspectives on several of the topics explored earlier.

Although many who write about divorce appear to have a certain type of couple in mind, it is important to emphasize at the outset the diversity among divorcing couples. Although a majority of divorces involve minor children, two in five do not. Even though many long-married couples di-

1

vorce, a majority of marriages that end do so before the couple's fifth wedding anniversary. Although most divorced spouses will remarry in fewer than five years, a significant minority will never remarry. And, of course, divorce occurs in all social classes and ethnic groups. These facts mean that there is no stereotypical couple (if there ever was) around which one can structure marriage, divorce, and remarriage policy. The law must serve this diversity of families with different needs.

Just as divorcing couples vary, so does no-fault divorce law. As Herma Hill Kay explains in chapter 1, although the broad concept of divorce without fault has now been accepted throughout America, the national norm does not reflect the pioneering California regime, where unilateral divorce is available without delay. Many states require a considerable waiting period if only one party proposes a no-fault divorce, and in a few states including New York, no-fault divorce is available only by mutual consent.

Some lament the shift to no-fault divorce. They find it worrisome that in such a short time society so fully abandoned a regime under which, formally at least, the state carefully regulated when divorce would be permitted. Moreover, most states have skipped over, as it were, the idea of divorce by mutual consent to embrace unilateral divorce. Watching no-fault in operation, these critics bristle when they see that spouses can end their marriage without taking into account the interests of the children and that a guilty spouse can so readily sever marital ties from an objecting and innocent one.

Whatever sympathy there may be for this viewpoint, talk of reregulating divorce is virtually absent from the current discourse about reform. One reason is that in these times of moral uncertainty, where traditional religious values no longer dominate public policy concerning the family, there can be no easy agreement on which divorces we should to try to curb. Indeed, there is considerable sentiment for the proposition that only the spouses themselves can know the answer. Another reason society is likely to continue to delegate the decision to terminate a marriage to the realm of private ordering is that, as a practical matter, there is no very good policy alternative. The fault principle worked badly in practice. Simply giving one party a veto creates undesirable incentives and does not help when both parents put their own interests way above their children's. Nor does it seem promising to provide the children with an ombudsman or separate advocate who could block the divorce. The couple might then just live apart. Besides, how is an outsider to determine the best interests of a young child other than by imposing on the family the ombudsman's own values? There-

fore, the authors here assume that for the foreseeable future, states will neither require the moving party to demonstrate socially condemned behavior
by the other nor stop divorces in the name of the best interest of children.

In describing and assessing the no-fault divorce revolution, commentators accent different contexts. In the previous paragraphs the focus has
been on the grounds for divorce. But many take the no-fault regime to include as well the rules governing property division, spousal support, child
support, and child custody—those key issues that must be settled between
the parties beyond the bare fact of the divorce itself. Indeed, these are the
areas in which most no-fault critics have sought change and where, following the initial wave of no-fault enactments, most legislative action has centered. Even more broadly, discussion of no-fault comprehends not merely
the formal law and its changes but also the judicial application and enforcement of the divorce regime. Most widely, some look at no-fault as part of
the general environment in which the new system is functioning. That environment can include, for example, the roles of men and women in the labor force and in home life, the place of stepparents and biologic parents
after second marriages, and the public commitment to the financial well-
being of those involved in divorce. The chapters that follow attack the subject with a range of wide-angle and telephoto lenses.

Some writers and many state legislatures endorse the view that, whereas
it is right to remove fault as a ground for divorce, fault should remain a factor in the allocation of rights and responsibilities of individual couples
concerning both their financial matters and the custody of their minor children. One of the key actors in California's initial adoption of no-fault, Herma Hill Kay, challenges that view here, arguing instead that states nationwide should remove fault considerations altogether from the divorce process.

Many have charged that no-fault divorce has harmed women. It is
important to distinguish among different meanings of this claim. Some
have contended that women are worse off under no-fault than they were
under the fault system. But no-fault might be harmful to women in another
sense—one that is indifferent to women's treatment in the past. Rather,
women may fare badly as compared with some other standard—for example, as compared with how men fare or as compared with how women
should be treated. Still another perspective is that though women have always been shortchanged by divorce, the problem is more acute now that
the divorce rate is so much higher.

The chapters that follow examine these issues in a variety of ways. They present contrasting interpretations of how no-fault has functioned so far and several images of how it ought to function in the future. In addition to examining the consequences of no-fault, including its perhaps unintended consequences, this book addresses matters that the original no-fault reformers did not consider.

Has no-fault divorce undermined the ability of women to obtain physical custody of their children? Robert Mnookin's new findings on child custody desires, requests, and outcomes in California, reported and discussed in chapter 2, suggest that in most cases it has not. Nor does he find a large incidence of strategic bargaining whereby a divorcing spouse asks for more custody than he or she actually wants in order to obtain some other advantage in the settlement.

Have divorcing women suffered financially because they have lost bargaining power as a result of the shift in the grounds of divorce from fault to no-fault? Combining the results of her new New York study, reported in chapter 3, with the findings of earlier studies, Marsha Garrison concludes that, overall, they have not.

Do divorced women obtain significantly less property and spousal support under the no-fault regime than before? Reassessing the data presented in the most prominent study in the field, Lenore Weitzman's *The Divorce Revolution,* I argue in chapter 5 that they do not.

Yet all the authors here who address the issue agree that a large proportion of divorced women, especially those with young children, face very serious financial problems and a reduced standard of living. Hence, regardless of the role that the adoption of no-fault may have played, this plight ought to be a matter of high priority for future reform. What should be done?

A large proportion of women now deals with this predicament by remarrying fairly soon after divorce, although many do not. Some may be effectively pushed into a new marriage they might otherwise not wish to make. Other women seek to increase their earnings in the paid labor force. This may be difficult, given inadequate child-care facilities. In any event, many simply do not have this option. They are already working up to their earning capacity and have no real prospects of making more money, either because of discrimination in the marketplace or because of the limited skills they possess, having previously devoted themselves to homemaking. Some newly divorced mothers are forced actually to reduce their earnings once they become single parents because their former husbands are no longer available to shoulder some of the child-rearing and home-care duties.

Should society make divorced fathers pay more, and if so, on what basis? These are complicated and controversial questions about which the authors here have differing views. A longtime advocate of effective child support enforcement, Harry Krause, discusses in chapter 6 America's increased success in this direction. But he cautions that trying to meet the financial needs of children of divorce only from the wallets of their noncustodial fathers may be a wrong approach, arguing that many of them cannot meet, or in fairness cannot be expected to meet, the obligations being imposed on them. In chapter 5, I examine a wide range of grounds on which increased spousal support might be based, rejecting several theories that various writers have proposed and providing support for some others. Herma Hill Kay, in chapter 1, offers a program for a "nonpunitive, nonsexist, and nonpaternalistic" regime of financial rights and obligations of the parties. And what should be the role of stepfathers? Their highly ambiguous status is explored by David Chambers in chapter 4, where the law's traditional rejection of any special rights or obligations of stepparents is described and evaluated.

Should society better support the needs of divorced spouses and their children? Several authors here say it should. Deborah Rhode and Martha Minow argue in chapter 7 that society ought to stop trying to treat divorce as a private matter and accept public responsibility for its consequences. Since public policies have contributed importantly to gender inequality, reform, they argue, must extend well beyond domestic relations law. What exactly society should do differently is more controversial. Rhode and Minow offer a vision in which further divorce reform is but a part of a broader transformation of society and the roles of men and women. Kay concurs in this vision, but other authors here have less sweeping outlooks.

The reader will find some tension among the authors—for example, on subjects such as whether (and if so, how) wives who made economic sacrifices for their husbands should be compensated upon divorce, and whether (and if so, how) new family connections made by former spouses should influence their ongoing postdivorce financial obligations to each other.

All agree, however, that divorce reform is now at an important crossroads. This volume seeks to cast light on the various paths that future reform might follow.

1

Beyond No-Fault

New Directions in Divorce Reform

HERMA HILL KAY

> Discussion of divorce has too often started from the
> premise that divorce was an evil in itself, as if it was
> *divorce* that mattered. Whereas what matters is wedlock.
> —Karl N. Llewellyn, "Behind the Law of Divorce: II,"
> 33 *Col. L. Rev.* 249, 262 (1933).

> Given the existence of marriage and the fact that
> women work for no pay but with the expectation of
> security—that is, that their husbands will continue to
> "support" them—divorce is against the interests of
> women.
> —Sheila Cronan, "Marriage," in *Notes from the Third
> Year: Women's Liberation* 62, 64 (1971).

During the past twenty years, the United States has experienced a period of rapid change in the laws governing divorce. Touched off in
1969 by California's adoption of the nation's first divorce code that dis-
pensed entirely with traditional fault-based divorce grounds and completed
in 1985 when South Dakota added a no-fault provision to its list of fault-
based grounds, the concept that marriage failure is itself an adequate reason
for marital dissolution has been accepted by every state.[1] Viewed from a
broader historical perspective, however, the shift from fault to no-fault as a
statutory basis for divorce did not begin in 1969, nor was it fully completed
in 1985.[2] The history of divorce in Anglo-American law shows a movement
from the total unavailability of permanent divorce under the jurisdiction of
the ecclesiastical courts in England prior to the reign of King Henry VIII,
through a limited traffic in parliamentary divorces during the latter part of
the seventeenth and eighteenth centuries, to the conferral of divorce jurisdiction upon the civil courts in 1857 in England and even earlier in some
American states.[3] From this perspective, the recognition of divorce for marital fault was itself a liberalizing repudiation of the earlier doctrine that
marriage was indissoluble. By the early twentieth century, all American

6

states (except South Carolina, which did not permit permanent divorce until 1948) had enacted laws authorizing courts to dissolve marriages for cause. The most widely recognized statutory grounds were adultery, cruelty, and desertion.[4] A few states unwittingly anticipated the subsequent no-fault ground of marriage breakdown by granting courts discretion to terminate a marriage for a cause deemed "sufficient," so long as the judge was "satisfied" that the parties could "no longer live together,"[5] while others recognized grounds for divorce that did not involve fault, such as incurable insanity or voluntary separation for a specified period of time.[6] Max Rheinstein characterized these early no-fault grounds as providing an "opening wedge"[7] for the more modern recognition that marriage breakdown is itself a sufficient basis for dissolution.

Formidable religious, social, political, and economic barriers had to be overcome before these modest wedges successfully pried open the door that led to no-fault divorce.[8] Between 1966 and 1970, however, four influential groups concluded, after respectively studying the contemporary divorce laws in England, California, and the United States, that divorce based on fault no longer represented wise social or legal policy. The documents issued by these groups—the report of the Archbishop's Group in England,[9] the responding report of the English Law Commission,[10] the report of the Governor's Commission in California,[11] and the original version of the Uniform Marriage and Divorce Act promulgated in 1970 by the Commissioners on Uniform State Laws,[12]—all proposed instead that the exclusive standard for marital dissolution be a judicial finding that the marital relationship was no longer viable.[13] Despite the respect these reports commanded, however, none of them enjoyed full legislative acceptance. Opposition to such a complete shift in the basis for divorce led in each case to uneasy compromise. The final product to emerge from each of these studies—the English Divorce Reform Act 1969,[14] the California Family Law Act of 1969,[15] and the 1973 version of the Uniform Marriage and Divorce Act (UMDA)[16]—all differed from the original proposals, chiefly by retaining marital fault as a factor that could be considered in determining whether the marriage had broken down.[17] The controversy and compromise are reflected in the reception of the recommendations for change in the grounds for divorce among the American states. Although the no-fault principle is firmly established in all states as a statutory basis for divorce, its formulation varies across the states, and it forms the exclusive basis for divorce only in a minority of states.[18] Nevertheless, the impasse that had for so many years prevented meaningful reform of the grounds for divorce in both countries had been broken,[19] and the new approach continues to spread among the American states.[20]

While the primary objective of the modern American no-fault divorce reform movement was to change the grounds for divorce, related reforms were proposed as well in the laws governing other core issues of family dissolution. These proposals were initially limited to an effort to remove the punitive function formerly performed by the fault doctrine from such questions as alimony, property distribution, and child custody.[21] The no-fault principle is most intuitively appealing when it is invoked to permit the legal termination of a marriage that both spouses agree has ended in fact. In that context, the recognition of marriage breakdown is tantamount to legalization of divorce by mutual consent, and the elimination of fault as a basis for resolving the related issues of property, support, and child custody appears appropriate. Family dissolution has been analogized in such cases to the winding up of a partnership; much of the emotional work of terminating the marriage relationship may have been accomplished before the case goes to court.

As Lawrence Friedman has pointed out, however, "No-fault goes beyond consensual divorce. Either partner can end a marriage simply by asserting that the marriage has broken down."[22] Divorce by unilateral fiat is closer to desertion than to mutual separation. Unlike divorce based on mutual consent, unilateral divorce is apt to produce unexpected emotional stress and financial dislocation that exacerbates the upheaval accompanying family breakdown. The fault doctrine may have served to lend emotional vindication to the rejected spouse, as well as a measure of financial protection and status as the preferred custodian of children. If so, greater justification may be required in those cases for eliminating that doctrine from the related core areas of support, property distribution, and child custody.

Adequate justification may be found in the ideal of marriage as a relationship characterized by the continuing existence of a mutual loving commitment between the spouses. It follows that once the marriage is no longer viable, neither its legal existence nor its related legal incidents should become weapons used to obtain revenge for the breakdown or to extort a favorable settlement. But if fault is withdrawn, the party formerly able to invoke that doctrine may be left in a vulnerable position both when negotiating a dissolution agreement and when litigating the matter in court.[23] This vulnerability may be lessened or avoided if the elimination of fault is accompanied by a clear specification of appropriate substantive standards capable of ensuring fair treatment to both parties to replace the punitive philosophy inherent in the former approach. Unfortunately, however, the recommendations designed to create such specifications contained in both the 1966 California Governor's Commission report and the 1970 draft of the UMDA were not accepted in the 1969 California Family Law Act or the 1973 version of the Uniform Act.[24]

Instead, as Mary Ann Glendon has pointed out, the prevailing approach in the United States has been to rely on judicial discretion to decide contested cases under general standards without requiring any meticulous judicial scrutiny of the private agreements negotiated by the parties in non-contested cases.[25] And as Lenore Weitzman has demonstrated in her award-winning study of practice under the California no-fault law, many judges exercised their discretion in ways that failed to protect the vulnerable party, thus impoverishing many dependent women and the children in their custody.[26] Drawing on Weitzman's study and those of others, Glendon concludes that "more than any other country among those examined here, the United States has accepted the idea of no-fault, no-responsibility divorce."[27]

It is perhaps not surprising, then, that proposals to eliminate fault from the distribution of property, the award of spousal support, and decisions affecting the custody of children have not yet received nationwide acceptance. Freed and Walker reported that, as of August 1988, fault had been excluded as a factor in property distribution and/or maintenance in seventeen states (although ten of these seventeen did permit consideration of economic misconduct) and expressly retained as a factor in twenty-two states and the District of Columbia.[28] The same authors reported that marital fault had been excluded as a factor in awarding alimony in twenty-nine states, that marital fault may be considered as a factor in determining the alimony award in eleven states and the District of Columbia, and that marital misconduct remains an express bar to alimony in eight states.[29] The authors offer no comparable analysis of the impact of marital fault upon child custody awards. They noted in an earlier study, however, that at least four states have prohibited judges from considering the conduct of a proposed custodian that does not affect the custodian's relationship with the child.[30] Moreover, the most commonly adopted reform in child custody standards—the nearly nationwide experiment with joint custody[31]—was initially proposed as a development consistent with the no-fault principle.

At the present time, therefore, the translation of the no-fault principle into the financial aspects of divorce, particularly spousal support and property distribution, as well as its relevance to decisions concerning the custody and support of children, remains unfinished business in most states. Still to be hammered out are the guiding principles that will shape and give content to that project. Our choice of those guiding principles will, in turn, be significantly influenced by our assessment of the impact of no-fault divorce on contemporary family life.

Weitzman's assessment is clear. She has concluded that "the divorce law revolution . . . transformed the legal norms for marriage by articulating, codifying, and legitimating a new understanding of the marital partnership and marital commitment in our society."[32] She goes on to point out that the new understanding encourages husbands and wives to place their individual self-interest ahead of the family unit, and she questions whether this societal norm is an appropriate one.[33] This assessment leads Weitzman to recommend principles designed to minimize the financial impact of divorce upon wives in traditional marriages.[34] As Weitzman's own research clearly demonstrates, however, wives who devote themselves to homemaking and child rearing, becoming dependent upon their husbands for support and status in the process, are ill-prepared for independence upon divorce.[35] If we wish to preserve traditional marriage as a viable future option for women who do not work outside the home, we must reform marriage as well as divorce.

I have suggested elsewhere that, although the law should not penalize women at divorce whose earlier marital choices left them financially dependent upon their husbands, neither should we perpetuate a legal framework for marriage and divorce that encourages couples to choose gender roles that are financially disabling for women in the event of divorce.[36] Yet, even if we imagine that many or most future marital unions will be composed of economically self-sufficient individuals, the presence of children normally entails periods of dependency for caretaking parents that may impair their financial security if divorce ensues. It seems necessary, therefore, that divorce law must provide what Jeremy Waldron has termed the "fall-back" rights that marital partners can rely on for protection if their mutual affection fades.[37]

The fall-back rights we create during this next phase of contemporary divorce reform should be designed for a society in which the context of family life is changing rapidly. Today, it is normal for family life to occur outside of marriage, and marriage itself may be expected to continue its present trend toward norms of greater equality between husband and wife. Some observers expect that marriage may eventually be redefined to become available to homosexual as well as heterosexual couples.[38] We need to create a legal framework sufficiently flexible to permit the flourishing of a human intimacy that is the basis of loving commitment in all its variety and that, in turn, fosters the nurturance and guidance of children.[39]

The thesis of this chapter is twofold: first, these fall-back rights must consist of clear substantive standards for the just resolution of the core issues of family dissolution, and second, we must formulate those standards so as to keep them free of punitive, sexist, or paternalistically protective overtones. Only then can we hope to complete the project that began with the no-fault divorce reforms: to create a legal framework for family dissolution that is perceived by all parties as fair and that will facilitate a healthy emotional transition between marriage and divorce. Such a framework should enable all family members to be as free as possible of anger, bitterness, and anxiety stemming from the dissolution process itself, and to help them rebuild postdivorce lives that are relatively unscarred, if not unaffected, by the earlier family breakdown.

In what follows, I will examine existing and emerging standards in light of that underlying goal. I will provide in the second part a brief overview of various legal innovations that have appeared in the wake of the no-fault divorce reforms. Most of these developments have been traced in detail elsewhere; my aim in this part of the chapter is to bring the parts of this story together in one place and to show how these early innovations have prepared the way for the next period of divorce reform. Drawing on this overview, I will then attempt to sketch out in the third part a nonpunitive, nonsexist, and nonpaternalistic framework for family dissolution, including an examination of several proposals newly adopted or currently under consideration in California designed to respond to Weitzman's critique of the no-fault reforms.

Beyond No-Fault: Alternative Approaches to Financial Distributions and Child Custody
Financial Distributions

Property Distribution. Twenty years ago, the American states recognized two vastly different marital property regimes. Eight states had adopted a version of the civil law community property system, in which the spouses share ownership of property acquired after marriage by the efforts of either spouse. The remaining states and the District of Columbia followed the English common law, which, as modified by the nineteenth-century Married

Women's Property Acts, recognizes the individual ownership of each spouse in the property that spouse acquires. Although the community property states routinely divided marital property at divorce, not all the common law states did so. Reporter Robert J. Levy informed the Commissioners on Uniform State Laws in 1969 that seventeen common law states and the District of Columbia either failed to authorize the transfer of one spouse's property to the other upon divorce or prohibited or restricted such transfers.[40]

The states continue to be divided between common law and community property adherents, but two important developments—reform of the common law distribution rules and a redefinition of the meaning of property—have occurred to soften those differences. First, forty common law states and the District of Columbia now authorize courts to make an equitable distribution of property upon divorce, in the form of either a transfer of title or an award of maintenance.[41] These states differ, however, on whether all property held by either spouse or only marital property is available for distribution. In a majority of these states separate property—defined as property acquired prior to marriage, property acquired after marriage by gift or inheritance, and property excluded by agreement of the parties—is not available for distribution.

A spirited debate over the appropriate standard for property division accompanied the drive for broader distribution authority in many common law states.[42] The disputed question is whether property should be divided equally between the spouses at divorce or the court should be given discretion to apportion the property equitably, usually after considering a list of statutory factors. A consensus appears to be developing that the equitable distribution laws have not lived up to their promise of providing a fair apportionment of assets between the parties. Two observers of judicial practice under the New York Equitable Distribution Law concluded in 1984 that "with few exceptions the courts are not treating the wife as an equal partner."[43] And Weitzman prefers equal division because her research indicates that women tend to receive smaller awards under equitable distribution laws than they do under equal division provisions.[44] Glendon criticizes equitable distribution because of the potential it holds for unfair and even arbitrary judicial action, which could give rise to widespread public dissatisfaction with the courts;[45] Suzanne Reynolds argues, however, that a preference for equal division, at least in principle, hampers courts in taking adequate account of the needs of a dependent spouse, thus undercutting the goal incorporated in the UMDA that property division, rather than alimony, should serve the primary function of providing postdivorce support.[46]

The community property states have not escaped the debate over a proper standard for distribution. Although equal division may be more easily justified in community property states (where sharing principles exist during marriage in the form of undivided equal vested shares) than in common law states (where any sharing principles are deferred until marital dissolution), only three of the eight community property states expressly mandate an equal division upon divorce.[47] Three other community property states, however, presume that the division will be substantially equal unless one party can show that another distribution is warranted.[48]

Grace Blumberg discerns a movement toward equal division in both community property and common law states.[49] If her perception is accurate, experience with administering an equal division principle under the equitable distribution laws may prompt the common law states to consider instituting sharing principles at the commencement of marriage rather than at its termination. Such a development is facilitated by the Uniform Marital Property Act (UMPA), promulgated by the National Conference of Commissioners on Uniform State Laws in 1983.[50]

The second major development affecting property distribution in the wake of the no-fault divorce reforms can be characterized as an effort to redefine the nature of property. The struggle initially centered around employment-related benefits, such as pensions, goodwill, disability benefits, and severance pay. More recently, it has attempted to encompass the increased potential for production of income represented by a professional degree and license to practice.[51] Weitzman has coupled her defense of the equal division standard with a strong recommendation that "career assets," including "enhanced earning capacity," must be included in the distribution pool, asserting that their omission "makes a mockery of the equal division rule."[52]

The movement to redefine property to include career assets as part of the pool for distribution on divorce has met with mixed results. It has been most successful in capturing employment-related assets such as pension and retirement benefits or the goodwill created by a spouse's efforts during marriage. Blumberg reported in 1986 that all community property states and many equitable distribution states treat any pension interest earned during marriage as marital property.[53] Similarly, Homer Clark states that, as an abstract proposition, the goodwill of a spouse's business conducted during the marriage is generally treated as property subject to division on divorce in both community property and common law states.[54] He adds, however, that there is little agreement over the definition of goodwill or how it should be valued.[55] The treatment of disability benefits, including worker's compensation disability coverage and that portion of personal injury recoveries attributable to future inability to work, is less well settled. Blumberg has argued powerfully that these benefits ought to be classified according to the nature of the assets they replace, so that a benefit designed to replace future wages would be classified as separate property if, regardless of the disability, the marital community had been terminated by separation or divorce at the time the wages would have been earned.[56]

In contrast to the general acceptance of pensions, goodwill, and other wage replacements as property, virtually all the states that have faced the issue to date[57] have resisted the characterization of professional degrees or licenses as property subject to division upon divorce.[58] Many of the courts have accepted the reasoning of the Supreme Court of Colorado:

> An educational degree, such as an M.B.A., is not encompassed even by the broad views of the concept of "property." It does not have an exchange value or any objective transferable value on an open market. It is personal to the holder. It terminates on death of the holder and is not inheritable. It cannot be assigned, sold, transferred, conveyed, or pledged. An advanced degree is a cumulative product of many years of previous education, combined with diligence and hard work. It may not be acquired by the mere expenditure of money. It is simply an intellectual achievement that may potentially assist in the future acquisition of property. In our view, it has none of the attributes of property in the usual sense of that term.[59]

The New York Court of Appeals' interpretation of its Equitable Distribution Law to define a license to practice medicine as marital property in *O'Brien v. O'Brien*[60] is the sole exception to the majority view. The court rested its rejection of the prevailing opinion on a narrow statutory basis: "Decisions in other States rely principally on their own statutes, and the legislative history underlying them, and . . . the New York Legislature deliberately went beyond traditional property concepts when it formulated the Equitable Distribution Law."[61]

Any influence the *O'Brien* case might have had in turning the tide on this issue was undercut by its unique statutory rationale: several states have declined to follow New York's lead, adhering instead to the majority view that professional degrees are not property.[62] I have indicated elsewhere my own view that a property classification is not the best way to prevent loss to a spouse who has invested in the other spouse's education or enhanced earning capacity.[63] I will spell out below my perception that courts and commentators are using the so-called degree dilemma as the context for creating a hybrid form of award that has some of the characteristics of both property and alimony in order to resolve the distributional problem created by one spouse's acquisition of enhanced earning capacity.[64]

Spousal Support Awards. The law governing alimony has been in need of reconceptualization since the nature of the award changed from an allowance paid during marriage to a wife living separate from her husband under an ecclesiastical decree of divorce from bed and board to an order by a civil court compelling a husband to continue to support his ex-wife after a judicial decree of absolute divorce.[65] The punitive philosophy underlying the fault doctrine of divorce served to mask the fundamental question of why, once marriage lost its character as an indissoluble status and became instead a contract terminable for cause, one spouse should have any obligation to support the former spouse. If divorce could be granted only at the behest of an innocent spouse against a guilty one, alimony could be viewed in theory at least as an award in the nature of punitive damages for marital misconduct. That the innocent spouse had been forced to terminate the marital status because of the wrongdoing of the other spouse could be seen as sufficient injury to justify the award.

Now that marriage has become a contract terminable at will, the need to reexamine alimony is even more pressing than before. Ira Ellman has convincingly demonstrated that "no-fault reform created a sea-change in [the] legal environment"[66] surrounding traditional alimony. As he spells out the altered situation, "The man who wants to end his marriage now simply files a petition alleging that it is irretrievably broken; there is no defense against such an allegation. The wife seeking alimony, property division, or child support has no leverage to demand such compensation as the price of her husband's 'freedom,' but must rely instead on the substantive law governing these issues. Thus, the law of alimony and property now count in a way neither did before."[67]

In this context, the concept of alimony as a permanent award, modifiable by further order of the court and terminable in the absence of contrary agreement by the remarriage of the wife or the death of the husband, virtually disappeared. Instead, several techniques emerged in practice that have had the common result of changing permanent alimony into a temporary allowance. These included "step down" awards with a future non-modifiable termination date,[68] and the introduction of "rehabilitative" alimony, designed as a temporary award to enable the dependent wife to acquire the necessary training to find a job and become self-supporting.[69] Weitzman reports that alimony awards following marriages of short (less than five years) duration were virtually eliminated following the enactment of the no-fault divorce law in California.[70] In cases involving marriages of longer duration, particularly those of more than twenty years, appellate courts have attempted case-by-case control of lower court judges insensitive to the needs of older displaced homemakers by reversing awards found to be insufficient.[71] Dissatisfied with this means of control, legislatures in several states have enacted more recent statutes designed to set clearer standards for alimony. Some of these initiatives, and others proposed by commentators, will be discussed below.

Child Placement and Support

Child Custody. Although decisions concerning the placement of children at divorce have never been free from considerations of parental misconduct, the chief determining factor until very recently has been the sex of the proposed custodian. That factor, however, has favored both fathers and mothers at different historical periods. The father's right to custody of his legitimate children was virtually absolute at common law,[72] while the mother's right arose only after the father's death. By the late nineteenth century, American courts had created a rebuttable presumption that the custody of a young child should normally go to the mother.[73] Although the maternal presumption has largely disappeared today,[74] debate continues over its constitutionality[75] and its wisdom.[76]

The demise of the maternal presumption left courts dependent on the "best interests of the child" standard, commonly supplemented by a statutory list of factors to be considered.[77] Critics agree that the "best interests" standard fails to provide adequate guidance to judges.[78] Several writers have proposed standards designed to ensure greater certainty, as well as fairness, in divorce custody cases. Chief among these proposals are a directive that custody should be awarded to the child's "psychological parent," who may or may not be a biological parent,[79] and another that custody should go to the child's primary caretaker.[80]

Other commentators seek to avoid an all-or-nothing decision granting sole custody to one contestant by favoring joint legal or physical custody in both parents, a solution claimed to be consistent with the no-fault philosophy.[81] Despite its rapid acceptance by most American jurisdictions in one form or another,[82] joint custody remains controversial among family law scholars,[83] child welfare experts,[84] and feminists.[85] One writer seeks to meet these and other objections by offering an alternative to the present adversary divorce procedure: a "cooperative custody" model that would require the state to "structure parental interaction through a combination of joint custody, mediation, and active judicial management, which together create a cooperative custody system."[86] In California, the requirement of mandatory mediation in contested custody cases[87] has apparently reduced the number of cases in which courts must decide the issue.[88] Drawing on empirical studies, Carol Bruch questions whether these reduced litigation figures reflect either enhanced parental cooperation and satisfaction or improvements in the welfare of children.[89] She notes further that in California the combined effect of mandatory mediation and joint custody has produced a dramatic increase in the number of joint custody awards, speculating that "many of these mediated joint custody agreements appear to be the product of strong pressures to compromise rather than the expressions of shared parental conviction envisioned by the Civil Code."[90]

Child Support. The no-fault divorce reforms did not, by and large, change the standards for setting child support.[91] Recent congressional enactments, however, promise major changes in this area. In 1984, Congress required states to develop guidelines for setting awards.[92] Implementing regulations provided that the guidelines must yield a specific numerical amount that can be used as the basis for the child support award.[93] Many have hoped that this process will yield not only more uniform but also larger and thus more "adequate" awards. The effectiveness of the guideline strategy for that purpose remains to be seen. In 1988, Congress enacted legislation that requires judges and other decision makers to use the guidelines as a rebuttable presumption in setting child support awards.[94]

Bruch has provided a thoughtful critique of the issues that should be addressed by those drafting or evaluating such guidelines.[95] She then points out that virtually none of the guidelines has taken into account the nonmonetary child-rearing contributions of the primary custodial parent. In an important insight, she distinguishes two reasons for assessing parental income: first, to determine the amount of the child support award and, second, to allocate the support burden between the parents. She also provides an incisive analysis of the factors that should be considered in balancing the support rights of first families against those of subsequent families.

Obtaining an adequate support award is only the first step. A second major problem has been the inability of many recipients to enforce their awards. Weitzman calls the failure of fathers to pay child support a "national disgrace."[96] The Child Support Enforcement Amendments of 1984[97] represent a partial response to this problem. The main thrust of this act, which also mandated the creation of the child support guidelines discussed above, was to require that states provide mandatory wage-withholding procedures that would be triggered whenever payments are one month in arrears.[98] The act also provided for interception of federal and state tax refund checks to be applied to past-due support obligations. Congress went even further in 1988, mandating that by January 1, 1994, states put in place mandatory withholding arrangements even before the noncustodial spouse is in arrears.[99] These provisions should aid substantially the collection of child support awards.

New Directions in Divorce Reform
Fixing No-Fault: The California Legislature Responds to Weitzman

Lenore Weitzman's book, *The Divorce Revolution*,[100] has focused national attention on the plight of divorced women and their children. In response to her findings, feminists began agitating for renewed legislative reform of the financial consequences of divorce.[101] Marygold Melli notes that others also have become concerned, including those who are opposed to, or uneasy about, the idea of no-fault divorce itself, as well as those concerned about increases in public welfare payments.[102]

Because her book was perceived as critical of the California law, and because the California Legislature regards itself as a leader in divorce reform, Weitzman's findings received particular attention in that state. State senators Gary Hart and David Roberti sponsored a resolution that created the California State Senate Task Force on Family Equity and charged it with reviewing Weitzman's book and making appropriate recommendations.[103] Weitzman encouraged these legislative efforts and served as a member of the Task Force. If, indeed, California's no-fault divorce law had unintentionally resulted in the impoverishment of many divorced women and their children, the California Legislature felt duty-bound to fix matters.[104] Because California's initiatives in divorce reform have been watched closely in other states, the work of the Task Force can be expected to receive similar scrutiny. Accordingly, its proposals deserve extended analysis here.

The Task Force, which issued its final report on June 1, 1987, began by considering Weitzman's book, but its deliberations encompassed a broader field. It chose to emphasize "the need to equalize the results of divorce, focusing especially on assuring adequate economic protections for the older homemaker and minor children."[105] It decided not to address two potentially significant issues, viewing them as beyond its charge: (1) whether to recommend that California should return to a fault-based system of divorce and (2) whether to propose the substitution of an "equitable" division of property rather than the existing mandatory equal division.[106]

The final report of the Task Force does not contain any serious critical evaluation of Weitzman's study.[107] Judging from its investigations,[108] the Task Force simply concluded that the findings and trends Weitzman reported "are indeed serious problems which need to be addressed," and it recommended twenty-three specific legislative proposals intended "to serve as a starting point for enhancing equality and equity in the economic outcomes of divorce."[109] In what follows, I will briefly describe its major proposals and indicate their current status. In the next section of this chapter, I will evaluate these and other proposals in light of the framework for future reform I present there.

Judiciary. Some commentators have blamed judicial insensitivity to the economic needs of divorced women and their children, rather than the no-fault law itself, for much of the adverse financial impact of divorce. Thus, in her review of Weitzman's book, Nora Jane Lauerman observes that "arguably, many of the economic problems faced by divorced women under the no-fault system are not caused by the provisions of the law itself. Instead, they stem chiefly from the judicial application of the no-fault law, combined with the general economic milieu of working women. . . . The applicable statutes are flexible enough to permit realistic, adequate awards but implementation depends on the individual judge's discretion."[110] Weitzman also recognized the central role played by judges in implementing the no-fault law. Accordingly, she recommended that only judges experienced in family law be assigned to family law calendars, and that mandatory programs be developed to train judges in the exercise of their discretionary power to set support awards.[111]

Although the Task Force did not propose a prior experience requirement for family law judges, it did recommend that the Judicial Council establish education and training programs for judges and other court personnel who are assigned to hear and decide family law matters. Furthermore, the Task Force directed that "this training should include instruction on the effects of gender bias in family law proceedings, and on the economic consequences of divorce for both women and men."[112] The Legislature promptly required the Judicial Council to carry out this recommendation.[113]

If the mandated training succeeds in raising judicial consciousness about the financial aftermath of divorce, we may expect more equitable orders at the trial court level. Although most family law judges are well aware of the practical problems of stretching scarce resources to cover two households instead of one, many have shown themselves in the past to be more solicitous of the male breadwinner than the female housekeeper. In an era when two paychecks have become necessary during marriage, judges must be alert for hidden biases that may unfairly disadvantage divorced women and the children in their custody.

Community Property. The Task Force report accepted Weitzman's recommendation that the definition of property be expanded to include career assets, adding that career assets classified as community property would be available for distribution on divorce.[114] Since all but one of the items Weitzman defines as "career assets" are already recognized as property in California,[115] the Task Force focused its discussion on the remaining item: the enhanced earning capacity of a spouse especially when represented by the attainment of a professional degree and license during marriage. The report enthusiastically endorsed[116] the New York Court of Appeals decision in *O'Brien v. O'Brien,*[117] which interpreted the New York Equitable Distribution Law to define a professional degree as marital property. Drawing on *O'Brien,* the Task Force recommended generally that the definition of community property be expanded "to include all forms of property and assets, tangible and intangible, including all career assets" and, in particular, that "enhanced earning capacity acquired during marriage be characterized as community property and subject to division upon dissolution."[118] The theoretical effect of this proposal would be to expand the pool of "property" available for current distribution. Since the enhanced earning capacity would be reflected in postdivorce income, however, the monetary amount would remain unchanged.

As noted earlier, however, *O'Brien* has not attracted any judicial followers in the United States.[119] Recent commentary appears to be divided over whether professional degrees and licenses should be classified as property.[120] So far there has been no legislative movement in California on this recommendation.

Family Home. The Task Force identified one particular community asset—the family home—as worthy of special treatment. Weitzman had reported considerable dissatisfaction among women with the current judicial practice of ordering the sale of the family home to comply with the equal division rule in the large number of cases where insufficient community assets existed to provide an offsetting award.[121] As she noted,[122] some California courts were quick to recognize the potentially harmful emotional, social, and economic consequences of dislocation to children and sought to deal with this problem by creating a practice that authorized a spouse having custody of children to live in the family home during a specified period of time.[123] The California Legislature codified this practice in 1984, stating that the purpose of an order awarding temporary use of the family home to the custodian of minor or adult disabled children is "to minimize the adverse impact of dissolution or legal separation on the welfare of the children."[124]

Noting that, despite this statutory authorization, many trial courts remain reluctant to defer an immediate sale of the family home, the Task Force proposed legislation that would require judges to consider deferring sale in all cases and would create a presumption favoring such an order where there are minor children in the home.[125] The Legislature implemented this recommendation by requiring the trial court, upon request of a party having sole or joint physical custody of a child, to determine whether it is economically feasible to consider ordering a deferred sale of the family home.[126] If the court finds that such an order is economically feasible, it shall consider a list of ten factors in exercising its discretion to grant or deny an order deferring sale of the home.[127] If the court grants a deferred sale of home order, it may specify the parties' respective responsibilities for the payment of routine maintenance and capital improvements, and it shall reserve jurisdiction to determine issues that may arise relating to the maintenance of the home and tax liabilities, as well as other matters. Unless the parties have otherwise agreed in writing, the court may modify or terminate the deferred sale order at any time. Finally, if the party awarded a deferred sale order remarries, or if there is otherwise a change in circumstances affecting the determinations made in granting the order or affecting the economic status of the parties or the children on which the order was based, the new law carries forward with minor changes the provision of the old law that created "a rebuttable presumption, affecting the burden of proof, . . . that further deferral of the sale is no longer an equitable method of minimizing the adverse impact of the dissolution or legal separation on the children."[128] Presumably, these new fall-back rules will influence the parties as they negotiate agreements concerning the family home.

Weitzman also recommended that long-married, economically dependent older wives should be able to retain the right to live in the family home regardless of the presence of minor children.[129] The Task Force concurred, proposing a deferred home sale order for "a supported spouse in a marriage of long duration where the court determines that the adverse impact on that spouse of loss of the family home is not outweighed by the economic detriment to the other spouse."[130] Senator Hart introduced a measure in 1986, which anticipated this recommendation by authorizing a court to "reserve jurisdiction and temporarily defer the sale of the family home where the adverse economic, emotional, and social impact on an older spouse in a marriage of long duration, which would result from the immediate loss of a long established family home, are not outweighed by economic detriment to the other spouse."[131] The bill failed. The Task Force, perhaps made cautious by this earlier defeat, stressed that its recommendation for deferring sale of the family home in favor of a dependent spouse in a marriage of long duration would constitute a "clarification of, and not a change in, current law," pointing out that "a deferred sale does not affect the equal division of property."[132]

Nonetheless, Senators Hart and Watson did not include a section to implement this recommendation concerning older wives in their successful bill discussed earlier dealing with deferred home sale orders where minor children are present.[133] And even the Task Force did not find it appropriate to endorse Weitzman's more forceful recommendation that the displaced homemaker be awarded the family home outright as an exception to the equal division rule.[134]

Spousal Support. Weitzman directs her harshest criticism of judicial practice under the no-fault laws at the failure of judges to award adequate spousal support orders. She points out that when the California Legislature shifted from fault to economic need and ability to pay as the basis for ordering spousal support, it identified three groups of women who were not expected to be self-sufficient: women who were the full-time custodians of minor children; older women who had been homemakers during lengthy marriages; and women in transition from homemaking to full-time employment who were in need of education or training.[135] Her research indicates, however, that California judges applying the no-fault laws did not observe these distinctions, with the result that "thousands of women are *unjustly* subjected to hardship."[136]

The Task Force accepted Weitzman's findings, and in response to her criticisms it proposed two new standards for spousal support, the first for marriages of short duration, the second for lengthy marriages. It recommended that the standard for support awards in short marriages should be "the standard of living established during the marriage."[137] The report explains that "the 'marital standard of living' standard provides a cut-off point for short marriages; *i.e.,* the spouse seeking support would not be able to take advantage of the increased standard of living of the supporting spouse, but would instead be bound by the standard of living established during the marriage."[138] This explanation assumes, consistent with Weitzman's data,[139] that the postdivorce standard of living of the supporting spouse will rise above that established during the marriage in marriages of short duration and that the supported spouse is not entitled to enjoy that increase. This policy may encounter theoretical difficulties in cases where minor children, who are usually thought to share the parent's financial success, live with the supported spouse.

In marriages of long duration, however, the Task Force proposed a different standard: "equalizing the standard of living of the two post-divorce households."[140] The report thus justifies the difference in standards: "A different standard is being proposed for marriages of long duration because of the longlasting, permanent effects of such marriages. In effect, the spouses have incurred lifelong responsibilities and benefits because of their long marriage."[141]

Although its reasoning is not entirely clear, the Task Force apparently envisioned that the older supported spouse should be able to continue to seek upward modification of the support award in order to keep pace with the supporting spouse's rising standard of living, for it sought to implement this proposal by recommending that courts be required to retain jurisdiction over spousal support in marriages of long duration. It declined, however, to specify the length of a "marriage of long duration," in order to avoid evasions by early divorce filings, relying instead on existing cases that used a similar concept.[142]

In addition to these proposed new standards, the Task Force also recommended other measures to increase the stability of the award and to improve its enforcement. Thus, the report recommended that the Legislature repeal the existing law that terminates spousal support upon remarriage;[143] that it require that any vocational evaluation report introduced as evidence of the supported spouse's earning capacity include a report on that spouse's ability to find employment commensurate with the standard of living established during the marriage, and require payment of the expenses of any training necessary to enable the supported spouse to produce a similar income level;[144] that it require that spousal support orders include a provision for an automatic wage assignment after one month delinquency in payment;[145] that it empower district attorneys to enforce spousal support in cases where there is no child support order, and provide full funding for this function;[146] and that the Judicial Council and the State Bar examine means of providing attorney fees at the beginning of litigation and of making the services of court-appointed experts available to spouses with limited income.[147]

These recommendations met mixed success in the California Legislature. It enacted a measure providing that spousal support orders would be based on the standard of living established during the marriage.[148] The provision contains no reference, however, to a requirement of equalizing the standards of living between postdivorce households following a marriage of long duration. An earlier measure, enacted in 1987 before the Task Force issued its final report, provided, with exceptions noted below, that "the court retains jurisdiction indefinitely where the marriage has been of long duration."[149] Contrary to the Task Force's recommendation that the length of a marriage of long duration not be specified, this measure contained a presumption affecting the burden of providing evidence that a marriage of ten years or more, measured from the date of marriage to the date of separation, is a marriage of long duration.[150] The Task Force recommendation to repeal the current law, which provides for the automatic termination of spousal support on remarriage of the supported spouse, has not been implemented. The Legislature enacted a measure subsequently vetoed by Governor George Deukmejian that would have implemented the Task Force recommendation requiring vocational evaluation consultants to report on the supported spouse's ability to find employment commensurate with his or her education, skills, age, and the standard of living established during the marriage, as well as the requirement that the costs of retraining the supported spouse be paid by the other spouse.[151] A measure that provided for automatic wage assignments was enacted and signed by the governor.[152]

Child Support. Weitzman's findings indicate both that child support awards are inadequate to cover the reasonable cost of raising children and that even these inadequate awards are not enforced.[153] She offered six recommendations for change: the establishment of realistic guidelines for child support awards based on the income-sharing approach; a requirement that parents support their children until they complete their college education, even though that would expand the support obligation beyond the children's age of majority at eighteen; the application of an automatic cost of living adjustment (COLA) to child support awards; the creation of a vastly improved state-administered system of enforcing child support awards; administrative monitoring of compliance, including the threat of incarceration for nonpayment; and finally, an effort to find more imaginative means for encouraging voluntary compliance.[154]

The Task Force agreed with Weitzman that the two most pressing problems affecting child support are inadequate awards and noncompliance.[155] It called attention to earlier legislative efforts to deal with both problems, in particular the Agnos Child Support Standards Act of 1984,[156] which set a uniform mandatory minimum award for child support derived from the amount that would otherwise be established as the need for that child under the AFDC program and Senator Hart's 1986 bill that required wage assignments to be included in all child support orders after January 1, 1987.[157] The Task Force found indications, however, that the Agnos Act was being treated as a ceiling, rather than a floor, on child support by some courts.[158] Moreover, it found that enforcement of child support remains a major problem.[159]

Despite these conclusions, the Task Force proposed little to address either systematic award inadequacy or ineffective enforcement. Instead, it offered several legislative proposals designed to remedy other perceived defects in existing law. Thus, it proposed that the age at which a parent's support obligation to an unmarried child ends should be increased from eighteen to twenty-one, regardless of whether the parents are divorced, married, or single. The Task Force believed this measure would be the "fairest and simplest" method for dealing with the problem of ensuring continued parental support for children.[160] A measure[161] designed to implement this recommendation was defeated on the floor in the closing moments of the 1988 legislative session. The Legislature did, however, add to the Family Law Act applicable to divorcing parents a provision already contained in existing law applicable to parents in intact families that continues a parent's duty of support to any unmarried child who is a full-time high school student and who resides with the parent until the child completes the twelfth grade or attains the age of nineteen, whichever occurs first.[162]

The Task Force's remaining child support recommendations provided helpful clarifications[163] and simplifications of existing law.[164]

Joint Custody. Weitzman found that no-fault divorce laws had very little impact on custody practices. Despite expectations that fathers would seek custody more often under no-fault, she found no increase in the percentage of fathers who sought or were awarded custody two years after the no-fault laws were enacted.[165] Following the enactment of California's joint custody law, effective in 1980,[166] preliminary data showed an increase in orders denominated "joint custody" awards, but observers reported that many were no different than orders earlier termed sole custody with "liberal visitation" awards.[167] Regardless of the nature of the legal standard for custody, however, Weitzman reported that "in the large majority of divorced families—between 67 and 85 percent, depending on how one classifies the joint physical custody awards—mothers continue to provide most of the nurturance and day-to-day care of their children."[168]

Weitzman made two recommendations for change in California's custody laws: the creation of a presumption favoring the primary caretaker as custodian and restricting joint custody to cases where the parents have agreed on such a plan.[169] The Task Force report contains no discussion of a primary caretaker presumption, so it did not endorse this recommendation. The Task Force did, however, recommend several changes to the joint custody statute. First, the Task Force recommended that Civil Code section 4608 be amended to require courts to consider a history of spouse abuse, along with its present consideration of child abuse, in determining the best interests of children.[170] A measure designed to accomplish this goal[171] had been defeated in the 1985–86 legislative session after it was amended to require that the spouse abuse allegation be subject to a "substantial independent corroboration" requirement. This amendment had prompted battered women's organizations and advocates to oppose the measure.[172] The Task Force received testimony indicating that an express provision requiring courts to consider evidence of spouse abuse still was needed.[173] Accordingly, the Task Force recommended such legislation without any "independent corroboration" requirement, although it specified that an initial finding of a history or pattern of spouse abuse or domestic violence would be necessary.[174] A measure designed to implement this recommendation was also amended to require "substantial independent corroboration" and met the same fate as the earlier effort.[175]

The Task Force's second recommendation was to clarify the existing joint custody provisions to indicate that no statutory presumption exists in favor of joint custody.[176] Citing testimony that some lawyers, judges, mediators, and parents believe that California law contains a presumption favoring joint custody, the Task Force indicated its concern "that this misinterpretation of California law could result in inappropriate joint custody orders and mediated agreements that would be detrimental to children and to parents."[177] In response, the Legislature added the following clarifying provision: "(d) This section establishes neither a preference nor a presumption for or against joint legal custody, joint physical custody, or sole custody, but allows the court and the family the widest discretion to choose a parenting plan which is in the best interests of the child or children."[178] The Task Force's further recommendation that a list of specific factors related to joint custody be inserted in the Civil Code was not implemented.[179] Its suggestion for creating a presumption against awards of joint physical custody in contested cases affecting infants three years old or younger[180] failed passage.[181]

Mediation. California's mandatory mediation provision for contested custody and visitation disputes states that its purpose is "to reduce acrimony which may exist between the parties and to develop an agreement assuring the child or children's close and continuing contact with both parents," and it directs the mediator to "use his or her best efforts to effect a settlement of the custody or visitation dispute."[182] Both the Task Force report and the report of the Advisory Panel to Senator Alan Robbins on the Child Oriented Divorce Act of 1987 agreed that legislation was needed to ensure that the settlement goal enunciated in the mediation law did not take priority over the best interests of the children who were the subjects of the dispute.[183] The Legislature implemented this recommendation by amending the statutory charge to the mediator quoted above to read as follows: "The mediator shall use his or her best efforts to effect a settlement of the custody or visitation dispute that is in the best interests of the child or children."[184]

The Task Force also recommended the development of safeguards to reduce undue coercion in the mediation process. Specifically, the Task Force was opposed to the local option rule contained in the mediation law that permits mediators to make a recommendation to the court concerning the custody or visitation order. The Task Force felt this power permitted the mediator to unduly influence the proceedings and discouraged the parties from negotiating in good faith without fear of influencing the outcome of the court proceedings. It recommended that the statute should be amended to provide for absolute confidentiality of the mediation process.[185] A measure designed to provide for further study by the Judicial Council of this and other Task Force proposals regarding mediation safeguards was enacted, but vetoed by the governor.[186] The Task Force's recommendation that mediation be made available in disputes over the implementation of existing visitation or custody orders and that persons requesting mediation in such postdecree situations be given access to mediation services within sixty days of the request was implemented.[187]

The work of the California Senate Task Force on Family Equity represents an important first step in a new direction. Its successful major proposals, discussed above, will provide new fall-back rights that go far toward improving the administration of justice in divorce litigation in California. In addition, these new rules will serve to guide negotiated settlements in more appropriate directions.

Toward a Nonpunitive, Nonsexist, and Nonpaternalistic Framework for Marital Dissolution

Despite the profound changes in American divorce law over the past twenty years, we have not yet fully accepted divorce as merely constituting, along with death, one of two alternative ways to end a valid marriage. As Dr. Judith Wallerstein observed after studying a group of divorcing families for a period of ten years: "Divorce has two purposes. The first is to escape the marriage, which has grown intolerable for at least one person. The second is to build a new life. Everyone who initiates a divorce fervently hopes that something better will replace the failed marriage—and this second-life-building aspect of divorce turns out to be far more important than the crisis. It is the long haul of divorce that matters. How people succeed in translating the hope for a better life into a reality is the critical, unexamined issue in the postdivorce years."[188]

Our failure to accept divorce as a normal social occurrence has contributed to our continuing to treat legal divorce as a civil action in the nature of a claim for tortious injury, where blame is determined and damages assessed. As the philosophy underlying the no-fault reform spreads from the grounds for divorce to other aspects of the dissolution proceeding, we should begin to change our punitive view of divorce.[189]

Once we move from treating divorce as a shameful event to seeing in it a necessary and appropriate corrective for an unwise or undesired marital choice, we can evaluate the contemporary proposals for divorce reform in a different light. Because punishment is not our goal, we will no longer try to preserve marital fault as a means of allocating property or determining spousal support. Other goals can then assume more prominence in the process of reform. Moreover, because of our societal commitment to ending sexist stereotypes, we will no longer give priority to mothers over fathers as custodians of children; nor will we assume that women engaged in full-time demanding work are not interested in caring for their children. As we move to implement these goals, however, we must keep in mind the laws governing marriage. If we have learned anything from the work of Weitzman, Marcus,[190] and others, it is that we cannot expect to remedy the defects of marriage at the point of divorce.

The marriage laws traditionally reflect societal norms about the proper role and conduct of husbands and wives toward each other and in relation to their children. Although the norms may be universal, close attention to the experience of married life may disclose a divergent pattern. Sociologist Jessie Bernard has shown that men and women typically experience marriage very differently, with the result that marriage as an institution is more beneficial to men than to women.[191] This contrasting, sex-based pattern of marriage is reflected in the different attitudes toward divorce expressed by Llewellyn and Cronan in the two quotations that open this chapter. Thus, Llewellyn sees divorce as an insignificant rite of passage between marriage and remarriage: relationships that benefit men and that a man usually initiates. In contrast, Cronan sees divorce as a threat to women, even as she claims that women's experience in marriage is akin to slavery.

At the time Cronan wrote in 1971, the modern women's movement was less than ten years old.[192] Its early message was that women need not sacrifice their own potential in marriage. By individual effort, aided by legal and political attack on traditional attitudes and practices that kept women in their (secondary) place, women could overcome the time-honored separation between the family and the market. Women could achieve equality with men at work, while inviting men to share power with them in the home. Although this vision of the egalitarian family doubtless continues to influence many young women, others in the "postfeminist" generation appear to be having second thoughts about whether it is really possible to "have it all."[193] Today's feminists have recognized that institutional supports available in other industrialized Western countries for working mothers are not provided in the United States.[194] Despite misgivings about substituting dependency on the state for dependency on husbands, feminists are in the forefront of political efforts to secure federal legislation that would create child-care programs as well as parental and nurturing leave opportunities for parents and adult children of both sexes.[195]

The availability of institutional support for child care, helpful though it would be, is insufficient to alter the root problem of female dependency at divorce. That problem is the result of three interlocking factors: (1) women and men are socialized differently in our culture; (2) as a result of that socialization, women are overwhelmingly responsible for the nurturance of children and care of the elderly and infirm, whether or not they work outside the home for pay; and (3) these two factors combine to mean that women in the work force are viewed as secondary workers who are commonly segregated in female occupations, paid less than men, have fewer opportunities for advancement than men, and are marginalized by their male colleagues even if they succeed in penetrating the inner sanctuaries of power associated with male-dominated higher-level jobs. Despite more than twenty-five years of experience with federal and state laws prohibiting discrimination in employment based on sex, these three factors taken together mean that, in most cases, marriage is still the most promising opportunity open to women who want to raise their standard of living. If the marriage terminates in divorce, leading to the immediate decrease in the income available to households composed of women and children that Weitzman reports,[196] remarriage is the most efficient path to an immediate return to a higher standard of living.[197] Marriage, it seems, is both a long-term cause and a short-term cure of female poverty.

Cronan's solution to this dilemma was an appeal to all women to join in an effort to abolish marriage as a legal institution.[198] Her appeal has gone unheeded. Instead, feminists have taken on the project of restructuring marriage in ways that are designed to alter the traditional roles of the spouses and thus to make marriage less disabling to women.[199] If this project is successful, the future impact of divorce on women may be radically different. Although divorce would no doubt continue to be emotionally traumatic, representing as it does the failure of an attempt to create a lifelong loving commitment between two people,[200] the marital termination itself might no longer entail a severe financial disadvantage.

Nevertheless, even if spouses enter marriage as equals, the fact remains that in our culture most people marry for love.[201] Love is characterized by romantic, subconscious factors that prompt otherwise self-interested individuals to engage in the sharing behavior and mutual bonding that characterize our ideal of marriage. As a result, we must expect that married couples will make choices based on the assumption that their marriage will endure for a lifetime, and not with a view to its earlier termination by divorce. It follows that one spouse may choose a course of action that fails to protect her (or him) against that contingency. We need, therefore, to devise a legal framework for divorce that will safeguard those who do not maximize their separate interests, but instead engage in unselfish, sharing behavior.[202]

A nonpunitive, nonsexist, and nonpaternalistic framework for marriage dissolution, then, should begin with recommendations that encourage sharing behavior during marriage without penalizing such behavior at divorce. In what follows, I will discuss several examples of the kind of substantive standards such an approach requires.

A good place to begin is with reform of the marital property laws. Common law states should consider adopting a marital property system that initiates a sharing principle at the inception of the marriage and that provides for equal management of the common property. The Uniform Marital Property Act provides a convenient model.[203] Community property states like California that have departed from the original Spanish-Mexican regime by treating the income from separate property as separate should consider adopting the Uniform Act's broader commitment to sharing principles that treats such income as community property when acquired after marriage.[204] The recognition of an equal ownership in marital property not only promotes shared management during marriage but also serves as a rationale for an equal division of that property when the relationship ends in divorce.

I am not persuaded, however, that the agenda for marital property reform should include an expanded definition of property that would capture the enhanced earning capacity represented by a professional degree and license. For reasons that I have given elsewhere,[205] I prefer to approach the degree dilemma through an analysis of the loss incurred by the supporting spouse rather than by attempting to divide the gain realized by the supported student spouse.[206] That loss occurs only if the marriage ends before the expected increase in the student's capacity to produce income as a professional practitioner has been realized and its financial benefits shared by the spouses. When the marriage is terminated before that realization occurs because the professional spouse wishes to acquire a new mate, we may feel that the supporting spouse is badly treated. The no-fault philosophy, however, does not support the use of property law as punishment even in these circumstances. At the same time, that philosophy need not require that the supporting spouse be left without remedy.

As we have seen,[207] virtually every court that has considered the degree dilemma has declined to characterize the student spouse's enhanced earning capacity as property, concluding instead that the enhancement is an appropriate factor to be taken into account in setting the spousal support award or making an equitable division of property. There are at least three problems with the spousal support approach. The first is that the availability and amount of spousal support is discretionary with the court, and not a matter of right. The second is that spousal support awards normally terminate on the remarriage of the supported spouse or on the death of the supporting spouse. The third is that enforcement of such awards is notoriously difficult. The choice of a spousal support order rather than a property disposition in this context, however, does have the advantage of flexibility. Since support orders are usually modifiable, they can be adjusted to changed circumstances such as the professional spouse's unexpected career developments or inability to continue working. What is needed is an award that can combine the flexibility of a support order with the permanence of a property award.[208] The New Jersey courts seem to be in the process of creating such a hybrid concept in the form of an award of "reimbursement alimony" that does not terminate upon remarriage.[209] Such an award should also survive the obligor's death and serve as the basis for a claim against the estate.

As presently stated, however, "reimbursement alimony" recaptures only the monetary contributions made toward the professional education. That is too limited a recovery to compensate the supporting spouse adequately for the loss incurred. Ira Ellman has proposed a broader remedy in the context of his general theory of alimony to accompany the no-fault divorce reforms.[210] Ellman offers an economic reformulation of alimony designed to encourage sharing behavior during marriage by compensating a spouse for loss of earning capacity that resulted from having made a rational marital investment producing gain to the other spouse that survives the divorce.[211] The payment he proposes is unrelated to the benefit conferred on the other spouse, to the standard of living enjoyed during the marriage, or to the needs of the investing spouse. Rather, he measures the payment by the alternative use the investor could have made of his or her efforts: an investment in his or her own earning capacity.[212] Ellman conceives of this claim as one asserted by one spouse (usually the wife) against the other (usually the husband) and therefore necessarily limited by the husband's capacity for payment. Ellman's theory rewards an investor spouse for the ability to choose a marital partner with the aptitude and perseverance for lucrative self-development. His approach also confers a higher recovery upon an investor spouse whose own capacity for self-development is greater than a less talented or ambitious investor spouse whose loss of earning capacity is relatively small. Finally, Ellman's theory denies recovery for bad investments, where the investor's loss does not result in gain to the other spouse.[213]

Applying his theory to the specific case of a wife who supports her husband while he attends graduate or professional school, Ellman concludes that some wives will recover, but others will not. The wife who delayed her own education while supporting her husband but was divorced at his graduation will have a claim equal to the added earning capacity she would have had at divorce if she had gone to school herself. If the marriage lasted until her subsequent graduation, she may still have a claim measured by the impact of the delay on her earning capacity. The wife who does not return to school, but instead stays home to raise children and become a homemaker might recover half of her lost earning capacity to spread the loss involved in raising children.[214] Ellman concludes, however, that "the woman who supported her student-husband while holding the same job she intended to keep anyway has suffered no loss in her earning capacity, even though she expected to share in his. Her lost expectation is not compensable and she has no claim."[215]

Ellman concedes that this result may appear "ungenerous," but he sees little alternative, given his position that lost earning capacity is essential to a claim.[216] He could be more generous if he took account of the possibility that the wife may have decided to remain in a relatively nondemanding job after she married a husband whose increased earning capacity would render unnecessary her own greater economic self-development. If so, then she has suffered a loss that, presumably, Ellman's theory would recognize.

I am not persuaded that the wife whose investment did not turn out to produce a benefit for her husband should be left without a remedy. Her loss of earning capacity is no less real because of his disappointing performance. If we want to encourage sharing behavior during marriage by limiting its risks upon divorce, we should permit the wife to recover her loss whether or not her husband gained from her investment. Ellman's economic point that a prudent wife would invest in herself rather than her husband where she would be a more promising investment is undercut by the sociologic fact of our romantic approach to marriage. If Ellman is right, presumably the husband would also recognize that the wife's breadwinning potential is greater than his own and would agree that she should be the subject of their marital investment. Such men appear to be rare, however, and even when they exist, their decision to give priority to their wives' careers would encounter severe negative male peer pressure that might act as a powerful deterrent.

If Ellman's approach, modified as I have suggested to recognize the wife's loss without regard to whether it produced a gain for her husband, is combined with the New Jersey theory of reimbursement alimony, the wife who has engaged in sharing behavior during the marriage will be compensated for her loss even though she will not share in her husband's future gain. Such an outcome is consistent with both the no-fault philosophy and with the principle that encourages sharing behavior during marriage.

In a state with a marital property system based on sharing principles, an equal division of marital property combined with an expanded approach to reimbursement alimony of the kind described here will go far toward providing financial equity between the spouses at divorce. Despite the desirability of such a doctrine, however, and perhaps even its ultimate fairness as applied to future couples, I doubt that it provides adequate current protection for the older homemaker whose marital choices have long since been made and who is no longer capable of becoming self-supporting.

As we have seen, the plight of the older homemaker figures prominently in Weitzman's critique of the impact of the no-fault divorce law, and the California Task Force on Family Equity gave first priority to redressing her situation. Only one of its three major recommendations directed toward that goal, however, was adopted. Neither its proposal to expand the family home award to be available to older homemakers without custody of children nor its suggestion of a special support standard designed to equalize the standard of living in postdivorce households following lengthy marriages was enacted. The only successful measure resulting from the work of the Task Force specifically directed at the older homemaker is the provision that courts retain jurisdiction over the support award in marriages of long duration. I believe that these or similar proposals should be reconsidered by the California Legislature. But given its recent rejection of them, I question whether it is a good idea for California to implement an Ellman-like general theory of reimbursement alimony immediately. At the very least, such an approach would need to be phased in gradually and prospectively, with a grandmother clause to safeguard the interests of the traditional homemaker.

A second area that requires further examination is the substantive standards governing child custody decisions. The California Legislature has, as we have seen,[217] responded to the Task Force report by negating the inference that a statutory presumption favoring joint custody exists in California. It has also expressly subordinated the goal of settlement in mandatory custody mediation to the overriding concern for the best interests of children. Both of these measures represent sound policy. But the likely outcome of their enactment is to increase judicial discretion in the decision-making process and with it the uncertainty surrounding the custody decision. Measures designed to reduce this uncertainty in the child placement decision remain necessary.

That does not mean, however, that the Task Force's failure to support Weitzman's proposal for a primary caretaker presumption was mistaken. The predictability that such a presumption brings to custody awards is purchased at the cost of legitimating the maternal preference under an easily penetrated veneer of gender neutrality that effectively excludes the vast majority of fathers as potential custodians. Contemporary social, cultural, and economic factors all tend to inhibit fathers from any realistic commitment to qualifying as the primary caretaker of children. Indeed, the normative effect of such a legal preference actually might tend to discourage fathers from participating in the care of their children during marriage while reinforcing the existing cultural directive that women ought to regard mothering as their primary role. As I have suggested elsewhere,[218] the legal system should not facilitate the continuance of the conventional practice of designating a single primary caretaker for children. Instead, we should foster the nonsexist practice of shared parenting for infants and children. If we are successful in doing so, the parents who have experienced this behavior during marriage are more likely to wish to continue that practice after divorce, and to do so voluntarily.

Martha Fineman's recent attack on joint custody in the context of mandatory mediation[219] has prompted me to reconsider my thinking, but not to change my conclusion. I share many of her doubts about the value of mandatory mediation. I believe, however, that Fineman goes too far in her zeal to dislodge social workers from their victory in what she sees as a turf battle against lawyers for ownership of the "property" of controlling custody decision making.[220] In the course of her critique, she unnecessarily discards the therapeutic approach to family dissolution,[221] even though that approach preceded and is not inherently linked to the more recent penchant for mandatory mediation. Indeed, in 1969 the California Governor's Commission on the Family proposed the use of that approach implemented through the creation of a family court as essential to its recommendation for no-fault divorce.[222]

I do agree with Fineman, however, that "the best interest of the child test must be replaced"[223] in the form in which it is presently implemented. I continue to believe that the least detrimental approach to child placement at divorce is one that encourages the divorcing spouses to reflect on their continuing roles as parents within the supportive context of a judicially supervised family court staffed by well-trained and experienced mental health professionals.[224] In my view, the experience with mandatory mediation, in light of the legislative withdrawal from joint custody as a preferred solution to the child placement decision, suggests that the California Legislature should reconsider the family court proposal.[225]

California, having led the country into no-fault divorce, is now undertaking a responsible reexamination of the consequences of its earlier action. The results of that reappraisal may serve to ignite a second wave of divorce reform capable of building a nonpunitive, nonsexist, and nonpaternalistic framework for marriage dissolution on the foundation of the no-fault philosophy.

Conclusion

We have not yet, in considering divorce reform, fully grasped the implications of Llewellyn's point. Shorn of its conventional context, his point simply was that divorce is not an end in itself. Rather, it is a legal device that permits the termination of a marriage during the joint lifetime of the spouses. Divorce indeed makes possible new beginnings, but the opportunities it affords are not limited to remarriage. We have high cultural aspirations about the laws shaping marriage and family life. But all we need require of a divorce law is that it do no harm. A divorce law restricted to fault does harm by preserving legal unions that are emotionally nonviable, creating incentives for evasion and blackmail.[226] A no-fault, no-responsibility divorce law does harm by favoring the economically independent party over the dependent party, creating incentives to distort the law of property in search of just solutions. A framework for a nonpunitive, nonsexist, and nonpaternalistic system of marriage dissolution built on sharing principles can minimize, if not entirely eliminate, the financial harm done by divorce. More sweeping cultural change is, however, required to alter the context within which family life is lived in our society.

2

Private Ordering Revisited
What Custodial Arrangements
Are Parents Negotiating?

ROBERT H. MNOOKIN

ELEANOR E. MACCOBY

CATHERINE R. ALBISTON

AND CHARLENE E. DEPNER

In the wake of the no-fault revolution, as Kay so well documents in her chapter of this book, both the standards and procedures concerning child custody have been transformed.[1] Presumptions in favor of maternal custody have given way to custody rules that call for individualized determinations of the child's best interests, with no preference to either parent by reason of gender.[2] Indeed, as Kay suggests, many states now authorize, and some even encourage, joint custody arrangements in which both parents share responsibility for custody following divorce.[3] Moreover, with respect to custody issues, the legal system now seems geared to emphasize dispute resolution, not the regulation of family life of postdivorce families. State laws now explicitly recognize the legitimacy of "private ordering"—the notion that divorced parents should have substantial freedom to negotiate their own financial and custodial arrangements within the framework of state law.[4]

Legal scholars and advocates have written a great deal about these changes in the formal law and have made a variety of claims about the advantages and disadvantages of a gender-neutral best-interest standard, an emphasis on coparenting or joint custody, and a legal regime that promotes

Eleanor E. Maccoby is the Barbara Kimball Browning Professor of Psychology Emeritas at Stanford University. Catherine R. Albiston is research assistant, Stanford Child Custody Study. Charlene E. Depner is coordinator for research, California Statewide Office of Family Court Services, and former study director, Stanford Child Custody Study. The authors would like to thank Forrest S. Claassen, Kim Powlishta, and Sue Dimiceli for their assistance.

private ordering. But there is surprisingly little systematic empirical evidence about how custody issues are in fact resolved at the time of divorce. The best-interest standard, because of the discretion it provides to the court, is said to create uncertainty about judicial outcomes and thus increase the likelihood of conflict.[5] Scholars have acknowledged that most custody conflicts are resolved through negotiation rather than adjudication, but little reliable information exists about the proportion of divorcing parents who are in conflict over custody or the number of cases that require mediation, court-imposed evaluations, or adjudication.[6]

Much of the recent debate over custody standards and procedures has concerned issues of gender, and whether the new regime (or certain of its elements) systematically and unfairly favors fathers or mothers. Advocates for women have claimed, for example, that under the best-interest standard, mothers are now frequently losing custody to fathers[7] and that the possibility of joint custody and the emphasis on gender-neutral custody standards have operated to deprive women of a critically important bargaining chip when faced with attempts to reduce spousal and child support in divorce negotiations.[8] Advocates for fathers counter that the best-interest standard is gender neutral only in theory, not in fact, and that in actual operation judicial biases favoring mothers perpetuate a maternal presumption.[9] Good empirical data could surely inform these debates. It would be useful to know: What proportion of divorcing mothers prefer sole custody at the time of divorce? Do the preferences of fathers frequently differ? When parental preferences are in conflict, how is that conflict resolved? How many cases are actually subjected to judicial determination?

Interest and concern has also been expressed about joint custody and coparenting following divorce, with prominent feminists and child advocates joining in on all sides of the debate.[10] Some have claimed that joint custody, with its emphasis on the rights and responsibilities of both parents following divorce, is the best way to create gender equality because it aims to make the roles of mothers and fathers the same.[11] Moreover, "frequent and continuing contact with *both* parents" following divorce, has been proclaimed to best serve the interests of the children.[12] But critics have asserted that the possibility of joint custody has distorted the divorce bargaining process in ways that disfavor women and harm children.[13] Joint custody may frequently be used, according to the critics, to resolve custody conflicts between parents who are fundamentally at odds with each other and lack the ability to cooperate in parenting following divorce.[14] Once again, information about the actual operation of the legal system would be helpful. How common is joint custody? How frequently is it imposed by courts or used by mediators or warring lawyers to resolve highly conflicted divorce custody battles?

The Stanford Child Custody Study, longitudinal research involving over 1,000 California families who filed for divorce between September 1984 and March 1985, addresses these and other issues. This chapter presents some of our findings based on our initial analysis of 908 California families that we studied between the time their divorce petitions were filed and their final decrees were granted. Because our study took place in California, the next section gives essential background about current California law, as well as our sample and our methods. We then report and discuss our findings. We conclude the chapter with some suggestions concerning further research, as well as the broader implications of what we have learned.

Background
California Law

California has been in the vanguard of the family law revolution, and its legal system at the time of our study reflected both a rejection of sex-role stereotypes and an emphasis on private ordering. During the time the families in our study were securing their divorces, state law provided that custody should be awarded on the basis of the "best interest of the child" standard, with an explicit provision that the gender of a parent not be the basis for preference.[15]

Since 1979, California custody law has done more than simply formally insist on gender neutrality; it has also expressed the policy of assuring children "frequent and continuing contact with *both* parents."[16] In 1979, California became the first state in the nation to adopt a statute that explicitly authorized joint custody awards upon divorce. Indeed, it established a presumption in favor of joint custody when both parents requested it. It also authorized a court to order joint custody in a disputed case.[17] Moreover, the statute suggests that in cases where the parents cannot agree on custody, the preferences of the more cooperative parent—that is, the parent more willing to accept a custodial arrangement that provided for continuing contact of both parents—should be favored.

In addition, California law emphasizes private ordering by explicitly differentiating between *physical* custody and *legal* custody. In 1983, the legislature provided a statutory definition of each. Physical custody has to do with which parent has responsibility and control for the child on a day-to-day basis, and joint physical custody involves custodial arrangements whereby both parents have responsibility for the child for "significant periods." Legal custody, on the other hand, has to do with "the right and responsibility to make decisions relating to the health, education and welfare of the child." Joint legal custody is a situation in which both parents have these rights and responsibilities.[18] This differentiation between legal and physical custody allows parents more flexibility in negotiating custody arrangements. Finally, the statute allows the divorce judgment itself to reflect any parental agreement concerning the allocation of responsibility between parents who have joint legal or joint physical custody.

California divorce decrees now contain information about both physical custody and legal custody. When we refer to custody in this chapter we are referring to these legal labels, and we will ordinarily distinguish between physical custody and legal custody. The common combinations found in California divorce decrees are:

1. *Mother physical custody—mother legal custody.* This is the traditional arrangement in which the mother has sole responsibility for the day-to-day care and custody of the child, along with the various legal rights that go with legal custody. The father usually has the right to visit his children on a "reasonable" basis.

2. *Mother physical custody—joint legal custody.* Under this arrangement, the mother has ongoing day-to-day responsibility for the care of the child, but the father has the legal right to participate in decisions including but not limited to education, religion, and medical care.

3. *Joint physical—joint legal custody.* Both parents retain full legal rights and responsibilities, including the physical custody of the child. In this form, the child presumably resides for some significant amount of time in the home of each parent. As we will describe, there is a considerable range of actual arrangements under this label.

4. *Father physical custody—joint legal custody.* Here the father is the primary custodian, and the child presumably lives in his household, but the mother has the right to participate in various decisions concerning education, religion, and medical care.

5. *Father physical custody—father legal custody.* Here, in addition to having sole responsibility for the child's day-to-day care, the father

also exclusively holds the legal rights concerning education, religion, and medical care.[19]

A California divorce proceeding is initiated when either parent files a petition. Among other things, in all divorces in which there are minor children, the petitioner is required to make some request for physical and legal custody. For both physical and legal custody, the form provides three options: sole mother custody, sole father custody, and joint custody. After the other parent receives notification that a petition has been filed, he or she normally has thirty days to respond. The form for the response provides an opportunity for the respondent also to make a request for physical or legal custody. California law permits either parent to request a hearing concerning interim financial or custodial arrangements during the pendency of the divorce proceedings by filing an order to show cause.

California law also emphasizes the resolution of custody disputes outside of court. Since 1981, California has mandated mediation for parents engaged in any sort of custody dispute as a precondition for a court hearing on the matter.[20] The purpose of mediation is to help parents resolve their custody conflict through negotiation, without the necessity of a contested adjudicatory hearing.

This mediation is usually court-annexed, but a mediator chosen by the parents may also be used. If mediation fails to resolve the conflict over custody, the family proceeds to a custody evaluation again usually performed by a court-appointed evaluator but occasionally done by an evaluator of the parents' choice.[21] Each party receives a copy of the evaluator's report. If disagreement over custody continues after the evaluation, each parent may respond to part or all of the report before there is a contested hearing. Even during the hearing, parents may settle the custody dispute before the judge decides.[22] Throughout this process, there are many opportunities for parents and their lawyers to negotiate a settlement. Ultimately, a judge will adjudicate the few remaining custody disputes.

Our Sample

Our analysis is based on a sample of 908 divorcing families (1) who filed for divorce in San Mateo or Santa Clara County between September 1984 and March 1985 and (2) who had received a final divorce decree determining the custody of the children by July 1988.[23] We secured our sample in the fall of 1984 and the spring of 1985 by examining San Mateo and Santa

Clara court records. We established three eligibility requirements for families to be a part of our study: (1) the petition for divorce had to have been filed between September 1, 1984, and March 31, 1985, in Santa Clara or San Mateo County; (2) the petition had to reveal that at the time of the filing, there was at least one child under sixteen years of age from this marriage; and (3) at the time of the filing, the couple had been separated for no more than fourteen months. About 1,990 families from the nearly 7,000 court divorce petitions filed during the relevant period met our eligibility requirements. We were able to enroll in our study approximately 60 percent of the eligible families.[24]

For the families included in our study, information was collected from two sources: (1) court records and (2) three rounds of telephone interviews with parents. From the court records, we learned which parent was the petitioner and what this parent requested for physical and legal custody. We also learned if a response was filed and, if so, whether the respondent requested some other form of custody. In addition, we determined whether the divorce was uncontested[25] and whether either or both parents were represented by counsel in the divorce proceedings. We also determined whether, because of a disagreement concerning custody, the case had been referred to court-annexed mediation. Under California law, if mediation fails, a custody evaluation is prepared before a contested custody hearing takes place. We examined the record to determine whether there had been such an evaluation. Finally, from the final judgment and any appended separation agreement, we determined the physical and legal custodial arrangements incorporated into the decree.

In addition to this information from the court records, we conducted three rounds of parent interviews. The primary mode was a structured telephone interview, which typically lasted slightly more than an hour. This interview focused on the processes by which the divorcing couple arrived at their custody and visitation decisions and on family functioning following separation. The first telephone interview typically took place two to three months after the divorce petition had been filed ("Time 1 interview"). The modal period of separation before filing was two months. Consequently, our first interview usually occurred within six months after the couple had separated. The second interview ("Time 2 interview") was done a year after the first interview—eighteen months, in the usual case, after the couple had separated. The final round of telephone interviews took place approximately three years after the first.[26] In some cases in which a parent could not be interviewed by phone, a mail interview was sent to eligible parents. Of the 908 families included in the present analysis, we secured interviews for both parents for 411 of the families (45 percent). For 344 families (38 percent), we were able to interview only the mother, and for 153 families (17 percent), we interviewed only the father.

Measures and Terminology

Before reporting our results, we will describe our measures and explain some of our terminology.

1. *Parental desires: what do parents want in terms of custody?*

In our first interview, we sought to learn what custodial arrangement each parent would prefer with respect to the divorce judgment. We asked what he or she would "personally like" in terms of physical custody and legal custody. For respondents who were confused by the terms *legal* and *physical* custody or requested a definition, the interviewer explained what we meant by each. What we were trying to get at was *not* what a parent *asked* for in their legal papers but what they really wanted. We used the parents' responses to this question as an indication of their desires.

2. *Parental requests for custody*

From the court records, we determined what physical and legal custodial arrangements were requested by the petitioner and, if there was a response, by the respondent. We called this requested custody.

3. *Custody outcomes*

By custody outcomes, we mean the forms of custody awarded in the divorce decree.

4. *De facto residence*

As previously noted, families seek a variety of custodial arrangements in the divorce decree, but these do not always define the actual living arrangements of the children. For this reason we determined for each family where the children actually resided.

In our parent interviews, we asked that they describe for us in detail what portion of each twenty-four-hour period the child spent with each of the parents in the two-week period preceding the interview. We also asked whether the last two weeks were typical, and if not, we determined whether there was a regular pattern that differed from the last two weeks. If there was such a pattern, we obtained a detailed report of it.

Using this information, we categorized for each time period each family's de facto residence as follows:

  a. *Mother residence* includes those families in which the child spent more than ten overnights in a two-week period with the mother.
  b. *Dual residence* includes those families in which a child spent four or more overnights in a two-week period with each parent.
  c. *Father residence* includes those families in which the child spent more than ten overnights with the father.[27]

The decision of how to draw the boundaries for dual residence was, of course, somewhat arbitrary, but we were reassured in our decision to use a measure of four overnights with each parent in a two-week period by how most parents responded to another question. In our interviews, we asked them, "Do your children now live with you, your spouse, both of you, or someone else?" There is a strong correspondence between the parents' responses and our measure of de facto residence. If the child spent three or fewer overnights with the father, over 90 percent of the parents said the child resided with the mother; if three or fewer overnights were spent with the mother, over 90 percent of the parents said the child resided with the father. In a majority of cases in which the child was spending four or more overnights with each parent, the parents characterized the child as living with both of them, although many others were described as residing primarily with the mother.[28]

5. *Measuring legal conflict*

In addition to examining the extent to which custodial preferences of the parents differed, and whether their requests in their legal papers for custody coincided or not, we developed a legal conflict scale to measure and compare the extent to which parents disagreed over the custody and visitation determinations found in the divorce decree. The scale was constructed with information from two sources: (1) parental responses to a question that asked them how much conflict there had been up to the time of the divorce judgment about the arrangements for custody and visitation and (2) examination of the court record for objective evidence of legal conflict.

We combined the evidence from both court records and parental ratings of conflict to create for each family a 4-point conflict scale that categorized the levels of conflict as follows: Level I—"negligible" conflict; Level II—"mild" conflict; Level III—"substantial" conflict; and Level IV—"intense" conflict.[29]

Constructing a conflict scale that uses both the parents' subjective evaluation of the intensity of the conflict over custody *and* court record data is preferable to using either source of information alone. The obvious disadvantage of a measure that simply asks the parents to rate the level of conflict is that different parents could rate similar legal conflict in a very different way depending upon their own, perhaps idiosyncratic, subjective appraisal. For example, in order to avoid any implication that the children had been upset by parental conflict over custody, some parents might give a very low conflict rating even though the court record clearly indicated intense battling requiring judicial intervention. Conversely, in a case in which the divorce was entirely uncontested and there was no evidence that the other parent disagreed with the petitioner's custody request, a sensitive father might nevertheless rate the custody conflict as 7 on the 10-point scale because he remembered a single argument with the mother over the custodial arrangements at the time of separation. Since our goal was to measure legal conflict, we therefore took into account discrepancies between the interview and court record information.

We also concluded, however, that it would be inappropriate to use court records information alone, for the cold court record could be misleading. An uncontested divorce, for example, might have involved intense negotiations *before* the petition was filed. On the other hand, some thick court files might reflect the lawyering style of certain attorneys more than the actual degree of legal conflict. For example, some lawyers as a matter of course file an order to show cause and demand a hearing concerning interim custody and support issues during the pendency of the divorce petition after they file the petition. We never categorized such cases as "uncontested," although from our discussions with attorneys we learned that in many instances these requests for orders to show cause do not represent substantial legal conflict. (Indeed, in many instances, the motion led to a formal interim agreement between the parents that probably could have been secured by a phone call from one attorney to the other rather than through the motion.) In other circumstances, the court record made it clear that a case should be assigned to a high conflict level even though the parents gave a low rating. For example, a visitation dispute that was referred to the court-annexed mediators was treated as a Level III conflict, even if the mother gave a low rating. We believe that cases requiring court-annexed mediation typically had substantial conflict regardless of the parents' subjective appraisal. Similarly, we concluded that cases where the court record indicated that there was a need for a formal custody evaluation belonged in the "intense" category.

Results

In our analysis we set out to answer some basic questions concerning the dispute resolution process at the time of divorce. Our initial questions concern the relation between parental desires for custody and parental requests, and between parental requests and custodial outcomes. What proportion of parents want sole custody of their children following divorce, and how do mothers and fathers differ in this regard? To what extent do parents' legal requests concerning custody conflict? What is the role of lawyers in this process, and how do they influence custody requests? How do all these factors affect custodial outcomes?

A second set of questions focuses on the relation between the official custody outcome and the actual custodial arrangements following divorce. How closely do parents follow the official arrangements? How do high conflict families cope with joint physical custody?

Our final questions concern issues of legal conflict. What patterns of conflict arise during divorce negotiations? What is the relationship between custody requests and legal conflict? How does conflict affect satisfaction with the final settlement? These questions address both the nature of this process and the attitudes and preferences parents bring to the negotiation. The answers provide insight into motives and behavior of divorcing parents that are largely outside the purview of the court system in private ordering.

We approach these questions in this chapter through descriptive statistics, largely using marginal analysis, not cross-tabulations or multivariate analysis. Thus, we have not attempted to evaluate the extent to which such factors as income, education, or length of marriage may affect behavior. Nor have we used the longitudinal dimensions of our data—three interviews over time—to explore the dynamics of causation. Our analysis does demonstrate, however, the extent to which the gender of a parent still makes an important difference in what custodial arrangements mothers and fathers desire, what they ask for in the process, and the custody awards themselves, notwithstanding the formal changes in California law. The analysis also shows the extent to which joint physical and joint legal custodial arrangements are now found in California divorce decrees, and whether in fact dual residential arrangements have become common.

Physical Custody

Parental Desires. In our first interview, we asked each parent what he or she would personally like in terms of residential custody, regardless of what in

Table 2.1. What Parents Wanted: Physical Custody

Custody Wanted	% of Mothers[a] (N = 735)	% of Fathers[a] (N = 537)
Mother	82.2	29.4
Father	1.8	32.4
Joint	14.6	35.4
Split	0.7	1.9
Other	0.7	0.9
	100.0	100.0

[a] In 81% of the families, the mother responded to this question; in 59% of the families, the father responded.

fact had been or would be requested in the legal proceeding. Our initial question concerned what parents wanted in terms of the custodial arrangements following divorce.[30]

The results for those parents who responded to this question are shown in table 2.1. The difference between the desires of mothers and fathers is conspicuous. The overwhelming majority of mothers responded that they wanted to have physical custody of their children. Of the 735 mothers answering this question, 82.2 percent said they personally wanted maternal custody. About 15 percent of the mothers indicated a desire for joint physical custody, but less than 2 percent said they wanted the father to have physical custody.

For fathers the pattern of desires expressed for physical custody is radically different from the pattern for mothers. Roughly equal proportions of the fathers desired joint custody, father custody, and mother custody. Nearly 70 percent of the 537 fathers responding expressed a desire for a form of residential custody other than mother custody. There may well be some selection bias here that is worth noting. We were able to secure interviews with 537 of the 908 fathers in our sample families. We suspect that the fathers who did agree to participate in our study might on average have been more involved with their children than the fathers we could not locate or who refused to participate. Had we been able to interview every father in our 908 families, a somewhat higher percentage of fathers—perhaps one half—might have expressed a desire for maternal custody.[31] Nevertheless, our results indicate that there are large numbers of fathers who would personally prefer joint physical custody or father physical custody over mother custody.

Table 2.2. Physical Custody: Parents' Requests by Parents' Desires

Requested on Petition	% of Mothers[a]				% of Fathers[a]		
				Wanted			
	Mothers (N = 605)	Joint (N = 107)	Father[b] (N = 13)		Mother (N = 158)	Joint (N = 190)	Father (N = 174)
Mother	78.4	32.7	—		35.4	11.1	12.6
Joint	6.9	31.8	—		18.4	38.9	19.0
Father	0.5	3.7	—		1.9	6.3	37.4
No request	14.2	31.8	—		44.3	43.7	31.0
	100.0	100.0			100.0	100.0	100.0

[a]Excludes 10 mothers and 15 fathers who wanted/requested split or nonparental custody.
[b]Because percents based on such a small group would be misleading, no figures are given.

Table 2.3. Concurrence between Custody
Wanted and Custody Requested

	Physical		Legal	
	% Mothers (N = 695)	% Fathers (N = 501)	% Mothers (N = 714)	% Fathers (N = 507)
Requested what they wanted	82.7	56.5	75.4	74.9
Requested more than they wanted	5.1	8.8	17.2	14.8
Did not request as much as wanted	12.2	34.7	7.4	10.3
	100.0	100.0	100.0	100.0

Note: Parents who wanted split or nonparental custody are excluded. If a parent made no request, it is presumed that the request of the other parent was acceptable to him or her and was that parent's request by default.

The Relationship of Custody Desires to Custody Requests. We compared parental desires with what parents actually requested on the divorce petition or response filed in court. Tables 2.2 and 2.3 show the results. Several conclusions are worth emphasizing.

First, the results suggest that mothers are more likely to act on their stated desires than are fathers. It is interesting to compare, for example, the behavior of mothers who said they wanted maternal custody with that of fathers who said they wanted paternal physical custody. For the mothers, nearly 80 percent requested sole maternal custody on the petition or response. For the fathers, on the other hand, less than 40 percent requested sole paternal custody, even though these fathers had indicated that this is what they wanted.

Second, many fathers did not bother making a physical custody request by filing a petition or response. Forty percent of fathers who told us what they would really like in terms of custody failed to make *any* request. On the other hand, only 17 percent of the mothers failed to make a request. One reason a parent might not have made a request for physical custody in the legal papers could be that the other parent as petitioner had already requested what he or she wanted. To explore this possibility, in every case where one parent made no request, we examined what the other parent had sought in the petition. This analysis revealed that in 64.5 percent of the 110 cases where the mother made no request, the father in fact had petitioned for the mother's stated preference. For the 193 fathers who made no request, on the other hand, the mother made a consistent request in only 35.1 percent of the cases. Indeed, because mothers requested sole custody in such a high proportion of cases, only for those nonrequesting fathers who desired mother custody was it true that the mother was typically requesting what the father wanted.

This comparison of desires with actual requests reveals that some parents asked for *more* physical custody than what they said they wanted, whereas others asked for *less* than what they said they wanted. In divorce bargaining, of course, it is possible for parents to ask for more custody than they really want as an attempt to make a better deal for themselves in the negotiation process. For example, a father who wanted the mother to have sole custody might nonetheless petition for joint custody in an attempt to persuade the mother to accept a less generous financial arrangement. Indeed, our data show that 31 of the 158 requesting fathers who wanted maternal custody in fact asked for joint physical custody or father physical custody. The data indicate that some mothers might be playing this game as well; out of the 107 mothers who expressed a desire for joint physical custody, 35 requested sole maternal custody in their papers. Interestingly, out of the 190 fathers who wanted joint physical custody, only 12, or 6 percent, asked for sole father custody.

We found, as table 2.3 indicates, that 9 percent of the fathers and 5 percent of the mothers requested more physical custody in their petition or response than they indicated they had wanted. This might suggest at first glance that fathers are more inclined to engage in strategic conduct than mothers. But recall that for all those mothers who wanted maternal physical custody (some 80 percent of the mothers in our sample) it was not possible for her to request more physical custody. She preferred sole custody and could request no more than sole custody. Indeed, when we examined the behavior of those mothers who indicated a desire for joint custody, the proportion who asked for more custody was substantially higher than for any group of fathers. Finally, it must be remembered that some parents might have requested more custody than they desired because their preferences at the time the petition or response was filed were in fact different from their preferences at the time of our initial interview. (It should be noted, however, that for most of the parents in our sample, we ascertained their preference within a month or two of when the petition or response was filed.)

The most striking finding that emerges from table 2.3 concerns the substantial proportion of fathers who did not request as much physical custody as they indicated they would like. Indeed, when we took into account those cases in which the father simply did not file a petition or response and instead treated the mother's request as his own, it turned out that over a third of the fathers in our sample did not ask for as much physical custody as they had indicated they wanted. For those fathers who wanted joint custody, over half either made no request or requested sole mother physical custody. The behavior of those fathers who wanted father physical custody is particularly interesting in this regard. Less than 40 percent asked for father physical custody. As table 2.2 shows, nearly 20 percent asked for joint custody, about 13 percent asked for mother physical custody, and over 30 percent made no request whatsoever.

It is possible that fathers were less likely to file a petition or response asking for custody because they felt less strongly than mothers about the custodial arrangements. In our Time 1 interview, we asked parents to rate themselves and their spouse on a 10-point scale on their "feelings about custody, where 1 is someone who doesn't really care much about which kind of custodial arrangement is made and 10 is someone who is extremely determined to get the exact custody they want." When we compared self-reports for mothers who wanted sole custody and fathers who wanted joint or sole custody, mothers rated themselves somewhat higher than fathers on their feelings about custody (mean for mothers = 8.8; for fathers = 8.4). These means, however, are both very high, and the difference between them, while statistically significant, is small. We also compared fathers who wanted joint or sole custody and filed a request to those who wanted the same forms of custody and did not file a request. Again, fathers who filed a request rated themselves somewhat (and significantly) higher (8.6) than fathers who did not file a request (8.0). Thus, it appears that though many fathers genuinely want to live with their children, fathers who feel more strongly about custody file a request, whereas those who do not feel so strongly are less likely to act on their desire for custody.

To What Extent Do Parental Requests Conflict? The comparison of the desires of mothers and fathers would suggest the possibility of conflict in a high proportion of cases. But an examination of the petitions and responses suggests that there was a conflict between what the mother was asking for in her legal papers and what the father was seeking in only about 20 percent of

Table 2.4. Concurrence of Spouses' Physical Custody Requests

Requests of mother and father do not conflict.	78.1%
Both parents request a higher level of custody than their spouse wants them to have.	21.5
Both parents request a lower level of custody than their spouse wants them to have.	0.5
	100.0%

Note: Includes only families with petitions requesting mother, joint, or father custody. Less than 1% of the families had one or both parents requesting some other form of custody.

the cases. In the other 80 percent, there was no conflict either because the parental requests were the same or because no response was filed.

Table 2.4 shows the extent to which the parents concurred in their request for physical custody. Two points are worth emphasizing. The first is that in a very high proportion of cases—78.1 percent—the requests of the parents did not conflict. This does not necessarily mean, of course, that it was easy for these parents to agree on the custodial arrangement. Substantial bargaining might have occurred in some of these cases before a petition or response was filed. Nevertheless, it indicates that by the time the legal proceedings in the divorce were initiated, in most cases there was no remaining conflict concerning physical custody.

The second point is obvious but important. In theory parental requests could conflict for either of two reasons: (1) the petitioner might have sought more custody for himself or herself than the respondent requested; or (2) the petitioner might have been seeking *less* custody for himself or herself than the respondent requested. In practice, nearly all the conflicts involved each parent wanting *more* custody than the other would provide. In less than 1 percent of the cases was there a conflict between the petition and the response because one parent was requesting a form of custody that would give the other parent more custody than he or she requested.

Outcomes in Cases without Conflicting Requests. Table 2.5 shows the outcome for physical custody in those 693 cases where the parents' requests did not conflict. The pull toward mother physical custody is obvious. For nearly 500 of these 693 the request was for mother custody, and in 90 percent of these, the final judgment indicated that sole physical custody was in fact awarded to the mother. For the 47 cases in which the request was for father custody, a somewhat lower percentage—75 percent—resulted in sole phys-

**Table 2.5. Physical Custody Outcome
When Parents' Requests Do Not Conflict**

	Request[a]		
Outcome	Mother (N = 496)	Joint (N = 148)	Father (N = 47)
Mother	90.1%	31.1%	12.8%
Joint	6.1	54.1	6.4
Father	2.8	7.4	74.4
Split	1.0	7.4	6.4
	100.0%	100.0%	100.0%

[a]Excludes two families with petitions requesting split or nonparental custody.

ical custody for the father. It is worth noting that there were over ten times as many cases in which the uncontradicted request was for *mother* physical custody than for *father* physical custody. Moreover, when the request was for mother physical custody, only 10 percent of the cases led to some other form of judgment, whereas when the request was for father physical custody, about 25 percent of the cases resulted in some other form of judgment.

An examination of those cases in which the uncontradicted request was for joint physical custody indicates a similar pull toward mother custody. Only slightly more than half these cases resulted in a joint physical custody decree. More fundamental, over 30 percent resulted in mother physical custody, and about 7 percent resulted in father physical custody. In other words, the proportion resulting in mother custody was four times higher than that resulting in father custody.

Outcomes in Cases with Conflicting Requests. An analysis of the 190 cases where the parents made conflicting physical custody requests shows that the mothers' requests were granted about twice as often as the fathers' requests. Of these 190 cases, the mother was granted the custody she requested in 115 cases, the father was granted the custody he requested (or more) in 50 cases, and the remaining 25 cases resulted in a compromise between the two requests in the custody allocated.

Table 2.6 reveals that the most common form of conflict arose when the mother requested sole physical custody and the father requested joint physical custody. In nearly 70 percent of these cases the divorce judgment pro-

Table 2.6. Physical Custody Outcome When Parents' Requests Conflict

Mother's Request: Father's Request: Outcome	Mother Joint (N = 124)	Mother Father (N = 52)	Joint Father (N = 14)
Mother	68.6%	46.2%	0.0%
Joint	25.8	36.5	42.9
Father	2.4	9.6	42.9
Split	3.2	7.7	14.2
	100.0%	100.0%	100.0%

Note: Excludes four families with petitions requesting split or nonparental custody.

vided for sole physical custody for the mother. In about a quarter of the cases the result was joint physical custody. In the few remaining cases, either the father got sole custody or there was split custody with each parent taking one or more children. In other words, in about 30 percent of these cases the father denied the mother sole physical custody.

The second most common form of conflict—and probably the most intense—involved each parent requesting sole physical custody. This was true for about 5 percent of our sample, some 52 cases. Two important observations can be made about these cases. First, the outcome was sole maternal custody five times as often as sole father custody. Thus, in 46 percent of the cases, the mother got her preferred outcome, whereas in only 9.6 percent did the father get his preferred outcome. Second, in over a third of the cases in which the mother and father each requested sole custody, the outcome was joint physical custody. This suggests that joint physical custody is sometimes being used, whether through negotiation or adjudication, to compromise this extreme form of conflict.

The other form of conflict was rare. In only 14 cases was there conflict because the mother requested joint physical custody and the father requested sole custody. Only in this category does it appear that mothers and fathers were equally successful in securing their desired outcome.

Summary for Physical Custody. With respect to physical custody, our findings might be summarized as follows. First, the overwhelming majority of mothers wanted sole maternal custody. The fathers who responded to our interview were much more divided, with roughly equal proportions desiring mother, father, or joint physical custody. Mothers and fathers acted on their desires in very different fashions. Mothers were more likely than fathers to file legal papers seeking what they indicated they wanted. Over a quarter of the fathers did not request as much physical custody as they said they wanted, perhaps because they did not feel as strongly about custody as the fathers who did. In other words, there was less conflict between what parents requested than with what they said they really wanted. Our evidence suggests that in about 10 percent of the cases a parent asked for more physical custody than they said they wanted. This was consistent with the notion that some parents engage in strategic bargaining behavior concerning physical custody. What was more common, however, were cases in which fathers requested less physical custody than they said they wanted. Finally, we looked at outcomes in those cases in which the parents had made conflicting requests, and it appears that mothers were about twice as likely as fathers to secure their requested outcome.

Legal Custody

California divorce decrees now distinguish between *physical custody,* which presumably relates to which parent has the legal right to control where the child lives and day-to-day child rearing, and *legal custody,* which relates to the parental power to decide a child's religion, education, and medical treatment. In our interviews with parents, we asked about their desires concerning legal custody. From the court records, we determined what a parent requested in terms of legal custody, the extent to which parental requests initially conflicted, and the outcomes in terms of the divorce judgments.

Desires with Respect to Legal Custody. As table 2.7 indicates, there was much greater similarity between the desires of mothers and fathers with respect to legal custody than was true with respect to physical custody. A majority of both mothers and fathers wanted joint legal custody. For mothers, about 60 percent indicated a desire for joint custody, with the remainder indicating a desire for mother legal custody. For fathers, the percentage preferring joint legal custody was even higher. Seventy-five percent of the fathers wanted joint legal custody, about 17 percent wanted father legal custody, and 6 percent desired mother legal custody. In short, a majority of both mothers and fathers wanted joint legal custody, and most of the remainder suggested a desire that they (not their spouse) should have sole legal custody.

Table 2.7. What Parents Wanted: Legal Custody

Custody Wanted	% of Mothers[a] (N = 728)	% of Fathers[a] (N = 520)
Mother	38.5	6.0
Father	0.3	17.3
Joint	60.8	75.5
Split	0.3	0.8
Other	0.1	0.4
	100.0%	100.0%

[a] In 80% of the families, the mother responded to this question; in 57% of the families, the father responded.

Comparison of Requests with Desires. When requests in the divorce petitions and responses are compared with stated desires, a strong pull toward joint legal custody is indicated (see table 2.8). On the one hand, for those who said they preferred joint legal custody, there was very little slippage in terms of requests. For the 443 mothers who expressed a desire for joint legal custody the overwhelming majority either requested joint legal custody or made no request in circumstances where the father had requested joint legal custody. Only 10 percent of such mothers asked for sole legal custody. For fathers, the pattern is even more striking: all but 2 percent of the fathers who wanted joint legal custody either made that request on a petition or a response or made no request in circumstances where the spouse had requested joint legal custody. Moreover, many parents who expressed a desire for sole legal custody ended up requesting joint legal custody or filing no request in circumstances where their spouse had petitioned for joint legal custody. This was true for over 40 percent of the mothers, and nearly 70 percent of the fathers.

Conflicting requests were rare with respect to legal custody. In only 95 cases, or about 10 percent of our sample, did mothers and fathers petition for different forms of legal custody. Almost all of these were cases in which the mother asked for mother legal custody and father asked for joint legal custody. In nearly two-thirds of the cases, only one parent made a request, and that request was usually for joint legal custody. When the two parents made the same request, that request was almost always joint legal custody. (For legal custody requests, the numbers of cases for the various combinations of

Table 2.8. Legal Custody: Parents' Requests by Parents' Desires

			Wanted				
	% of Mothers[a]				% of Fathers[a]		
Requested on Petition	Mother (N = 280)	Joint (N = 443)	Father[b] (N = 2)		Mother (N = 31)	Joint (N = 393)	Father (N = 90)
Mother	53.2	10.6	—		22.6	0.8	4.4
Joint	38.9	68.6	—		29.0	60.5	43.3
Father	0.0	0.0	—		0.0	1.3	26.7
No request	7.9	20.8	—		48.4	37.4	25.6
	100.0%	100.0%			100.0%	100.0%	100.0%

[a] Excludes 3 mothers and 7 fathers who wanted/requested split or nonparental custody.
[b] Because percents based on such a small group would be misleading, no figures are given.

Table 2.9. Percent of Joint Legal Custody Outcomes for Different Combinations of Parental Requests

Father's Request	Mother's Request				
	Mother Custody	Joint Custody	Father Custody	No Request	Total
Mother custody	—	—	—	18%	24%
	(3)	(5)	(0)	(17)	(25)
Joint custody	85%	98%	—	93%	94%
	(67)	(228)	(0)	(136)	(431)
Father custody	83%	100%	—	36%	71%
	(12)	(11)	(1)	(14)	(38)
No request	32%	89%	—	46%	67%
	(152)	(247)	(1)	(13)	(413)
Total	49%	93%	100%	78%	79%
	(234)	(491)	(2)	(180)	(907)

Note: Excludes one family who requested nonparental custody. In some cases no figures are given because percents based on such small numbers would be misleading.

parental requests are shown in the parentheses at the bottom of the cells in table 2.9.)

Outcomes. Whether the requests conflicted or not, the outcome was usually joint legal custody. Table 2.9 shows for each combination of requests the percentage of cases that resulted in joint legal custody. In 611 cases, nearly two-thirds of our sample, one parent requested joint custody and the other either agreed or filed no request. As table 2.9 shows, nearly all of these cases resulted in joint legal custody. Moreover, when there were conflicting requests, if either parent asked for joint legal custody, that was usually the outcome. For example, in 67 cases the mother asked for mother legal custody and the father requested joint legal custody. In 85 percent of these cases, the result was joint legal custody. As table 2.9 shows, the only important exception was in circumstances when the father made no request and the mother requested mother legal custody. In sum, for 79 percent of our entire sample, the divorce decree provided for joint legal custody; mother legal custody was the outcome for nearly all the remaining cases.

Obviously this tendency for California divorce decrees to provide for joint legal custody is recent. Before 1979, there was no statutory reference to any form of joint custody. The growth of joint legal custody is suggested by pilot studies conducted by Michael Wald and Eleanor Maccoby. They and their seminar students examined a sample of the court records of divorce decrees granted in Santa Clara County during October 1979 (before any joint custody legislation went into effect) and October 1981 (shortly after the first provisions were enacted). In the 1979 decrees, only 25 percent of the judgments provided for any form of joint custody.[32] In 1981, 37 percent of the final decrees provided for some form of joint custody.[33] In contrast, in our study, involving divorces granted between 1985 and 1988, 79 percent of the decrees provided for some form of joint custody.

The prevalence of joint legal custody poses a number of interesting questions. The most basic is, to what extent do parents behave differently because they have joint legal custody? Are they more likely to consult with respect to education, religion, or medical care? In cases in which the mother has physical custody but the father has joint legal custody, are those fathers more likely to remain involved with the children? Are they more likely to comply with support orders? We hope to explore these questions in subsequent work that will be a part of the Stanford Child Custody Study, although the methodological problems in making many of these comparisons are substantial.[34]

Table 2.10. Custodial Decrees

Physical Custody	Legal Custody	Percent
Mother	Mother	18.8
Mother	Joint	49.3
Father	Father	1.8
Father	Joint	6.6
Joint	Joint	19.6
Other		3.9
		100.0

Note: $N = 908$.

Summary of Custodial Outcomes for Physical and Legal Custody

Table 2.10 summarizes the distribution of custodial decrees for combinations of physical and legal custody. Our examination of court records suggests that in about half the cases (49.3 percent) the decree provided for mother physical custody and joint legal custody. In an additional 19 percent of the cases, the mother had sole physical and legal custody. In nearly 20 percent of the decrees, the parents had joint physical and legal custody. In slightly over 8 percent of the cases the father had physical custody, and in most of these the parents had joint legal custody.

The Role of Lawyers

Does the presence of lawyers influence the sorts of custody parents are requesting or receiving? We addressed this issue by first determining from the court records who had legal representation in the divorce proceedings. As table 2.11 indicates, in 80 percent of our sample, one or both parents were represented by legal counsel in the divorce proceedings. Both parents were represented in nearly half (47 percent) of the cases. When only one parent consulted a lawyer, that parent was much more likely to be the mother than the father.

Mothers were more commonly represented by counsel for two reasons. First, petitioners are usually much more likely to be represented by counsel than respondents. Table 2.12 reveals that petitioners in our sample followed this pattern and that mothers were the petitioners in about two-thirds of the cases. Indeed, the percentage of father petitioners represented by counsel

Table 2.11. Legal Representation

Who Has a Lawyer?	Percent
Mother only	24
Father only	9
Both parents	47
Neither parent	20
	100.0%

Note: $N = 898$. Includes only those parents for whom we have information regarding employment of a lawyer. No information exists for 10 cases.

Table 2.12. Legal Representation: Gender of Parent by Petitioner Status

	% with Lawyer	
	Mother	Father
Petitioner	79	76
	($N = 613$)	($N = 295$)
Respondent	55	45
	($N = 292$)	($N = 606$)

(76 percent) was not statistically significantly different from the percentage of mothers who were petitioners and were represented by counsel (79 percent). Second, when mothers were respondents, they were more likely to be represented by counsel than fathers who were respondents. As table 2.12 indicates, 55 percent of the mothers who were respondents were represented by counsel, and only 45 percent of the father respondents were. This difference is statistically significant.

Involvement of Lawyers and Frequency of Joint Legal Custody. Given the prevalence of joint legal custody, we were particularly interested in learning whether the presence of lawyers affected the diffusion of this form. Families were divided into four groups: (1) neither parent had a lawyer, (2) only the mother had a lawyer, (3) only the father had a lawyer, and (4) both parents had lawyers.

It appears that the involvement of lawyers did have an impact on both

Table 2.13. Percentage of Joint Legal Custody Outcomes as a Function of Attorney Involvement

Who Has a Lawyer?	N	% Joint Legal Custody
Neither parent	183	50
Mother only	224	73
Father only	81	89
Both parents	430	92

Note: Includes only those cases for which we have information regarding employment of a lawyer. No information exists for 10 cases.

requests and outcomes. As table 2.13 shows, in cases in which both parents were legally represented, the outcome was almost always joint legal custody. At the other extreme, joint legal custody was awarded to only half the families in which neither parent had a lawyer. When only one parent was represented, the frequency fell between the two extremes.

The presence of lawyers seems to have influenced legal custody requests, also. First, we found that parents with lawyers were more likely to request joint legal custody than those without lawyers. Second, we examined desire-request discrepancies and looked at the cases in which a parent said they desired sole custody but nonetheless requested joint legal custody. Those with attorneys were more likely to request joint legal custody, with 50 percent of the mothers and 52 percent of the fathers doing so, even though they said they desired sole legal custody.[35] In short, lawyers appear to have encouraged their clients to ask for joint legal custody. This is consistent with the fact that more joint legal custody was awarded when at least one party had an attorney.

Perhaps the most striking evidence that lawyers are key in bringing about a high proportion of joint legal custody outcomes flows from our analysis of one particular subgroup where the numbers were large enough to make some interesting comparisons. There were 150 cases in which the mother requested mother legal custody and the father made no request. In 68 percent of these cases the mother was in fact awarded mother legal custody, but in 32 percent, the result was joint legal custody. The presence of lawyers differentiates these two outcome groups, as figure 2.1 illustrates. Joint legal custody was almost always awarded if both parents had an attorney, was

Figure 2.1
Mothers Who Filed Uncontradicted Requests for
Mother Legal Custody: Relationship between Joint
Legal Custody Decrees and Legal Representation

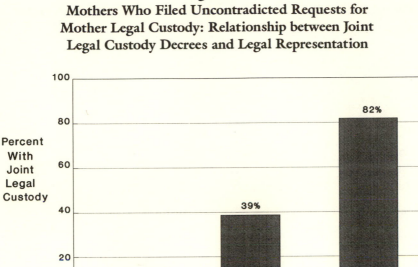

extremely rare if no attorneys were involved, and was intermediate when only the mother had an attorney. (In none of these cases did only the father have an attorney.) This would suggest that lawyers appear not only to encourage their clients to request joint legal custody but also to push for joint legal custody even when this has not been specifically requested on the petition or response.

Involvement of Lawyers and Physical Custody Outcomes and Requests. A similar four-way grouping of cases according to the presence of attorneys was related to the physical custody outcomes. Cases were divided into four groups: (1) there were no attorneys, (2) only the mother was represented, (3) both were represented, and (4) only the father was represented. We then calculated the percentage within each group that had various custodial outcomes. The results, as seen in figure 2.2, show that the relationships were more complex than for legal custody.

Regardless of group, mother physical custody was the most common

Figure 2.2
Physical Custody Outcome as a Function of Legal Representation

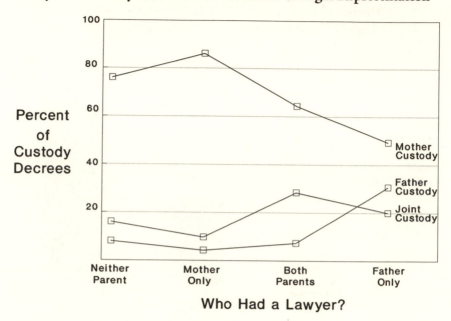

Who Had a Lawyer?

Note: Excludes thirty-four families with split or nonparental physical custody and ten families with missing information regarding employment of lawyers.

outcome, ranging from a low of 49 percent of the cases when only the father had a lawyer, to a high of 86 percent when only the mother did. Father physical custody was quite rare, with one exception. When the father had the only lawyer, he gained physical custody about a third of the time. Joint physical custody, on the other hand, was highest in those cases when both parents had legal counsel, with about 25 percent of them sharing physical custody. Mother physical custody was more common when only the woman had a lawyer, father custody when only the man had a lawyer, and joint custody when both were legally represented.

In short, for physical custody, those with an attorney were more likely to gain custody than a parent of the same gender without a lawyer, but it is hard to determine the causal relationship. Do parents who are willing to fight harder for custody hire lawyers, or do lawyers convince their clients to fight for custody? Other factors, such as economic and educational status, no doubt substantially mediate these relationships, but these must await further analysis.

We also explored the extent to which having a lawyer may influence the discrepancy between what parents say they desire and what they request in their legal papers. Lawyers may encourage their clients to make custody requests they may not otherwise make. The discrepancy between what parents said they desired in terms of custody during the interview and what they actually requested could indicate a lawyer's influence.

For physical custody, there was no relationship between a mother's having a lawyer and a desire-request discrepancy. Mothers nearly always requested what they wanted—86 percent who made a request in a petition or response in fact requested the form of custody she said she preferred, which was almost always mother custody. This was not true for fathers. Fathers with attorneys were *more* likely to request what they wanted than fathers without. Indeed, only 21 percent of fathers without counsel even made a request, whereas 80 percent of fathers represented by counsel did so. These differences are statistically significant.

Our analysis suggests that the probability of either a father or a mother asking for more physical custody than his or her stated desire—thus possibly using custody as a bargaining chip—was higher among those parents with a lawyer than those without. As noted, only a small number of fathers and mothers requested more physical custody in the petition than they indicated they desired in their interview: 35 mothers and 44 fathers. Of the 35 women who said they desired joint physical custody but in fact requested sole physical custody, 30 (or 86 percent) were represented by counsel. In our sample as a whole, only 70 percent of mothers were represented by counsel. For fathers, 41 of the 44 men who asked for more custody than they said they desired were represented by counsel, and only 55 percent of all fathers in our sample were represented by counsel. There is, of course, no way to know for certain whether these requests represented strategic behavior and, if so, whether the lawyer encouraged the request. Nonetheless, the results show that a parent represented by a lawyer is more likely to ask for more custody than he or she says she wants, although it should be emphasized that the total number of parents who did this was a small proportion of our entire sample.

The Relations between Official Custody Outcomes and Where Children Spend Time

Because the legal judgment is only a piece of paper, an important question is the relation between what a divorce decree says about custody and where children actually live. In our interviews, we asked how many nights the

Table 2.14. De Facto Residence by Custodial Decree

Physical: Legal: De Facto Residence	Mother Mother (N = 159)	Mother Joint (N = 425)	Custodial Decree Joint Joint (N = 177)	Father Father/Joint (N = 70)	Split (N = 31)
Mother	84.3%	85.6%	39.6%	8.6%	32.3%
Dual	5.7	8.0	42.9	14.3	12.9
Father	2.5	4.0	13.0	70.0	16.1
Split	3.1	1.9	2.8	1.4	32.3
Other	4.4	.5	1.7	5.7	6.4
	100.0%	100.0%	100.0%	100.0%	100.0%

Note: Excludes 45 families missing de facto residence data for the period concurrent with or subsequent to the decree as well as 1 family with nonparental custody decreed.

children usually spent with each parent to determine de facto residence categories.

Table 2.14 shows for each sort of custodial decree the percentage of cases falling into various de facto residence categories. It is clear that most children who were assigned the sole physical custody of one parent were actually residing with that parent.[36] Thus, in about 85 percent of those cases in which the mother was awarded physical custody, all the children were in fact residing with the mother. For cases in which physical custody was assigned to the father, 70 percent in fact resided with the father. It is worth noting, however, that when the father was awarded physical custody, the drift toward dual residence or mother residence was much greater than the drift in cases where the mother was awarded physical custody. Nearly 23 percent of cases resulting in father physical custody were dual or mother de facto residence, whereas only 11 percent of cases resulting in mother physical custody were dual or father de facto residence.

Although about 20 percent of our total sample had joint physical custodial decrees, less than half of these families maintained a de facto dual residential pattern (42.9 percent). Indeed, a nearly equal proportion of these cases (39.6 percent) resulted in de facto mother residence. Once again, we see the pull toward mother custody. The percentage of joint physical custody cases that result in de facto mother residence was three times greater than the percentage resulting in father residence (39.6 percent versus 13 percent). Although over half of the families with joint physical custody decrees did not have de facto dual residence by our definition, nevertheless about 16 percent of our total sample did in fact have dual residence. Because there were enough families with mother physical or father physical custody who in fact had de facto dual residence, the percentage of the total sample that had de facto dual residence was nearly as high as the percentage with joint physical custodial decrees.

Custody Conflict: What Are the Patterns?

Most divorcing families with children have very little legal conflict concerning custody or visitation prior to judgment. About 70 percent of the cases in our sample had either "negligible" (38 percent) or "mild" (32 percent) conflict (Levels I or II). Indeed, for families who experienced "negligible" conflict, the divorce was uncontested *and* the parental interview information suggested that there was no basic disagreement concerning what the divorce decree should say about the custodial arrangements (Level I).

The evidence suggests, however, that for about 30 percent of our sample, the resolution of the legal issues concerning custody and visitation was not so easy. These families cited "substantial" (Level III) or "intense" conflict as measured on our 4-point scale. Of the 781 cases measured on our conflict scale, 141 (18 percent) had court-annexed mediation. Of these, 47 were assigned to Level III, or "substantial" conflict, based on parental reports of moderate conflict and the absence of a custody evaluation. The remaining 94, or two-thirds, however, were classified as Level IV, or "intense" conflict, owing to either parental reports of high conflict or the presence of a custody evaluation, or both.

In addition, there were 47 other cases that did not involve mediation that we categorized as "intense," or Level IV. For 70 of the 140 Level IV cases, there was a court-ordered custody evaluation. Following this, the custody issue was usually resolved without the need for a contested trial. Only 32 of these high-conflict-evaluated families proceeded to a contested trial,[37] and of these, in only 13 instances did the court actually adjudicate the custody or visitation provisions of the judgment.[38]

The Relation between Custody Requests and Conflict. Our analysis suggests that the odds of whether there will be conflict were very much affected by what the father requested in the petition or response, but not by the mother's request. If the father requested mother physical custody, whether combined with mother legal custody or joint legal custody, only 10, or 12 percent of the cases fell into the "intense"-conflict category. On the other hand, for fathers requesting joint physical custody, 30 percent of the cases involved "intense" conflict, and for fathers requesting father physical custody, 41 percent fell into the highest category. As it turns out, about 71 percent of the "intense"-conflict families (Level IV) involved fathers who initially requested joint physical custody or sole father custody, although only 37 percent of families in all four conflict levels had fathers making such requests.

For mothers, there were no significant differences in proportions falling into the four conflict categories, when we compared mothers who requested mother physical custody and those who requested joint physical custody. The one group that was different was composed of those few mothers requesting father physical custody, for which there were very few high-conflict cases (10 percent). The differences, however, were not statistically significant.

Custody Outcomes and Conflict Levels. We were also interested in examining the conflict levels for different custody outcomes. We were particularly interested in exploring whether intense or substantial legal conflict was more or less common in cases in which the result was joint physical custody or father custody as compared with mother physical custody.

As it turned out, the average level of conflict in cases in which the result was father physical custody or joint physical custody was higher than for those cases in which the outcome was mother physical custody, whether with joint legal custody or not. Indeed, the highest overall mean was for joint physical custody cases (mean = 2.4).[39] Perhaps more important than the difference in the overall means, however, were the differences in the proportion of cases in the highest conflict category. Twenty-seven percent of the joint physical custody cases involved "intense" conflict compared to only 11 percent or 16 percent for either of the mother physical custody categories. When one adds those families with "substantial" conflict, it appears that over a third of the families that ended up with joint physical custody experienced high levels of legal conflict in reaching a decision. It should be emphasized that in only a handful of cases did a court actually adjudicate this conflict and award joint physical custody. Instead, nearly all these high-conflict cases were ones in which the parents reached this result through negotiations that were often protracted and acrimonious. There is also some evidence that court-annexed mediation may encourage joint physical custody, even though some claim that joint physical custody only prolongs conflict between warring parents.[40]

We also looked beneath the legal labels and compared the level of conflict for families with each of our three de facto residential patterns. Interestingly, we discovered that there were no statistically significant differences in mean conflict levels among de facto mother, father, or dual residence families. This result posed something of a puzzle: if families where the legal decree provided for joint physical custody had higher levels of conflict than families with other physical custody decrees, why is it that families with de facto dual residence did not have higher levels of conflict than families with other de facto arrangements?

We discovered the answer to this puzzle by comparing the de facto residence for high- and low-conflict joint custody families. (We treated Levels I and II as low; Levels III and IV as high.) Figure 2.3 shows the de facto residential patterns for the 62 families with joint physical custody who experienced high conflict—either "substantial" or "intense" conflict. It

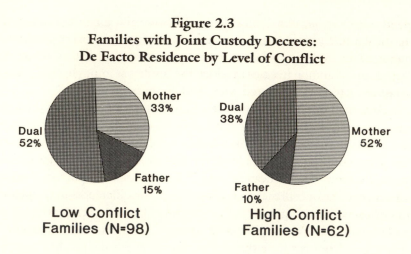

Figure 2.3
Families with Joint Custody Decrees:
De Facto Residence by Level of Conflict

compares their residential arrangements with the 98 low-conflict joint physical custody families—those with either "negligible" or "mild" conflict. The results are striking. In over half (52 percent) of the high-conflict joint physical custody families were the children in fact residing with the mother; they were spending only three or fewer overnights in a two-week period with the father. This was true of only 33 percent of the low-conflict families. Put another way, in two-thirds of the low-conflict joint custody families, children in fact maintained dual residences by spending four or more overnights with the father, but this was true of less than half (48 percent) of the high-conflict families.

Thus, it appears that in a number of high-conflict cases, the parents resolved their custodial conflict by incorporating joint physical custody into the divorce decree while having the children in fact reside with the mother. Did these families shift from dual residence to mother residence after the decree? Or had the children always resided with the mother, and the custody conflict was simply resolved by putting a joint physical custody label on this relationship? A preliminary analysis suggests no statistically significant differences in overnight stability over time among high- and low-conflict joint physical custody families. This at least suggests that some custody conflicts are being resolved with joint physical custody decrees, but the children actually reside with the mother and spend comparatively little time with the father.

In our interviews we asked each parent to rate how satisfied he or she was with the present arrangement for the children "in terms of the time they spend with each parent" on a scale of 1 to 10, where 1 meant completely unsatisfied and 10 meant completely satisfied. Interestingly, mothers in high-conflict families expressed almost the identical mean level of satisfaction (6.6) as mothers in low-conflict families (6.9). On the other hand, fathers in high-conflict families were less satisfied with these arrangements than fathers in low-conflict families (mean for high-conflict fathers = 4.8; mean for low-conflict fathers = 6.3). This evidence is certainly consistent with our conclusion that in cases in which there is conflict between the parents over custodial arrangements or visitation, the children end up with the mother more often than with the father. Moreover, it suggests that in high-conflict cases in which each parent wants to spend more time with the child, parental satisfaction with the outcome depends not on the legal label but on how much time the parent is actually spending with the child.

Conclusion

Our research suggests a substantial amount both of continuity and of change in terms of the actual operation of the legal system in California. Only further research in other states, however, will show to what extent divorcing families in California are characteristic of all divorcing families.

Mothers plainly remain the primary custodians of children following divorce, and it appears that there are very substantial differences between mothers and fathers with respect to custodial preferences. Gender differences in expressed desires and behavior among parents remain real and substantial after divorce as well as before. The overwhelming majority of mothers want to be the children's primary custodian. Although a surprisingly high percentage of fathers indicate they would prefer some physical custodial arrangement other than mother custody, there is much less legal conflict than one would expect simply by comparing the stated preferences of mothers and fathers.

Our findings contradict the claims of those who suggest that mothers are losing custody in a high proportion of cases. When one looks at those cases in which the mother and father make different custodial requests in the divorce proceedings, the evidence suggests that mothers secure their preferred outcome twice as often as fathers. Indeed, it appears that many fathers would prefer some custodial arrangement other than mother physical custody, but most never request such an arrangement in the judicial process.

While mothers remain the primary custodians of children after divorce, it is unclear whether this is due to judicial discretion or proper application of the best-interest standard. The accusation that judges perpetuate the maternal presumption seems somewhat unfounded, as very few cases in our sample were actually decided by a judge. It is unclear, however, what pressures may or may not be applied through the process of mediation and evaluation of the family.

Why did so many fathers in our study not request the form of physical custody they said they wanted? It is possible that fathers who told us they wanted custody meant it less passionately than mothers who told us the same. Evidence does suggest that mothers felt more strongly about custodial arrangements than fathers did. Fathers, however, rated themselves very high on their desire for custody, and we cannot discount these strong feelings solely on the basis that they were not as strong as those of mothers.

Fathers might also have been responding to what they believed was the social expectation that women are "supposed" to have custody and that fathers should not request it except in unusual circumstances. Another possibility is that the custodial desires of the mothers and fathers were almost equally strong but that many fathers realized their wishes were not realistic either because they were less experienced in the day-to-day management of the children's lives or because they expected to find it too difficult to coordinate the demands of their jobs with the demands of child rearing. Perhaps the fathers agreed to mother physical custody when it was clear that she had both more experience with the children and a work situation that could be better coordinated with family demands. Actually taking on major child-rearing responsibilities would be a large step for many men, and they may hesitate to make the commitment even though they genuinely want to live with their children.

The evidence concerning joint custody suggests substantial change. Joint legal custody was the outcome in a large majority of cases in the two counties we studied. Moreover, it appears that lawyers were important change agents in this regard and often may have suggested joint legal custody in situations where one or both parents had not otherwise considered it.

It remains to be explored what meaning, if any, the joint legal custody label has in terms either of the process by which parents make specific decisions concerning education, religion, or medical care or, more broadly, of how parents—particularly the father—view the parental role following divorce. The fact that joint legal custody carries with it so little by way of actual consequences probably explains why it has become so popular. Lawyers for mothers no doubt tell their clients that they are giving up nothing of importance in agreeing to joint legal custody. The parent with whom a child is residing, absent some explicit agreement to the contrary, can still make all the important day-to-day decisions for the child, and in this sense, joint legal custody does not undercut a mother's dominant role. On the other hand, the label may have important symbolic consequences. For fathers, it may well be taken as confirmation of their continuing parental rights and responsibilities, and it is at least possible that this confirmation may lead to greater paternal participation in the child's life following divorce.

We found that joint physical custody was the outcome in nearly a fifth of these California divorces. Although this legal label is meant to suggest that the parents are going to substantially share day-to-day child-rearing responsibilities, in a significant number of joint physical custody cases in our study—particularly the high-conflict cases—the children in fact resided with the mother and spent three or fewer overnights in a typical two-week period with the father. Nevertheless, in about 16 percent of the families in our study, the child in essence did have two homes and was spending four or more overnights with each parent in a two-week period. In other words, for about a sixth of the families both the father and the mother appear to have had substantial, if not equal, ongoing child-rearing responsibilities whether or not they had joint physical custody decrees.

It appears that in a number of cases involving "intense" parental conflict, the outcome was joint physical custody. It should be emphasized that this was not directly the result of judges' decisions. Of the tiny number of cases that judges in fact decided, only 4 resulted in this outcome. Instead, it appears that the use of joint physical custody to resolve some disputes was more the result of the negotiations between the two parents, often with the involvement of a mediator or through negotiations by attorneys.

Although joint custody was the outcome for a substantial number of high-conflict cases, we cannot say whether pressure for settlement under mediation was taking precedence over the best interest of children in these cases. The parents might simply have been more aware of the joint custody option as a result of mediation or more willing to agree to it within the mediation context. It is too early to conclude from these findings that the use of joint physical custody should be discouraged as a matter of policy, or even that parents, mediators, and lawyers should be told that this outcome is never appropriate in cases where there is "substantial" conflict between the parents. One would need to very carefully consider the consequences for divorce bargaining if new rules were established that attempted to prohibit joint physical custody in such cases. More fundamentally, one would need to know more about the effect on children of dual residential arrangements where the parents had "substantial" conflict in the process of divorce.

It is evident that gender still matters, in both the desires and behavior of parents concerning custody of their children. Overwhelmingly, mothers wanted physical custody of their children, and fathers' desires were more evenly divided among mother, joint, and father custodial arrangements. In addition, mothers were much more likely than fathers to act on their desires by filing a specific custodial request. Similar percentages of mothers and fathers, however, desired joint legal custody. These data indicate that though policies concerning standards for custody decisions may be gender-neutral, social realities still produce gender differentiation between parents.

Finally, our research confirms that in the overwhelming majority of cases, it is the parents, often with the involvement of lawyers, who resolve issues concerning custody and visitation following divorce. For 30 percent of our sample there was significant conflict, and for some 15 to 20 percent the conflict appeared to be serious. Our examination suggests that the intensity of the conflict was a function of what the father asked for, and the odds of conflict were much greater when the father requested either joint physical custody or physical custody for himself. Only 13 of our cases (1.4 percent), however, required a judicial determination concerning custody or visitation. Most parents—indeed, 70 percent of our sample—appeared to have little if any conflict concerning the custody or visitation provisions of the divorce decree.

3 The Economics of Divorce
Changing Rules, Changing Results

MARSHA GARRISON

The package of reforms that accompanied the establishment of no-fault divorce has been widely criticized as unfair to women and the children in their custody.[1] Critics argue that, as a result of the reforms, women fail to receive sufficient property or income following a divorce. To use the words of Lenore Weitzman, they claim that the "major economic result of the divorce law revolution is the systematic impoverishment of divorced women and their children."[2]

This claim is, of course, a serious and troubling one. At today's divorce rates, as many as half of all American marriages will be affected by divorce law.[3] Moreover, women and children are the most rapidly growing segment of the poor.[4] We need to know if the new divorce rules have indeed exacerbated this trend—and if changed rules can ameliorate it.

The claim that no-fault divorce reforms have resulted in women's impoverishment has thus far rested more on assumption than on careful consideration of the empirical evidence, however. Although some researchers have found that women and children are financially worse off under no-fault regimes than they were under fault rules, the independent impact of changes in the divorce transfer rules, as opposed to the enactment of no-fault divorce grounds, has not been assessed. Nor has the separate role of judicial discretion been determined. Indeed, we do not really know whether the divorce law revolution bears any responsibility for the changes in property and income distribution that have been discovered.

This chapter provides an assessment of the currently available evidence on the responsibility of the no-fault revolution for divorced wives' declining fortunes. It utilizes published data concerning divorce outcomes before and after the introduction of no-fault reforms in several states, as well as new, previously unpublished, data based on my own research on divorce outcomes before and after introduction of an equitable property distribution

The research described in this chapter was funded by the Alfred P. Sloan Foundation.

75

law in New York. The New York data are particularly valuable because they examine changes in financial outcomes associated with change in the alimony and property rules during a time when the divorce grounds did not change.

The first part of this chapter describes the critique of no-fault, and the evidence and assumptions upon which it has been based. The second part describes the New York data on alimony, child support, and distribution of the marital home, and the third compares the New York data with other available research, with the aim of assessing the validity of the claims made by no-fault's critics.

The Critique of No-Fault: The Evidence

The claim that the shift to no-fault divorce has negatively affected the economic well-being of divorced wives and children has been supported by evidence of two types. Surveys of postdivorce income in the no-fault era have demonstrated that the incomes of wives tend to substantially decline following divorce while those of husbands tend to increase.[5] Although these income surveys have not purported to demonstrate that divorced wives were better off in the fault era, research in several states[6] has shown that wives generally fared worse following no-fault divorce reforms than under the old fault regime.[7] More specifically, in most surveyed jurisdictions, it appears that the likelihood of receiving alimony,[8] the duration of alimony awards,[9] and the proportion of marital property awarded women decreased[10] following no-fault reforms, while the proportion of family debt women were required to pay increased.[11] The claim that divorce law reform has resulted in women's impoverishment, however, also rests on several assumptions that have not been subjected to rigorous scrutiny.

Causation or Correlation?

The first assumption is that the reported declines in property and/or alimony and child support awards that followed the advent of no-fault were, at least in part, *caused* by no-fault. Correlation is not equivalent to causation. Demonstrating a causal link between the enactment of no-fault divorce laws and declining awards to divorced women is particularly difficult, for several reasons.

First, no-fault laws were frequently coupled with changes in the property/alimony rules themselves, which makes it difficult to assess the independent impact of the climactic change no-fault might have occasioned from the impact of literal changes in the transfer rules. For example, at the time no-fault divorce grounds were enacted, most states followed California's lead in placing greater emphasis on need and employability as factors in determining whether alimony was appropriate, and for how long.[12] With increased emphasis on need and employability, it would not be surprising if alimony awards were to decline in the absence of any changes in the rules regarding fault. Moreover, the transfer rules might have been changed without the adoption of no-fault divorce. Perhaps more to the point today, they might be changed once again while retaining the no-fault regime with respect to the grounds for divorce.

The causation question is further complicated by the significant social and economic changes that occurred during the same period—the 1970s—as did the no-fault revolution. The decade witnessed, along with no-fault, continuing changes in women's employment and in public attitudes toward marriage and divorce. The proportion of married women in the work force continued to rise,[13] and the decade witnessed even more profound differences in social attitudes toward women's work; employment for married women, even those with young children, became not merely acceptable but expected. The changes in women's work were accompanied by equally profound changes of attitude toward marriage and divorce. Not only did the divorce rate skyrocket[14]—evidence of increased social acceptability for divorced status—but public opinion about marital obligations shifted. By the 1980s most of the American public seemed to agree with the shifts in postdivorce income distribution that critics of no-fault have noted; for example, they favored alimony on the basis of need and for a transitional period only.[15] Given the considerable discretion enjoyed by judges under the fault regime, it would not be in the least surprising if these various social, economic, and attitudinal changes had an impact on divorce awards, apart from any legislative change.

Causation Hypotheses

Assuming that the no-fault revolution did cause the noted declines in income and property transfers to divorced wives, how it would have done so remains obscure. In some cases legislatures mandated results, but more often the results were not required by the new legislation and may even have run counter to the legislature's expectations. For example, the California no-fault law did not on its face make it harder for mothers of young children—a group whom Weitzman found experienced a dramatic decline in spousal support[16]—to obtain alimony.[17] Indeed, by eliminating the fault requirements,[18] the law created the possibility that more women in this group would receive alimony.

The principal hypothesis that has been offered to explain how no-fault divorce has yielded reduced economic outcomes for divorced wives postulates that women have less bargaining power in the no-fault era because they have lost the ability to block a divorce.[19] Under the fault regime, as marital fault sufficient to provide grounds for divorce was difficult to establish,[20] a wife who did not want a divorce could, in many cases, prevent her husband from obtaining one by contesting the action. The bargaining power hypothesis presumes that wives used this leverage by trading the ability to block a divorce for a better financial settlement. Under unilateral no-fault divorce, this bargaining leverage is lost.[21] In short, the theory attributes divorced wives' lower economic expectations to the change in the grounds for divorce.

An alternative (or concurrent) hypothesis suggests that the judiciary has misunderstood or abused its discretion under the new rules.[22] The judicial discretion hypothesis is an ambiguous one as judges had ample discretion under the fault rules to achieve the same results that have accompanied the movement to no-fault. Thus, the judicial discretion theory must be tied to some aspect of no-fault reform in order to link no-fault with the changes in economic outcomes that have been noted. Perhaps, as some commentators have suggested, the no-fault regime changed the "climate" of judicial decision making by promoting the notion of formal equality between the spouses.[23] The elimination of the fault requirement could also reduce income and property awards to divorced wives by altering the judicial perception that alimony and marital property were entitlements of an innocent spouse.[24]

These two hypotheses, implicitly or explicitly, have played a considerable role in shaping reform proposals. Both hypotheses have produced a general preference for bright-line rules—for example, equal rather than equitable property distribution—that will lessen the need for bargaining chips and simultaneously reduce judicial discretion.[25] Many of the reform proposals also reflect an implicit assumption that we need not worry too greatly about the precise mechanism by which the decline in awards to divorced wives has occurred; no matter what the cause, clear directives to judges can improve the results for women.

Reliance on such an assumption is, however, highly questionable; we should not forget that the reason reforms are being proposed in the first place is to make up for the failures of past reform measures. Take the case of property distribution. Weitzman indicates that, in adopting an equal division rule, the California legislature thought that it was merely codifying past practice.[26] Weitzman's research, however, revealed that women had in fact received more property under the old regime.[27] Lack of information about present outcomes affected the debate over equal distribution and, to some extent, determined the impact on women. Yet many women's advocates have continued to urge equal over equitable distribution on the basis of scattered, anecdotal reports that women typically get less than 50 percent of marital property in equitable distribution jurisdictions.[28] McLindon's 1987 report on New Haven, Connecticut, was the first to systematically describe outcomes under an equitable property distribution scheme in the no-fault era. Although he found that awards had declined, women still obtained more than half the property on average, and in three of four income groups they obtained more than two-thirds.[29] McLindon's report may not, of course, be representative of national trends; he also found alimony awards far more frequently than has been reported elsewhere.[30] But it does strongly support the need for evidence rather than anecdote as a basis for reform.

The Varied Revolution

The New Haven example just noted illustrates the reform movement's inattention to the diversity of no-fault reforms and the economic outcomes that have been reported in varying jurisdictions. Critics of the divorce revolution have too often assumed *a* revolution, without careful consideration of the fairly extensive differences in no-fault regimes.[31] These differences are important not only for the challenge they present in formulating reforms but also for the research possibilities they offer. One would expect that, to the extent that the no-fault revolution played a role in promoting declining property and income transfers to women, different regimes would translate into different results. Moreover, these differences should throw some light on the causation issues just described.

Take a simple example. In a handful of states—including my research site, New York—it is still impossible to obtain a no-fault divorce without the consent of both spouses.[32] In these states the bargaining power of the spouse who does not want a divorce is preserved; any decline in wives' awards of property and/or alimony following the introduction of no-fault in this very limited form should be attributable to other factors. In other states, a no-fault divorce cannot be obtained unilaterally without a fairly substantial period of separation.[33] Here the bargaining power of the spouse is partially preserved. In sum, if reduced bargaining leverage has played a major role in producing lower divorce awards to wives, one would expect that wives would fare best in states without unilateral divorce, second best in those that require a waiting period, and worst in states that permit unilateral divorce upon demand.

One researcher, using U.S. census data, has already attempted such a comparison.[34] Peters compared alimony, child support, and property awards to divorced wives in states that granted unilateral, no-fault divorce with those in states that did not and found results identical to those predicted by the bargaining hypothesis. Although the strength of Peters's conclusions is weakened by the fact that she lumped together states that require only a waiting period—indeed some with fairly modest waiting periods[35]—with states that do not permit unilateral divorce at all, she did find results predicted by the bargaining hypothesis. The differences were modest,[36] but nonetheless statistically significant at a fairly low confidence level.[37] Peters's report thus provides some support for the bargaining hypothesis, but her conclusions have been neither replicated nor refuted in any other study.[38] No one has compared outcomes in states that enacted different no-fault schemes—for example, a waiting period rule and a unilateral option rule. Nor has anyone examined the impact of changed alimony or property rules that were enacted outside the context of a no-fault reform.

Currently available data[39] do provide some opportunity for such comparative analysis, as the no-fault reforms enacted in the various jurisdictions in which research has been done were not uniform. For example, research reports are available describing divorce outcomes before and after no-fault in California, Connecticut, and Ohio. California adopted a unilateral no-fault option without a waiting period and with an equal property division rule.[40] Connecticut and Ohio both adopted a scheme that required a separation or a spousal agreement as the no-fault basis for a divorce.[41] Neither state adopted an equal property division rule. In Ohio the property division rules were not changed at all; in Connecticut the only change was to add criteria that the judge was required to consider when dividing the property.[42]

My research in New York provides additional data to enlarge the possibilities for comparative analysis.[43] The addition of the New York data is particularly helpful in assessing the various causation issues for several reasons. First, New York's limited no-fault option (adopted in 1966) requires spousal agreement[44] and thus has preserved fault regime bargaining chips. Second, unlike all other jurisdictions in which research has been conducted, New York's equitable distribution scheme was not enacted as part of a comprehensive no-fault reform.[45] Finally, the equitable distribution law enacted by the New York legislature and the changed alimony rules that accompanied it are fairly typical of the transfer rules that accompanied no-fault; the role of fault was deemphasized,[46] while need and employability were stressed as factors for determining alimony.[47] As a result of these various factors, the New York data considerably enhance the possibility of assessing the independent impact of changes in the divorce transfer rules as opposed to changes in the grounds for divorce. The next section will briefly describe the New York research, and what it has revealed about the impact of a change in the divorce transfer rules, independent of no-fault reforms, on alimony, child support, and distribution of the marital home.

The New York Divorce Reform Experience
How the Law Was Changed

Prior to the 1980 reform, New York was one of a handful of states that did not have a marital property distribution scheme[48] and that retained traditional, fault-based, alimony rules.[49] The new law brought New York law into the mainstream by establishing an equitable property distribution rule and introducing the concept of rehabilitative alimony.

New York's equitable distribution law as a fairly typical one. It applies only to property acquired during the marriage and additionally excludes gifts (except between spouses), inheritances, and personal injury awards from distribution.[50] Property is to be distributed based on a number of specified factors,[51] as well as "any other factor which the court shall expressly find to be just and proper."[52] Although the legislation itself is silent as to whether marital fault may be considered, the courts quickly ruled that fault should play a role in distribution only when egregious.[53]

The equitable distribution law was linked with legislative changes in the determination of alimony awards. The legislature specified that any alimony award (renamed maintenance under the legislation) was a factor in determining a property award.[54] It also introduced consideration of the property distribution into the alimony decision,[55] along with spelling out in more detail than the previous statute traditional factors for awarding alimony and eliminating fault as a basis for denying it and occupancy of the marital residence.[56]

Although these changes would not, on their face, appear to disadvantage women, a legislative memorandum explaining the new statute indicates that an award of maintenance "should rest on the economic basis of reasonable needs and the ability to pay."[57] According to the memorandum, permanent maintenance may be necessary "in marriages of long duration, or where the former spouse is out of the labor market and lacks sufficient resources, or has sacrificed her business or professional career to serve as a parent and home-maker,"[58] but the primary objective of maintenance is to "award the recipient spouse an opportunity to achieve independence."[59] This language, which has been cited approvingly by the New York Court of Appeals,[60] suggests that courts should, in general, award maintenance for short-term "rehabilitative" purposes. The revised alimony law thus closely resembles those typically adopted as part of no-fault reforms in its emphasis on need and employability.

Research Methodology

Data were drawn from the files of 900 divorces filed in 1978, two years before enactment of the equitable distribution law, and from the files of 900 divorces filed in 1984, four years after the law's passage. Within each year, the cases were selected in equal numbers from an urban (New York County, that is, Manhattan), suburban (Westchester), and an upstate (Onondaga, that is, Syracuse, N.Y., and its immediate environs) county.[61] Within each county, cases were chosen on the basis of case category: 100 contested,[62] 100 consensual,[63] and 100 default[64] divorces were randomly selected from each county for each survey year. From the contested cases it was possible to collect comprehensive data, including detailed financial information on income and assets, occupation, education, and health.[65] Information in the other case files was more limited, and it was typically impossible to ascertain spousal income or the value of assets owned and transferred.

Characteristics of the Sample

The couples in my sample were married for an average of 11.7 years in 1978 and 11.1 years in 1984.[66] These averages are considerably higher than the average marital duration reported by California researchers,[67] but roughly comparable to those reported by other researchers in the Northeast.[68]

The proportion of the sample with children and the average number of children were also relatively close to the figures reported by other Northeast

Table 3.1. Percentage of Wives Awarded Alimony, by Year

Case Category	1978 (N = 926)	1984 (N = 946)	Difference
Total sample	32	21	−11
Total divorce population	21	12	− 9

Note: $p < .001$

researchers.[69] In 1978, 67 percent had children; in 1984, 60 percent did so. The average number of minor children per couple was 1.3 in 1978 and 1.1 in 1984.[70]

Age and income information was available only for the contested sample. Among this group (which also had a longer average marital duration and more children than the total sample), the average age of husbands was 40.3 years in 1978 and 40.9 years in 1984; wives averaged 37.2 years in 1978 and 38.2 years in 1984. Average family income for this group ($53,702 in 1978, $47,057 in 1984)[71] was also considerably higher than median family income in the three surveyed counties according to census reports.[72]

The Aftermath of Reform

Alimony and Child Support. Among the 1978 cases, alimony was awarded in 32 percent of all sample cases, and 21 percent of all divorce cases within the three surveyed counties.[73] In 1984, alimony was awarded in only 21 percent of all sample cases[74] and 12 percent of all divorce cases within the three surveyed counties, a statistically significant decline (see table 3.1).

More dramatic changes occurred in regard to the duration of alimony awards (see table 3.2).[75] In 1978, when alimony was awarded, it was permanent in 78 percent of the sample cases and 81 percent of cases within the total divorce population. In 1984, when alimony was awarded, it was permanent in only 37 percent of the sample cases and 41 percent of the cases within the total divorce population. The decline was, again, statistically significant. The change was also consistent across case categories[76] and across counties.[77]

The greatest impact of the decline in alimony fell on long-married wives (see table 3.3).[78] Although wives married twenty or more years were, in both study years, more likely to receive alimony than their counterparts in shorter marriages, the awards to these wives also declined the most. In

Table 3.2. Percentage of Alimony Awards Permanent, by Year

Case Category	1978 (N = 289)	1984 (N = 186)	Difference
Total sample	78	37	−41
Total divorce population	81	41	−40

Note: $p < .001$

Table 3.3. Percentages of Wives Awarded
Alimony, by Year and Length of Marriage

Length of Marriage	1978		1984		Difference
	%	(N)	%	(N)	
Under 5 years	14	(214)	11	(277)	− 3%[a]
5 to 10 years	26	(254)	17	(220)	− 9%[b]
10 to 15 years	37	(163)	24	(176)	−13%[c]
15 to 20 years	43	(114)	28	(127)	−15%[d]
20 or more years	54	(158)	34	(139)	−20%[e]
Total sample	32	(903)	21	(939)	−11

[a] not significant
[b] $p < .02$
[c] $p < .01$
[d] $p < .02$
[e] $p < .001$

1978, 54 percent of wives in our sample married twenty or more years received an alimony award, but in 1984 only 34 percent did. The decline for wives married less than five years, by contrast, was much smaller (from 14 percent to 11 percent).

Wives with custody of minor children were, in both survey years, significantly more likely to obtain alimony than were wives without custody (see table 3.4). The general decline in alimony awards, however, did affect wives with custody to a slightly greater extent than wives without custody; the likelihood of wives with custody obtaining alimony declined by 36 percent, and the likelihood of wives without custody obtaining alimony declined by 32 percent.

The decline in the likelihood and duration of alimony awards cannot be

Table 3.4. Percentages of Wives Awarded
Alimony, by Year and Custody Status

Custody Status[a]	1978		1984		Difference	% Change
	%	(N)	%	(N)		
With custody[b]	39	(471)	25	(378)	−14	−36
Without custody[c]	19	(337)	13	(409)	− 6	−32

[a]Cases involving split or joint physical custody are excluded from this portion of the analysis.
[b]$p < .001$
[c]$p < .05$

Table 3.5. Percentages of Wives Receiving
Alimony, by Year and Employment Status

Employment Status[a]	1978		1984		Difference	% Change
	%	(N)	%	(N)		
Employed[b]	37	(169)	26	(208)	−11	−30
Unemployed[c]	64	(95)	52	(79)	−12	−19

[a]These figures apply only to the contested cases, the only group for which employment information is available.
[b]$p < .10$
[c]$p < .05$

completely accounted for by changes in surveyed wives' employment or income. Between 1978 and 1984 wives' employment did increase. In contested cases (the only group for which employment information is available), employment among wives rose from 64 percent of the total group to 73 percent. If the 1978 relation between alimony and employment held constant, one would predict alimony awards to decline by three percentage points.[79] But alimony awards within the contested group instead declined by fifteen percentage points (from 45 percent to 30 percent). Moreover, alimony awards to unemployed wives declined over the survey period along with awards to employed wives; the likelihood of an unemployed wife receiving alimony declined by 19 percent as compared to 30 percent for employed wives, a relatively modest difference (see table 3.5). Unemployed

Table 3.6. Average Alimony Awards ($ per month), by Year

Category	1978 $1984	(N)	1984 $1984	(N)	% Change
All Sample Cases					
Total sample[a]	276	(923)	171	(948)	−38
Total divorce population	101		93		− 8
All Alimony Awards					
Total sample[b]	824	(291)	841	(192)	7
Total divorce population	652		606		− 7
(Onondaga and Westchester counties only)					

[a] $p < .01$
[b] not significant.

wives in lengthy marriages (over ten years) experienced an even sharper drop in the likelihood of obtaining alimony than did the general pool of unemployed wives. Of this group 74 percent received alimony in 1978 as compared to 58 percent in 1984, a 22 percent decline. Additionally, wives' average income did not increase substantially over the survey period. In 1978 wives in contested cases earned an average of $14,470, and in 1984, $15,130.[80] It is thus unlikely that alimony awards declined because wives were more capable of self-support through their own earnings.

The average alimony award for the total divorce population did not decline dramatically between 1978 and 1984, even when zero awards were included (see table 3.6). For both years, however, the averages varied substantially among categories[81] and counties.[82] Wives with low incomes also experienced a much greater decline in the level of alimony than did high-income wives. The mean alimony award for wives earning less than $10,000 declined from $754 per month to $370 per month, while the mean for wives earning $20,000 to $40,000 held constant at $79 per month.

Child Support. Although alimony awards declined only marginally, the level of child support declined much more substantially (see table 3.7).[83] The average monthly child support award for the total sample was $502 in 1978 and $376 in 1984.[84] The average award per minor child declined from $273 to $216. Although it was possible to compute average awards for the total divorcing population in only two of the three survey counties,[85] here again the average fell markedly.

Table 3.7. Average Child Support Awards ($ per month), by Year

Case Category	1978 (N = 475)	1984 (N = 410)	% Change
Total Sample			
Total[a]	502	376	−25
Per child[b]	273	216	−21
Total Divorce Population			
(Onondaga and Westchester counties only)			
Total	480	342	−29
Per child	248	190	−23

[a]$p < .01$
[b]$p < .01$

Table 3.8. Percentage Distribution of Child Custody Decisions, by Year

Custody Decision	Total Sample		Total Divorce Population	
	1978 (N = 538)	1984 (N = 467)	1978	1984
W physical custody	88	82	88	84
H physical custody	5	9	7	9
Split	4	4	3	3
Joint physical custody	3	5	3	4
Joint legal custody	22	42	17	35

$p < .05$ for overall shifts in physical custody

The decreases in child support awards cannot be explained by changes in custody outcomes, as changes in the physical custody of minor children were quite modest (see table 3.8).[86] In both periods, wives obtained physical custody in more than four out of five cases, even though provisions for joint legal custody rose dramatically during the survey period from 22 percent to 42 percent. Moreover, although husbands were slightly more likely to obtain physical custody in 1984 than in 1978, in both years child support awards were made almost exclusively to wives. Only two fathers in 1978 and one in 1984 received support awards.

Table 3.9. Percentage Distribution of
Marital Home Awards (Owned), by Year

Disposition of Marital Home	1978 (N = 396)	1984 (N = 396)
Title to W without payment to H	31	31
Title to W with payment to H	3	4
Occupancy to W	16	8
Total Occupancy to W	50	43
Title to H without payment to W	14	16
Title to H with payment to W	6	12
Occupancy to H	2	2
Total Occupancy to H	22	30
Present sale	27	26

Distribution of the Marital Home. In both 1978 and 1984 approximately two-thirds of the surveyed couples owned a home (64 percent in 1978, 68 percent in 1984).[87] In both survey years the home was jointly owned in 88 percent of all cases. Average equity for the contested sample[88] was $61,665 in 1978 and $83,968 in 1984.[89]

Change in the disposition of the family home, whether rented or owned, was fairly modest between the two survey years. Among renters, wives were slightly more likely to keep the family home in 1984 than they were earlier (52 percent in 1978, 57 percent in 1984),[90] but the change was not statistically significant.

Among home owners, husbands were slightly more likely to retain occupancy of the marital home[91] under the new regime as compared to the old one, but once again the difference was statistically insignificant (see table 3.9). In 1978 they obtained outright ownership 20 percent of the time. In 1984 they obtained outright ownership in 28 percent of the cases. Wives, by contrast, received outright ownership in 34 percent of the 1978 cases and 35 percent of the 1984 cases. The increase in husband ownership came largely at the expense of occupancy orders on behalf of wives (16 percent in 1978, 8 percent in 1984). On the other hand, the increase in husband ownership was largely offset by cash settlements with wives. Thus, generally speaking, the modest shift in the distribution of the marital home that occurred between

**Table 3.10. Percentages of Wives Awarded Marital Home
(Rented or Owned), by Year and Length of Marriage**

Length of Marriage	1978		1984		Difference
	%	(N)	%	(N)	
Under 10 years	41	(269)	40	(238)	− 1[a]
10 or more years	62	(312)	52	(312)	−10[b]
Total Sample	52	(581)	47	(550)	− 5

[a] Not significant.
[b] $p < .02$

1978 and 1984 seems to have been one in which wives were losing occupancy but gaining money instead.[92]

The decline in occupancy awards was not matched by any increase in the probability that the home would be sold. Sales occurred in 27 percent of the 1978 cases and 26 percent of the 1984 cases. This pattern occurred in both the contested and consensual cases.[93] Nor, when the home was sold, was there any decline in the proportion of the net proceeds received by divorcing wives. In 1978 wives received less than half of the proceeds of a current sale in 6 percent of the cases; exactly half in 73 percent of the cases, and more than half in 20 percent of the cases. In 1984, they received less than half in 8 percent of the cases, exactly half in 72 percent of the cases, and more than half in 20 percent of the cases.[94]

Despite the overall lack of dramatic change over the survey period in regard to the disposition of the marital home (rented and owned), long-married wives were adversely affected to a surprising degree; the decline in awards to this group was also statistically significant (see table 3.10). In 1978 wives married ten or more years obtained occupancy of the family home 62 percent of the time, and wives married less than ten years obtained the home 41 percent of the time. In 1984, wives married ten or more years obtained occupancy of the home 52 percent of the time, and wives married less than ten years obtained the home 40 percent of the time. The decline in awards to long-married wives is largely accounted for by a corresponding increase in awards to husbands (from 14 percent in 1978 to 24 percent in 1984).[95] The direction of change was consistent across case categories, although it was more pronounced in the consensual and default cases than in those that were contested.[96]

The relationship between custody and disposition of the marital home varied less substantially over the survey period. Neither the differences in occupancy awards[97] nor ownership of the marital home was statistically significant.[98]

Assessing the New York Research Data
Alimony and Its Duration

The likelihood of an alimony award and the permanency of those awards declined after the introduction of New York's equitable distribution law in a way closely parallel to the declines noted in states that experienced no-fault reforms and that have been associated with no-fault's introduction (see table 3.11). In New York, as in the surveyed no-fault jurisdictions, the number of divorced wives receiving alimony declined somewhat over the survey period; the number of permanent alimony awards dropped quite precipitously. Table 3.11 demonstrates that all surveyed jurisdictions show substantial declines in the overall proportion of wives receiving alimony and, with the exception of Spokane County, Washington, substantial declines in the likelihood of receiving permanent alimony as well.

What can we infer from these results? The New York data demonstrate that the introduction of no-fault divorce, with the resulting elimination of the bargaining leverage it might offer wives, is not necessary to trigger substantial declines in the likelihood of receiving alimony. In New York reduced awards coincided with changes in the property/alimony rules themselves without any accompanying change in divorce grounds. The New York data thus fail to support the hypothesis that loss of bargaining leverage has reduced alimony awards to divorced wives. The data suggest instead that where both the grounds and the underlying entitlement rules were changed simultaneously, it was the latter, not the former, that mattered most.

The Spokane County, Washington, data cast further doubt on the bargaining leverage hypothesis. There the introduction of no-fault divorce was not associated with any reduction in the level of permanent alimony awards. But prior to the introduction of no-fault in Spokane County, the proportion of wives receiving permanent alimony was already low compared to other surveyed jurisdictions after the introduction of no-fault. This suggests that the rehabilitative, short-term alimony concept was sufficiently well accepted in Washington, before no-fault, that no-fault itself made no appreciable difference.

Table 3.11. Percentages of Wives Awarded Alimony and Percentages of Alimony Awards that Were Permanent, by Jurisdiction and Year

Research Site Divorce Grounds[a]	Year 1 Alimony % Permanent %	Year 2 Alimony % Permanent %	Difference	% Change
Cuyahoga County, OH[b] (UW)	26	18	− 8	−31
	60	30	−30	−50
New Haven, CT[c] (UW)	59	30	−29	−49
	99	60	−39	−39
Los Angeles/San Francisco, CA[d] (U)	20	15	− 5	−25
	62	32	−30	−48
Spokane County, WA[e] (U)	10	7	− 3	−30
	38	40	+ 2	+ 5
San Diego, CA[f] (U)	66	30	−36	−55
	46	37	− 9	−20
NY/Onondaga	21	12	− 9	−43
Westchester/NY (M)	81	41	−40	−49

[a] Divorce grounds: U = no-fault divorce, unilateral option; M = fault divorce and no-fault divorce based on agreeement; UW = fault divorce, no-fault based on agreement, and unilateral no-fault with a waiting period.

[b] McGraw, Sterin, and Davis, "A Case Study in Divorce Law Reform and Its Aftermath," 20 J. Fam. L. 443, 473–75 (1981–82).

[c] McLindon, "Separate but Unequal: The Economic Disaster of Divorce for Women and Children," 21 Fam. L. Q. 351, 362, 364–65 (1987).

[d] L. Weitzman, The Divorce Revolution, 164–65, 167 (1985). Weitzman's reported data on the duration of alimony awards is confined to Los Angeles. Id. at 164.

[e] Welch and Price-Bonham, "A Decade of No-Fault Divorce Revisited: California, Georgia, and Washington," 45 J. Marriage & Fam. 411, 415 (1983). Welch and Price-Bonham also report on divorce outcomes before and after no-fault's introduction in Clark County, Georgia. The Clark County results appear to be strongly influenced, however, by the fact that one judge decided all divorce cases within the county during the initial period surveyed and half of them in the second year; analysis of his decisions by the researchers indicated that his no-fault divorce settlements differed little overall from either his fault divorce settlements or the no-fault divorce settlements of the new divorce judge. Id. at 412. Because of this apparent bias in the Clark County data, this part of Welch and Price-Bonham's findings are excluded from my analysis.

[f] Seal, "A Decade of No-Fault Divorce: What It Has Meant Financially for Women in California," 1 FAM. Adv. 10, 12 (1979). The 66% figure includes token awards of $1, excluded by the other researchers. Seal does not indicate how many of the awards are for token amounts. Weitzman, however, indicates that token awards were received by 19% of Los Angeles wives and 17% of San Francisco wives in 1968; 11% of wives in both cities in 1977. L. Weitzman, supra note d at 167. If San Diego award patterns are consistent with those of other large California cities, the percentages of wives receiving more than token alimony in San Diego would be approximately 48% in 1968 and 19% in 1976.

The Washington and New York experiences together suggest that the introduction of no-fault divorce is neither a necessary nor a sufficient condition to trigger declines in the level of alimony or the likelihood of permanent alimony. In contrast to what some have supposed, loss of wives' bargaining power resulting from the abolition of fault appears to have been a rather unimportant factor in determining financial outcomes in these jurisdictions.

A comparison of the research results in relation to the grounds for divorce within the surveyed jurisdictions lends further support to this viewpoint. Of the six surveyed jurisdictions,[99] broadly similar declines in the level and permanency of alimony accompanied no-fault reforms. But the no-fault features adopted by these states differed considerably; California and Washington adopted pure unilateral no-fault regimes, New York had a fault regime offering no unilateral no-fault option, and Connecticut and Ohio adopted mixed legal systems offering unilateral no-fault divorce only after a waiting period.[100] If the bargaining leverage of fault were a key factor in producing higher alimony awards, one would expect different results: the greatest declines should occur in the unilateral no-fault states, and the least in the fault state (New York), with Connecticut and Ohio falling somewhere in the middle.

On the other hand, a comparison of the research results does suggest that legislative changes in alimony and property rules are correlated with reduced alimony awards. California's no-fault law went into effect in 1970; by 1972, a decline in alimony was apparent.[101] By contrast, between 1966 and 1972 in Ohio there was no legislative change and no significant change in alimony awards.[102] Ohio's no-fault law went into effect in 1973; by 1978 changes in alimony awards almost identical to those that occurred in California were apparent.[103] Similarly, twelve years after New York introduced no-fault divorce by mutual consent, alimony awards, particularly in regard to duration, were more like alimony awards before no-fault in California and Ohio[104] than the post-no-fault awards then current in these states. After New York's legislative change in the alimony and property rules, however, similar declines occurred. In sum, that such similar changes occurred at different dates and within the context of such different legal regimes suggests that, whereas legislative action on no-fault divorce grounds has not been centrally related to declining alimony awards, the ancillary alimony reforms that have typically accompanied no-fault (or, in New York, enacted independently of no-fault) have played a major role in producing the changed outcomes.

In some respects, this seems to be exactly what was intended. For example, as noted earlier, many legislatures intended to restrict alimony to wives who could not support themselves.[105] The two models to which states adopting no-fault typically turned—the California law and the Uniform Marriage and Divorce Act[106]—both envisioned alimony as a remedy limited to the needy spouse, and permanent alimony as a remedy limited to the older spouse whose prospects of gainful employment were dim.

The cases of Washington and New York provide interesting contrasts in the role of legislative change in the alimony rules. The level of permanent alimony in Washington did not decline after no-fault divorce was introduced, but both the proportion of permanent awards and the percentage of wives receiving alimony were, before no-fault was introduced, lower than in any other surveyed jurisdiction after no-fault's introduction. Here the judiciary had introduced the concept of short-term alimony, declaring that state policy required a divorced wife to "seek employment, if possible, and not give her [a] permanent claim for alimony against her husband."[107] The shift to no-fault thus did not mark any shift in the alimony rules. In New York, by contrast, the alimony statute prior to the statutory changes that accompanied equitable distribution had been judicially interpreted to mandate permanent alimony absent an agreement to the contrary. And, as we have seen, the legislature's intended change in that pattern was followed by altered outcomes.

Although the results thus appear to be generally consistent with legislative intent, the data also suggest that the exercise of judicial discretion has been an important factor in producing changed outcomes (see table 3.12). More specifically, in some jurisdictions, judges appear to have been overzealous in attaining the legislative goal of encouraging self-sufficiency for divorced wives.

If legislative intentions were controlling, one would expect that long-married housewives would not experience any significant diminution in the likelihood of receiving alimony, and that wives in short marriages, employed wives, and wives without custody would be significantly less likely to receive alimony after revision of the alimony rules. As table 3.12 indicates, in California, economic outcomes for these women initially failed to meet legislative expectations, but did so five years later. According to Weitzman, what produced the shift was appellate decisions chastising trial-level judges for overzealous interpretation of the new law.[108] The New York and Connecticut data suggest that judges may initially have been similarly overzealous in applying the law to some groups and that corrective measures, at the judicial or legislative level, may be necessary.

Table 3.12. Alimony Awards in Relation to Marital Duration, Employment, and Custody, by Year and Research Site

Research Site	Year 1 Alimony	Year 2 Alimony	Year 3 Alimony	Difference/ % Change
New Haven, CT[a]				
Long-married house-wives (15)[b]	80		75	− 5/− 6
Long-married wives (15)	84		50	−34/−40
Housewives	61		45	−16/−26
Short-married wives	n.a.[c]		n.a.	
Employed wives	60		26	−34/−57
Wives with custody	n.a.		n.a.	
Wives w/o custody	67		17	−50/−75
Los Angeles and San Francisco, CA[d]				
Long-married house-wives (10)	44	34	64	+20/+45
Long-married wives (15)	39	31	46	+ 7/+18
Housewives	24	18	26	+ 2/+ 8
Short-married wives (5)	13	5	5	− 8/−62
Employed wives	15	10	13	− 2/−13
Wives with custody	22	15	22	0/ 0
Wives w/o custody	13	10	11	− 2/−15
Westchester/Onondaga, NY				
Long-married house-wives (10)	74		58	−16/−22
Long-married wives (20)	54		34	−20/−37
Housewives	64		52	−12/−19
Short-married wives (5)	14		11	− 3/−21
Employed wives	37		26	−11/−30
Wives with custody	39		25	−14/−36
Wives w/o custody	19		13	− 6/−32

[a]McLindon, "Separate but Unequal: The Economic Disaster of Divorce for Women and Children," 21 *Fam. L.Q.* 351, 362, 363–64 (1987).

[b]The minimum marital duration required to be counted as a "long-married" wife and the maximum marital duration required to be counted as a "short-married" wife are noted in parentheses following these designations for each study.

[c]n.a.: The research report does not report alimony rates for this group.

[d]L. Weitzman, *The Divorce Revolution*, 168–69, 176–77, 185–86 (1985).

All in all, a comparative examination of the research data strongly suggests that the legislative rules regarding divorce entitlements and judicial interpretation of those rules have been more important determinants of divorce outcomes than loss of bargaining power available under the fault regime.

The Amount of Alimony and Child Support

There is a quite remarkable consistency across all surveyed jurisdictions in the level of support per minor child awarded in the period following whatever reform was studied (see table 3.13). In constant 1984 dollars, these awards ranged from $182 to $234 per month. Given the variety of legal regimes and locations (with probable differences in cost of living) that was involved, the uniformity of these figures is striking. Moreover, of the three jurisdictions in which I could determine what proportion of the payor's income went to child support, New York, with the most restrictive divorce grounds, fell in the middle. Hence once again, the bargaining leverage of fault does not seem to have provided any tangible benefit; children in New York fared no better than did their counterparts in unilateral and mixed no-fault regimes.

The data on the amount of alimony awarded are more difficult to interpret as researchers have seldom made clear whether the average alimony award they report includes or excludes zero awards. Weitzman does provide an average that excludes zeros: it is only 5 percent less than in Westchester and Onondaga counties, New York. While a comparison of two research reports is hardly definitive, this difference seems quite insubstantial given the fact that one of the surveyed New York counties is among the wealthiest in the nation. The Onondaga County average ($446) is indeed less than that reported by Weitzman.

The Marital Home

A comparative survey of the marital home data again fails to support the bargaining hypothesis (see table 3.14). The bargaining hypothesis would predict that outright awards of the marital home to wives would decline most in unilateral no-fault jurisdictions and little or not at all in a mutual no-fault jurisdiction, with declines in a mixed jurisdiction somewhere in the middle. This is not precisely what happened. As table 3.14 demonstrates, outright awards to wives did decline quite dramatically in California (−36

Table 3.13. Alimony and Child Support Awards, by Year and Research Site in $1984

Research Site	Year 1	Year 2	% Change
Cuyahoga County, OH[a]			
Avg. support per minor child	237	214	−10
Avg. alimony award[b]	378	323	−15
Support % (gross)	13	12	− 8
New Haven, CT[c]			
Avg. support per minor child	242	234	− 3
Avg. alimony award[d]	234	160	−32
Support % (gross)	34	29	−15
Los Angeles, CA[e]			
Avg. support per minor child		217	
Avg. alimony award		573	
San Diego, CA[f]			
Median support per minor child	296	182	−39
Median alimony award	224	182	−19
Spokane County, WA[g]			
Avg. support per minor child	214	220	+ 3
Avg. alimony award[b]	386	362	− 6
Westchester/Onondaga, NY			
Avg. support per minor child[h]	248	190	−23
Avg. alimony award	652	606	− 7
Support % (gross)	29	24	−21

[a]G. Sterin and J. Davis, *Divorce Awards and Outcomes: A Study of Pattern and Change in Cuyahoga County, Ohio 1965–1978*, 94–95, 132 (1981).
[b]Method of computing average unclear.
[c]McLindon, "Separate but Unequal: The Economic Disaster of Divorce for Women and Children," 21 *Fam. L.Q.* 361, 369 (1987).
[d]Average includes cases with zero awards.
[e]L. Weitzman, *The Divorce Revolution*, 171, 265 (1985). Although Weitzman also conducted research in Los Angeles, she provides child support figures only for San Francisco. *Id.* at 265.
[f]Seal, "A Decade of No-Fault Divorce: What It Has Meant Financially for Women in California," *Fam. Adv.* 10, 12 (1979).
[g]Welch and Price-Bonham, "A Decade of No-Fault Divorce Revisited: California, Georgia, and Washington," 45 *J. Marriage & Fam.* 411, 415 (1983).
[h]The average support figures are for Onondaga and Westchester counties only.

**Table 3.14. Disposition of the Marital Home (Owned),
by Year and Research Site**

Research Site	Year 1 Disposition	Year 2 Disposition	Difference/ % Change
Cuyahoga County, OH[a]			
To W outright	49	39	−10/− 20
To W w/pay	3	11	+ 8/+267
To H outright	23	15	− 8/− 35
To H w/pay	2	7	+ 5/+250
Sold	17	21	+ 4/+ 24
New Haven, CT[b]			
To W outright	82	37	−45/− 55
To W w/pay or occupancy	13	26	+13/+100
To H outright	16	32	+16/+100
To H w/pay or occupancy	0	5	+ 5/+500
Sold	2	17	+15/+750
Los Angeles and San Francisco, CA[c]			
Sold	10	33	+23/+230
San Diego, CA[c]			
To W outright	66	42	−24/− 36
Westchester/Onondaga, NY			
To wife outright	31	31	0/ 0
To W w/pay or occupancy	19	12	− 7/− 37
To H outright	14	16	+ 2/+ 14
To H w/pay or occupancy	8	14	+ 6/+ 75
Sold	27	26	− 1/− 4

[a] G. Sterin and J. Davis, *Divorce Awards and Outcomes: A Study of Pattern and Change in Cuyahoga County, Ohio 1965–1978*, 109 (1981). The numbers do not add to 100 because of a separate listed category entitled "maintain joint" (5% in each survey year). The nature of these arrangements is unclear. *Id.*

[b] McLindon, "Separate but Unequal: The Economic Disaster of Divorce for Women and Children," 21 *Fam. L.Q.* 351, 362, 363–64, 376 (1987). According to McLindon, these numbers add to more than 100 because, in some cases, multiple houses were involved. *Id.*

[c] L. Weitzman, *The Divorce Revolution*, 78 (1985). Weitzman does not describe who actually gets the marital home, but instead provides data on the distribution of equity. Under no-fault, equal division increased from 23% to 35% of all cases while the percentage of cases in which wives received a majority declined from 61% to 46%. *Id.*

[d] Seal, "A Decade of No-Fault Divorce: What It Has Meant Financially for Women in California." *Fam. Adv.* 10, 12 (1979). Seal's figures apparently lump together cases in which wives received the home with and without payment to the husband. *Id.*

percent in San Diego), a unilateral no-fault jurisdiction, not at all in New York, and more modestly in Ohio (−20 percent), a mixed jurisdiction. But they declined the most (−55 percent) in Connecticut, another mixed jurisdiction like Ohio.

In contrast to the alimony results, however, the New York data before and after introduction of equitable distribution do not correspond to the reported pattern in surveyed jurisdictions before and after no-fault. Whereas outright awards of the marital home to wives declined and sales increased in the other surveyed jurisdictions after no-fault divorce was enacted, after the passage of New York's equitable distribution law outright awards to wives and sales remained remarkably constant. Moreover, the proportion of partial awards (title with payment, or occupancy only) did not go up markedly in New York after equitable distribution's advent as they did in the other surveyed jurisdictions after the introduction of no-fault.

It is also notable, again in contrast to the alimony results, that New York's dispositional pattern regarding the marital home prior to the equitable distribution law's enactment appears to correspond more closely to the pattern in other surveyed jurisdictions after no-fault was enacted than that reported before no-fault. Overall, under the old New York regime, New York wives were no more likely to obtain the marital home than were their no-fault counterparts in other surveyed jurisdictions. Indeed, the proportion of wives who obtained the home outright in New York under the old regime (31 percent) was lower than in any of the other jurisdictions after no-fault (49 percent to 82 percent); sales occurred more frequently under the old New York regime than in the other jurisdictions after no-fault except California with its equal division rule.

In sum, the New York marital home distribution data appear to be somewhat analogous to the Washington alimony data. Recall that permanent alimony awards did not decline in Washington after the introduction of no-fault because, apparently, the short-term alimony concept was already well established within the existing fault regime. In New York, the proportion of outright home awards to wives did not decline because, apparently, the shared equity concept was already well established within the existing fault regime. This fact is more notable given the absence in New York, prior to the equitable distribution law, of any formal property distribution scheme.[109] The high rate of joint home ownership made distribution a necessity; in the absence of other legislative guidance, New York judges and litigants apparently adopted norms that were generally in keeping with those prevalent in no-fault jurisdictions.

But with complete data available for only three jurisdictions, and considerable diversity in outcomes among those jurisdictions, firm conclusions about what factors—bargaining, judicial discretion, legislative pronouncement—played the most significant role in determining outcomes are difficult to draw. For example, the disposition of the marital home in relation to custody varies greatly from one jurisdiction to the next. In California, Weitzman indicates that the presence of minor children in a parent's custody made no difference in the disposition of the marital home;[110] in New Haven, by contrast, custodial parents received the family home 71 percent of the time after no-fault (down from 98 percent before), even though awards of outright ownership or occupancy to wives generally occurred in only 50 percent of cases overall.[111] Although the difference here would appear to be due to California's equal division rule, the Ohio researchers also report that, though custody was correlated with a greater likelihood of retaining the marital home prior to no-fault, after no-fault the difference disappeared.[112] Moreover, the various research reports do not typically provide comprehensive data on the marital home and report results in nonuniform ways. For example, most of the reports describe the likelihood of the wife obtaining title to the house in contrast to sale, but Weitzman's California research reports only on the overall distribution of home equity; it is impossible to determine from her data what proportion of wives actually obtained the house, as opposed to a share of sale proceeds.[113]

How Much Certainty Does the Research Data Provide?

As with the marital home distribution data, it is necessary to exercise caution in interpreting the research data as a whole. Several factors enhance the interpretive problems.

The first is the shortcomings in much of the research. Some of the research is based on samples that are quite small.[114] Several of the research reports fail to indicate whether results are statistically significant.[115] Almost none provides information on changed outcomes in relation to spousal income and employment, which might be expected to have a strong influence on outcomes independent of the impact of legal changes. Moreover, the research reports typically report outcomes in ways that make comparisons difficult.

The second is researchers' inability to control for background variables that might influence outcomes. For example, because the research has almost universally compared outcomes before and after legal reforms have gone into effect,[116] it fails to provide any sense of long-term change; it is possible that some of the changed outcomes noted by researchers reflect gradual development that is unrelated to reform of the legal rules. Additionally, as noted earlier, recent years have witnessed profound changes in social attitudes toward divorce that might themselves have been responsible for changes in divorce outcomes.

Controlling for these variables would, of course, be difficult and costly. One would have to do research over a fairly lengthy period and compare outcomes in states where no legal change occurred with those in states where it did. Although my New York research provides some data for the latter type of comparison, no one has attempted a comprehensive research project that would provide both a time and interjurisdictional perspective.

Because of these problems, one must interpret the research data cautiously. Although the available data provide little support for the bargaining thesis, they do not provide conclusive evidence in favor of any other theory either.

Conclusion

A comparative examination of divorce outcomes in states that have adopted different legal regimes suggests that the factors that determine the direction and pace of legal change are numerous and complex. Divorce courts respond to legislative command, the decisions of appellate courts, and changing social norms, as well as their own past practice, in shaping outcomes in specific cases. The bargaining chips of litigants are similarly varied.

Overall, it seems unlikely that the adoption of no-fault grounds for divorce has played the dominant role in producing reduced awards to divorced wives. Specific changes in the alimony rules themselves are more clearly related to declines in the likelihood of receiving alimony and its duration. Data on distribution of the marital home similarly fail to provide strong support for the theory that no-fault divorce itself produced changed outcomes. This suggests that states are unlikely to influence significantly the financial status of divorced women by eliminating unilateral no-fault divorce and imposing either a substantial waiting period or a mutual consent requirement.

The data suggest that the process by which changed outcomes have occurred is complicated, but they also suggest that reform can come through more than one avenue as well. Appellate courts in some jurisdictions appear to have been highly successful in shaping results at the trial level;[117] legislative action thus does not seem to be essential for meaningful reform.

What is essential for reform is information. Although research to track the results of statutory enactments is always useful, it is time for legislatures making divorce law policy to find out what happens *before* initiating significant legal change. It is probable that more Americans experience divorce than any other type of legal proceeding; the outcome of a divorce may shape the future life of family members for years to come. We need to know what happens before drastically revising legal standards and entitlements. Only when acting on the basis of full information can policymakers ensure that divorce law truly comports with the needs and interests of American families.

4 Stepparents, Biologic Parents, and the Law's Perceptions of "Family" after Divorce

DAVID L. CHAMBERS

The drama of divorce always contains at least two characters, a woman and a man, and often a third, a child born to the woman and the man. If you have read the other chapters of this book, you have rarely encountered any of the other persons who may be affected by a divorce, such as the children of either person from a prior marriage, or later spouses or partners of either party, or later born children of either party—all the persons who are or become stepchildren or stepparents. You have not encountered them because, in this country, with minor exceptions, they are all ignored by the law bearing on the divorce of the original couple.

Stepfamilies abound in this country today. Mavis Hetherington, in her continuing study of a group of divorced mothers with custody of children, has found that 70 percent of the mothers were remarried by six years after divorce.[1] Constance Ahrons and Lynn Wallish have recently studied a sample of divorced couples and their children in Dane County, Wisconsin, located through court records, and found that three years after divorce 89 percent of the children had at least one parent who was currently remarried or was cohabiting with another person. In only 11 percent of families were both parents without a new partner.[2]

Frank Furstenberg has made estimates for all American children, not just children of divorce. He calculates that about one-fourth of all children born in the early 1980s will live with a stepparent before they reach majority.[3] And many children experience a parental divorce more than once; their custodial parent remarries and then divorces again. It has recently been estimated that over 40 percent of couples who marry when one or both of them have children from a prior marriage or relationship divorce within five years of their marriage.[4]

The increasing number of children who have one or more stepparents has attracted the attention of the psychological and social sciences, generating within the last decade a highly productive surge of research on the stepparent relationship. At least forty empirical studies resting on non-clinical samples were published in the United States in the decade between 1976 and 1985, dwarfing in quantity the research conducted before then.[5] As ever, the reviewers of the new research identify critical unanswered questions, but all recognize the vast expansion of available information.

By contrast, over the last decade the stepparent-stepchild relationship has attracted only a modest amount of writing by legal scholars.[6] Why so little has been written is not difficult to understand. Legislators and others who shape public policy have tended to consider the biologic parent relationship the only legally significant relationship in a child's life. Adequate financial support for children is a critical social problem in the United States today, but stepparents are neither blamed as a source of the problem (even when they have divorced a custodial parent) nor widely conscripted as part of the solution.

This chapter relates some of the findings of the recent research on the stepparent relationship and the small, halting ways in which stepparents who live with children are coming to be seen as legally relevant individuals in children's lives. In the course of the exploration, we will see that even if the law becomes less single-minded about biologic relationships and somewhat more attentive to steprelationships, it is not easy to prescribe what the legal position of the stepparent ought to be.

I focus almost solely on the position of persons who have married a biologic parent after that parent has been divorced.[7] Doing so permits concentrating on two divorces of possible interest to the law: first, the divorce of two biologic parents and the effects of the custodial parent's remarriage on the legal position of the absent parent and the new stepparent and, second, the later divorce of a custodial parent and stepparent and the legal consequences of that divorce for all three parent figures.

The Varieties and Ambiguities of the Stepparent Relationship

Any consideration of laws or regulations bearing on stepparents must contend with the immense variety of stepparent relationships, a variety that, in one sense, closely mirrors the variety of relationships children form with biologic parents. The biologic parent-child relationship varies, after all, from the remote position of the man who impregnates a woman and never lives with their child, perhaps never knows of the child's existence, to the central position of the primary caretaking parent, who becomes the most important figure in the child's life.

The major difference between the biologic relationship and the steprelationship is that most of us hold in our minds a paradigm of what biologic parent relationships ought to look like, a clear model for thinking about responsibilities and entitlements. For most Americans, the paradigm is the nuclear family of man and woman married to each other and living with their children. Even for the father who never marries the mother or lives with the child, we share deep-seated notions of the significance of blood and the responsibilities that flow from intercourse. Toward their children, to reach back to Blackstone, parents owe "an obligation laid on them not only by nature itself, but by their own proper act in bringing them into the world."[8] We may have little agreement about appropriate roles for absent biologic parents in the day-to-day lives of their children (an uncertainty that helps create our uncertainties about the appropriate roles of stepparents), but we at least have a fairly clear vision of the core attributes of biologic parenthood.

The stepparent relationship, by contrast, lacks—and, I would argue, cannot possibly obtain—a single paradigm or model of appropriate responsibilities. As a starting point, children acquire two dramatically different and irretrievably "normal" forms of steprelations—the stepparent who is married to a custodial parent and with whom the child lives (a "residential stepparent," if you will) and the stepparent who is married to the noncustodial parent and whom the child sees, if at all, on visits. Both are wholly acceptable relationships, yet dramatically different in terms of children's typical experiences in them.

Even if we consider residential stepparents only, we still lack a single paradigm for the normal relationship of stepchild and stepparent. Whereas the biologic relationship always starts at a common point, the point of conception, and thus offers a roughly predictable progression over the course of the child's life, the residential steprelationship begins at widely varying points in children's lives. The child who begins to live with a stepparent while still an infant is likely to develop a different relationship and bond with the stepparent than the child who begins the relationship as an adolescent.

In cases in which the biologic parents have been divorced (in contrast to cases in which one of the biologic parents has died), the course of the stepparent-child relationship is especially difficult to predict because of the very existence of the nonresidential parent and the variations in the frequency and quality of the visits between the child and the nonresidential parent. Indeed, the range of family compositions in the lives of children one or both of whose parents remarry is vast. Ahrons and Wallish in their study of divorced families cataloged, three years after the divorce, whether the parents had remarried (or recoupled), whether the new partners brought children of their own into the union, and whether the parent and stepparent had new children after their union. They found eighteen patterns of family composition among the ninety-eight couples they studied.[9]

It is thus unsurprising that in the burst of research on stepfamilies within the last decade, researchers have confirmed that stepparents and stepchildren come into these relationships uncertain what to expect and what is expected of them. As they begin a stepparent relationship, neither stepparents nor stepchildren have available to them a set of clear norms to guide their behaviors.[10] As Judith Wallerstein has said, "Becoming a stepparent is like arriving in the middle of a very complex conversation. It takes a lot of effort to catch up and to keep up."[11]

To the extent that we do have an image of the stepparent relationship provided to us from our culture, it is a bleak one. Our very use of language reveals an expectation that the stepparent relationship will be detached or uncomfortable. As a metaphor, "stepchild" describes a neglected issue or subject. When people are told stories with identical content with the storyteller varying the family positions of the characters, persons identified as "stepmothers" are described afterward by the listeners in substantially less positive terms than those described as mothers, sisters, aunts, or nieces.[12] Cinderella's stepmother was wicked. Hamlet's stepfather was evil. In 1989, a B-grade thriller entitled *Stepfather II* came out of Hollywood billed as "the shattering conclusion to one of the scariest films ever made." He's "coming home," the advertisement continued, "to slice up more than just the cake!" How many tales do you know of stepparents who were loving or kind? Some researchers believe that our cultural images of the stepparent increase the awkwardnesses of the relationship for those who are entering them.[13]

For residential stepfathers, perhaps only one aspect of their roles and responsibilities toward their stepchildren is reasonably clear from the beginning. Apparently, nearly all residential stepfathers perform as parent in one important respect: those who are working nearly always contribute to the financial support of the children with whom they live; many in fact provide all the financial support.[14] In fact, demographers are now so accustomed to regarding children living with a parent and stepparent as economically secure in comparison to children living with a single parent that, in reporting on the status of children, they typically group those in biologic families and stepfamilies together under the single label of "two-parent families."[15]

Apart from this role as provider, however, the relationship between many stepparents and stepchildren remains unclear and uncomfortable well beyond the initial stages. In his study of children with a residential stepparent, Furstenberg found that children were much less likely to say they felt "quite close" to their stepparent than to say they felt "quite close" to their custodial parent and much less likely to say that they wanted to grow up to be like their stepparent than to say they wanted to be like their custodial parent.[16] In fact, about a third of children living with a stepparent did not mention that person when asked to name the members of their family. Nearly all named their noncustodial parent, even when they saw him or her erratically.

By much the same token, about half the stepfathers in the Furstenberg study said that their stepchildren did not think of them as a "real" parent, about half said that the stepchildren were harder to love than their own children, and about half said that it was easier to think of themselves as a friend than as a parent to the stepchildren. Stepparents had difficulty figuring out their appropriate role in disciplining the child and determining how to show affection for the child. Many stepparents and children remain uninvolved or uncomfortable with each other throughout the years they live together.[17] Some researchers have even attributed to the awkwardness of the stepparent relationship the somewhat higher divorce rate in the early years of second marriages.[18]

Part of the difficulty for stepparents, as Furstenberg's questions themselves may suggest, is that many may believe that they are expected to be seen as a true "parent," an equal at caretaking and counseling, even when they recognize that that role is unlikely to be attainable. To be sure, not all stepparents have difficult relations with their stepchildren. Some—many of those in the other half of Furstenberg's respondents—come to see themselves as a parent and are viewed by children as such. Many others attain a comfortable relationship with the child but not in the role of a parent, establishing themselves over time not as an adult authority figure but as an adult companion and adviser. Those stepparents who prove least comfortable in the stepparent role are often those who find themselves stuck in the role of "other mother" or "other father," seen by themselves and the child as being in a parent role, but competing with and compared unfavorably with the noncustodial parent. Hetherington's research suggests that, at least for residential stepfathers, the best strategy for gaining acceptance and building a strong relationship with a stepchild is to start slowly, supporting the mother in *her* parenting role and building over time toward a more active involvement.[19]

Ultimately, the difficulty for stepparents in our society may be due in part to a want of social imagination, to an incapacity to recognize that, especially in the context of divorce, it will commonly be very hard for a stepparent either to hold a role identical to the biologic parent or, as the partner of the child's biologic parent, to become just a friend. The difficulty in many families of finding the right name for the child to call the stepfather reveals this problem. Neither "Dad" nor "Jim" seems quite right, but they appear to be the only choices. We conceive the stepparent role to be analogous to roles we already know. We expect the stepparent to be "like" someone—and he or she usually falls short.

What we have been unable to do here, as we have been unable to do in so many contexts in which people are perceived as different—the deaf, those from other cultures, those of other colors—is to learn to embrace the differences. The residential stepparent is, after all, in the unique and potentially resourceful position of being the person in the world closest to the person to whom the child is closest, while free of some of the baggage of having a long-term and biologic link with the child. Perhaps it is impossible to forge coherent or flexible middle views. Perhaps it is psychologically inevitable that children will see a stepparent with whom they live as a person assigned to take the place of the absent parent. The least that can be said is that we as a society do not regard the advent of stepparenthood as we do the arrival of a new baby—as a treat that offers the opportunity for rich relationships.

The awkwardness of the stepparent relationship might be thought to suggest that children would in general be better off if their custodial parents did not remarry and that the law ought in general to discourage the formation of stepfamilies. That is not what the current state of research suggests. Most children living with a custodial mother become much better off economically upon their mother's remarriage. Whether they are typically better or worse off in other respects is uncertain. Research that attempts to measure the developmental effects on children of any life event—a parent's remarriage, parents' divorce, whatever—is fraught with difficulties, and thus research on the developmental effects of a parent's remarriage on children is predictably inconclusive. Clinical studies often find that children living with stepparents have adjustment problems and other difficulties, but so do children living with a single parent; empirical research typically finds few systematic differences between children raised in stepfamilies and children raised in other family configurations.[20] In short, insofar as the needs of children are concerned, economic considerations suggest that remarriage is typically beneficial and other considerations point in no definitive direction.

The Law Ignores the Stepparent

How has family law conceived the stepparent relationship? The stepparent as parent? As friend? As someone in between or as someone entirely different? Family law, as a formal matter, has largely ignored the relationship. In the substantial majority of states, stepparents, even when they live with a child, have no legal obligation to contribute to the child's support; nor does a stepparent's presence in the home alter the support obligations of a non-custodial parent. The stepparent also has had no authority to make decisions about the child—no authority to approve emergency medical treatment or even to sign a permission slip for a field trip to the fire station. State law has had only one mechanism—adoption—to permit a stepparent married to the custodial parent to formalize a role with a child.

On the breakup of a marriage between a biologic parent and a stepparent, the stepparent again has been ignored by the law unless the child has been adopted. In the absence of adoption or some extraordinary circumstances noted later, the law in nearly all states imposes no continuing financial obligations on the stepparent regardless of the extent of support he or she has provided while living with the child. Similarly, except in unusual circumstances, the law has not treated the stepparent as an appropriate custodian for the child or aided the stepparent in continuing a relationship with the child through visitation. On the death of a stepparent, laws of intestate succession nearly always exclude stepchildren from the list of relations who will share in the estate.

In the next section, I discuss scattered court decisions and unusual state and federal statutes that impose greater responsibilities on stepparents or give them more opportunities for custody of children. These decisions and statutes, however, have probably affected very few stepparents' or stepchildren's lives, except in the context of families receiving welfare. The vision of the stepparent relationship that the dominant state of the law conveys is thus most consistent with an image of the stepparent as stranger or, at most, as a friend, a relationship that often includes warm feelings but that in itself carries no legal consequence. The stepparent becomes something more only by adoption, an event that converts the friend into a full legal parent, passing over all intermediate possibilities. Katherine Bartlett, in a provocative article, has identified and criticized this view of parenthood as an "exclusive" status—the stepparent as either all or nothing, full parent or stranger.[21]

Another, less bipolar view of the current state of the law is possible. It is that the law has, without intention, created a largely neutral environment for the stepparent relationship, leaving it open to the two biologic parents, the stepparent, and the child to fashion whatever sort of relationship seems appropriate to them.[22] Apart from minor annoyances regarding the stepparent's lack of authority to authorize medical treatment and other acts for which a parent's consent may be necessary, the stepparent can behave like a "mom" or "dad" day by day in the relationship or just be a friend and the law will not interfere. The stepparent and the noncustodial parent can share parenting functions in any way they wish. Stepparents can contribute as little as they choose to the children's financial support without fear that the state will compel a larger contribution. Conversely, they can contribute a great deal without fear of altering the support obligations of the absent parent or of binding themselves to continued support if the marriage to the custodial parent ends. Or with the consent of the biologic parents, they can adopt the child, and, on divorce, if the parents agree that the child can live with or have visitation with the stepparent courts will typically give force to their agreements.

In this view, the law projects no fixed image of the stepparent relationship—neither stranger nor friend nor parent. It is simply a relationship based on consent, to be shaped by the inclinations of the adults and the child. Of course, this neutral view of the stepparent relationship may also be thought unhelpful. The law's failure to announce a model or image of the stepparent relation may be thought to contribute to the confusion that stepparents feel over their expected role. Perhaps so. Yet, so far as I can find, no social scientist writing about the stepparent relationship has blamed their confusion, even in part, on the law's failure to establish a clearer image of the appropriate stepparent relationship.[23]

When the Law Recognizes the Stepparent Relation

In the United States, the earliest widespread statutory recognition of the stepparent relationship probably occurred in the Workers' Compensation acts adopted by nearly all states in the early years of this century to provide for the dependents of workers injured or killed in work-related accidents. Through these acts, some states provided coverage for all persons actually dependent on a worker, others for specific relations who were eligible if dependent. Under either approach, stepchildren actually dependent on a worker were typically provided for.[24] Congress, in the Social Security Act provisions for benefits upon death or disability, continued this form of recognition of stepchildren. Since 1939, Social Security benefits have been available to the stepchild of a deceased covered worker, if the worker had been living with the child for a prescribed period at the time of the worker's death.[25] The extent of coverage for stepchildren, however, has always been narrower than that for biologic children, for the latter are covered whether the parent lives with them or not. Nonetheless, the fact of the coverage of stepchildren, even if limited, is noteworthy.

The drafters of Workers' Compensation and Social Security laws were seeking to ensure that children actually dependent on working adults continue to receive support when the adults are no longer able to provide it. The coverage of stepchildren reflects, appropriately, an awareness that stepparents who are working almost always contribute to the support of the children with whom they live. More broadly, quietly, and fundamentally, the coverage of stepchildren recognizes the stepparent relationship as a socially approved relationship—persons whose coverage would not be objected to by employers or by other workers, those without children, who are forced to contribute to the Social Security fund.

So far as I can tell, at no point has the coverage of stepchildren by Workers' Compensation or Social Security laws been regarded as controversial. The absence of controversy probably has two sources. First, at the time of the enactment of the original Workers' Compensation acts and the Social Security Act amendments of 1939, most residential stepparents where men who had married not divorced women, but widows. In these families, no surviving male parent could have been expected to provide support. Second, even in cases in which there had been a divorce, the coverage typically, though not always,[26] occured in a manner that had no felt cost to any of the parties. The biologic parents, the stepparent, and the child were all typically pleased by the coverage of the stepparent, for it came to the child at no greater price than any of them would have had to pay otherwise.[27] In most of the other contexts I am about to discuss, the recognition of the stepparent relationship costs someone something and someone feels like a loser: an absent biologic parent opposes adoption or wants to reassert custody; a stepparent objects to being excluded from consideration for custody or to being pursued for child support; a custodial parent objects to a decrease in a public assistance check because of a stepparent's presence.

Over the fifty years since stepchildren were added to the Social Security Act, as we are about to see, a few other state and federal statutes have dealt with the residential stepparent relationship. So have court decisions in a variety of contexts. While these official pronouncements have altered very little the lives of most stepparents and stepchildren, they are nonetheless instructive about the occasions when governments have accorded legal significance to family relationships in the late twentieth century.

The small changes in the law have not been due to lobbying efforts by stepparents themselves, for they are not a well-organized political force in this country.[28] They have had no voice in the legislatures comparable, say, to that of the senior citizen groups that have advocated for grandparent visitation statutes. Rather, three major initiatives in late-twentieth-century public policy bearing on children have been responsible for shaping recent changes in the law. In large part, the three reflect a direct concern not for the steprelationships themselves but for larger or different issues that happen to bear on them. The three are the efforts to reduce public welfare expenditures, the efforts to provide income to nonpoor mothers and children through the enforcement of child support, and the efforts to recognize and protect children's long-term emotional ties with significant caretakers. Each of these policy initiatives bears on stepparents, but each is affected at all points by the continuing, even growing, drive to recognize and enforce children's biologic relationships. In America, blood is not merely thicker than water; it is thicker than usual.[29]

The Reduction of Welfare Expenditures

For several decades, critics have complained about the inadequacy of the nation's system of public welfare benefits for low-income families with young children. Yet, since the early 1970s, most welfare reform by Congress and the states has taken the form not of striving to ensure that state-provided grants for children are adequate for their needs but of shifting as much of the costs of welfare as possible from the government and onto those whom the state views as appropriately responsible "family" members. How Congress and the states have defined the responsibilities of various family members reveals, of course, social judgments about the significance of various relationships.

By far the largest part of the effort to shift costs has focused on absent biologic parents, particularly fathers. These efforts began in 1950, but have accelerated in the last fifteen years with the adoption of three substantial amendments to the program of Aid to Families with Dependent Children (AFDC). Through these amendments, the most recent in 1988, Congress has sought to force the states to make more substantial efforts to collect child support from absent biologic parents. The legislation has grown from the perception that most children receiving AFDC have an absent parent, a conviction that such a parent ought to be compelled to contribute, and a hope that, if the states expended more effort, such parents could be forced to pay. (And each new piece of legislation, as Harry Krause discusses in chapter 6, seems to have been successful in the sense of offsetting, even if only slightly more each time, the total governmental expenditures on public assistance for children of divorced parents.)

Under the federal legislation, states must identify absent biologic parents, establish orders of support against them, and, under the newest legislation, require employers after 1994 to deduct from wages all amounts of child support that are due. Except for the first fifty dollars secured each month, the child on AFDC receives no financial benefit from the absent parent's payments: all moneys recovered are kept by the state and federal governments. [30]

Beyond its central focus on absent biologic parents, the federal welfare legislation includes a few provisions that deal directly with stepparents. These are complex, and since each state has some freedom to vary the details of the welfare system, they are difficult to describe simply. In capsule form, the federal AFDC program was originally conceived to provide assistance to children living with one parent only (particularly to children living with widowed mothers). If the child had two nondisabled parents, they were expected to provide for the children out of their own labors. The federal government has permitted but not required states to treat residential stepparents as if they were biologic parents and thus to exclude a child from AFDC coverage when the child lived with a stepparent and a biologic parent. [31]

If a state does not elect to treat the stepparent as a parent under its laws (and only about six states do), then it must treat the child as eligible to be considered for AFDC. But the state must, under federal law, take the income of the stepparent married to and living with the custodial parent into account in determining the child's financial need and hence the size of the grant the child and the caretaker will receive. [32] If the income of the stepparent is sufficiently high, the child will receive no grant at all. Only the income of stepparents actually married to the custodial parent and living with the child is to be deemed available to the child. By contrast, the income of a residential companion of a custodial parent, no matter how parentlike a relation the person has with the child, may be considered only to the extent that the companion actually provides support to the child.

For all its complexities, the pattern of federal welfare laws paints a fairly coherent congressional vision of proper familial responsibilities. Its chief feature is that biologic parenthood is primary, more important than any other relationship, entailing obligations that endure through time without regard to the residence of the parent or child. Only a termination of parental rights can end the obligations.[33] At the same time, though biology is primary, the stepparent who lives with a child and is married to the child's mother is, by law, more than a stranger. For no person other than a residential stepparent must the states *assume* that the person's income is made available to the child.

The welfare rules, as they apply to stepparents, are as interesting for their limits as they are for their reach. The federal government and the states have been ardent, rabid even, in their efforts to reduce welfare costs by finding ways to impose the costs on others, but, under the federal legislation, no pressure has been put on the states to treat residential stepparents *exactly* as if they were biologic parents. Nor has any pressure been applied to the states to seek support after divorce from a stepparent who has lived with a child for many years but no longer does so. Congress, however frugal, recognizes that there are limits on the extent to which our culture perceives stepparents as responsible for children. And even the statute that requires states to treat the income of a residential stepparent as available to children can be seen less as a judgment that stepparents have a moral obligation to provide support than an empirical guess, almost certainly accurate, that stepfathers who are married to the mother and residing with a child nearly always do so in fact.

The legislation requiring the income of a residential stepparent to be taken into account can nonetheless, like many other welfare rules, have perverse and undesirable effects on children. The rules work only to their financial disadvantage. The stepfather's income is relevant only for reducing the amount of public support for the child. Such a result, given the fact that most stepparents actually do provide support, may seem defensible.[34] Nonetheless, because welfare grants, even at their highest, are so meager (well below the poverty level in all states), any rule that reduces the amount of a grant to a child creates in recipients a sense of injustice and a pressure and ready rationalization for evasion. Thus, rather than marry, a mother with a relationship with a working but low-income man may choose to protect her welfare grant by living furtively in a relationship outside of marriage that may well be less stable and less satisfying.[35]

The Collection of Child Support for Children Not Receiving Welfare

Until recently, most children whose parents were divorced received either no financial support from their absent parent or far less support than they were entitled to by law. The consequence was many angry custodial parents and their children living at even lower standards of living than they otherwise would have. The recent move by legislatures to increase the collections of child support marks the second theme that has directly and indirectly affected stepparents. Obviously, this theme overlaps the first one—the efforts to reduce welfare costs—but it differs in that these efforts to increase child support payments have been intended primarily to benefit middle-class families.

The two most recent federal amendments to the AFDC statute merge welfare and nonwelfare families insofar as child support is concerned. They do so through an aggressive flexing of federal muscle. In the past, the federal government left the content of family laws outside the welfare context entirely up to the states, and the Reagan administration took office in 1981 hoping to return even more welfare decision making to the states. Despite this, Congress, through the AFDC amendments, conditioned the states' full federal reimbursement of their welfare costs on their making more concerted efforts to collect child support not only on behalf of children receiving AFDC but also on behalf of other children with absent biologic parents, including those from high-income families. The United States now has a formal federal policy declaring the enduring primacy of the biologic relationship for all children. To be sure, nothing in federal law prohibits the states from making stepparents concurrently liable for the support of children, but federal law does require that, in the absence of a termination of parental rights, biologic parents be compelled to support their children and even that the amount of the support follow state-developed uniform guidelines.[36]

Independently of the federal government, many states had also been improving their systems of child support collection from absent parents. Very little of this legislation directly mentioned stepparents. A few states have had statutes that imposed financial liability on residential stepparents during the course of a marriage,[37] but, outside the welfare context, these statutes have had little operative content: while children are living with a stepparent and a parent, the state has few occasions to inquire into family finances to make sure that parental figures, step or biologic, are devoting their income to the support of their children.

During the course of a marriage between a parent and stepparent, there is nonetheless one set of questions bearing on the stepparent's responsibilities that frequently arises. These are questions about the effect of a second marriage on preexisting child support obligations. In most states the law is fairly settled: a custodial parent's remarriage does not alter the extent of the liability of the absent biologic parent, even though most absent parents, particularly fathers, probably believe that their former wife's remarriage should reduce the extent of their responsibility for child support. Conversely, though some variation exists among states, the new stepfather cannot obtain a reduction of any child support he may owe for children from a prior relationship by pointing to his de facto responsibilities for new stepchildren, even though he may feel the strongest sense of responsibility (and the greatest psychological pressure) for the needs of his new wife and her children.[38] In nearly all states, only the biologic relationships count. A few states, however, seem to be considering rules that look at the economic position of new units formed by either the custodial or the noncustodial parent and exploring ways to take into account the new incomes and new expenses in the reconstituted families.[39]

The issue of the liability of a residential stepparent for the support of stepchildren is also raised, from rare time to time, upon the breakup of the stepparent's marriage to the custodial parent. Here again, the starting assumption in all American states remains that, whatever state statutes provide during the course of a marriage, no liability survives for the stepparent on the breakup of the marriage to the custodial parent. The stepparent relation is consensual and time-bound. Upon a second divorce, children are expected to fall back upon the support payments of the noncustodial biologic parent, regardless of the length of time the stepparent lived with the child and regardless of the lavishness of the support provided by the stepparent during the marriage to the custodial parent. This general rule has been applied by courts even in some cases in which a child seems to have an unusually compelling claim for continuing support. Thus, the Utah Supreme Court recently dealt with a divorce case in which a woman was divorcing for the second time. She had been pregnant by her first husband at the time of their divorce, and the second husband, though knowing the truth, had signed the birth certificate as the father at the time of the child's birth. The second husband then lived with the child for several years, during which time the biologic father neither paid support nor visited the child. The court held that, since the second husband never formally adopted the child, he had no obligations to pay support on the breakup of his marriage to the mother.[40]

To be sure, common law equity notions of estoppel might have been used by the Utah court to impose liability. In fact, the lower court in Utah had adopted such a theory—that the person who holds himself out as a father and behaves as a father cannot later be heard to deny that he has the responsibilities of a father—to impose liability at the trial level. A few other American appellate courts have imposed liability in somewhat more common circumstances—in cases in which the stepparent during the course of his marriage to the custodial parent had actively sought to discourage the noncustodial biologic parent from having any contact with the children.[41] In such cases, courts have sometimes made clear, however, that judges may not impose liability simply on finding that a strong bond has developed between a stepparent and child or that the stepfather has generously supported the child during the course of the marriage. Some judges have expressed the fear that expanded rules of liability for stepfathers on divorce might discourage men from marrying women who have children from prior relationships.[42]

The very modest movement of American courts and legislatures toward imposing continuing responsibility on long-term stepparents stands in stark contrast to the law in England and Wales, where the rule since the 1950s has been that the stepparent may be held liable to contribute to the support of the child on the divorce from the biologic parent if the stepchild had been living with the stepparent and treated as a child of the family before the separation.[43] Rather few English appellate cases have dealt with trial court judgments imposing liability in these circumstances, but one case, characterized by a British commentator as the "leading case,"[44] stands in marked contrast to the Utah case above. In the English case, the marriage of the mother and stepfather lasted only six months and the stepfather lived with the woman's two children for only three months. The stepfather was ordered to pay an amount per week only slightly less than the amount ordered to be paid by the biologic father, and the appeals court upheld the decision.[45]

What could explain the difference in the sensibilities of the English, our legal cousins, and the Americans on the issue of the continuing responsibility of stepparents? One difference, which caught me by surprise when I first read it, is that the English rule may have originated less out of a sense that stepfathers have a moral obligation to support children who have become financially and emotionally dependent on them than out of a sense that stepfathers are often morally at fault for the breakup of the marriage between the children's biologic parents.[46] The stepfather is seen as a home-wrecker, responsible for the child's imperiled financial condition.

A more recent statement by England's Law Commission painted the responsibility of the stepparent as supplemental to that of the biologic father and commented that the stepfather "shall be regarded as having taken the risk of having to maintain [the stepchild] to the extent that the first husband failed to do so." This statement of an assumption of risk may be merely conclusory or it may reflect the commission's beliefs about what the average English citizen accepts as the responsibilities that flow from marrying a woman with children.[47] Whatever the attitudes of English citizens, I suspect that the current state of American law comports with current American attitudes. Most Americans, I suspect, believe that biologic fathers ought to continue to pay support after a mother's remarriage, that stepfathers ought to make their income available on top of the absent biologic parent's support payments while they live with a stepchild, but that upon divorce the responsibilities of stepfathers end.

Will American sensibilities alter over time? Some empirical evidence suggests that when residential stepparents enter children's lives, the children generally see their absent parents less often than they did before.[48] I have already mentioned the findings that, despite the ambiguities of the stepparent relationship, many individual stepparents do form strong emotional bonds with their stepchildren. They are seen by the child as "parent." And, of course, there is ample corresponding evidence that biologic fathers who do not live with their children will not pay child support unless compelled to do so and that they visit their children less and less as time passes, whether or not the mother remarries. In the future, we may come to view residential stepparents as replacing absent parents and assuming some or all of their responsibilities.

Given the strong public support for policies to ensure adequate support for children without public expenditure, it is possible to imagine in the future the development of rules imposing some continuing liability on stepparents after divorce. Stepparents might, for example, be required to make contributions either until the custodial parent remarries or for some limited period of years. Stepparents, that is, would be responsible for cushioning the blow from the sudden loss of income they have made available to the child and on which the child has become dependent.

Protecting or Fostering Children's Attachments

Under American law as it has generally existed, a stepparent may acquire formal authority to make decisions in a stepchild's life or serve as custodian for a stepchild only with the consent of one or, usually, both biologic parents. In the eyes of the law, stepparents become what the biologic parents permit them to become.

Over the last few decades, changes have occurred in the law regarding stepparent adoption and custody that have made it easier in some states for courts to recognize the attachments children develop with stepparents. At the same time, in a manner familiar in other contexts in which judges must resolve children's custody, legislatures have provided little clear guidance from about how to deal with the cases in which adoption or custody is proposed.

Stepparent Adoption. Adoption entails the termination of the parental rights and obligations of one or both biologic parents and the assumption of those rights and obligations by a new adult. A biologic parent disappears as a legally relevant person and is replaced by someone else. Adoptions by stepparents today typically occur, as they always have, with the explicit consent or acquiescence of the parent who is about to be replaced. Laws that once permitted adoption to occur only when there was such consent (or acquiescence or deliberate "abandonment") have now, however, commonly been expanded to permit courts to approve adoptions by stepparents in a wider range of cases, including some in which the noncustodial biologic parent strenuously objects to the adoption.

The new statutes vary widely among the states.[49] Some states have adopted the Uniform Adoption Act, which permits adoption by a stepparent without the noncustodial parent's consent in cases in which the parent "for a period of at least a year has failed significantly without justifiable cause to communicate with the child or to provide for the [child's] support."[50] Some other states, such as California and Michigan, require a period in which a parent both fails to communicate *and* fails to pay support. A few states have enacted statutes that appear to make stepparent adoption much more readily available, permitting courts to authorize adoptions if consent is being "unreasonably withheld contrary to the best interest of the child."[51]

Almost no information is available about actual patterns of stepparent adoption in this country or about the impact of adoption on the relationships between stepparents and children. For those interested in people's own conceptions of family and how they use laws to validate those conceptions, distressingly little is known about what stepparents and custodial parents consider when deciding whether to seek adoption or about what biologic parents consider when deciding whether to consent.[52] What we are able to calculate is that only a small percentage of stepparents actually adopt their stepchildren,[53] despite the fact that the high proportion of children of divorce who never see or receive support from their noncustodial parent[54] suggests that the number of stepparents eligible to adopt, even over the absent biologic parent's objection, must be very large. We know nothing about what distinguishes the families in which adoption occurs from the families in which it does not. We do not even know whether stepparent adoptions are increasing in frequency. Because of the more generous standards for stepparent adoption and a supportive atmosphere today for stepparent involvement in children's lives, we could guess that more are occurring. On the other hand, as child support enforcement against absent fathers has become more effective in some states, more custodial parents may wish to hold onto this source of income.[55]

Just as we know little of the incidence of or motivations for stepparent adoption in the United States, so likewise we know almost nothing about the effects of such adoptions on children. No researcher has ever compared children who were adopted by their stepparents with children living with a stepparent but not adopted in order to learn whether adoption affects children's sense of well-being or even clarifies roles within families.[56]

In the absence of empirical information, I must fall back on the adoption statutes themselves and on reported decisions of courts for the attitudes they convey about stepparents and family composition and about the values to be derived from stepparent adoption. The expanded provisions are themselves revealing for their implicit views about family.[57] The old view of the family was that parenthood, when the parents had been married to each other, persisted as long as the parent chose. The new view has two aspects. The first is that children form new bonds and that it is appropriate for the state to ratify them. The second (also reflected in neglect and abuse laws) is that it is appropriate to terminate old bonds when a biologic parent fails to meet certain responsibilities.

What is interesting, and, in fact, a little bizarre, is the adoption statutes' implicit conception of the responsibilities of the biologic parent. In states that permit a court to dispense with the father's consent only when there has been both failure to communicate and failure to support, a parent can usually prevent a child from being adopted by the stepparent by making occasional payments of child support, even though the parent never visits or otherwise communicates with the child in any manner.[58] In fact, in some states, the adoption may be prevented by support payments that are extracted from the parent without his consent and thus are no evidence of any concern or affection whatever for the child.[59] At the same time, in those states that permit a court to dispense with the parent's consent when there has been *either* a failure to communicate *or* a failure to support, an adoption can go forward over the father's objection even though he has visited with the child regularly, so long as he has willfully failed to make support payments.[60] In the context of children receiving welfare payments, the willful failure to pay support may not indicate any lack of concern for the child's well-being or lack of involvement with the child, for the parent knows that almost all the payments he makes are kept by the state and not forwarded to the child. In short, in some states, any amount of support money can prevent an adoption and, in other states, no amount of attention, no matter how great, can prevent one. In both types of states, what turns out to be significant about some biologic relationships is cash.

The anomalies of stepparent adoption do not end with the provisions for defining the circumstances in which the court can proceed without the consent of the biologic parent, for at the core of these statutes is a more unsettling issue. Facing a request for adoption, the judge, even after making a determination whether to proceed without the absent parent's consent, is supposed to make a separate inquiry into whether adoption by the step-parent will serve "the best interests of the child." In any given case, especially one in which the biologic father is protesting, the judge may well be puzzled whether the child will really be any better off if adopted. The immediate benefits to the child from permitting the adoption may be hard to measure— the child is, after all, already living securely with the stepparent who pro-poses to adopt. Custodial parents and adoptive stepparents would probably claim that they want the adoption to produce family unity and stability and to improve a child's already close relationship with the stepparent.[61] Given what we know about stepparents' uncertainties about their roles, they may be right about adoption's value for these purposes. On the other hand, as Jessie Bernard once commented, "It is doubtful if the kind of man who is willing to adopt his wife's children would be any less conscientious in his behavior toward the children without the legal sanction of adoption."[62]

For the court, the most tangible reason for permitting the adoption may be that the mother wants the child to share her new last name or that the children can obtain access to health insurance and other benefits through their stepfather only if he adopts them.[63] At the same time, the judge can easily perceive at least one possible harm from permitting the adoption—the biologic parent, now protesting, and the child will lose all legally protected opportunities for contact with each other, and many, perhaps most, adoptive stepparents expect that the child will have no further contact with the absent parent after the adoption.[64]

The contested cases of stepparent adoption put before judges the most elemental of decisions about the definition of family in a context in which judges can have little idea what the effects of their actions will be. Facing such choices, at least a few judges in appealed cases (and an unknowable number of others in unappealed cases) have imaginatively sought to evade the awesome finality of termination and adoption by straining to find authority to permit the adoption while at the same time ordering continued visitation for the biologic parent.[65] Some other judges have cajoled the custodial parent and stepparent into agreeing to visitation before entering the order of termination and adoption and then enforced the coerced agreement.[66]

A comparison with England may again be instructive, for, as with child support, the English have sought ways to accord legal significance to biologic relationships and steprelationships simultaneously. Adoption in which a stepparent supplants a biologic parent has been regarded much more warily in England than in the United States. At one point in the 1960s, for example, England's Association of Child Care Officers, the organization representing adoption workers, recommended that stepparent adoption be prohibited altogether in cases of children whose biologic parents had been married.[67] Although stepparent adoptions are typically approved when unopposed, the number of such adoptions has declined significantly from the 1960s to the 1980s.[68] Instead England has contrived mechanisms other than adoption to permit formal recognition of the stepparent relationship without ending the relationship with the biologic parent. Together with the custodial parent, a residential stepparent may, under certain circumstances, apply for a form of "joint custody" of the child or, in other cases, for custodianship.[69] The English joint custody permits the stepparent to make legally recognized decisions on behalf of the child, but does not end the support obligations or visiting privileges of the noncustodial parent.

Stepparent Custody after the Death of or Divorce from a Biologic Parent. The elemental reordering of families also occurs in another context—on occasions when a stepparent proposes to become the primary custodian for a child. Sometimes changes of custody occur without hostility, with all affected family members agreeing on a placement with a stepparent. On the death of a custodial parent, for example, all family members may agree that the children will be best off if left with a longtime stepparent.

On occasion, courts become involved in formally adjudicating a stepparent's request for the custody of stepchildren over the objection of another parent, either after one parent's death or at the point of divorce. Probably no more than twenty-five appellate cases have been decided in the United States over the last two decades in which a stepparent and biologic parent have contended for custody. How many more cases have been decided by trial courts and not appealed is, as usual, impossible to say. Of course, in the United States today, relatively few parents die during their children's minority. Moreover, for at least two reasons, it is also probable that few residential stepparents seriously consider seeking custody upon divorce, let alone contesting the issue in court. First, most residential stepparents are men, and father custody after divorce, even among biologic fathers, remains much less frequent than mother custody in this country.[70] Second and more fundamental, most stepparents themselves probably believe that the children belong with (and to) the biologic parent.

In the occasional cases in which judges must choose between stepparents and biologic parents, they face much the same ineffable choices that they do in the context of disputed stepparent adoptions. The appellate opinions recording these decisions are not a pretty sight.[71] I have read them as much to observe judges' attitudes toward stepparent-stepchild relationships and their ways of characterizing the stepparent and the biologic parent as I have to learn the developing state of the law. Whichever way one reads, it is difficult to perceive consistent patterns. The widely differing results of courts in these custody cases should not come as a surprise, however. The incoherent pattern of outcomes and the murky and inconsistent discussions of the governing rules almost certainly reflect our society's conflicting and unresolved attitudes about stepparents, even when loving, and about biologic parents, even when indifferent.

Here are some of the ways these attitudes display themselves. For dealing with custody disputes involving stepparents, only one state appears to have adopted legislation that treats them by name as potential custodians,[72] and only a few others provide general authority for courts to consider requests for custody by long-term caretakers.[73] Even the Uniform Marriage and Divorce Act, which deals at length with issues of custody on divorce, never mentions stepparents and implicitly relegates a stepparent who wishes custody to search for other sources of statutory authority for any claims. Courts in some states have thus simply held that they had no jurisdiction to consider a petition by a stepparent for custody, even after a child has lived with the stepparent as her only caretaker for many years.[74]

Most courts that find jurisdiction to resolve a claim by a stepparent for custody have to rely on legislation drafted without stepparents in particular in mind. Some state courts have taken jurisdiction by fiat, simply failing to discuss the basis for their authority to decide. Others in cases with a compelling case for placement with a stepparent have stretched, brazenly, the language of a custody statute that seemed to apply to biologic parents only.[75]

When courts have found a basis for jurisdiction, they have then had to grapple with the standard to apply. Are biologic parents and the residential stepparents competing for custody to be treated as equals or does the biologic parent stand in a preferred position before the court? Courts' opinions might have included revealing discussions about the importance of preserving biologic ties or the importance of preserving continuity of caretaking or frank discussions of the rights of biologic parents to the custody of their children regardless of children's needs. Unfortunately, nearly all the discussion is unilluminating. Courts fuss over statements of the standard without explaining what considerations are affecting their inquiry.

Consider, for example *Henrikson v. Gable,* a recent Michigan case involving a dispute between a residential stepfather and a biologic father after the death of the custodial mother.[76] The children, aged nine and ten, had lived in the stepfather's household since infancy and regarded the stepfather as their dad. The biologic father had rarely visited or called. A trial judge, after a long hearing, left the children with the stepfather. Wrestling with the case on appeal, the appellate court found two statutory provisions pointing in conflicting directions—one provision creating a strong preference for biologic parents and the other creating a strong preference for keeping children in "established custodial environments" under prior court orders. Then the court without anything that can generously be called reasoning held that the first section trumped the other and directed the children's return to their biologic father. The court drew on earlier state appellate decisions that make little sense either individually or as a group and at least some of which announce a different standard than the appellate court in *Henrikson* applied. Courts in some other states have candidly complained that the decisions of their own state's courts have not been wholly consistent.[77]

In a substantial number of cases, courts with a strongly sympathetic case for a stepparent simply seem to impose on the stepparent the toughest standard that that person can meet, proclaiming with vigor the rights of biologic parents and the presumptions in their favor but keeping the standard just weak enough that the stepparent can win.[78] In some cases, courts have said in one part of their opinion that there as a strong preference for biologic parents but, in the end, found that the best interests of the child controlled and placed the child with the stepparent on the basis of a standard that seemed to treat the stepparent and biologic parent as equals.[79]

Not all courts, of course, go out of their way to rule for stepparents. Forced to choose between a long-term custodial stepparent and an absent biologic parent who has regularly visited, some courts have, without much explanation, decided that children are better off returned to their biologic parent.[80] Others, dealing with cases in which the biologic parent has had little contact with the child, seem to stretch to place custody in the biologic parent.[81]

Courts also vary widely in the ways they depict the stepparents and biologic parents themselves. Appellate cases that end by ruling for a caretaking stepparent typically recite at length and with warmth the child-tending acts of the stepparent and the passive behavior of the biologic parent. The court speaks of a stepmother who treated a stepchild "as if he were her own child" or "as a member of her own family."[82] Or they refer to the stepparent with approval as the child's "psychological father"[83] or "psychological parent."[84] Not surprisingly, the highest praise for stepparents in custody cases is that they have performed in the way the court believes an ideal blood parent should behave. Courts sometimes in fact have a tone of wonder: look, they seem to be saying, at how far beyond the call of duty this stepparent went for this child.[85]

The cases in which the appellate courts rule for the biologic parent have a different tone. In these cases, the court typically says very little about the behavior of either the biologic parent or the stepparent. They say nothing about parenting acts at all and stress instead some statutory rule or presumption. When courts rely on blood, they have often found little to say.

That courts have not acted consistently and cannot explain cogently why they do what they do should not surprise us. These cases in which a stepparent and a biologic parent contend for custody are often even more difficult than they appear. The choice is not so simple as preserving blood ties versus preserving continuity, for blood ties themselves commonly offer continuity both in the sense of roots and in the sense of ties of desired affection yearned for, often by both absent parent and child, over the years. Conversely, the caretaking stepparent offers more than just continuity. In these custody cases, the stepparent has typically been living with and sharing the bed of the biologic parent for many years. She or he has been caring for the child with the endorsement and involvement of the custodial parent. The stepparent has been "the person closest to the closest relative a child can have."[86] The stepparent may not be blood, but she has been far more than a nurse or a friend.

Katherine Bartlett, in her fine article criticizing America's absorption with parenthood as an "exclusive status," recommends dealing with cases such as *Henrikson* by fashioning rules that permit courts to order shared custody between biologic parents and long-term caretaking third persons or by ordering continued visitation between long-term caretakers and children.[87] As she points out, many courts are beginning to find authority to order visitation for stepparents and other caretakers. She has even found one court that ordered joint legal custody between a stepmother and a biologic mother upon the death of the custodial father.[88] If courts and legislatures move toward the adoption of such rules, I hope that they turn out to be ones that courts rarely impose, that they will be designed instead to set a stage for conversations and negotiations between biologic parents and caretaking stepparents (and children old enough to participate) in which all come to acknowledge the needs of the others.

Some Concluding Words and Reluctant Recommendations

The starting point of my discussion of the law as it relates to stepparents was that there is no law relating to stepparents. That, of course, proved to be a mild overstatement. Still, American states today impose few obligations on stepparents during the course of their marriage to a custodial parent and no obligations after they leave the marriage. What stepparents do for children they do by choice. States have expanded the occasions when stepparents may assume the formal legal status of parent through adoption but the status of parent is almost never thrust on a stepparent[89] and always requires the concurrence of both biologic parents or the concurrence of one biologic parent and the substantial default of the other.

Just as the law imposes no obligations, so also it gives stepparents no rights in children. Biologic parents have claims in their own voice. Their desires for custody or visitation are usually acknowledged as important apart from the interests of their child. By contrast, the occasional cases in which a stepparent is given custody of a stepchild rest entirely on a court's judgment of the needs of the child, not at all on the interests of the stepparent.

In most regards, this state of the law nicely complements the state of stepparent relationships in the United States. Recall the inescapable diversity of such relationships—residential and nonresidential, beginning when the children are infants and when they are teenagers, leading to comfortable relationships in some cases and awkward relationships in others, lasting a few years and lasting many. In this context, it seems sensible to permit those relationships to rest largely on the voluntary arrangements among stepparents and biologic parents. The current state of the law also amply recognizes our nation's continuing absorption with the biologic relationship, especially as it informs our sensibilities about enduring financial obligations.

We could, of course, ask the law to serve a quite different function. Instead of using it to reflect current social attitudes about family, we could try to use it to shape those attitudes. We could, that is, use laws to announce a particular vision of the appropriate stepparent relation, seeking to clarify for stepparents the roles they are expected to perform. But what vision would we choose to impose? Without some new social consensus about either children's needs or adults' responsibilities, is there some new vision we would select? And, even if we developed a new vision and embodied it in rules that, say, treated long-term residential stepparents as equals with biologic parents, eligible for visitation and custody and subject to orders of support, it is far from clear whether such rules would lessen the uncertainties that stepparents experience as they enter or live within these relationships. Even if prospective stepparents learned about new laws or, more diffusely, even if new laws contributed in some modest way to a general understanding of social expectations, most of the confusions of the stepparent role would surely persist. The uncertainties almost certainly inhere in the unpredictable diversity and complexity of the relationships themselves.

If I were forced to recommend specific new rules, I am more confident about what I would prescribe regarding stepparent adoption and child custody than I am about rules I would propose regarding support. My suggested rules for adoption and custody would flow in large part from considerations not much explored in this chapter but developed elsewhere in the family law literature.[90] Both because of ideology and because of theories of child development, I favor maintaining ties for children with persons who have been important in their daily lives. Thus, I find attractive some aspects of the current law regarding stepparent adoption—for example, stepparents through adoption voluntarily obligate themselves to contribute to the long-term support of the children and put themselves into a position in which they are considered appropriate persons for custody or visitation. At the same time, I have doubts about the further attribute of adoption that dictates an end to children's legally protected opportunities for contact with the absent biologic parent. I would thus favor exploring some of the middle grounds that England has been trying or that Katherine Bartlett suggests.[91]

Regarding custody and visitation at the end of the marriage of a parent and a residential stepparent, I would recommend that states strive to encourage parent figures to work our resolutions that they and the child find acceptable and that encourage opportunities for children to have continued contact with persons who lived with them for substantial periods.[92] When parents and stepparents simply cannot agree, I would favor in cases of divorce involving young children, a strong presumption for placement with the parent or stepparent who has been the child's long-term primary caretaker,[93] and, in cases in which a custodial parent has died, I would recommend a presumption for leaving the child with a long-term residential stepparent if the stepparent has been substantially involved in the child's caretaking.[94] In both sorts of cases, I would almost always permit generous visitation with an absent biologic parent. These rules regarding stepparents would, by their very nature, be applied only in cases in which a stepparent came forward seeking a continuing relationship with a child. Nothing in these rules imposes obligations on the residential stepparent who never develops a close relationship with a stepchild and has no desire for continuing contact.

Prescribing rules for child support during and after a remarriage is a greater challenge. During a second marriage, if a custodial parent marries a person with a substantial income, should the absent parent's child support order be adjusted to reflect the new standard of living the children maintain? Similarly, should a stepparent with biologic children from an earlier marriage be permitted to pay less support to the biologic children to reflect the greater expenses he incurs in supporting his new family? The traditional answer to both of these questions has been no. On the other hand, under new child support guidelines, at least a few states would apparently permit continuous adjustment of support at the payor's request to reflect, at each point, the actual living arrangements and incomes of all affected adults and children. Deciding on the wisest approach is difficult. Any rules permitting the downward adjustment of existing support obligations to take into account remarriages risks encouraging undesirable behavior—custodial parents may avoid remarriage to prevent a reduction in support, and noncustodial parents may enter into new marriages in part to punish their former spouses. On the other hand, any rules that fail to take into account new relationships will, in some cases, lead to transfers from a payor (or family unit) already living at the margin to another family unit living more comfortably. (Consider, for example, the case in which, after divorce, a low-earning man supports a woman and her children while paying child support for children living with his former wife and her higher-earning new spouse. These cases are not the norm, but they are not rare either.) My own pragmatic resolution of this problem would be to continue to provide that the remarriage of either the custodial or the noncustodial parent does not, in itself, mark an occasion for recomputing child support but that, if the custodial parent or the state seeks an upward adjustment in a support award to reflect inflation (or the increased earnings of the supporting parent), the actual current standard of living of both family units would be taken into account in determining whether and how much of an adjustment to grant.

Prescribing rules for child support *after* the breakup of a marriage between a stepparent and a biologic parent is also difficult but for different reasons. It is difficult because rules imposing support obligations on a stepparent necessarily involve coercing an unwilling stepparent, and, as we have seen, the stepparent relationship, even among residential stepparents, takes so many forms. Of course, as with many rules relating to divorce today, it would be possible to give courts authority to compel a stepparent to pay support and then to prescribe a set of criteria that the court is expected to take into account in fixing an amount—criteria such as the length of time the stepparent lived with the child, the extent of support the stepparent actually provided, and the extent of support the biologic parents provided during the marriage.

Sad to say, courts have applied similar loose criteria for many years in fixing child support orders for biologic children at the point of divorce, and most observers have been dismayed by the lack of uniformity in the orders produced. As we have seen, Congress has in fact now insisted that states develop and follow more precise dollar guidelines in fixing support orders for absent biologic parents. Evenhandedness in the application of loose criteria is likely to be even more of a problem in the context of stepparents, where there is no general agreement about the obligation of support at all. To be sure, precise guidelines might be developed for residential stepparents—say, one year of support *after* divorce for each two years the stepparent lived with the child. Such guidelines could be justified on the basis of equitable notions that adults should be responsible for dependencies they have fostered and encouraged. Nonetheless, I am uncertain what the effects of such rules would be on people's willingness to enter into marriages with custodial parents. And what is more fundamental, I am uncertain whether most Americans really believe that someone who makes voluntary contributions toward another's support should be considered obligated to continue those contributions simply because the other, even a child, becomes dependent on them. I am thus reluctant to recommend such a change in the law. For now, I think that states can justly continue the current rule that stepparents cannot be compelled to provide support to stepchildren after divorce.

5 Dividing Financial Interests on Divorce

STEPHEN D. SUGARMAN

This chapter addresses the financial impact of no-fault divorce, especially its alleged harmful impact on women.[1] We can assess no-fault's impact from quite different perspectives. One encompasses contrasting what has happened under the new regime with what it promised. It turns out that not much can be made of this comparison, however, because divorce reformers did not seem to have given the question a great deal of thought. Certainly, no representations were made that, as a result of no-fault, women would fare better financially than in the past or that they could look forward to a standard of living after divorce equal to that of their former husbands.[2] Rather, no-fault divorce primarily sought to rid domestic relations law of the bad features of the old system—bitter recriminations, private detectives, cooperative lying about adultery, the stigma of being divorced, and so on.

At the same time, no-fault advocates surely did not intend to make women financially worse off.[3] But, according to several observers, the new system, unintentionally, has had this result. On this view, no-fault divorce might be described as yet another example of good liberal intentions gone (at least partly) awry.

This seems to me to be the main (although by no means the only) theme of Lenore Weitzman's enormously influential book *The Divorce Revolution,* which compares outcomes under the new regime with outcomes under the old. The first part of this chapter explores that sense of "impact." Yet my conclusion is the opposite of Weitzman's. Reexamining her data, I argue that there is little reason to think that women as a class are importantly worse off financially under California's unilateral, no-fault divorce system than they were under the pre-1970 fault regime (or would be were the fault regime still in place). This does not, I should emphasize, speak to whether women fare well, or as well as they ought, under no-fault, but only to their comparative position (generally poor) under both the old and the new systems.

The remainder of this chapter explores "impact" by comparing the current regime with what the rules for dividing financial interests between husbands and wives on divorce should be.[4] The second part examines several approaches that are favored by others but that I consider to be unproductive. First, I explain my objections to partially reintroducing the fault principle—either by employing it around the fringes of divorce law for cases of extreme misbehavior or by trying to base no-fault divorce rules on presumptions of fault. Next, I scrutinize and reject the contention that convincing solutions for divorce law may be found in analogies to traditional contract law or partnership law.

The third part examines behavioral incentives. This material is designed to canvas in a systematic way how divorce law might influence conduct at various points in the couple's relationship—premarital, during marriage, on divorce, and postdivorce. The significance of these behavior-shaping forces to divorce policy is importantly empirical—how much do they really matter? There are few firm data on this question, however, and I have my doubts about their magnitude.

In the final part I explore a variety of fairness claims upon which no-fault rules might be based. I criticize as unconvincing the assertion that the financial goal on divorce ought to be to equalize the (long-run) standard of living of the former spouses. In the process I argue that Weitzman's claim that under no-fault divorce women fare drastically worse financially than do men is exaggerated.

I also criticize theories for allocating financial interests on divorce that are rooted in detrimental sacrifices that one spouse is said to have made to the advantage of the other. I offer instead three separate fairness-based arguments that I think have considerable persuasive power in determining what is just for divorcing couples. One is rooted in the principle of necessity, a second rests on the right to fair notice, and the third I call merger over time.

The chapter ends by sounding a theme of Deborah Rhode and Martha Minow's chapter: ought there not be some collective responsibility for the financial well-being of spouses after divorce?

Fault and No-fault Outcomes Compared

Are women *importantly* worse off under the no-fault regime than they were under the fault regime? I do not believe that Weitzman's California data, comparing results before and after the adoption of no-fault in 1970, demonstrate that they are—despite her interpretation to the contrary. Rather,

Table 5.1. Percent of Divorcing California Husbands and Wives Who Obtain a Family Home (or Its Equity), by Year

	1968	1977
No house to divide	60	54
Majority to wife	24.5	21
Majority to husband	6.5	9
Equal division	9	16
	100%	100%

my reading of her data is that however poor the financial position of just-divorced women may look under no-fault, this basically reflects a long-standing pattern. My conclusion certainly does not imply that the no-fault system is necessarily fair to women but rather that, on the whole, it is not importantly more unfair to them than was the fault system.[5]

It is conventional to say that there are two categories of financial interests to be allocated on divorce—property and future earnings—with separate principles and mechanisms governing their division. Since this is what the law formally does and is how Weitzman attacked the problem, I will adhere to this convention.[6]

With respect to property, I believe Weitzman's data primarily show that more than half of divorcing couples do not have a significant amount of (conventional) property to divide up.[7] Therefore, for those couples the wife cannot be importantly worse off on this dimension under no-fault as compared with the old system. Neither now nor then has there been anything significant to award to her.

Other divorcing couples, however, have one and ordinarily only one important piece of property to divide, and that is the couple's home. So the question I asked of Weitzman's data is, do women get the family home significantly less often under the no-fault system? As I read table 5.1, which I have constructed from information reported in Weitzman's book, the differences are very small; for example, women obtain a majority interest in the family home less often about three and a half times out of a hundred. Put differently, Weitzman's data suggest that for every one hundred divorcing couples, fewer than a handful of homes go to men post-no-fault where they went to women pre-no-fault. More houses were equally divided in 1977; but more couples owned houses then.[8]

Table 5.2. Percent of Divorced California Wives
Awarded Spousal Support, by Year

	1968	1972	1977
No spousal support	81	87	83
Some awarded	19	13	17

Table 5.3. Percent of Divorced California Wives with Different
Lengths of Marriage Awarded Alimony, by Year

	1968	1972	1977
Under 5 years	13	5	4
Over 10 years	31	30	38

When I look at the data on spousal support from future earnings, I see the same general picture. The story was supposed to be that before no-fault women were regularly awarded alimony and for life, whereas now they often obtain no spousal support, or lower amounts, and then only for short periods. But Weitzman's data show (a point she properly makes a great deal of) that fewer than 20 percent of divorced California women were awarded alimony in 1968.[9] In brief, it is a myth that alimony was routinely imposed under the fault system.

How does the no-fault system compare? As table 5.2, again constructed from Weitzman's book,[10] shows, between 94 and 98 percent of women were treated the same under both systems in terms of whether or not they were awarded spousal support. Put the other way, between two and six women in a hundred do not get alimony who previously did. I do not deny that this is a change, but it hardly seems an important change.

In table 5.3 spousal support award data are presented in terms of the duration of marriage.[11] It reveals that women with short-duration marriages (under five years) fared somewhat better under the fault system, but that those with longer marriages (over ten years) are probably doing slightly better under the no-fault system. This result is hardly consistent with the stories often told about no-fault in which the longer-term married woman is seen as having been most victimized by the change. Once again, this by no means argues that long-term married women are treated well by divorce law; it addresses only their relative treatment under the two regimes.

Do women who receive spousal support receive less (in constant dollars) than those who received awards under the old system? Not as I read Weitzman's data. Those with awards in the 1968 sample received an average of about $300 a month (in 1984 dollars).[12] By contrast, those with awards in the 1977 sample received a mean of about $575 a month and a median of about $367 (in 1984 dollars).[13] To be sure, since the 1977 sample included proportionately more longer-married women receiving spousal support awards, as compared with the 1968 sample, one might predict somewhat higher average awards, but given the data Weitzman reported, I do not think I can adjust for that. Therefore, at least I can say that the change to the no-fault regime does not seem to have been accompanied by lower sums being awarded to those women who receive awards. Nor does Weitzman claim this has happened.

What about the duration of the awards? Remembering that 81 percent of women before and 83 to 87 percent of women after received no award, nonetheless, did those who received awards in the past at least have longer awards? Here there does indeed, at least at first blush, seem to be an important distinction between the two regimes. Whereas 62 percent of the awards were said to be permanent before, only 32 percent were after.[14]

But this does not tell the whole story. First, many women remarry fairly soon after their divorce (within five years) and typically under the old rules their "permanent" awards then ended. As a result, for those women a longer guarantee turned out not to be important in terms of the money they received.

Second, alas, large numbers of men have always defaulted on their continuing spousal support obligations, and increasingly so as the date of divorce recedes in time. Therefore, once again the value of a permanent award is often less than the legal formality suggests. None of this is to imply that it is either fair or unfair for support awards to be of permanent duration. But these factors make me quite skeptical about whether that extra one third of women with permanent awards in 1968 (constituting about six in a hundred women divorced that year) actually found the durational feature of their award a significant advantage in practice.

In sum, I am simply unconvinced that Weitzman's data from actual court records show that California women as a group fare importantly worse under no-fault as compared with how they fared under the fault system.[15] Yet, when one reads her book one is led to the opposite conclusion. Why is this?[16]

For her, the point is to focus on those cases where there is some property to divide and where some alimony or spousal support is awarded, and to demonstrate for such cases a statistically significant change in result. I, in contrast, am looking at all divorced women and am considering the magnitude of any shifts that have occurred in that context. Thus, where Weitzman finds lots of change and an alarming trend, I see that overall things are pretty much the same as always.

Which is the more helpful view of the data? Weitzman has performed a very valuable function. Not only has she collected and analyzed extremely interesting information, but by doing so she has played a key role in making further divorce reform an important policy issue. But the problem I have with her emphasis upon a comparison of the old and new systems is that it suggests a solution I am confident she would reject.

That is, suppose the law were changed so that the patterns of property and spousal support awards under no-fault were altered, and women were no longer, in Weitzman's terms, worse off under no-fault than before. Would that "solve" the problem? To the contrary, surely most policy analysts concerned about the situation of women after divorce, including Weitzman, would be wholly unsatisfied with such a result. Or suppose that Weitzman had found that women were better off under no-fault to the same extent that she found them worse off. Would no-fault then be seen as a big success story? I somehow doubt it. Instead, I imagine, Weitzman would have written a different book, but still emphasizing the financially weak postdivorce position of women—something like "the far-from-finished divorce revolution."

Ironically, even though I strongly believe that getting women back to where they were financially under the fault regime is very much the wrong goal of divorce law, it is perhaps oddly good for the political future of women's interests that Weitzman found the changes she did. Otherwise, it might have put the discussion of further divorce reform on the back burner, or at least cast it in a less appealing light.

Nevertheless, for those who are concerned about the plight of women under no-fault divorce, Weitzman's research convinces me that what is required as a persuasive theory, or at least a well-argued program, for allocating financial interests on divorce that is not at all anchored in a comparison with how women fared under the fault system.[17] That will be the focus of the remainder of the chapter.

Some False Starts

A Residual Role for Fault?

My discussion will assume that we will not go back to a system of conditioning divorce upon fault-finding in individual cases. Nonetheless, I will air here some ideas about potential residual roles for fault in a no-fault scheme.

Even if the decision to grant a divorce is not based on fault, the rules pertaining to financial rights (and the custody of children) could depend upon marital conduct, as remains the case in some states and in other countries today. Plainly, the rhetorical force of an attack on the California-style no-fault system can be enhanced if set in the context of an innocent and a guilty spouse. For example, a specific case of a faithful, older woman who has been cruelly abandoned by her husband for another woman may evoke in many people the feeling that this woman should have special financial entitlements even if she should not be able to block the divorce.

Although my purpose here is not to try to make the case for the California-style no-fault divorce regime, my assumption is simply that, overall, the social costs of considering fault, even when restricted to determining the divorcing couple's financial rights and duties, are thought to outweigh the benefits—even though that means abandoning the attempt to "do justice" in individual cases. That someone may not like the way no-fault divorce works when the other spouse is unilaterally divorcing her or him, but likes it when it is the other way around, hardly demonstrates that the shift to a thoroughgoing no-fault regime was a mistake.[18]

Yet the exclusion of fault considerations from the parties' financial settlement need not be an all-or-nothing matter. For example, even relatively pure no-fault accident compensation schemes still typically recognize a residual role for fault in extreme cases.[19] In workers' compensation, intentional self-injury, on the one hand, bars worker claims, and especially bad employer conduct, on the other, leads either to an enhanced compensation award or the right to sue in tort on top of the workers' compensation award. Even in New Zealand, where accident law has essentially been obliterated and replaced with a comprehensive accident victim compensation plan, victims still retain the right to sue, in extraordinary cases, for punitive damages.

Analogously, we could maintain a role for fault in that small proportion of divorce cases involving especially reprehensible conduct. One way to do that would be to apply to such situations different rules for property division and spousal support.[20] Alternatively, perhaps, the wronged spouse could be allowed a separate tort suit for damages that would supplement the basic no-fault rules of domestic relations law.[21]

In either event, however, I believe we would have considerable difficulty in achieving a social consensus as to what sort of conduct in the marriage context is to be considered equivalent to the malicious or despicable behavior that generates punitive damages in torts cases today. I imagine that simple adultery would not; on the other hand, spousal battering probably would. Yet other situations might be quite ambiguous.

Without reasonably clear standards, however, we run the risk of reinjecting fault into nearly every divorce case. Indeed, in order to ward off the risk of a suit for legal malpractice and for whatever bargaining leverage it might bring, divorce lawyers could be strongly tempted routinely to include a tort claim (or a claim for an enhanced, fault-based, divorce award) on behalf of every one of their clients. That would surely be an undesirable result if the social goal was to have an essentially no-fault system that provided extra financial compensation only to victims of extreme marital behavior thought to occur in, say, 5 percent or fewer of the cases. One strategy for preventing such an outcome would be to restrict extra awards to cases involving essentially physical, rather than emotional, harm. But given the American tort law experience in other contexts, it is by no means clear that excluding all emotional harm–based claims in the divorce setting would be either a desirable or an administratively feasible screening device. Hence, on balance, this approach may be rather more alarming than attractive.

Irrebuttable Presumptions of Fault?

Some people might ideally prefer the law to be based on fault, believing that the propriety of the conduct of the parties during the marriage should be the key determinant of their financial rights and obligations on divorce. At the same time they may conclude that it is not desirable to try to administer a regime that requires determining in each case who is in the wrong. Might we instead sensibly run a no-fault system that seeks to approximate fault through the use of irrebuttable presumptions? I doubt it.

Surely, deeming either the party who files for divorce or, alternatively, the one who is sued to be the innocent one, and the other party the guilty one, would be unacceptable, especially in view of the undesirable incentives such presumptions would create. So, too, I think the public would find it wrong to adopt a regime premised on the assumption that men (or women) are usually at fault. Nor does it seem fair to view as the innocent one either the primary caretaker of the children (where there are children), or the lower earner, or the one who does not want to remarry immediately, or any other non-fault category that I have been able to think of.

Even if there were considerable overlap between fault in many specific cases and the criterion used, the problem is that the simultaneous over-inclusiveness and underinclusiveness of any such criterion makes it highly offensive when those irrebuttably presumed against are not in fact at fault and when those who are in fact at fault fall outside of the presumption.

To be sure, we effectively presume fault in other areas of the law, such as in tort law when we impose strict liability on manufacturers of defective products. Yet, at least in that setting, the risk of liability can be planned for, insured against, and ultimately distributed among the purchasers of the product, any one of whom might have had the bad luck to encounter the dangerous item. But this is simply not analogous to the marriage and divorce setting. Presumed fault liability here is more analogous to a rule that would jail anyone found in possession of what turned out to be stolen goods with no consideration given to how the defendant actually obtained them (for example, as a bona fide purchaser or through an unsuspicious gift).

This difficulty with using presumptions of fault does not make it un-acceptable for the law intentionally to favor, say, women or, say, primary caretakers—so long as that preference is based upon reasons other than the presumed fault of the other spouse. This does highlight the need for those "other reasons" to be convincing, however. Otherwise, critics may be tempt-ed to characterize specific proposals as irrebuttably presuming, for example, that the man or that the woman is at fault.

Marriage as Contract?

Can marriage be thought of as a contract in which fairness is found by applying ordinary contract principles to determine the allocation of the husband's and wife's financial rights and duties on divorce? I do not think so.[22]

Marriage, at least in this century, is typically said to be best understood as a status, rather than as a contractual, relationship. Yet I believe that ordinary contract law provides a much better analogy to the law governing the marriage relationship under the fault system than under the no-fault regime.

By this way of thinking, marriage in the past was like a long-term contract for an indefinite period in which both parties made promises for a lifetime together. When one breached, this was supposed to lead to the award of damages to the other in the form of property transfers and alimony obligations.

Today, however, although we can still talk about marriage as a contract, under pure no-fault divorce like that available in California, it is more like a contract-at-will from which either party can unilaterally walk away. There is no place for the concept of breach and resultant damages. The analogy, rather, is to the way we traditionally have thought about employment relationships, where an employee could quit and an employer could discharge for any reason. Interestingly enough, employment relationships in modern times are increasingly subject to "wrongful discharge" limitations that give rise to suits for damages, indeed sometimes punitive damages, against the breaching party. But since "wrongful discharge" is clearly rooted in bad conduct, this analogy does not fit modern marriage law so long as we are going to stick to no-fault principles.

The upshot is that, under no-fault, the contract law analogy provides no guidance for the allocation of the couple's property, and if it says anything about spousal support, it would appear to reject it. Although "no-fault, no-responsibility" divorce law might be what society wants,[23] it is not persuasive to reach that normative solution simply by pointing to the law of contracts-at-will. The question is whether our society's values concerning marriage "contracts" are the same as those concerning contracts-at-will, and to determine that requires looking outside of contract law to see what our values are.

Marriage as Partnership?

Perhaps a better legal analogy to no-fault divorce can be found in partnership law. The idea is that through marriage the man and woman have joined together (50-50?) in an economic partnership, which, like partnerships generally, can be dissolved by either party. On the ending of the marriage partnership, like other partnerships, there is to be a winding up of the partnership's activities and a distribution of the partnership assets. In traditional partnership law there are some special tortlike rules governing unusual cases where one partner is seen to take unfair advantage of the other party by breaking up the partnership. But since these turn on fault and are thus inconsistent with my assumptions about no-fault divorce, I put them aside here.[24]

Under the partnership analogy all earnings generated by the couple during the marriage would seem to belong to the partnership, as would any
things bought with those earnings and any earnings left unspent and saved
or invested. In traditional financial partnerships, ongoing distributions are
often made that exceed the immediate consumption needs of the partners.
These sums cease to be partnership assets, and the individual partners can
separately invest them or spend them as they wish. In the marriage setting,
however, it is as though, as a general rule, all the extra income and asset
appreciation of the partnership is simply retained and reinvested in the
partnership. But given the nature of marriage partners, as contrasted with
ordinary financial partners, this seems right.

At the same time, just as financial partners contribute only some of their
property to the typical partnership, certain items of property belonging to
the husband and wife could be seen as outside the marital partnership and
not subject to division on the marriage's termination. They might include
assets the parties bring to the marriage and do not commingle with other
marital property, and those gifts and inheritances separately received by
either party during the marriage and maintained separately.[25]

If marriage under no-fault is to be seen as a conventional partnership, no
formal distinctions would be made between long- and short-duration marriages; to be sure, in long-duration marriages, there might be more assets to
distribute. So, too, the family home would not be treated differently from
any other asset. The implication of minor children would be ambiguous
since there is no obvious counterpart in ordinary partnerships. Does gaining custody mean that you have obtained a partnership asset, or merely that
you have assumed a partnership liability for which you should be
compensated?

Most important, under the partnership analogy there would be no
spousal support. That is, in the traditional partnership, even though the
partners agree to make their earning capacity available to the partnership
during its lifetime, they ordinarily just walk away from the dissolved partnership with all their own human capital. This applies both to the human
capital they brought to the partnership and to any enhanced human capital
they gained during the operation of the partnership.

As with the contract law analogy, however, it does not follow that there
should be no spousal support obligation after a no-fault divorce just because there seems to be no parallel in partnership law. We could adopt this
solution to make the analogy complete, but that requires first making up
our minds as to what is socially desirable.

Traditional financial partners, of course, may anticipate certain problems of partnership breakup and, if they wish, enter into alternative arrangements at the outset. For example, they might want to agree to certain buy-out provisions, or notice provisions, or postpartnership client-sharing provisions, in order both to induce each other to form the partnership initially and, in case of a falling out, to govern their financial relationship on terms different from what the default rules of partnership law provide. They also might agree to be other than 50-50 partners originally. Perhaps married couples could also be encouraged to make specific agreements in advance. But, in fact, nowadays nearly no one does so. (This practice seems largely restricted to the very rich and those entering into second marriages who want to protect the financial interests of children of the first marriage as against the second spouse.)

In view of that, and on the grounds that marriage is a very special sort of financial partnership, we could instead try to think about what special partnership terms marrying couples would likely agree to, a topic I will explore more fully below. But this, of course, takes us away from using the provisions of current partnership law as the basis for resolving the couple's financial rights and obligations.

Finally, we could, of course, keeping fairly close to conventional terminology, decide to treat the parties to a marriage partnership as permanently joining their human capital upon entering into marriage. Alternatively, we could decide to give the divorcing parties back their premarriage human capital but divide between them their enhanced earning power. Or we could elect to divide enhanced human capital only under certain circumstances, such as when one spouse made a specific financial sacrifice for the other. Or we could elect to have rules for human capital sharing that are meant in some way to replace the fault-based part of regular partnership law that we have excluded from divorce law. But the question is, *should* we treat human capital in one of those ways (or in other ways)? Imagining that we could do it, and further recognizing that our solution can then fit reasonably comfortably into only moderately altered partnership law models, hardly provides the answer.

Behavioral Incentives

This part explores the prospects of divorce law serving a behavior-channeling function at various stages in the relationship between the couple. The idea is that divorce rules could be selected on the ground that they promote socially desirable conduct and discourage socially unwanted conduct.

One way to think about desirable incentives is in terms of what private agreements would-be husbands and wives might make if they were actually to face up to the contingency of a no-fault divorce and to plan for that possibility in a rational way. The important assumption here is that the parties would find it in their mutual interest to include incentive features in such an agreement that would maximize their mutual well-being. Of course, individual couples might have reason to prefer quite different terms that a uniform no-fault divorce law could not accommodate. Nevertheless, there might be widespread consensus on certain matters. Divorce law, at least to the extent it reflected these norms, could then be seen as a kind of standard form marital partnership agreement governing the allocation of financial interests on the ending of the marriage.

If this idea were pressed far, it might generate interest in providing the details of divorce law to couples who are about to marry, so that those who wanted a different deal might actually negotiate variations on the standard form (or there might be several standard forms from which the parties could select). There are, however, considerations that cut the other way. First, I believe there would be reluctance to introduce officially the reality of frequent divorce into a celebratory occasion that pretends to the contrary. Second, I would be concerned that at the time of marriage the parties would not negotiate rationally with each other over the divorce contingency. Because entering into marriage in our society is thought more often to be the result of romantic love than hard-headed business bargaining, there is reason to fear that many individuals would not insist upon terms that would sufficiently protect themselves. On the other hand, some couples might choose to incorporate into their agreements extravagant promises intended more to symbolize their anticipated undying love than to deal realistically with what would seem right if love faded.

Moreover, there are considerations relevant to a desirable divorce law that go beyond what the couple might prefer. First, society at large may also have legitimate interests in how the parties to a marriage and divorce behave. Second, were unmarried couples really to negotiate a marriage and divorce deal as business dealings are traditionally negotiated, both specific individual would-be spouses, and possibly men in general, would have considerably more bargaining chips (and hence would be in a superior bargaining position). In thinking about designing a divorce law that would stand in for the solution that the parties would reach, would we really want to take into account such mismatches in bargaining power? Or would we not instead want to think in terms of couples making arrangements from, at least in some respects, more equal initial positions?

With these considerations in mind, I turn now to illustrate a number of ways in which financial rules under a no-fault regime could influence the actions of the couple, a topic that has begun to engage the attention of economists. Before starting down the list, however, I offer two caveats. On the one hand, it is critical to consider whether the financial incentives that any proposed divorce law creates will actually affect conduct in an important way. If not, then the instrumental use of these rules for behavior-channeling purposes loses much of its relevance. On the other hand, as I will explain in the next section on fairness considerations, providing behavioral incentives is unlikely to be the only purpose of divorce law even if its contours promise significantly to sway how people act.

Whether or Not to Marry

One place to begin is at the beginning, with the question of the impact of divorce rules on marriage. One reviewer of Weitzman's book argued that if her proposed pro-wife reforms were enacted, men would become reluctant to marry and that one consequence would be that divorced women over age thirty-five would be far less likely to remarry than today.[26] Whether this prediction is right is another matter, but it raises an important issue. Surely we can agree that the state should not create significant incentives not to marry.

At the extreme, clearly the divorce regime could significantly deter marriage—at least if it could not be altered by agreement, and if living together outside of marriage did not carry the same financial consequences. Suppose, for example, that on divorce each party completely owned the other party's human capital, or suppose the rule was that on divorce a woman owned both her own and all of her former husband's human capital. This is not to argue that even such regimes as these would necessarily eliminate marriages. To be sure, such rules would give women considerably strengthened economic power as compared with the present system; indeed, where unilateral no-fault divorce is permitted, they could elect to walk away from a marriage at any time and for any reason and take their husband's earning capacity with them. Yet women could, of course, choose not to exercise all their power, and, in the end, many would not do so—if for no other reason than that to press their rights to the full would cause many former husbands to stop working or to flee into hiding, leaving the assertive wife with nothing. With that in mind, many men, in order to gain the advantages of marriage, might be willing to take the risk that, if their marriage did end in a divorce, they would not in fact have to turn over all of their future earnings to their former spouse.

Of course, people today are not actually suggesting that on divorce women be awarded all of their husband's human capital, and even very pro-wife reforms that are being proposed may not have an important impact on entry into marriage. Still, given the growing acceptability of cohabitation outside of marriage, this is a factor to look for—a constraint perhaps—in designing a divorce law regime. After all, it is not only society's interest in marriage that is at stake; it hardly helps women to be handed such future economic clout as to prevent them from obtaining their more important current objective of getting married.

I have so far considered the law's potential impact on men's willingness to marry, but there is the other side as well. Elizabeth Landes has theorized that a legal policy against the award of spousal support on divorce discourages women from marrying; and she found just such an effect through an empirical study, albeit as measured by a weak data set.[27]

To Specialize or Not in Certain Functions during Marriage

Several scholars have suggested that certain divorce rules may be desirable in order to help couples arrange for their preferred allocation of marital roles.[28] They suppose that it is often the mutually advantageous thing for couples to specialize, with the woman (usually) not taking on a paid work force role and emphasizing, instead, having children, running the household, and emotionally supporting her spouse.

But these analysts suggest that this desired specialization of function may not come about if women fear that on divorce they will be left financially unprotected and without the ability to earn much money themselves. Given such fear, the wife might enter the paid work force after all—to the couple's detriment as the couple sees it. The wife makes this second best choice so as to create, in effect, an insurance policy against the contingency of divorce. On the other hand, this line of reasoning goes, if divorce law promised to compensate women for forgoing the development of their own earning capacity, then the law could pave the way for women to invest in their husband's (and family's) human capital instead of their own. With the security of such divorce rules, the woman might follow her (and the couple's) preferred path and stay at home.

Notice here that even though individual couples may see such specialization of function as good for them, others might well object to what they see as society promoting such specialization—both symbolically and by actually facilitating such role separation. These objectors, who typically want largely to rid our society of gender-linked roles, would prefer that individual couples bear short-term losses for what would be claimed as longer-term gains for people generally. In short, there may be a clash between what the couple prefers given the society they confront, and what others want a new society to look like (or what couples might prefer were society changed).

In any event, even if the idea of facilitating specialization had considerable appeal in theory, I wonder how important this incentive is (or would be) in practice. Many women today invest in their husbands and their children, rather than in their own economic independence, but seemingly without the divorce law protections favored by those scholars concerned about specialization. Indeed, this is an important part of Weitzman's complaint. Of course, perhaps there would be even more specialization of function were more generous divorce guarantees made to women—and less so if such guarantees were lacking and women became more aware of how financially precarious certain role specialization could be in a world of unilateral no-fault divorce.

To Initiate Divorce Proceedings or Not

Whereas many people want the state to be neutral as to whether couples divorce, others would like to discourage divorce, especially where minor children are involved.[29] Despite this difference of opinion, surely we can agree that we do not want rules that promote divorce. To pick up the specialization-of-function theme again, the other side of the coin is that if divorce laws do not provide certain protections for women, and if women choose to invest in their husbands and children anyway, then husbands may later find themselves in a position where they are tempted to exploit their spouses by divorcing. The argument here rests on the assumption that by having children and devoting themselves to home life, women often contribute disproportionately to the couple's well-being at the early part of the marriage, whereas men's most important contributions often come later once their earnings peak.[30] Where that is true, the claim is that after the woman has done her part, divorce law should deny the man an incentive to expropriate her contribution by divorcing before doing his share. Without such protection in the divorce laws, it is argued, the law gives men who have enjoyed benefits without repaying them too great an incentive to pull out of the marriage.

Without doubting that many middle-aged men in our society may be in a position to exploit their wives in the way this model assumes, the extent to which men actually initiate divorce proceedings for that reason is uncertain.[31] Another way to put it is to ask how much less likely are men to seek divorce if the price of leaving were significantly increased in cases where the family pattern fits this model. In general one might anticipate that taxing divorce would serve to discourage it. But the specific issue here is the elasticity of demand for marital freedom of men who would be subject to the burden of compensating for benefits obtained in the way imagined here, and I do not think we have good data about that.

Quite apart from the specific concern about husbands expropriating their wives' past contributions to the marriage, it might be imagined that, in general, the party with more financial independence is more likely to initiate a divorce, so long as he or she can hold onto that economic advantage. In principle, then, increasing the cost of divorce to the financially stronger party could reduce that party's propensity to split.

On the other hand, it is also worth noting that by requiring compensation to lower earners in order to remove the financial incentive for higher earners to divorce them, we at the same time economically position more dependent spouses to initiate divorce proceedings. Fairness considerations aside, this factor undercuts the idea that imposing an exit tax on higher earners, payable to their lower-earning spouses, necessarily reduces the incentive for divorce.[32]

Whether or Not to Cooperate during the Divorce Process

No-fault divorce in California is supposed to be obtainable simply and unilaterally. But in practice, either party often can choose to make the proceedings easy and friendly or nasty and burdensome for the other. I think we could agree, other things being equal, that the desirable social policy under a no-fault regime would be to discourage spouses from making the process of obtaining a divorce trying for each other.

Of course, the no-fault principle itself is meant to promote cooperation by making legally irrelevant to the grant of divorce conduct of the parties during the marriage that, when fought over by them and their lawyers, is thought to have the effect of both protracting the divorce process and making it arduous on both sides. The additional behavioral incentive point here is that no-fault divorce law's financial allocation rules may also have a significant impact on how people behave once one or both decide there is to be a divorce. For example, if one side foresees that she (or he) will be drastically worse off financially after the divorce, that may create a strong incentive to delay the divorce as long as possible, by forcing protracted negotiations over children and financial matters.[33] Of course, the financially stronger party should be in a position to bribe the other not to hassle and delay, but that may require a certain rationality in the bargaining process that may elude a significant share of divorcing couples.

How to Act after Divorce

Both the parties and society have interests in the former couple's postdivorce behavior, including such matters as how hard the former spouses work, how much contact the noncustodial spouse has with their children, and whether the former spouses remarry. Divorce law rules can play a role in these matters.

Like any income transfer mechanism, divorce law can create disincentives concerning postdivorce work effort. Suppose the man is ordered to pay spousal support to the woman in an amount that will vary as both his and her future incomes vary. For example, he may be asked to pay 25 percent of his earnings minus 25 percent of her earnings. Such an order can discourage both from earning more income because each party nets less from every extra dollar he or she might make.

From the woman's viewpoint (in our example) an order requiring the husband to transfer even a fixed sum of income or wealth, either monthly or as a lump sum, can affect her decision to enter the paid labor force. Even though in this case she will not lower her spousal support by becoming employed, nonetheless, if the standard of living such a transfer provides is sufficient, all things considered, she may simply elect not to become employed at all.

Normally, there is strong public sentiment in favor of encouraging people to make productive use of their abilities in the paid labor force. To the extent that this sentiment applies to the divorced couple setting, it suggests the desirability of fixed (and perhaps time-bounded) transfers between spouses. Of course, the price that must be paid to overcome these employment disincentives may be unacceptable. For example, it could mean abandoning ongoing transfers that carefully mesh with need or ability to pay and that might otherwise be desirable. Moreover, at least where the care of minor children is involved, there is considerable controversy over whether the divorced custodial parent (typically the mother) should enter the paid labor force.

On the whole, social policy currently favors promoting the visitation of children by noncustodial parents. The divorce rules may influence such conduct, although the direction is not entirely clear. Does having the non-custodial spouse regularly pay money to his former wife and children actually prompt him to visit more? Or do ongoing financial obligations lead to disputes that cause her to block access to the children?[34]

Finally, most people probably do not want divorce law to discourage remarriage. From that perspective it would, other things being equal, seem advantageous for the payee of spousal support to receive either a fixed sum or time-bounded payments rather than payments that terminate on remarriage. Should the subsequent marital situation of the payor of support affect his (or her) continuing obligation to the previous spouse? Such adjustments could influence a decision to remarry at all, to remarry someone who brings children along, and to have children in the new marriage. But no assessment of incentives alone can resolve these questions because at stake here is the meaning of fairness as between first and second families which is necessarily implicated in any resolution to this issue. This brings me to questions of fairness generally.

Fairness Considerations

Once it can be agreed upon what constitutes marital property as contrasted with individual assets of the spouses[35]—and assuming for this purpose that the spouses' human capital is not marital property—I think that most people are comfortable today with the notion that fairness, at least presumptively, suggests an even split of the divorcing couple's marital property.[36] After all, once it is recognized that the couple might have consumed all that they together earned or were given, it strikes most people as intuitively right that they should divide whatever is left unspent. Moreover, both the law and practice seem to be moving in that direction. But as mentioned earlier, apart from the family home, these rules are usually not very important. This is especially so for those many low-income divorcing couples who have debts that roughly equal, and sometimes exceed, their meager assets.

Therefore, the important controversy concerns what claims the spouses might fairly have to each other's future earnings—or to an adjustment in the allocation of their marital property *because* of considerations rooted in their anticipated future income. This is an acute controversy because if women generally are going to fare significantly better in the couple's division of their financial interests on divorce, a convincing case is going to have to be made that they are entitled to more of their former husbands' postdivorce income than they now obtain. Again, this is particularly important for relatively lower-earning couples, where the only way that husbands can typically contribute to the postdivorce financial well-being of their former wives is through spousal support.

Just as the previous part canvassed a series of behavioral incentives that might sensibly influence divorce policy, this part reviews several possible fairness-based norms. My main theme is that fair principles for dividing future income are far less evident than others suggest.[37] Although I reject several norms that have been prominently endorsed, I offer three other principles that I find reasonably persuasive.

The Equal Living Standards Principle

Perhaps Weitzman's most frequently quoted finding is this: "The research shows that, on the average, divorced women and the minor children in their households experience a 73 percent decline in their standard of living in the first year after divorce. Their former husbands, in contrast, experience a 42 percent rise in their standard of living."[38] I contend that not only is this conclusion both exaggerated and misleadingly precise, but also that, in any event, such disparities by themselves say nothing about the fairness of the way no-fault divorce is functioning. Following that discussion I search for what arguments might be made on behalf of the principle that no-fault divorce should assure former spouses equal living standards and find nothing persuasive.

Without explaining precisely where her calculations went astray, Saul Hoffman and Greg Duncan have already shown that Weitzman's much-repeated finding about the decline in divorced women's living standards is inconsistent with previous research, implausibly large, and incompatible with other data she reports.[39] They suggest that a 30 percent decline in living standards for women in the first year of divorce, rather than the 73 percent Weitzman claims, is far more likely to be typically the case. Although 30 percent is by no means a trifling amount, the difference between the two estimates is dramatic.[40]

It is also not clear that the most sensible time period for comparing the financial circumstances of the former spouses is the first year after divorce.[41] When I think about the point one year after divorce, I imagine that relatively few men or women have remarried, and that, whereas he is probably both settled back into his job and settled into new quarters, her life, especially if she has their children, may be still very much in transition.[42] Admitting that this is a loose generalization and that its accuracy in individual cases may depend, for example, upon the time between when the marriage broke up and when the divorce occurred, it will serve to make my point. Let us now consider instead the situation that might pertain if we compared the living standards of former couples three or five or ten years after divorce. By then, many more women may have entered the paid labor force or may have increased their earnings.[43] Also, many women and even more men would be remarried and both burdened with new responsibilities and aided by a new spouse. As a result, it is certainly possible that the differences between the earlier divorced men's and women's living standards would be considerably less than they appear to be one year after divorce.

If this surmise is right, then the wisdom of measuring men/women differences for the first year after divorce depends on what the purpose of the measurement is. If, for example, we are interested in how financially well positioned the former spouses are to carry on with their lives as singles, then Weitzman's approach seems to make sense. If instead (or in addition) we are interested in long-run financial consequences of divorce as reflected in terms of the former spouses' standards of living, then it would have been better if Weitzman had provided similar data for periods of time longer removed from the initial divorce.

I also have some concerns about how one goes about making comparisons between men's and women's living standards after divorce. I will assume initially that the goal is to concentrate on comparing incomes, rather than trying to measure utility levels. Even so, one must contend with the matter of "imputed" income. For example, economists point out that the rental value of the family home to whoever is still living in it creates imputed income. So do do-it-yourself activities. Consider, for example, as Weitzman recognizes, that wives traditionally do most of the housework and that after divorce former husbands are deprived of this benefit, and thus have a lowered standard of living to that extent. I could not find any indication that these imputed income items were included by Weitzman in the measurements reported in her book. Another question is whether the comparison should be in terms of gross income or, say, income after taxes and reasonably necessary work expenses (including child-care expenses). I would think that the latter, although perhaps more difficult to ascertain, would be a more appropriate basis of comparison. It would appear that Weitzman used gross income figures in her study.[44]

Next, if there are children and one spouse has primary physical custody, then a comparison of the spouses' living standards somehow has to take into account the expenses of the children. One solution would be to assume that child support awards (or payments) take care of that need. On this approach, one would exclude the child support from both the payor's and payee's income and would ignore the existence of the children. But if, realistically, the custodial spouse spends more than the child support payments for the needs of the children, this is an inadequate solution that would overestimate the financial condition of the custodial parent. Understandably, then, Weitzman sought to compare the living standard of the noncustodial parent with how well the custodial parent (usually the woman) and the children can together live on all of their income.[45]

Yet, an approach that considers only the financial burden of the children and gives no weight to the nonfinancial benefits that children produce takes us back to wondering about the wisdom of the initial choice to compare incomes rather than utility. To be sure, sometimes the children are a drag that neither party wants. Parents without physical custody may clearly value the leisure they have obtained more than whatever benefits they would derive from custody of their children. In these situations, men-women differences (where women have custody) are reduced, rather than exaggerated, by looking at income differences. But where women have physical custody of the children and men feel that they have, as a result, lost something terribly important to them, it is deeply troubling to compare the former spouses' living standards in terms that treat the children solely as a liability. And as Robert Mnookin points out in chapter 2, substantial numbers of divorcing husbands claim they want more physical custody of their children than they are able to obtain.[46] Since it is unclear how one would go about dealing with this consideration, this just reinforces the ambiguity that surrounds the measuring of former spouses' comparative states.

Nonetheless, let me assume that, even after taking into account all the points just made, recently divorced men were still shown to enjoy a significantly higher standard of living than recently divorced women. Indeed, I am willing to assume for these purposes that men's living standards typically go up and women's down. Is that unfair? I do not think we can possibly say so without having a theory of what would be fair. Such disparities would certainly show that divorce, at least initially, is financially bad for women (and children) and good for men, and might, for example, be the basis for predicting that men would be more likely to initiate divorce than women. But until it is shown that fairness requires equal living standards, these differences would only be facts.

Although Weitzman does not, as I see it, really try to *argue* for the equal living standards norm, at several places she seems to endorse it.[47] Just what is the case for it? I am still trying to figure that out.

While it is in some sense true that in the typical marriage vow the couple agrees to support each other forever, they also in the same sense promise to love each other and stay married forever. Since they are free to change their minds about the latter, something more needs to be added to the equation to explain why the former obligation would nonetheless continue. There are, after all, many marriages that end in less than one year, and a majority end in less than ten years, often without children.[48] And if the equal standard of living principle is not meant to apply to all marriages and forever, on what basis is it meant to be limited? Once we go down that road—for example, for a period of five years, or for as long as the marriage lasted, or only for marriages lasting more than fifteen years—then it is really some other principle that is being applied.

Although women typically begin their divorces with lower standards of living than their former husbands, it is also the case that they typically enter marriage with lower personal economic prospects in the paid labor force. Even though it may be that men as a class have partly caused women's condition in the job market, I do not see why the particular man, who now happens to be a former husband, should be responsible for redressing this much larger social problem. In short, I think that a case for society-based income transfers from men to women, or strong affirmative action plans favoring women over men in employment settings, would be easier to make than the case that a former husband should remain a lifetime provider for his former wife.

Another puzzle is whether, under the equal living standards idea, the lower earning spouse would be assured only some specified standard of living that is once and for all determined at the time of the divorce. That, however, would not seem to capture the point as I see it. Rather, is it not the idea that their future financial condition is to be bound up with both of their financial futures just in the way that it would have been had they remained married (even though they did not)? But implications of that, it seems to me, are disquieting in other ways. What, for example, are we to do about all the changed circumstances that occur when they go their separate ways—such as a second marriage (and the assumption of new family obligations) and then, possibly, a second divorce?

In the end, the case for equal standards of living seems to me to rest on a tautology: the spouses were equal partners in marriage, and everything they have, including their future income potential, is theirs and is to be divided equally on divorce. But this begs the question of whether the moment of marriage should indeed be seen to merge their human capital together, and a convincing case for that has yet to be made. In the sections ahead I consider other principles by which one spouse might fairly be thought to obtain rights to at least some of the human capital of the other.

Need

Many no-fault divorce laws now emphasize meeting "need" as a key basis for determining the division of financial interests on divorce—at least with respect to spousal support.[49] How justified is this norm? One fundamental problem we face in answering that question arises from the uncertainty about what is meant by "need."

Are we to focus on what sum, if any, is necessary to keep the spouse in question out of poverty, as defined by the official poverty level or by the Bureau of Labor Statistics' budget for a low-income household? Or is need more of an "opportunity" or "transitional" notion, such as what is needed for someone to take steps to become reasonably self-sufficient (such as to go to school, or to have job training, or to have time to pull one's life together)? Or does need have psychological overtones that make it important for people not to descend to a significantly lower income/social class? On this latter view, because people become accustomed to certain life-styles, they soon "need" more money than they might otherwise. If this sounds like an odd notion of need, notice that the Social Security system's method of providing benefits to elderly wives and widows was originally sold to Congress in 1939 on grounds of need, with benefits based upon the earnings of husbands. As a result, the wife's standard of living during the marriage becomes important in determining how much Social Security she gets.

Is it possible to select among the various notions of need in a convincing and principled way? I once thought that progress on this question could be made by thinking about it in terms of John Rawls's "original position."[50] We would ask ourselves what system of rules people would prefer if they did not know, for instance, whether they would be men or women, earners or not, or married or not. But I am now doubtful that this approach takes the analysis anywhere. If nothing else, Rawls's "difference principle" already calls for a societywide scheme of equalized incomes (except where inequality can be justified, generally on incentive grounds, as making the worst off better off). In the absence of such a world, it is exceedingly tricky to decide how to apply his principles to but one area. Indeed, as I have already noted, one of the important controversies about divorce law is why it ought to serve to reduce inequalities between the sexes arising from forces outside the marriage relationship.

Necessity

Nonetheless, there is at least one need-related concept that perhaps can be convincingly carried over from other areas to divorce law. It is the notion of necessity, and from it would follow the conclusion that a former spouse can be said to have a duty to support the other former spouse in order to avoid grave financial hardship.

Necessity-based rights arise when one is critically dependent upon another and the dependent one is thought fairly to have a claim for assistance from the one specially positioned to provide it. For example, if a guest in your home becomes ill, you can hardly eject the person out into the cold night where he is quite unlikely to be able to care for himself.[51] Nor can you properly refuse a sailor the use of your dock when it is needed to protect the sailor from the life-threatening dangers of a storm.[52]

Note well that properly invoking the necessity doctrine depends upon a showing that it is right to single out the one who is asked to provide the support from among all of society. That is why, for example, you may be said to have a duty to provide comfort to a hiker caught in a snowstorm who happens to discover your isolated cabin, but not to the needy panhandler whom you and many others pass on the street.[53]

Analogously, a divorcing spouse appears to be a very appropriate person to single out as having the duty to prevent the other spouse from suffering a severe hardship, especially since the now needy party would ordinarily have been financially dependent upon the other spouse during the marriage. Moreover, the couple's past intimacy alone may be seen as a convincing basis for imposing this duty. On that ground, for example, a necessity claim would also accrue at divorce to a spouse who had long been a substantial earner but only just became disabled and incapable of self-support.

Yet there are problems with a divorce regime that rests on the principle of necessity. On the one hand, by analogy to other necessity cases, this would seem to impose a duty to support the other at only some minimum, severe-hardship-avoiding level, and that may be thought far more miserly than is instinctively sensed as just. On the other, it is ambiguous how long a necessity-based claim ought to last. Certainly at some point—but *when* is rather difficult to say—after the intimate connection between the parties is long over and there has been time for the dependent one to make choices about his or her future, it no longer seems justified to single out the former spouse as the responsible party, even if the other remains in dire need.

A further problem is that although the needy party may seek to impose a duty arising out of necessity on the other former spouse, where both are fairly poor the latter may not be able to afford to discharge it or could do so only through a significant self-deprivation. Alas, in all too many cases to-day, the financial question being decided on divorce is less how to share affluence than it is how to allocate poverty. This suggests that society as a whole may have a larger role to play here. Indeed, the question whether it would not be better for government to plan in advance for predictable situations of necessity by adopting a sensible public income transfer scheme designed to discharge this duty is one to which I will return in the conclusion.

The Expectations of the Parties

Does what the divorcing spouses financially deserve from each other turn on a thoughtful appreciation of the "expectations" of husbands and wives? The idea here is that fairness requires that people's legitimate expectations be reinforced through the law. The main difficulty with this line of thought is that, for the most part, it has the analysis reversed. Since we live in a time when there are no consensus expectations on so many issues concerning marriage and divorce, what we are actually looking for here are new norms to adopt that will then serve to create expectations in the future.

It is true that more and more couples today are marrying, knowing that they might later divorce. In this new state of affairs, we could inquire as to what they expect to be their rights and obligations if their marriage ends. But, because of social uncertainties, asking them is not likely to be terribly revealing. For example, at the broadest level, do couples expect that they should be able to make a clean break or do they expect to have ongoing financial claims on each other long after their emotional and physical inti-macy has ended? I think most people's feelings would be rather fuzzy.[54]

When a marriage ends in divorce, the spouses, of course, suffer disappointed expectations in the sense that they had earlier anticipated the mutual sharing of their combined earnings in the future. But this hardly tells us whether they mutually expected that the higher earner would share post-divorce earnings with the lower earner in the event their marriage terminated. In the end, I believe that any arguments couched in the language of expectation, if persuasive, would rest more securely on some other ground.

Unjust Enrichment

One such ground might be "unjust enrichment." Consider again the familiar examples of those wives who have invested in their husband's career and/or in their home life instead of in their own future earning capacity. While this may seem like a revisit of the section on incentives, the point here is different. Now the claim is not that a woman needs a certain divorce law regime in order to get her to act as the couple wishes or in order to keep the man from exploiting and then divorcing her. The point is, rather, that when there is a divorce, unless she is awarded a fair return on her investment, he may be unjustly enriched at her expense.[55]

I have several problems with this idea, however. First, consider some of its ambiguities. Determining what might be a fair return on the wife's investment is a complicated matter. Should it be a share of the husband's enhanced earning power? Or should it be measured by the wife's opportunity costs? Or should we concentrate instead on what it will now take to boost her future earning capacity? Over these choices there is today considerable controversy, even among those who favor the idea of some spousal entitlement in these settings.

Furthermore, it is not self-evident that this approach would, on balance, actually favor women. After all, because they live on their husbands' income, for example, significant numbers of women are enabled to attend college or to obtain other further training after they are married. Indeed, it is possible that this pattern is more common than the opposite. That alone would not dispose of the matter, however, since those could be the very cases in which the couple is much less likely to divorce.[56] The point is that the potential impact of rules concerning rights in the other party's enhanced earning power ought to be studied very carefully before being adopted, if we wish to avoid renewed criticisms about "unintended" effects of reforms.

More generally, I am troubled by the basic idea that through self-sacrifice one spouse would earn rights in the other's enhanced earning power, or "career assets," as Weitzman terms it. The strongest way I can think of to put the claim goes like this: "I sacrificed something for us, expecting us to benefit in the future. Now that we are getting divorced, because of my sacrifice, I, standing alone, am in some way disadvantaged and, you, standing alone, are in some way advantaged. If I am not compensated, you will be unjustly enriched at my expense and that would be an unfair outcome." This statement emphasizes both a loss on one side and a gain on the other. It rests on an asserted expectation of future gain, and on an asserted causal connection between the sacrifice made and the present plight.

Three familiar examples are typically said to fit this claim. In the first example, the wife works as a secretary while the husband goes to medical school. Now he is a professional, and she is not, and their marriage breaks up. In a second scenario, they have kids. She stays home to raise them while he pursues his career. Then their marriage breaks up. And third, rather than working on her own career, she gives dinner parties and otherwise socializes with his business friends while he pursues his career. Then their marriage breaks up.

But are these scenarios really examples of the generalized pattern I set out above? Often they are not. For example, in the secretary/medical student situation, it will frequently not be true that it was her sacrifice that enabled him to go to medical school. This is not to deny that she sacrificed for them. Perhaps her working enabled him to go to school without borrowing (or with borrowing less), or perhaps it enabled them to get married while he was in medical school. But he often would have gone to medical school anyway.

The same point can apply to the mother-at-home example. Frequently, it is not that her conduct enabled him to pursue his career (which he would have pursued anyway), but rather that it enabled them to have children. Again, this is not to deny that she sacrificed her career development for them. But that is different from saying that her sacrifice was the cause of his career development.

Even the "corporate wife" role is, at least sometimes, more a matter of pleasure for her than more salary for him, even if going to conventions, company picnics, and the like keep her from exploiting her own income potential.

Moreover, these three are hardly the only examples of detrimental sacrifice in marriage. Suppose, for example, he drops out of high school so they can get married and together have their baby she is carrying. He goes to work at a gas station. Now he has sacrificed his career opportunities for them and is disadvantaged when their marriage later breaks up.

Or, as another example, suppose they both sacrificed by delaying having children, working hard to save money for the time they could afford to be parents. Before that happens, however, the marriage breaks up. But whereas one party has a new partner, the cómplaining party does not. The latter is left disadvantaged by not readily being able to have children now, whereas the other party takes half of their savings along to the new partner and promptly starts a family.

Or suppose one spouse, say the husband, passes up an opportunity to move to a new job for the sake of the family's stability, and the marriage later breaks up. Maybe the wife not only gets the kids but moves away. He now says that whereas he sacrificed for them, he does not get the long-run benefit that was envisioned—being together with the children.

This brings me back to the earlier example in which she stays home and cares for the kids while he pursues his career. Suppose he argues that he sacrificed his leisure time by working especially hard at the office so that they could afford to have kids, but now that the marriage breaks up he is left with a loss and she a gain, assuming she gets the kids and he does not.

As a final example, suppose he works overtime to the point of haggardness, while she spends lots of time at fitness centers. He enjoys having a fit and lovely wife. Then their marriage breaks up, and she takes her good health and good looks with her. He is stuck with his ulcer.

The point of these examples is to show that there are many circumstances, besides the three with which I began, in which one party has sacrificed for the benefit of the marriage, expecting a long-run benefit that is not realized. Moreover, not only is that party now disadvantaged by the sacrifice, but also the other party takes advantages obtained during the marriage away with her or him. Are all these advantages and disadvantages to be carefully accounted for and redressed on divorce? Or should all of them be seen as risks of disappointed expectations that are simply to be assumed as part of the risk of divorce?

Of course, as illustrated by my examples, it is not only money that the disadvantaged partner may sacrifice or that the advantaged partner may take away. But it is not clear to me why that should be required if the case for spousal compensation is based on a theory of "unjust enrichment."

Furthermore, there are additional problems lurking here even in the three initial examples—where the wife puts the man through medical school, or stays home to have children, or entertains his business colleagues. First, if he does have higher earnings because he was able to focus on his career, then often they will have already benefited as a couple from those higher earnings. If so, is her sacrifice ever considered repaid? For example, suppose the doctor and his wife live together for ten high-income years after he completes his training. Has she not by then already obtained a fair return on her investment? If so, when has that occurred?

Second, basing entitlements at divorce upon a careful accounting of investments and earning power enhancement could lead to enormous differences that I find bizarre. For example, the wife who helps put her husband all the way through medical school presumably will be entitled, even after ten or twenty years of marriage, to a great deal more compensation than would one who married and supported him starting in his third year. So too there will presumably be radically different treatment of the woman who, ten years ago, instead of marrying him lived with him while in medical school, or of one who was his girlfriend and was supportive of him in various ways, but married him only afterward.

All these factors make me think that unjust enrichment is the wrong way to think about divorce. The three typical examples upon which that theory rests are perhaps better understood as illustrating that, because of social conditioning in our society, marriage very often means quite different roles for men and women—which roles coincide with women on divorce being financially dependent and men financially independent. From that perspective, maybe it would be better to base women's claims for support on divorce on how long they functioned in the wife's role. Norms based on marriage duration are examined in the next two sections.

Merger over Time

The unjust enrichment concept seems to put enormous weight on the relationship between the parties during the critical years when the other spouse happened to most increase his or her earning capacity, rather than on the total length of the marriage relationship. So, too, the equal standard of living norm seems indifferent to the length of the marriage, as though the couple's human capital merges during the wedding ceremony.

A different approach is to see the spouses as merging into each other over time. In this model, the longer they are married, the more their human capital should be seen as intertwined rather than affixed to the individual spouse in whose body it resides. This idea is consistent with the notion that human capital needs constant renewal—a regular tune-up, repair, and parts replacement model, if you like. After a while, one can less and less distinguish between what was brought into the marriage and what was produced by the marriage. Moreover, the longer the marriage, the longer the spouse in a dependent role has likely submerged her or his independent identity and earning capacity into the marital collective.

One way to implement such a concept would be to give each spouse a percentage interest in the other's human capital/future earnings based upon the duration of the marriage. For example, one might obtain a 1.5 percent or 2 percent interest in the other for every year together, and presumably this interest would survive the remarriage of either party. Such a regime might be subject to minimum vesting rules restricting when the right accrues (such as after three or five years of marriage), and it might possibly be subject to a ceiling (such as 40 percent or twenty years).[57]

One clear attraction of this model is that it works to the benefit of long-term homemakers as compared with those with only brief marriages. So, too, it would call for far more spousal support for long-term homemakers as compared with long-term marriages where the earnings of the spouses had been fairly even.

Treating human capital as called for in the merger over time model would make it, in a certain sense, analogous to the typical pattern we see with conventional marital property. That is, at the beginning of the marriage the property the couple has (apart from wedding gifts) is generally thought to be the separate property of the one who brought it to the marriage. But over time, more and more of their property becomes theirs collectively, as it is either obtained with their earnings or results from the commingling of formerly separate property with other marital property.

Although I believe that many people would find this merger over time principle fair, it is not the only norm I can imagine that increases the lower-earning spouse's claim as the marriage lengthens.

Fair Notice

A different model I call "fair notice" would guarantee support to a lower-earning divorced spouse for a period of time based on the length of the marriage. The level of support would be based upon the other spouse's ability to pay and would be intended, to the extent possible, to minimally disrupt both spouses' living standards for the period of the support. This approach is based on the general idea that a party ought to have a duty to provide adequate notice before terminating what was intended as (and may well have become) a long-term relationship.

Marriages, like long-term contracts generally, are not like impersonal quick market transactions where parties can easily find other sellers and buyers. In such long-term relationships, where people know the contract may end, where they know there will likely be dependence, where fault rules are not going to be available to police the contract's termination, and where no insurance is available to cushion the loss that one side might suffer on the ending of the deal, special contract-ending arrangements seem appropriate. At a minimum, I believe that the parties are entitled to some fairness-based, mutual insurance–like rules designed to protect against what can be very unequal burdens of termination. Specifically, each should be required to give the other substantial notice before he or she can cut off the support the other has grown to rely upon. Thus, for the period of the notice, the couple's financial affairs would remain largely intertwined.

In this model, the filing of the divorce action would likely trigger the notice period. Although some might favor a uniform notice period for all divorces, it seems to me that the length of the notice period required is more sensibly related to the length of the marriage. I base this on the fact that it typically takes longer to unravel dependencies of longer duration. Whether the notice period should be equal to the marriage's length, or to half or a quarter of it, and whether it should be subject to a maximum are questions I put aside for now.

Since in cases of extremely short marriages, the time it takes after the filing to achieve the divorce would generally be sufficient notice, this model's operation would be consistent with the typical lack of postdivorce spousal support in such marriages today. Similarly, it would be broadly consistent with what is commonly termed "rehabilitative alimony"—spousal support for a modest and fixed term—that is often awarded in marriages of modest duration. This model would also call for considerable notice in long marriages, thus perhaps demanding longer spousal support than Weitzman found is being awarded to older, long-married divorcées generally.

Let me illustrate how the fair notice model differs from the merger over time model. Whereas under both models lower earners in ten-year marriages would be entitled, other things being equal, to substantially more money than they would be in five-year marriages, the nature of their entitlement differs. In the fair notice scheme, the couple would, generally speaking, continue to fully share their income for a fixed period based on the marriage's duration—for example, for five years after a marriage of ten years. By contrast, in the merger over time plan, the couple shares their income for the rest of their lives, but the proportion they share is less—for example, 20 percent after ten years of marriage.[58] The fair notice model has the advantage, if it is indeed an advantage, of leading to a clean financial break between the former couple. The merger over time model has the advantage of providing the lower-earning spouse a secure (at least in principle) long-term financial base upon which to rebuild an economic future. (In practice, under both models, many couples might elect to convert these periodic payment obligations to one-time lump sum settlements at the time of divorce.)

One potential conceptual difficulty with the fair notice norm arises when the lower earner brings the marriage to an end. First consider the case where the lower earner has behaved in a way, even a socially undesirable way, that leads the higher earner to want a divorce. In such a setting, given the no-fault philosophy, I do not find it troubling that under the fair notice principle the higher earner, in effect, has to buy his or her freedom from the other over time. But where the lower earner wants out of the marriage (say, to marry someone else) and the higher earner does not, I suspect that some will find dismaying the idea that the moving party is entitled to a period of notice. I have considered whether this objection might be avoided by entitling to notice only the party who is sued for divorce. But I have rejected that solution on the ground that it gives too much bargaining power to the higher earner. In the end I conclude that the objection to entitling a divorce-seeking lower earner to a notice period is not a telling criticism. After all, that party could have remained in the marriage, thereby imposing an even longer duty of support on the other. By announcing an intention to end their marriage, the moving party, in effect, informs the other that his or her future obligation is limited.

More deeply at stake here, I believe, is something that is at stake in all the models considered in this part that would impose on the higher earner the duty to provide, out of future earnings, support for the lower-earning former spouse. In those cases, however few in proportion, in which the lower earner is seen by the other to be significantly and primarily at fault in the breakup of the marriage, it is likely to be galling to the higher earner to have to turn over postdivorce earnings whatever the earlier nature and duration of the couple's marriage. And since men typically are the higher earners, this is a concern that I believe men have about any reforms that would significantly increase the financial burdens of divorced men generally. This anxiety traditionally resulted in legal rules that freed husbands from alimony and more generous property-sharing burdens when their wives were guilty of adultery. That sort of result, however, is fundamentally at odds with the no-fault concept and should be rejected. Assuming, therefore, that no individualized inquiry into fault is to be made, then I see no proper basis for reducing husbands' burdens generally just because some wives are wrongdoers, especially when no adjustment has been made the other way on account of the fact that some husbands are wrongdoers.

The real question in this no-fault world becomes whether there ought to be some sort of social insurance scheme that, among other things, would help spread the risk that higher-earning spouses might individually be imposed upon unfairly.

Conclusion

When all is said and done, because of the limited spousal and child support that they currently are forced to pay, divorced men under today's regime are generally able to take on new family responsibilities and, without having to boost their earnings far above their former level, they can contemplate supporting a new household at a standard of living that is not too far below that of their old family. Indeed, they can even imagine financially coping with a new wife who brings children along. By contrast, divorced women, especially those with children, generally find themselves under great economic pressure to remarry if they wish to regain anything of the standard of living they had while married.

Put this way, many people conclude that this imbalance is unfair. Certainly many people will not like the image of a divorced woman being forced into another marriage that she might not otherwise choose to make. And many will not like the female dependency implications of both sides of this equation—that a woman must marry to achieve a familiar standard of living and that a man would think in terms of having to support his new wife (and perhaps her children from a former marriage).

Yet, to return to a theme discussed earlier, is not the imbalance between men and women basically true before a first marriage as well? Because of inequalities in the financial prospects of men and women in the paid labor force, marriage is at the outset a more promising route to a higher standard of living for women than it is for men. Although we may object to those inequalities between men and women, I ask again whether divorce law is the place to correct them. Moreover, even if we observe individual women sacrificing their own careers in individual marriages, is not the point of most feminist writing about this that such behavior is more a matter of general cultural pressure than oppression by individual husbands? On that basis, again, a collective solution seems more fitting.

I have in this chapter put forward several grounds that would justify a legal policy of spousal support on divorce and that could lead to higher levels and a greater frequency of spousal support than Weitzman found in California. Some of these grounds rest on incentive concerns, assuming we can agree on the intended behavioral objectives and that we believe there is at least a substantial chance that conduct would actually be shaped by such rules. Others derive from fairness norms, three of which I find at least somewhat persuasive and have called "fair notice," "merger over time," and "necessity." Although these different justifications can be seen to call for somewhat different implementing solutions, a crude synthesis would seem to argue for a spousal support formula that reflects primarily the duration of the marriage and the individual financial prospects of the parties on divorce.

But ought there not be some public responsibility here as well? The Social Security system currently provides non-means-tested financial support to dependent spouses (the overwhelming proportion of whom are women) on the occasion of the death, disability, or retirement of their family's main breadwinner—at least when those dependent spouses are elderly or caring for a minor child. And those benefits are related to the past wages of the spouse who no longer is earning income for the household. Ought not that program be expanded, or some new program of reasonably similar design be constructed, to alleviate the substantial risk lower-earning spouses take that divorce will be a financial shock? The precise basis for financing this sort of social insurance benefit—that is, the extent to which higher-earning divorced spouses, marrieds in general, and earners in general should contribute—I save for another time (although I note that there is considerable room in such a scheme for redistributive features of the sort found in Social Security that could go a long way to ease the financial plight now faced by the poor single mother).

What seems clear to me now is that with such a public financial base in place the debate over new ways of allocating private financial interests between divorcing husbands and wives would be much less divisive. Those championing women's interests would feel less of a need to reach so far, and those defending men's interests would feel less threatened. To be sure, to support social insurance benefits on the occasion of divorce is to open one up to the charge that this fosters even more divorce. Yet not only am I skeptical about how true this charge is, but I do not think we can be very optimistic about the future of marriage and the family if we insist that these relationships be importantly glued together by financial dependence and obligation.

6 Child Support Reassessed
Limits of Private Responsibility
and the Public Interest

HARRY D. KRAUSE

Looking back at over twenty years of work with the legal parent-and-child relationship and, more specifically, the child support obligation,[1] I am increasingly concerned about current trends. Tension is mounting between (1) society's continuing need for a functioning family infrastructure, (2) the modern "me-generation's" emphasis on the individual's *rights* ("liberty and happiness"), (3) traditional financial responsibility for dependents (spouse and children), and (4) the care-giving capacity of the one-parent family. These tensions have become greater than the loosened framework of the modern family (or less formal, more casual relationships now competing with marriage) can reasonably be expected to handle.

At least since the time of President Lyndon Johnson, politicians have concerned themselves with the "breakdown" of the American family and have emphasized the importance of family policy.[2] Ever sharper ideological disagreement now divides the political right and left.[3] They have one thing in common: neither side's proposals are likely to reconstitute the "American family," whatever that was.[4] Standing alone, current proposals to grant pregnancy leave[5] or to subsidize day care[6] are inadequate to that task—as inadequate as are calls to return to a moral past[7] that has been superseded by new facts.[8]

In the 1970s, divorce reform and child support reform seemed revolutionary. Looking back, we see that those "reforms" amended traditional approaches and brought adjustments, but left in place many traditional concepts—perhaps too many. True, no-fault divorce ended the state's role in the divorce decision, but divorce by consent had been available all along.[9] Moreover, the state soon reasserted its interest by reregulating the financial

My thanks go to Steve Sugarman and Frank Zimring for constructive criticism and thoughtful suggestions, and to Marion Benfield as well as Eva and Peter Krause for their comments on earlier drafts.

166

consequences of divorce, which strengthened the legal meaning of marriage where it matters: after divorce. The (consequent?) increase in premarital, nonmarital, and postdivorce cohabitation[10] has led to the demand—somewhat successful in several states—that cohabitation give rise to legally enforceable economic rights and obligations parallel to marriage.[11] And the enormous increase in births to unmarried mothers—which strained the welfare system to the breaking point—has led to the multibillion-dollar, government-assisted child support enforcement industry.

Child support is my immediate topic. I shall put aside exciting related questions regarding the continued legitimacy of interspousal support liability in the ongoing marriage and after divorce, and concerns as to what reasonably should be the treatment of property accumulation in the modern marriage.[12] My focus will be on the rationale of the parental child support obligation (1) in the ongoing family, (2) after divorce, and (3) when the absent parent has never participated in a family or similar social setting.

The very success of the federal child support enforcement legislation[13] ($4 billion are now collected annually)[14] raises provocative new questions. What level of support obligation is consistent with modern perceptions of family ties? Is the father's demotion from cherished patriarch to absent parent entirely irrelevant to his obligations? Should a "second class" (noncustodial) parent pay "first class" support? Is the mere existence of a "biological link" enough? How much support is enough? Will rigid enforcement of high levels of child support, along with the risk of easy divorce and consequent de facto termination of the father-child relationship, prove to be a disincentive to responsible men to father children? Do we need a better balance between individual and social responsibility—in the children's *and* in society's best interests?

The Past: Little Interest in Child Support

In 1934, the American Law Institute's *Restatement of Conflict of Laws* characterized support obligations and their enforcement as "of no special interest to other states." The *Restatement* continued: "Since the duty is not imposed primarily for the benefit of an individual, it is not enforceable elsewhere."[15]

Twenty-five years ago, child support was not a public issue. Even if a child support obligation had been legally established, the absent father could all but choose not to pay. The obligation was rarely enforced effectively—especially not across state lines. Paternity—where in doubt—was rarely ascertained.[16] Dominant social work doctrine proclaimed that the father should *not* be brought face to face with his (theoretical) support obligation because enforcement might inconvenience the mother. In any event, since the AFDC system was paying for the child, support enforcement seemed quite unnecessary.[17] Feeble attempts to bring deserting fathers to accept responsibility were discounted with the argument that the funds thus collected would not benefit the children because collections would only be offset against AFDC entitlements.[18] Some went further and suggested that child support enforcement actually harmed the fragile black family structure by driving away fathers—fathers who liked the social tie but not the financial responsibility.[19] When Congress enacted the federal child support enforcement legislation in the mid-1970s, opposition came from many respected quarters—including even the League of Women Voters—and remained strong for a time.[20]

To be sure, not all the blame rested on social workers. When a welfare-related support action *was* brought, judges often saw fit to impose only token obligations, such as ten dollars per month. In short, despite widespread enactment of the Uniform Reciprocal Enforcement of Support Acts of 1950, 1958, and 1968, and explicit references to child support collection in early AFDC legislation,[21] *in practice* American law remained deeply insensitive to the enforcement of child support obligations.

Indeed, only thirty-five years ago, American law provided only a shaky basis for imposing a child support obligation on the father. An illustrative New Jersey case involved a medical necessity and arose within an *ongoing* family. Here are a few words from that case: "Suffice it to say that it appears that the question to be resolved here has not yet been passed on in the court of last resort, but that there are divergent views at law and in equity as to the fundamental nature of a parent's obligation to maintain an infant child awaiting decision."[22]

In the 1750s, Blackstone had said:

> The duty of parents to provide for the *maintenance* of their children, is a principle of natural law. . . . By begetting them, therefore, they have entered into a voluntary obligation, to endeavour, as far as in them lies, that the life which they have bestowed shall be supported and preserved. And thus the children will have a perfect *right* of receiving maintenance from their parents.
>
> And the manner, in which this obligation shall be performed, is thus pointed out. The father, and mother, grandfather, and grandmother of

poor impotent persons shall maintain them at their own charges, if of sufficient ability, . . . and if a parent runs away, and leaves his children, the churchwardens and overseers of the parish shall seize his rents, goods, and chattels, and dispose of them toward their relief.[23]

The Present: Enforcement!

Looking now at Blackstone's last sentence, we see the federal child support enforcement legislation and corresponding state law reforms. The intermediate past has been overcome.

The Federal Enforcement Initiative of 1974

The Office of Child Support Enforcement (OCSE) of the U.S. Department of Health and Human Services provides the following statistics for 1987: (1) 812,661 support orders were entered; (2) 268,766 paternities were established; (3) nearly 1.4 million parent-locate requests were filed, and 80 percent were filled within two weeks; (4) nearly $4 billion for support were collected, bringing to $23 billion the total collected since the inception of the program twelve years before; and (5) on average, $1.00 was spent to collect $3.68.[24]

When Congress enacted the sweeping legislation to strengthen enforcement of child support obligations across the nation, the primary goal was to reduce the federal cost of the AFDC program. Since then, the scope and purpose of the enforcement program have been broadened. It was recognized early that the objective of reducing the cost of AFDC programs could be secured more successfully if potential recipients were kept off welfare by extending the support enforcement program to them. But the program now reaches well beyond this group: support enforcement is available to anyone for a reasonable fee.[25] In terms of middle-class family support, this has made a significant difference—more than one-half of total collections are going to children who are not on the welfare rolls.[26]

State authority and state laws remain primary vehicles, but state enforcement agencies—now commonly known as "IV-D agencies," reflecting their location in title 42 of the United States Code—must meet standards imposed by federal law. The stimulator, overseer, and financier of state collection systems is OCSE. The "stick" waved at the states is loss of some of their federal AFDC funding. The "carrot" is federal funding for a considerable portion of the states' support enforcement programs, but only if they meet federal standards.

The Federal Enforcement Process

To summarize:[27] federal law requires state AFDC agencies to collect data, use the Social Security numbers of all AFDC applicants as identification, notify the state child support enforcement agencies when benefits are granted to eligible children, and open records to support enforcement officials. Applicants must assign their rights to uncollected child support to the state and must agree to cooperate in locating absent parents, in establishing paternity, in obtaining support judgments if none is outstanding, and in securing payments. In case of an applicant's unjustified failure to cooperate, AFDC benefits are withheld from the applicant, though not from children.

The states maintain parent locator services equipped to search state and local records for information regarding the whereabouts of absent parents. In Washington, D.C., OCSE maintains a sophisticated, computerized federal parent locator service with access to Social Security, Internal Revenue, and nearly all other federal information resources, except census records. When the absent (or alleged) parent is located, the state establishes paternity (if necessary and possible), obtains a support judgment, and enforces the obligation through either in-state or interstate proceedings. All states must cooperate fully with their sister states. Access to federal courts is provided, if necessary, and so is collection by the Internal Revenue Service. After collection, the state disburses child support payments, keeping detailed records and reporting to OCSE. To encourage local participation in child support enforcement, the state turns a portion of the proceeds over to the collecting unit of the local government.

The 1984 Amendments: Mandatory
Withholding and Discretionary Guidelines

In 1984, significant federal amendments asked the states to sharpen their laws and strengthen enforcement powers.[28] State laws now must require employers to withhold child support from the paychecks of parents delinquent for one month. (The 1988 amendments require immediate withholding by 1994).[29] State laws must provide for the imposition of liens against the property of defaulting support obligors, and credit companies may be informed of unpaid child support in excess of one thousand dollars. (By August 1988, eight states routinely reported child support debt to credit bureaus.)[30] Unpaid support obligations must be deducted from federal and state income tax refunds. Expedited hearings—judicial or administrative— are required in support cases. Following, extending, and anticipating various U.S. Supreme Court decisions,[31] statutes of limitation for the establishment of paternity must allow at least eighteen years after a child's birth. To give families receiving welfare some direct benefit from the father's support payments, the first fifty dollars per month are now paid directly to the family and not deducted from the family's welfare check.

The 1984 amendments announced that Washington will play a more active role in defining standards for acceptable state law on these questions. The amendments achieved one important objective long and effectively championed by David Chambers:[32] more effective methods of support enforcement will become the rule, specifically wage deduction to avoid default rather than (often counterproductive) jail and loss of job after default.

At least as important, the 1984 amendments require states to establish discretionary guidelines for child support awards. Toward that end, the amendments provide:

(a) Each State, as a condition for having its State plan approved under this part, must establish guidelines for child support award amounts within the State. The guidelines may be established by law or by judicial or administrative action.

(b) The guidelines established pursuant to subsection (a) shall be made available to all judges and other officials who have the power to determine child support awards within such State, but need not be binding upon such judges or other officials.

(c) The Secretary shall furnish technical assistance to the States for establishing the guidelines, and each State shall furnish the Secretary with copies of its guidelines.

(d) The amendment made by subsection (a) shall become effective on October 1, 1987.[33]

In response to the House Ways and Means Committee's request, a national panel was set up to advise concerning support guidelines.[34] That panel comprised a divorced women's advocate, a divorced men's advocate, a state support enforcement director, a child support judge, a state legislator, a court systems child support administrator, an economics professor, and a law professor (myself). After long debate and much compromise, we endorsed the following basic principles:

(1) Both parents share legal responsibility for supporting their children. The economic responsibility should be divided in proportion to their available income.

(2) The subsistence needs of each parent should be taken into account in setting child support, but in virtually no event should the child support obligation be set at zero.

(3) Child support must cover a child's basic needs as a first priority, but, to the extent either parent enjoys a higher than subsistence level standard of living, the child is entitled to share the benefit of that improved standard.

(4) Each child of a given parent has an equal right to share in that parent's income, subject to factors such as age of the child, income of each parent, income of current spouses, and the presence of other dependents.

(5) Each child is entitled to determination of support without respect to the marital status of the parents at the time of the child's birth. Consequently, any guideline should be equally applicable to determining child support related to paternity determinations, separations, and divorces.

(6) Application of a guideline should be sexually nondiscriminatory. Specifically, it should be applied without regard to the gender of the custodial parent.

(7) A guideline should not create extraneous negative effects on the major life decisions of either parent. In particular, the guideline should avoid creating economic disincentives for remarriage or labor force participation.

(8) A guideline should encourage the involvement of both parents in the child's upbringing. It should take into account the financial support provided directly by parents in shared physical custody or extended visitation arrangements, recognizing that even a fifty percent sharing of physical custody does not necessarily obviate the child support obligation.[35]

The establishment by the states of reasonable guidelines for setting child support obligations will ensure less arbitrary and diverse conceptions of the needs of the child and the father's ability to pay than have been applied in the past. The states' responses to the federal mandate are being evaluated.[36] For now I refer and defer to the analyses of others and add only one point: more consistent and coherent results would be achieved if federal (not state-by-state) law would set a national standard, with adjustments for regional variations in the cost of living. Having moved as far as we have with OCSE-sponsored national support enforcement, continued federal deference to state-by-state discretion seems misplaced.

The 1984 amendments injected federal initiative and authority more deeply into matters that previously had been viewed as reserved to the states. Nevertheless, when Congress signaled this policy by passing a Sense-of-Congress Resolution, it still insisted that "*state and local governments* must focus on the vital issues of child support, child custody, visitation rights, and other related domestic issues."[37] Specifically:

(a) The Congress finds that—

(1) the divorce rate in the United States has reached alarming proportions and the number of children being raised in single parent families has grown accordingly;

(2) there is a critical lack of child support enforcement, which Congress has undertaken to address through the child support enforcement program;

(3) Congress is strengthening that program to recognize the needs of all children;

(4) related domestic issues, such as visitation rights and child custody, are often intricately intertwined with the child support problem and have received inadequate consideration; and

(5) these related issues remain within the jurisdiction of State and local governments, but have a critical impact on the health and welfare of the children of the Nation.

(b) It is the sense of Congress that—

(1) State and local governments must focus on the vital issues of child support, child custody, visitation rights, and other related domestic issues that are properly within the jurisdictions of such governments;

(2) all individuals involved in the domestic relations process should recognize the seriousness of these matters to the health and welfare of our Nation's children and assign them the highest priority; and

(3) a mutual recognition of the needs of all parties involved in divorce actions will greatly enhance the health and welfare of America's children and families.[38]

The 1988 Child Support Amendments

The 1988 child support amendments[39] provide that, beginning in 1994, for all new or modified support orders, child support payments are to be withheld from absent parents' wages automatically and without regard to whether they are in arrears. Support guidelines must be used to determine child support obligations, and child support orders are to be reviewed every three years.

Federal standards for the establishment of paternity must be met, and the federal government will pay 90 percent of the cost of laboratory tests to establish paternity. Moreover, such tests may be required by the contesting party.[40] The legislation also mandates automatic tracking and monitoring systems, provides additional sources for the parent location service, and authorizes the establishment of a commission on interstate child support.

How Much Room is Left for Improved Enforcement?

Room for improvement remains. There are unexplained wide variations in collection performance from one state to another, arising from incomplete federal, state, and local implementation.[41] Better collection figures can and will come out of administrative improvements, stimulated by federal pressure. In August 1988, Wayne Stanton, the director of OCSE, admonished: "While collections have increased, child support agencies must become even more proficient at using every tool available to collect support from parents who are now simply walking away from their children. Much more State attention must be paid to collection efforts, such as using liens on personal and real property, as well as reporting delinquents to credit bureaus to cloud their credit."[42]

Despite OCSE's proud macrorecord described earlier, dismal microstatistics involving child support collections have been reported in numerous studies, prominently Weitzman's[43] and Bruch and Wikler's.[44] These studies do not focus on how much more is now being collected; rather, they show that in the samples the authors studied a lot of child support remains uncollected. It was reported by OCSE that "the aggregate amount of child support payments due for 1985 alone was $10.9 billion but payments actually received amounted to only $7.2 billion."[45]

Why is that support not collected? In order to concentrate on the really hard cases, we might put aside those in which the custodial parent supports the child adequately and, for reasons of her own, does not wish to impose on the absent parent. Ignoring such cases leaves only two alternative explanations of inadequate support. One is that the state makes an inadequate effort to enforce existing law, even though the law increasingly is up to the task. But as implementation of existing law is perfected—as it surely will be—only one explanation of why absent fathers do not pay will remain: they do not have the money to render adequate child support. Even now, I suspect that large numbers of defaulting fathers do not have (and never had) the missing money. Many a defaulting father's obligation, even if originally assessed fairly, does not correspond to his current economic circumstances, and current law or practice does not afford him an adequate opportunity to effect an appropriate modification.[46]

When one looks carefully at statistics and reality, it is reasonable to conclude that many fathers are not by themselves able to provide the support their children need to get a decent start in life, even if they try.[47] And to the extent we are now driven to see child support enforcement as the sole solution to childhood poverty, we are as wrong as those in the 1960s who saw the AFDC program as the sole appropriate source of support for female-headed families. To refresh my memory, I occasionally go to our local courts in a relatively affluent midwestern community—nothing like the big-city courts I also have studied—and spend a few hours seeing the parade of unemployed, and often unemployable, teenagers being confronted with unmeetable financial obligations arising, ironically, out of constitutionally protected conduct.[48] For those who have not seen these proceedings, David Chambers has described them graphically.[49]

I fear that our current emphasis on enforcing the father's obligation is clouding our judgment as to how much money we can realistically expect the father to provide. The detailed collection statistics at the bottom of the social pyramid reveal that at the AFDC level we currently spend nearly as much on collection as we collect—and in many states more.[50] Child support collection actually has been turned into an income transfer program from poor fathers to lawyers and welfare bureaucrats—something I had hoped we would avoid.[51]

On the fix-it-fast level, I have suggested that we institute facilitated, semiautomatic modification of prospective support payments to reflect the typical low-income father's often quickly changing ability to pay.[52] That would reduce or eliminate the accumulation of the hopeless arrears many fathers owe the government; by that I mean arrears that, short of winning the lottery, the father has no hope of every being able to pay. We should consider reinstituting forgiveness of such arrears, at least in the context of bankruptcy.[53] Nor am I completely at ease with the work product of our

National Panel on Child Support Guidelines.[54] These issues continue to concern me, but not here and not now.[55]

To sum up what I see, the next issues in child support include (1) the reality that many defaulting fathers simply do not have what it takes to support their children—as enforcement becomes comprehensive, fewer defaults will be due to irresponsibility, (2) my growing (if heretical) notion that it may not be fair to ask all absent fathers to foot the *entire* bill, and (3) the need to understand that children have a direct claim on society at large, along with their parallel claim on their parents. Let me now risk offering some caveats about over-emphasizing the paternal support responsibility.

The Future: Toward a Better Balance between Private and Public Responsibility
The Impecunious Father and His Welfare Child

In August 1988, the Census Bureau reported that, in 1987, the poverty rate (income below $11,612 for a family of four) for all children stood at 20.6 percent. Forty-nine percent of black children under the age of six were poor—one in two![56] I happily stipulate that the poverty measurement is subject to numerous doubts, ranging from its unrealistic derivation (three times a basic food basket) to its perverse disregard of the value of in-kind programs, such as food stamps, subsidized housing, medical care, and school lunches. Still, the poverty figure does provide a rough measure of well-being or its opposite. In most states, AFDC does not come close to meeting this minimum. In 1987, Alabama provided $147 per month for a family of four, and Mississippi provided $144.[57]

Our success in child support enforcement has not significantly improved the poorest children's lot, and it cannot, until we share between the poorest fathers and the taxpayer the cost of supporting all children at a responsible minimum level. My recommendation (and one I think not extravagant) when the 1984 amendments were proposed was that the welfare father's child support payments should not be deducted from his children's public welfare check until his payments have moved his children up to the poverty level.[58] Instead, we got the current fifty-dollar-per-month disregard[59]—a foot in the door, but hardly enough in terms of the children's realistic needs.[60]

The concrete reality of children's poverty speaks for itself, but who is listening? Along with the rest of our economy and shifting ideology, children have been "privatized." Why? The perception has taken hold that the absent father is solely responsible for support of his children and that if he does not pay enough, he is irresponsible—and worse, no one else is responsible. Realities predicted for the future, however, increasingly point away from the father.

In the so-called single-parent family, one parent (typically the mother) with one or more children constitute a household unit. Either she is divorced or she has never had a legal (and often not much of a personal) tie with the other parent. Increasingly, this is the social setting in which a significant proportion of our next generation is being raised.[61] But easy-come, easy-go marriage and casual cohabitation and procreation are on a collision course with the economic and social needs of children. This may sound like a moral value judgment, but it is a pragmatic assessment. The last two decades of piecemeal adaptations of traditional law to a changing society are not meeting the challenge. If the traditional social structure—the traditional, on-going two-parent family—is no more, can its ghost support traditional financial responsibility?

Senator Daniel Moynihan points out that by the millennium,

> we project that about three-quarters of American families will be of the "traditional" sort, whereas in 1960 nearly nine of ten families could be so described. In less than two generations the proportion of families headed by single persons will have doubled. . . . In the final two decades of the century we project the number of families will increase from 59.5 million to 72.5 million, which is to say a net of 13 million families. But of these additional households, only 5.9 million are expected to be "traditional" husband-wife families. Female-headed families will account for 5.8 million of the net increase, and male-headed families for 1.3 million. Put another way, in the period 1980–2000 the number of female-headed families will increase at more than five times the rate of husband-wife families.[62]

Can we afford to continue treating a phenomenon as widespread as one-parent child rearing as deviant? Can all problems attending one-parent child rearing be corrected simply by strict enforcement of child support obligations? Can we continue to limit social intervention to the prevention of outright starvation—at a level well below our official definition of a minimum standard? Are we dealing only with the failure of private responsibility?

As long and as hard as I have worked to raise child support consciousness (and sometimes have been criticized for that),[63] I now find it remarkable—even a little frightening—that the absent welfare father's child support obligation has become so quickly and so deeply the only true faith. Arguably, this was due in no small measure to an unlikely, if unwitting, political alliance between women's groups and a basically conservative, antiwelfare legislative constituency, the latter drawing its support from many real and perceived excesses of the Great Society of the 1960s and 1970s. Whatever the reason, putting it very bluntly, at the end of the 1980s the emphasis seems to be more on immorality—the culpability of the father—than on the needs of the child. This has dissipated any sense of urgency for legislative action to secure the financial welfare of children. By voting for tougher child support enforcement, state and federal legislators can congratulate themselves that something has been done for children—and at no public cost. In sum, our current intense preoccupation with the absent father's fault and irresponsibility had displaced awareness of the reality of the limited resources of many absent fathers. It has made a genuine dialogue over public responsibility much more difficult. Our justified insistence on the enforcement of the father's unmet legal obligation has unjustifiably eclipsed our need to understand that, ultimately, the adequate support of children is a public necessity.

The Rationale of the Parental Child Support Obligation

Turning to a more fundamental level than sheer inability to pay, I now want to have another look at the current validity of the traditional parental child support obligation. As Mary Ann Glendon,[64] Martha Minow,[65] Herbert Jacob,[66] and many others have pointed out, the dominant dilemma is that family loyalties today are not what they used to be: family responsibilities are understood as less binding than they were even a generation ago. But in contradiction to these facts of modern life, recent child support doctrine reflects a sharpening of traditional values and concepts governing family responsibility.

I do not have a clear answer to the question of what the most intelligent legal response should be to still evolving new perceptions of the family and new sexual-procreative life-styles. But I am fairly sure that now, after divorce reform, the answer must involve a radical redefinition of society's economic and social involvement with the parent-and-child relationship.

Tradition: Social and Economic Reciprocity. When Blackstone formulated the support obligation for the common law world,[67] he was looking at a world that was centered on the ongoing family. Divorce did not exist—even if the law did not entirely comport with London reality. Choosing to rest most of his case on natural law and what we now call sociobiology,[68] Blackstone did not say that the support obligation was founded on the reciprocal relationship of parent and child in the ongoing family, but I think it was. This reciprocity had an economic and a social component.

Economically, the support-obligated parent was entitled to the child's earnings until the child reached majority.[69] More important, economic reciprocity extended to the parent's old age.[70] Support received by the young child morally and legally obligated the adult child to support the aged parent. Thus, before we had Social Security, child support was an "investment" the parent made, to be recovered if needed. The law took this reciprocity literally: a child who had unjustifiably not been supported when young was absolved from the obligation later to support the parent.[71]

Socially, parent and child reciprocity involved an ongoing family life. Supporting parents had the emotional satisfaction of seeing their offspring grow up. They shaped their child's life. Nor did they owe very much. Blackstone said:

> No person is bound to provide a maintenance for his issue, unless where the children are impotent and unable to work, either through infancy, disease, or accident, and then is only obliged to find them with necessaries, the penalty on refusal being no more than 20s. a month. For the policy of our laws, which are ever watchful to promote industry, did not mean to compel a father to maintain his idle and lazy children in ease and indolence: but thought it unjust to oblige the parent, against his will, to provide them with superfluities, and other indulgencies of fortune; imagining they might trust to the impulse of nature, if the children were deserving of such favors.[72]

In short, the father did not owe much beyond food and clothing, and even that not for long. Today's "budget busters" were not yet in the picture. Long before medical bills could have seriously accumulated, the child would have died under the then prevailing standards of medical care. Education, if there was any, consisted of one-room schools. The main expense of schooling was the loss to the family of the child's earnings or potential contribution around the farm or in the family business. Today, ineligible for loans or tax breaks, middle-class parents often expend $20,000 per year for seven years—four years of undergraduate college followed by three years of law school—and that after having invested upward of another $100,000 in the same child before he or she turned eighteen.[73]

Modern Reality: Illegitimacy, Divorce, and De Facto Loss of Parental Rights. Today, fathers increasingly have assumed an active parental role in the ongoing family, but in stark contrast, the typical custody adjudication on divorce terminates the father's parental status,[74] at least in any meaningful sense.[75] This de facto termination of parental status comes at the very time we impose on the absent parent a child support obligation that typically is potentially far larger than what he might have shouldered, or was legally obligated to provide, in the ongoing family. Married parents do not legally owe their children a life-style that is consistent with their income and station in life. They may choose to rear their children in any reasonable way they see fit.

When the parents separate, however, the practicalities change. The decision-making power now is exercised by the custodial parent who, more often than not, is not the paying parent. In that situation, the custodial parent's reasonable choice of life-style largely controls. Without custodial control, the noncustodial parent may thus find himself (and in the future, herself) paying amounts well in excess of those the law would require him to provide if he had custody of his children. Further down the scale, unwed fathers typically never had, and even today rarely obtain, a social relationship with the children they are asked to support. Yet an Illinois court recently ordered an unmarried father to provide a college education for his nonmarital child,[76] whereas a father in an ongoing marriage has no such obligation.[77]

The point is that the absent parent may fairly claim that he is not getting his money's worth for the support he is obligated to pay, not on the economic or the social level. Today's enlarged child support obligation does not resemble what Blackstone was talking about.

Of course, times do change and traditional concepts take on new meanings. If the original rationale no longer holds, this does not mean that a newer rationale might not support what we want to do. Let us consider this next.

The Weakened Rationale of the Absent Parent's Support Obligation. I see a contradiction between lifting all "prior restraint"—social and criminal sanctions[78]—on consensual nonmarital sexual activity and then insisting on strict enforcement of a civil liability that often amounts to eighteen years of potentially extreme restrictions on the accidental (or in any event, absent) parent's life-style. I see an equally important contradiction on divorce, when we terminate the noncustodial parent's parental interest de facto and impose on him a greater and less flexible support obligation than the burden he shouldered in the ongoing family.

In other words, it does not seem at all obvious that the same (or a greater) level of parental responsibility that makes sense in the ongoing family should be grafted (1) onto consanguinity based on what is understood as permissible recreational sex or (2) onto the essentially terminated postdivorce relationship between the typical father and his child.

Please do not misunderstand, I was among the first to insist that financial responsibility be placed on absent fathers[79] and would be among the last to suggest that there be no responsibility. I am searching now for a level of responsibility that is commensurate with the social reality of the situation.

In a related context—where the unwed father seeks to assert his custodial right—the U.S. Supreme Court has seen fit to weave a pattern of preference for the social parent-and-child relationship. The biological father has been declared "odd man out." The Court's crucial phrase is that "the mere existence of a biological link does not merit equivalent constitutional protection."[80]

Consanguinity has a basic place in our culture and law, but it does not provide all the answers.[81] In the Supreme Court's considered view, the absence of a social relationship is sufficient to deny the biological, but unwed, father a right to object to his child's adoption. Some adaptation is needed to bring this perception to bear on our—one might say mirror-image—context. Just possibly, however, the mere existence of a biological link without a social link should similarly be deemed insufficient to justify imposing an unmitigated support obligation on the absent, especially the involuntarily absent, father. Conversely, as David Chambers suggests,[82] perhaps it is time to impose support obligations on stepparents, on those who have the social relationship though they lack the biological.[83]

The correlation, in fact, between a father's willingness to pay support and the quality of his personal relationship with his child has been pointed out by Judith Wallerstein and Shauna Corbin.[84] In terms of law, I think that it may be time to reflect the involuntarily lacking or impaired social relationship in the duty to support.

The absent parent's support obligation should be pegged at a level at which the cost of family failure—whether through divorce or because a family was not established in the first place—is shared equally by father and mother. Of course, I say nothing different here than what has been said so insistently by many advocates of the ex-wife and mother, and said with the greatest popular publicity by Weitzman.[85] So far we all agree. The problem is in the detail. What is a fair definition of equal cost, of equal sacrifice, to come out of family breakdown?

Even if many aspects of Weitzman's influential study have been questioned,[86] the basic findings are obviously accurate. There *are* irresponsible fathers, and there *is* considerable economic suffering by divorced wives and their children. That is not news. Accordingly, it is not at all my intention to cast doubt on or to belittle the mother's side of the story.[87] My argument goes to maintaining a balance. Let us also look fairly at the responsible father's side of the case.

Weitzman's oft-repeated[88] core charge that the father's standard of living after divorce goes up by 42 percent, whereas the ex-wife's and the children's standard goes down by 73 percent, is open to critical evaluation on a variety of levels.[89] But I do not want to bog down in that dispute. I simply want to establish the obvious: the fractured family has three sides—child, mother, and father. With all my prior work having been on the side of child support enforcement, I never have wasted sympathy on the absent father. But now that national support enforcement has alleviated the traditional nonenforcement scandal, I have come to think that sympathetic consideration for the responsible father may not be wasted, but deserved.

What I suggest we seek is a fair equalization of the cost of the alternative family behavior that has come to pass for normal, or at least acceptable, in our increasingly value-free social environment. I do not plan to develop here any specific adjustments to the child support formulas that have been enacted by the states in response to the federal mandate—and for which I may have some small measure of responsibility. Let us first consider whether there really is a third set of equities in the picture. If we accept the principle, specifics will readily suggest themselves for a "social relationship factor" in the definition of appropriate child support.

The connection between visitation and child support has been noticed even by the support-enforcement–minded Congress: "The Congress finds that . . . related domestic issues, such as child visitation and child custody, are often intricately intertwined with the child support problem and have received inadequate consideration. . . . It is the sense of Congress that . . . State and local governments must focus on the vital issues of child support, child custody, visitation rights."[90]

The states have not yet done so. So far, even when deprived of custody and visitation, the father finds little sympathy in the courts or legislatures when he argues that he should be allowed to retaliate by withholding child support.[91] And the counterargument is well taken: the child is not denying visitation, and the child should not suffer for the mother's disregard of a visitation order. Accordingly, courts have kept enforcement of child support and the issue of visitation separate,[92] with rare exceptions in unusual cases[93] and in even more unusual statutes.[94]

And indeed, what about the child? I certainly do not want to shortchange the child. But along with the need to pick up responsibility for the child of the father who is unable to pay, I think that there is a pragmatic 1980s rationale for reconsidering the level of personal sacrifice the absent father is asked to make for a child that is his in biology only.

To be sure, the lack of a social link between father and child—or social reciprocity as I called it earlier—has somewhat different implications in the case of the unwed father who has not lived with the child's mother than it does in the case of a divorced father who has lost custody. The latter more often maintains some social link through visitation. But the difference is one of degree only.

Society's Responsibility
Debt, Self-Interest, and the Social Security System

The former secretary of the Department of Health and Human Services, Otis Bowen, said: "Providing financial support for children is first and foremost a parental responsibility. A successful child support enforcement program enhances the lives of children who because of divorce, separation, or out-of-wedlock birth live with only one parent. Furthermore, collecting child support payments saves hundred of millions for taxpayers who must provide for families on welfare."[95]

As I see it, Secretary Bowen's view of the matter is correct, but incomplete. Why should any part of the child support burden be put on society? The answer is that economic reciprocity, as it once existed in the old-fashioned family and helped justify parental responsibility, today furnishes a pragmatic rationale for taxpayer subsidy. The modern system of Social Security provides old-age support for all retired workers and their spouses, regardless of whether they "invested" in children. Retirees who had no children are entitled to Social Security benefits—equally with those who shared their earnings with their children and had a hard time of it. To the argument that nonparents contributed to the system and that that is the basis of their claim, my answer is that their contributions were paid out long ago to retire their own parents. The fact is that the pensions nonparents expect to receive will be paid to them by other people's children—other people's children who have been forced by taxation to substitute them for their own parents.

I am not quarreling with the concept of social insurance, nor am I advocating that childless retirees be cut off. We must also understand, however, that children are only in part the private folly of their parents. Taxation has removed old-age provision from the family context. Taxation has nationalized that part of children's future earnings that might have gone to fund the retirement of their own parents. In exchange, the taxpayer should "preciprocate" by bearing an appropriate share of the cost of supporting those who will later bear the burden of old-age support for all.

In short, I think that society owes a more active role in supporting the rearing of children. Social recognition of this as a debt, not as a reluctant charity, seems to me as important as what we have already accomplished: raising the absent father's consciousness of his debt.

Drawing the elderly into this discussion has another dimension. In terms of family law, the elderly are becoming "obsolete."[96] Today's elderly no longer look first for help to their children; they look to the Social Security system, private pension plans, Medicare, Medicaid, home care, institutionalization, and other social provisions and services. In law even more than in fact, the extended family has given way to the nuclear family, even as—in fact but not yet in law—the nuclear family is giving way to the single-parent family.

Has society gone too far in the direction of accepting responsibility for the elderly[97] and fallen too short in what it does for children? The *New York Times* reports: "In the first half of the 1980's, the nation's elderly saw their median income rise by about 16 percent while that of the rest of the population either rose slightly, stayed about the same or fell."[98]

The economic share of children has been slipping. Senator Moynihan has said, "There are some 12 million poor children in the nation but for one reason or another, 5 million get nothing. A half century after the enactment of Social Security, we look up to find that insensate numbers of children are poor and that young children have seven times the poverty rate of the elderly."[99]

A partnership in child support is the appropriate goal. Martha Minow and Deborah Rhode favor treating "child support payments as a public concern, discharged primarily by parents but actively enforced and broadly supplemented by the government through social welfare programs, tax subsidies, and so forth."[100] David Chambers and I have thought for some time that in a few decades, our society may conclude that the enforcement of individual parental child support obligations, at least at full support levels, may no longer be good social policy.[101]

In democratic Western European welfare states, society insists on, but assists with, child support.[102] Typically, those systems accept the two most burdensome aspects of child support, health care and higher education, as primarily social, rather than private, responsibilities. Yet even the duties of providing sustenance and personal care are tempered by children's allowances, subsidized day-care arrangements, and subsidized housing.[103]

Abstract fairness in defining support obligations is not the only issue. A practical concern is that reproduction rates may drop to levels endangering our economy and the Social Security system. For women, the instability of modern marriage has raised to nearly unacceptable levels the economic risk of choosing a home and children over a career. For responsible men, rigorous child support enforcement may turn out to be a deterrent to "assisting" in the "production" of children. Given effective birth control, ready access to abortion, and the mutual risk of easy divorce, increasing numbers of couples even now choose to remain childless. Most already limit reproduction under the pressure resulting from both parties' pursuit of individual careers and the increasing expense of rearing a child. The time may be approaching when the opportunity cost of child rearing becomes prohibitive. Rational men and women may then choose not to have children, unless their economic security is assured by society at large. At that point, mothers and fathers who care or who have cared for children may have to be rewarded for their parenting services by meaningful tax reductions[104] and subsidies financed by an equalization-of-burdens levy on those who choose not to (or for any reason are unable to) accept the social responsibility of bearing, rearing, and supporting children.[105]

Our society's de facto delegation of the child-raising chore to the lower economic strata (especially unmarried, divorced, and unemployed women without adequate income)[106] requires a greater awareness on the part of couples with double incomes and no kids (our so-called DINKS) that their own future is in jeopardy. They should be asked whether they want to live in the kind of society that will be formed by an ever-increasing proportion of social outcasts—the inevitable product of continued disregard for the social and educational needs of the 25 percent of all (and 50 percent of black) children who even now survive under the poverty line.[107] If that question elicits no constructive response, they should be told that their own retirement is directly in jeopardy. Only a healthy, educated, and willing working generation will generate the necessary income to provide retirement for their predecessors in the workplace. In short, *having* children is not just a private matter—*and neither is not having children!*

The problem of our neglected and impoverished children is not simply the result of the failure of private responsibility. The problem we face cannot be corrected solely by enforcement of private monetary responsibility. We should take from parents what they can pay, but not more than they fairly should pay. Society cannot continue to limit social intervention to bare survival at a level well below our official definition of a minimum standard. Adequate financial and social support will turn a child from a social liability into a social asset. All of us must assume a fair share of the burden of decently raising the next generation. We are not doing that.[108]

The Custodial Parent's Need for Services

Money is not everything. Improved standards of economic assistance, in terms of a partnership between public aid and the child's parents, are but one aspect of a new public approach giving priority to the best interests of the child. We also should take a critical look at the relationship between the child and the custodial parent, and at the manner in which the mother takes care of her fatherless child. We cannot expect the absent parent to carry faithfully a full load of child support and refuse to look at the expenditure side. This has two aspects.

First, in fairness to the child and in analogy to the paying parent whose life-style is, in the best interest of his child, subjected to intensive scrutiny and often severe curtailment, the custodial parent should be held accountable that the money paid for the child's support is actually so used.

Second, honest concern for child welfare reasonably requires a routine check into the fitness for child rearing of single-parent homes—or, indeed, any home—without the implication of punishment or moral condemnation. Unlike some current child neglect laws, new laws should allow for the genuine cultural diversity and divergent life-styles that legitimately coexist in our society. We must develop new concepts of sharing caretaking responsibility between parent and assistance institutions. But a line against the inadequate parent must be drawn where the essential interests of the child are in jeopardy.

I learned long ago that the politics of this are fierce and angry,[109] all the more so because help for the child would have a statistically disproportionate impact in the African-American community.[110] But we must not be distracted by statistical appearances. For the sake of the children, I still think we must intervene in settings that are clearly inadequate for rearing children[111]—in settings that violate the civil rights of children.[112] Even if cocaine addicts have a right to their addiction, should they have the right to pass it on?[113] Should not children have a constitutional right not to be homeless,[114] not to live in welfare hotels,[115] not to grow up in Manhattan,[116] and not to be born drugged?[117] But here goes another article.[118]

What Can We Do in Times of High Deficits?

Quite immediately, we should focus tax rates and reductions on dependent children, not on joint returns triggered by a marriage certificate.[119] Driven originally by state law definitions of community income,[120] family tax relief has come primarily through income splitting by way of the joint return. The value of exemptions for dependents, even with a recent increase, pales by comparison. Wholly in line with this emphasis on the joint return, the recent family tax reform debate has long focused on the so-called marriage penalty, the difference between income tax owed by married and unmarried couples in the same or similar circumstances—demonstrating the self-centered political power of childless couples.[121] That debate culminated in a two-earner bonus provided under the Economic Recovery Tax Act of 1981.[122] That has been superseded by newer legislation, not least because the marriage penalty has been rendered less important by new nearly flat income tax rates.[123]

The real problem has been and remains that tax law has used marriage, not children, as the significant event. This approach has always been in conflict with the underlying justification of income taxation—ability to pay. Many modern forms of marriage have no bearing on ability to pay—or, more typically, marriage (or unwed cohabitation) reduces expenses through economies of scale and thus increases ability to pay.

For years, the marriage penalty debate has focused on the very reasonable question of why, for tax purposes, the married, two-earner, equal-career partnership established for emotional and sexual satisfaction should not be equated with the unmarried, two-earner, equal-career partnership established for the same purpose. Seen from that perspective, the marriage penalty complaint has obvious merit, even if the Internal Revenue Service and the courts have not agreed.[124] But this was the wrong question. Properly, the question should be why our tax law does not make a distinction between (1) the two-earner, equal-career partnership, married or unmarried, and (2) the wholly or partially role-divided family established for the purpose of raising children.

To both the wrong and the right questions, the appropriate answer is clear: married and unmarried DINKS should indeed be treated alike. We should discontinue the tax preference (or penalty) triggered by the technicality of legal marriage. Instead, tax recognition and relief should be focused on children, where they are (affecting ability to pay), and where they were (affecting the "former" mother's ability to earn in step with her childless sister)—that is, if our society considers expenses for child rearing on a higher level of social utility than, say, love boat cruises.

Where tax reductions have no effect, we should provide subsidies. We must ensure appropriate and necessary flexibility at the workplace for those who choose to parent, in terms of constructive day care for the children of full-time workers and part-time work without loss of long-run opportunity for those who choose to care for their children themselves. We must change employment practices to assist reentry into the economy of those who have parented, for their sake and that of the economy. A network of laws designed for full-time workers and based on workplace seniority now discourages needed change.

As for the argument that the federal budget will not stand for such new burdens, the good news is that the deficit, and ultimately perhaps the underlying debt, will soon be absorbed by the rapidly growing Social Security surplus, scheduled to be collected under laws now in place.[125] Even now, the budget is balanced in terms of current tax receipts and expenditures. The current deficit is all and only interest on the national debt,[126] nearly two-thirds of which was borrowed in the last eight years.[127]

Besides, there is misspent welfare money even in the current budget. I reject the usual military target—defense is not welfare and furnishes no useful comparison. The taxpayer, however, supplies more than $25 billion in "welfare" each year for "farmers,"[128] and not just for the romantic family farm of American history. The principal recipients of this "welfare" are agribusiness corporations[129] and adult individuals who have made bad business decisions, typically by borrowing irrational amounts to speculate in farmland.

The point is that we really can afford a major effort in this area. Can we afford not to step in? Recently, Justice William Brennan wrote, "In *The Republic* and in *The Laws,* Plato offered a vision of a unified society, where the needs of children are met not by parents but by the Government, and where no intermediate forms of association stand between the individual and the State. The vision is a brilliant one, but it is not our own."[130] Indeed it is not. We seem to be moving not toward a "unified society" but toward a fractured society in which the needs of children are "met not by parents" *and not* "by the government."[131]

At the welfare level, appropriate concern for the child requires a much more effective public contribution in terms of services and dollars to ensure the provision of basic necessities and to give the child a fairer start in life. At the well-off level, the argument is irrelevant—actor William Hurt is not hurt by paying $65,000 in annual child support for his six-year-old son, and the child has enough, even if the mother wants more.[132]

At the upper-middle-income level, the taxpayer would be wise to consider whether a proper public recognition of the social value of parenthood would not be the assumption of nonroutine health and higher education costs that now beggar responsible parents and that contribute to many responsible would-be parents' decisions not to have children. Above the welfare level and below the upper-middle-income level, my argument concerns the enormously wide stratum of those whom we like to flatter with the designation "middle class," but who all too often are but a notch removed from what we have come to call the "working poor." At that level, the call for more sympathetic concern with the financial plight of parents who are doing what they can and the argument for a better balanced role division not only between parents but between parents and public have their greatest strength.

Summary of Conclusions

Where we now are going is wrong. Although very impressive progress in child support collection from absent parents has been made, that very progress seems to have led us to overestimate, and consequently overemphasize, financial support that can be obtained from absent parents. Perhaps we also ask too much from those who have lost their social relationship with their child. Finally, it seems that we overestimate, and consequently overemphasize, the parental rights of the caretaking parent past the point where the latter's conduct conflicts with the best interests of the child. These three misunderstandings are displacing public consciousness of our shared responsibility for the unprecedented havoc that is threatening much of our next generation.

My thesis is simple: children have a right to a decent start in life. This right is the obligation of the father and equally of the mother, and in recognition of a primary and direct responsibility, equally the obligation of society.

1. The absent parent owes support commensurate with (a) his or her ability to pay, (b) the marital and sexual realities and expectations our society encourages or tolerates, and (c) his or her past and present social relationship with the child.

2. The custodial parent owes services and care in an environment conducive to the child's short- and long-term best interests (a) commensurate with his or her means and (b) subject to an objective minimum standard.

3. Society has a direct duty to the child to make up any shortfall (a) on the absent parent's side, by provision of money, and (b) on the custodial parent's side, by intervention when care is not provided at a level called for by a minimal definition of the child's best interests.

7

Reforming the Questions, Questioning the Reforms

Feminist Perspectives on Divorce Law

DEBORAH L. RHODE

AND MARTHA MINOW

Throughout the nineteenth and twentieth centuries, American commentators from a wide range of moral, legal, and political perspectives have presented divorce as a major social problem.[1] There has, however, been no consensus on what exactly "the problem" is. For some critics, it has been the growing frequency of marital breakdown. Others have been dissatisfied with the legal procedures for divorce, and a third group has been primarily concerned with socioeconomic consequences. The introduction of no-fault legal reforms in 1970 both reflected and contributed to controversies about what needed reform. The twentieth anniversary of no-fault legislation offers an opportunity to reconsider how problems surrounding divorce have been formulated, and what has been overlooked or obscured in the process.

Our central premise is that the legal issues surrounding divorce have been conceived too narrowly. Reform initiatives have too often treated divorce as a largely private dispute and have not adequately addressed its public dimensions. The following analysis, informed by contemporary feminist perspectives, underscores the complex relationship between ostensibly private realms of family life and public realms of state and market. A better understanding of those relationships should prompt a clearer understanding of the problems currently at issue in divorce reform.

In our view, the most pressing problems stem from the inadequacy of public commitments both to equality between the sexes and to the quality of life, especially for children, following divorce. Addressing those concerns will require more fundamental reforms, not just in divorce law but in the broader family, work, and welfare policies with which it intersects.

This chapter traces the direction of those reforms. Our objective is less to develop specific policy agendas than to suggest general principles that should guide analysis. In the process, we hope to further debate about the institutions, ideologies, and ideals that affect family life.

Public/Private Premises

To understand the limitations of contemporary divorce initiatives, it is first useful to identify the theoretical structure on which they draw. Divorce reform involves policy choices that rest on broader assumptions about the relationship between families and society. Traditionally, those policies have preserved certain public/private distinctions that are deeply rooted in American legal ideology. These distinctions have operated on two levels. Conventional doctrine has assumed a separation between both family and state and family and market.

The first of these boundaries, the one between family and state, has marked a zone in which most of the customary regulations governing contract, torts, and criminal behavior have not applied. The legal system's historic failure to punish marital rape, to respond effectively in cases of spousal or child abuse, or to enforce support obligations in ongoing marriages reflects long-standing concerns about shielding private relations from public oversight.[2] Reforms that have minimized state interference in the termination of marriage and enforcement of postdivorce obligations have extended this broader ideological tradition.

As much contemporary feminist scholarship notes, this image of family as private bears little correspondence to practice. On the most fundamental level, the state is deeply enmeshed in the family even when labeling it private and beyond judicial oversight. Governmental decision makers have determined what counts as private and what forms of domestic intimacy and inequality will be officially tolerated. So too, public policies concerning child care, tax, inheritance, property, welfare, and birth control have influenced ostensibly private family arrangements. Although the state's nonintervention in domestic matters traditionally has been defended as a means of safeguarding individual autonomy, the consequences of that policy are more complex. The result has often been to substitute private for public coercion and to expand some parties' liberty at the expense of others.[3]

Given the persistent sex-based disparities in social, economic, and political resources in this society, such laissez-faire policies are not gender-neutral. As in other contexts, the abdication of state responsibility on divorce-related issues has served to reinforce gender inequalities. These inequalities are not simply private concerns. The growing number of divorced women and children in serious need is a matter of profound public importance.

Similar observations are applicable to the other major public/private distinction underlying conventional legal ideology, the division between family and market. In the context of divorce, that distinction has encouraged decision makers to undervalue parties' noncommercial contributions in the home and to overlook gender inequalities in the workplace. Divorce reform mandates that have guaranteed formal equality between the sexes have failed to acknowledge, much less address, their persistent social and economic inequalities.

These inequalities reflect a complex interaction of gender socialization, family roles, and market practices. Women have traditionally assumed the bulk of homemaking tasks, a pattern influenced by cultural norms and employment discrimination. Females' lower earnings and restricted job opportunities have been one factor encouraging couples to assign primary domestic responsibilities to wives and primary breadwinning responsibilities to husbands.[4] Most available research suggests that women still perform about 70 percent of the housework in an average household and that working wives spend twice as much time on homemaking tasks as working husbands.[5]

Women's disproportionate assumption of "private" domestic responsibilities has constrained their "public" opportunities. Married women have been less able to assume the burdens of full-time work, particularly in demanding occupations that carry greatest social and economic rewards. Female labor participation over time reflects disruptions of childbirth, child rearing, and accommodation of the family's primary earner.[6] These disruptions, together with gender biases in the workplace, help account for the substantial gap between men's and women's earnings.[7]

It is common to criticize marriage for presuming and reinforcing the lower status of women in the labor market. At the same time, however, those marketplace disadvantages are mitigated by traditional family structures as long as the husband and wife remain together. In an ongoing marriage, the entire family shares in the salary advantages and job-related medical, insurance, and pension benefits that disproportionately accompany male jobs.[8] A wife is thus somewhat shielded from the full force of her disadvantages in a wage economy; she contributes her lower wages and uncompensated domestic labor to enhance the family's well-being without having to sustain herself and her children on that inadequate economic base.

In this light, marriage has presented a promise—between the members of the couple and also between the couple and society—that the costs of traditional gender roles will not be borne by women alone but will be spread more broadly throughout society.[9] Divorce, by contrast, represents the danger that a woman will be exposed to the full costs of uncompensated family duties and labor market disadvantages.

This danger has been inadequately recognized in divorce reform. Rather, we will argue, most reform strategies still bear the legacy of traditional public/private distinctions. The prevailing tendency has been to treat divorce as a matter for private ordering and to neglect the broader public forces that reinforce gender inequalities in employment and family roles. Our view of "the problem" in divorce contexts draws on an extensive body of feminist work in history, political science, sociology, anthropology, and law that challenges conventional public/private boundaries. In this work, the family and the state represent intertwined structures of authority: family roles shape and are in turn shaped by state policies and market forces.[10] Feminist scholars have carefully distinguished the ideology of the family from actual social practices and have emphasized the cultural construction of modern Western public/private distinctions.[11] Such distinctions are not fixed, and the point of much feminist analysis is both to challenge and to change conventional boundaries.

By extending this analysis to specific divorce-related issues, we highlight the need for new norms in policy debate. Our concern is to develop principles that are sensitive to the interconnections between public and private and that are committed to advancing both gender equality and the quality of family life. Although we believe that certain policy choices follow from such principles, our primary objective is not to work out the details of implementation. Rather, we hope to further debate over the assumptions about gender, work, and family relationships that underlie particular divorce reform efforts.

No-Fault Divorce: The Limited Agenda of Initial Reforms

Detailed histories of no-fault divorce are already available, and more will undoubtedly emerge, reflecting the needs and preoccupations of their age.[12] From this growing literature, we identify certain assumptions that guided architects of no-fault reforms, first in California and then in other jurisdictions. Our focus is on assumptions that have directed, and at times misdirected, analysis of gender equality, parental obligations, and public commitments.

The Limitations of No-Fault Reforms

The leading proponents of initial no-fault reform were lawyers, judges, and law professors. Their primary focus was on the legal grounds for divorce; their primary purposes were to reduce expense, acrimony, and fraud in resolving matters envisioned as essentially private concerns. What is, perhaps, most revealing about these original efforts are the issues that were not on the agenda. Early reform strategies neglected gender equality and public responsibilities.

Although no-fault initiatives coincided with the resurgence of a women's rights movement, proponents of these reforms generally were not seeking to remedy women's disadvantages under traditional family policies. Indeed, to the extent that gender equity appeared at all in discussions among decision makers, the focus involved equity for men. The dominant concern was beleaguered ex-husbands, crippled by excessive alimony burdens and threats of blackmail. Although this problem was grossly exaggerated, the absence of systematic data allowed policymakers to rely on anecdotal experiences to formulate the problem they sought to reform.[13]

In part, the absence of women's concerns from the debate reflected the absence of women. Those with greatest influence in policy-making—practicing attorneys, politicians, and family law experts—were overwhelmingly male.[14] The newly emerging women's rights movement was not significantly involved with early divorce reforms, in part because it was understaffed and overextended during this period, but more important, because the implications of such reforms were not yet apparent. Only as the divorce rate escalated and scholars concerned with women's issues began to chronicle its impact did the focus of debate begin to change.

Even when reformers identified gender equality as an objective, they relied almost exclusively on gender-neutral formulations. For example, they succeeded in eliminating explicitly sex-linked provisions (such as those granting alimony only to wives) and in reformulating rules for marital property distribution to require "equal" or "equitable" division of assets.[15] Yet as subsequent discussion suggests, such provisions have secured equality in form, but not equality in fact.

The assumptions underlying early reforms also marginalized the public implications of divorce doctrine. No-fault initiatives began from the premise that decisions involving the termination of marriage should rest with private parties; the public's responsibility was simply to provide efficient legal rules for processing their agreement and resolving any disputes. Within this framework, a couple's allocation of financial and child-rearing obligations appeared to be primarily matters for private ordering. If parties failed to reach agreement, their differences would be resolved under broad discretionary standards mandating equality or equity between the spouses in financial matters and the best interest of the child in custody contests. Public norms about the kinds of resolutions society should endorse receded to the background. As a result, the state was given little responsibility for guiding, enforcing, or supplementing judicial awards.

Paradoxically, this move toward private ordering failed adequately to acknowledge the diversity of private family circumstances. Those who framed and interpreted legal doctrine often overlooked the fact that marriages of different durations, formed during different decades with different expectations, could leave divorcing parties in sharply divergent situations. One single, discretionary standard was thought adequate to deal with circumstances ranging from a couple married for one year while the parties finished college to a couple married for twenty-five years while the woman worked in the home and the husband held paid employment.

Early no-fault reforms gave no special attention to the concerns of particularly vulnerable groups such as displaced homemakers with limited savings, insurance, and employment options; families with inadequate income to support two households (a problem disproportionately experienced by racial minorities); or couples with no children, no significant property, and no need for a formal adjudicative procedure.[16] Nor was child support central to the reform agenda; it appeared only as a side issue, buried within custody and other financial topics.

It bears emphasis what such a limited conception of public responsibility left out. The early reform agenda did not specify clear public norms concerning financial and child-care responsibilities to guide parties' decision making or judicial review. Nor did it mandate effective, affordable enforcement procedures for spousal and child support awards, or state subsidies where private resources were inadequate. Reformers also neglected the impact of postdivorce property divisions—such as the forced sale of the family home—on dependent children. And what was most critical, no-fault initiatives omitted criteria for assessing the outcomes of divorce, outcomes affecting not only the parties and their children but subsequent marriages, stepfamilies, and public welfare responsibilities.

In noting what was absent from the no-fault agenda, we do not mean to devalue its central objective. Reducing the acrimony, expense, and fraud associated with fault-based procedures was a goal worth pursuing in its own right. Given the opposition to liberalizing grounds for divorce, reformers may have been justifiably wary about raising other related issues.[17] But we also believe that the limitations of the original reform movement reflect not only what was politically expedient at that historical moment but also more fundamental conceptual inadequacies. By remaining wedded to traditional public/private distinctions, early divorce reform tended to amplify rather than redress gender inequalities. The reliance on private ordering and gender neutrality in a world that was not in fact gender-neutral and in which private resources and roles were unevenly distributed had profound costs.

These costs became more apparent as the divorce rate escalated. Research in the aftermath of no-fault reforms has found a sharp decline in single women's standard of living following divorce and a rise in men's.[18] The economics of divorce have also played a role in this nation's increasing feminization of poverty. Approximately 70 percent of all single-parent families are headed by divorced or separated women and half of all female-headed households are poor.[19] The ineffectiveness of legal responses to these patterns has been a continuing problem, both in initial and in more recent divorce reform efforts.

Alternative Conceptions: The Critics

Over the last two decades, no-fault divorce reforms have attracted increasing criticism.[20] Scholars from a variety of disciplines have emphasized how the practice of divorce law departs from its expressed promises of "equal" or "equitable" treatment. Other chapters in this book build on such scholarship in addressing the capacities and consequences of reform measures.[21]

Yet this criticism has not yet sparked the major policy reformulations that we believe are necessary. In our view, too much of the debate to date has centered on issues of cause and effect rather than broader normative concerns. For example, the scholarly dispute over the extent to which no-fault reforms are responsible for increasing poverty among female-headed households is as yet unresolvable.[22] In this, as in many contexts, it is impossible to isolate the impact of legal change from the social forces that helped produce it. The risk of emphasizing such issues is that they deflect attention from the fundamental limitations of initial and more recent reform efforts.

So too, most of the criticism that has influenced current divorce policy has left the law's traditional organizing assumptions intact. Although efforts to reform no-fault reforms have chipped away at the margins of the public/private distinction, its essential boundaries have remained. A steady stream of special commissions, legislative lobbying, and judicial education has produced some important initiatives, but their agendas fail to demand what is necessary: a comprehensive reformulation not only of divorce doctrine but also of family, work, and welfare policies.[23]

Yet we also believe that two central ideals underlying contemporary reform efforts, if more clearly developed, could lay the groundwork for broader changes. The first ideal seeks equality between men and women not just in formal rights but in actual status, power, and economic security. A second ideal seeks to promote the quality of family life; it envisions a diverse range of household structures that will encourage intimate partnerships among adults and minimize the hardships to children if those relationships terminate. These ideals, already implicit in recent reform initiatives, imply a fundamental reassessment of public/private distinctions.

Toward Gender Equality and the Quality of Family Life

In 1983, the *New York Times* described the move from fault to no-fault standards in divorce and marital property distributions as a shift from moral to economic principles.[24] This widely held view neglects the degree to which moral judgments underpin current standards. Distributional rules mandating equal or equitable division of marital property embody normative assumptions about what constitutes justice for divorcing couples. The focus has simply shifted from the moral conduct of the parties prior to divorce (who did what to whom) to the moral obligations that should be recognized following divorce (who is responsible to whom, to what extent, and for what duration).

In our view, these moral obligations should embody clearer commitments to equality between the sexes and the quality of life for children. Norms governing termination of a marriage should be consistent with the ideal to which marriage aspires—that of equal partnerships between spouses who share resources, responsibilities, and risks.[25] The economic losses resulting from the division of one household into two should not be unevenly distributed between divorcing men and women. Nor should these economic losses be disproportionately imposed on children, whose need for care and support endures regardless of their parents' abilities to share a household.

Gender equality and child welfare should become priorities in practice, not just theory, under contemporary divorce law. With these normative premises in mind, we turn to specific issues in the allocation of marital property, spousal assistance, and child support.

Marital Property and Sharing Principles

The ideal of marital partnerships has obvious implications for property divisions after divorce. Under partnership principles, the past and future labor-force earnings, benefits, and governmental entitlements of each spouse should be treated as shared family resources, potentially subject to distribution on divorce. Distributive decisions should depend on the parties' domestic as well as economic contributions to the relationship and on their future needs and earning potential. To realize this vision, the state needs to play a greater role in specifying standards for property allocation and ensuring their enforcement.

From a policy standpoint, this partnership framework is desirable both because it encourages cooperative commitments between spouses and because it serves broader egalitarian and caretaking objectives. In effect, sharing principles hold promise for bridging traditional public/private divisions between family and market. A partnership model can cushion the impact of persistent gender biases in couples' private allocation of homemaking tasks and in the public allocation of salaries and benefits.[26] By sharing their total resources, families can spread the risks and benefits of sex-linked roles, the remnants of a socioeconomic system that makes it difficult for any one individual to accommodate a full work and family life. Guided by a partnership vision, divorce law can take account of the interaction between the private choices of divorcing parties and the broader public policies and marketplace discrimination that have influenced such choices.

Not only do partnership principles promote gender equality; they also support caretaking commitments toward children and elderly dependents. Legal support for such sharing behavior is crucial in a society with notably inadequate policies toward child care, parental leaves, flexible scheduling, or meaningful part-time work.[27]

In principle, state standards that mandate either equal or equitable distribution of marital property could be consistent with this vision. In practice, however, their implementation has retained an emphasis on individual entitlements that undercuts sharing principles and reinforces gender inequalities.

Equal property division is the initial no-fault approach pioneered in California. By the late 1980s, about fifteen jurisdictions had adopted presumptions or absolute requirements of 50-50 splits of marital assets at divorce.[28] Yet this equality in formal treatment rarely emerges in actual experience. Part of the problem lies in restrictive definitions of property belonging to the community; for example, insurance and professional licenses are often not fully subject to division. Nor is future earning potential, which is many couples' only major asset.[29] Yet given the continued sex-based inequalities in labor market patterns and domestic responsibilities, married women have not had the same opportunities as men to develop marketable skills and experience.[30] An approach that ignores future earning capacity in defining marital resources will reinforce gender disparities.

Further inequalities arise from men's and women's different family responsibilities following divorce. Mothers retain physical custody of minor children in the vast majority of cases. As a recent California Task Force Report on Women and Family Equity pointed out, it is scarcely equal when the husband receives half the marital assets and the other half are shared by the wife and children.[31] Forced sales of family homes, which have increased since no-fault reforms and equal property initiatives, have also imposed disproportionate economic hardships on the custodial parent.[32]

Similar problems arise with standards that require not equal but equitable distribution of marital assets. Such mandates leave ample room for judges to impose their own assessment of individual conduct and individual entitlement. In some states, courts retain discretion to "do equity" by taking into account concerns inconsistent with sharing values, such as who "owns" particular assets. The result, according to a number of studies, is that husbands end up with a majority of marital property as well as with greater earning potential.[33] As in equal division jurisdictions, many equitable distribution states also restrict property subject to distribution in ways that penalize primary homemakers.[34]

Treatment of spousal professional degrees and nonvested pensions is a case in point. Most legislative and judicial decision makers have persisted in viewing these assets more as individual entitlements than as joint efforts even when they were earned during marriage. A common theory has been that professional degrees lack "traditional" features of property; they cannot be sold on the open market and they represent the cumulative product of education, effort, ability, and expenditures for which spouses assertedly do not expect compensation.[35]

Such approaches, which present property as if it were a tangible object rather than a legal construct, mask normative judgments even as they are exercised. "Traditional" features of ownership have always been open to redefinition, and spouses' expectations are in part a function of what courts and legislatures provide. So too, claims that nonvested retirement benefits should not be divided miss a basic point about the relationship of work and family dynamics in this society. The benefits in question represent deferred compensation that would otherwise have been available to support the wage earner's entire family.

Even jurisdictions that grant both parties a share in future assets often calculate the entitlement in ways that violate sharing principles. For example, in cases involving one spouse's professional degree, the other spouse often receives only compensation for out-of-pocket contributions such as books and tuition or for the market value of labor during the period in question. Such an approach rarely begins to compensate the nonprofessional spouse for forgone opportunities and the often permanent loss of earning potential that they reflect.[36]

We do not imply that professional degrees should be considered property while other career assets are treated as individual entitlements. Rather, in all cases involving such assets, spouses should be entitled to a proportion of each other's past and future earning potential commensurate with their contribution to the relationship and with the personal loss in earning potential that it has entailed. The same sharing principles that we advocate for spousal support generally should also be applicable to division of career assets.[37]

Finally, we believe that in cases involving extended marriages or minor children, there should be a presumption favoring deferred sale of the family home. In recommending such a rule, California's Task Force on Family Equity noted that residential moves intensify the trauma that children and traditional homemakers suffer as a result of divorce.[38] The disruption of established friendships and support structures, and the economic hardships involved in relocation, should be avoided for those who are most vulnerable.

Spousal Support

Although spousal support awards (traditionally labeled alimony) have never been common, most studies suggest that their frequency and duration have declined over the last two decades.[39] The current assumption is that fairness between the spouses is best accomplished through a "clean break," involving the distribution of existing assets and, in special cases, brief rehabilitative assistance. Since less than half of divorcing couples have significant assets to divide, and since conventional approaches to property division generally penalize primary caretakers, this represents a rather skewed concept of fairness.[40]

Statutes and judicial decisions currently governing spousal assistance often pay lip service to sharing principles and list a broad array of relevant factors to be considered (such as age, length of marriage, need, and financial as well as nonfinancial contributions to the relationship). However, no priorities among the factors are specified, and the rankings that have emerged in practice do not work in homemakers' favor. Recent surveys indicate that only about a sixth of divorced women receive spousal maintenance and two-thirds of these awards are for limited duration. Amounts are usually quite modest and only about half are fully paid.[41]

Many judges have disregarded sharing norms and declined to award substantial support except in extremely compelling cases. The prevailing attitude was well illustrated in one of Lenore Weitzman's judicial surveys. In response to a hypothetical situation in which a nurse supported her doctor husband through eight years of college, medical school, and residency, and then sought after divorce to attend medical school herself, less than a third of the surveyed judges would grant her four years of support; it appeared "unfair" to saddle her husband with such expenses since she was already able to support herself.[42]

Litigated cases involving older homemakers reflect similar insensitivity to the permanent costs of career sacrifice. Women with prolonged marriages and few if any marketable skills have been denied reasonable economic security on the assumption that they can become self-sufficient, often within highly unrealistic time intervals.[43] These displaced homemakers are losing not only their husband but also their primary identity and social status. They should not also be placed in constant financial risk or forced into jobs that are unsuited to their education and life experience. For marriages of extended duration, a "clean break" framework undermines sharing principles. An understandable goal—constructing separate futures for divorcing spouses—should not ignore the consequences of prior marital commitments.

Gender inequalities result not only from the inadequacy of initial spousal support and property awards but also from the costs of enforcement. High rates of noncompliance, together with states' failure to guarantee automatic wage withholding, subsidized legal assistance, or accessible and effective dispute resolution channels, translate into substantial economic insecurity.[44]

A serious commitment to sharing principles will require an expanded sense of both private and public responsibilities. Although formal doctrine generally acknowledges the factors that are relevant regarding spousal support, clearer priorities are necessary for their application. Legislative initiatives, appellate doctrine, and judicial education programs should seek to reduce idiosyncratic judgments and to ensure that less focus is placed on individual entitlements and more on partnership responsibilities.[45] Spouses who have sacrificed their own earning potential for the family's well-being or their partner's advancement should have a claim for compensation that is commensurate with their contributions and their sacrifices. The longer the marriage and less adequate a spouse's independent resources, the greater that claim should be. By taking into account the value of both contributions and sacrifices, courts can avoid penalizing a homemaker who would have difficulty demonstrating her entitlement if only one of these allocation principles was relevant.[46]

It will not, of course, be possible to measure forgone opportunities or the value of domestic contributions with any precision. Nor does it seem possible to establish bright-line rules that can avoid discretionary case-by-case judgments. But initiatives such as those recently proposed in California could prove effective at least in constraining discretion and educating trial judges and divorce lawyers about its appropriate exercise. For example, the California Task Force recommended that courts expressly and realistically consider the "reduced or lost lifetime earning capacity of a spouse as a result of having forgone or delayed education, training, employment or career opportunities during the marriage." The Task Force further proposed that the basis of support should be the "standard of living established during the marriage, except that in marriages of long duration, spousal support should serve to equalize the standards of living of both households after divorce."[47]

Such an approach has the virtue of acknowledging differences in family circumstances depending on the length of marital relationships. It also recognizes that extended sharing commitments carry permanent consequences and responsibilities. Since parties' economic circumstances after divorce are materially shaped by choices jointly made during marriage, neither spouse should bear a grossly disproportionate share of the costs of dissolution.

In order to translate these sharing principles into actual practice, the public must assume greater responsibility for enforcement of private obligations. Automatic wage withholding, along the lines recently mandated for child support, should also be routinely available for spousal maintenance. Subsidized legal assistance and accessible dispute resolution procedures are equally critical for any effective reform strategy.

Not all the gender disparities associated with divorce can, of course, be addressed through changes in divorce law. Particularly when marriages end after a relatively short period or the couple lacks adequate resources, husbands cannot be expected to compensate for all the disadvantages facing their divorced wives. Many of these disadvantages stem from deeper structural inadequacies in employment, welfare, health, pension, and child-care policies, and from the continuing legacy of sex-based stereotypes and socialization patterns. Broader initiatives in all these areas are necessary, as are targeted programs for particular groups of divorced women such as displaced homemakers and single parents.[48]

Gender inequalities are only part of the problem resulting from conventional approaches to marital property. A majority of divorces involve minor children, and frameworks preoccupied with formal parity between the spouses have too often marginalized concerns about the family as a whole.

Child Support

Throughout American history, women raising children alone have been financially at risk.[49] Despite the evolution from sex-linked to gender-neutral standards in child custody law, women continue to perform the vast majority of child-rearing tasks after as well as during marriage.[50] Any single parent faces the difficult task of juggling two roles: economic provider and primary nurturer. Women who assume this role confront additional barriers in the paid labor force, where the majority of female employees remain crowded in low-paying occupations with limited advancement possibilities.

The difficulties of single parenting in this society exact a heavy toll not only on women but also on their children. A child with divorced or separated parents has a disproportionately high likelihood of delinquency, poor school performance, and mental health difficulties.[51] Financial hardships often contribute directly or indirectly to these problems, and governmental responses have been highly inadequate. Few support structures, such as counseling services or subsidized child care, are available for single-parent households. Current welfare programs offer insufficient aid while degrading their recipients.[52] In theory, the financial needs of children in divorced families are to be met through support payments from noncustodial parents. In practice, this system has left millions of children unprotected.

Two perspectives on child support have traditionally informed public debate. From one perspective, support payments represent a redistribution of resources within the family unit. This makes child support controversies seem like other private disputes; the public role is simply to provide a forum for their efficient resolution. Under this view, the child's entitlement does not extend beyond what the parties specify or what a neutral judge is willing to order, unconstrained by clear public norms. From another vantage, child support payments reflect parental obligations that become subject to public oversight once the family separates. This approach envisions child support responsibility as private in the sense that it must generally be met through family resources. It is public only in the sense that the state defines minimum norms and provides limited aid in cases of indigency.

A third, still emerging, framework treats child support payments as a public concern, discharged primarily by parents but actively enforced and broadly supplemented by the government through social welfare programs, tax subsidies, and so forth.[53] We believe that only through this third approach can society respond adequately to children's needs.

Although this framework has not sufficiently shaped divorce policies, the public attention to parental support obligations has increased significantly since initial no-fault reforms. In part, this trend responds to well-publicized research about the insufficiency and nonenforcement of support awards, as well as to concerns about the resulting social welfare burdens. Courts routinely have approved support obligations based on unrealistically low estimates of child-rearing costs, and the value of these already inadequate awards quickly declines through inflation and noncompliance.[54] The problem is compounded by many women's willingness to make financial concessions and to decrease support requests in order to avoid custody and visitation battles.[55]

Partly in response to these problems, Congress expanded federal involvement through the Child Support Enforcement Amendments of 1984 and the Family Support Act of 1988. This legislation requires various procedures, including automatic wage withholding and state guidelines that must serve as rebuttable presumptions in establishing appropriate levels of child support.[56] Although the legislation's full impact has yet to be evaluated, certain limitations have already become apparent.

First, each state retains discretion in determining what support levels its guidelines will mandate, and existing standards have failed adequately to promote gender equality or child welfare. Three primary models for establishing guidelines have emerged. The first, an "equal living standards" approach, seeks to ensure that the child's household remains as well off as the absent parent's. In effect, the goal is to achieve rough parity in the consequences that follow from dividing one family life into two. Although we believe this framework is best suited to maximize child welfare, no state has yet adopted its formulation. Part of the resistance stems from difficulties in measuring relative standards of living and adjusting for changes in circumstances. The primary opposition, however, rests on the size of payments necessary to approximate equality, a particularly heavy burden if the noncustodial parent remarries and incurs new family obligations.[57]

A second approach involves "cost-sharing"; it attempts to divide the expenses of raising a child between the parents in rough proportion to their financial ability. Only California has adopted this framework, and policymakers in other jurisdictions have raised questions about its appropriateness.[58] A threshold problem concerns how to define the costs of child rearing. For example, since the custodial parent and the child jointly consume certain items, such as housing, disputes arise in allocating appropriate percentages of shared expenses to the child. Further problems involve valuing in-kind contributions, such as child care, in calculating both how much child raising costs and how much credit to give for a spouse's caretaking services. But if expenses were adequately defined and determined with reference to a family's predivorce living standards, this framework could well serve child welfare goals. Yet the failure to adopt such definitions has been one of the factors diminishing support obligations in the past.

The third, and most widely accepted model, involves "income sharing." It sets the support award at a level reflecting a specified percentage of the noncustodial parent's income. Underlying this framework is an assumption that all parents should contribute roughly the same proportion of their resources toward child support. The Federal Office of Child Support Enforcement has developed a variation of this approach, the "income shares" model. This framework reflects the same basic objective, but provides a somewhat more complex formula that takes into account the parties' combined income and number of children.[59] Neither variation of this model seeks to equalize mothers' and fathers' contributions to child-rearing expenses. Rather, the objective is to promote greater consistency in the percentage of income allocated to child support among different families.

Evaluation of these approaches requires detailed consideration. How much child support for families of varied incomes do they actually ensure? What incentives or disincentives do they create for parents to work or to increase their income? How equitable is the allocation of expenses between parents? How much do they focus on children's needs compared with adults'? Under what circumstances do courts depart from their requirements?

Although little evaluative research on these questions is available, preliminary analysis raises two sets of concerns.[60] The first emerges from certain obvious limitations in the guidelines' scope and enforcement. For example, under most existing approaches, support agreements need not provide cost-of-living adjustments, health care coverage, or support for dependents who are over eighteen. Insufficient provision has been made for custodial parents to remain in the family home and provide needed continuity in children's educational and neighborhood support structures. Bureaucratic bottlenecks and inadequate enforcement resources have left a wide gap between legislative mandates and actual practices.[61] However, such concerns could at least be addressed within current conceptual frameworks. A further line of criticism—and one we advance here—is more fundamental. In several crucial respects, recent child support initiatives reinforce the traditional public/private distinction and the gender biases it reflects.

First, current income-sharing guidelines incorporate a formal rather than substantive commitment to gender equality: they apply equally to men and women, but provide no public recognition of sex-based disparities in ostensibly private realms of work or family. By rejecting an equal living standards model and requiring minimal income transfers, states have permitted large economic gaps between custodial and noncustodial households. Since, as noted earlier, women generally retain physical custody, the result is to institutionalize gender inequalities.

A related problem involves biases in the definition of expenses and income under prevailing guidelines. For example, existing standards do not make sufficient provision for child-care costs, a major expense especially if a custodial parent needs to work.[62] Nor do the guidelines provide appropriate treatment of second families in determining available income. Generally they imply that if the noncustodial parent—usually the father—remarries and incurs new child-care obligations, those costs can reduce the funds available to children from the former marriage. In our view, support guidelines should not allow claims of a second family to diminish obligations to the first. The decision to have a child has irrevocable consequences and should imply irrevocable commitments. Those commitments need to be taken into account by parties contemplating a second family. Current guidelines send the wrong cultural message, create the wrong incentives, and reinforce a disturbing trend in parenting norms; an increasingly high percentage of fathers offer little economic or psychological support to children with whom they do not share a residence.[63]

Finally, although prevailing guidelines represent a significant shift toward a publicly articulated child support obligation, they reflect the traditional view that this obligation is to be satisfied by the private resources of the divorcing couple. Where such resources are insufficient to support two households, recent reform initiatives offer no remedy. Although child support legislation has been sold as a way to reduce poverty and welfare costs, it is hardly adequate to the task.[64] The families most in need often cannot depend on child support because the noncustodial spouse cannot be located or lacks sufficient income. These families are left to highly inadequate welfare programs such as Aid to Families with Dependent Children. Under current standards, three-quarters of all states provide assistance at less than 75 percent of the poverty level, and over half of all poor children are in families that receive no cash assistance.[65]

Despite recent progress, child support policy still remains hostage to characteristic limitations of divorce reform: an insufficient sensitivity to gender inequalities, a willingness to privilege interests of adults over interests of children, and undue reliance on private rather than public means of guaranteeing family support.[66] A different conceptual model is necessary to promote what should be our primary objectives: ensuring children's welfare and allocating the burdens fairly among men, women, and the state. The full details of this allocative scheme raise issues of income distribution and incentive structures that are beyond the scope of this chapter.[67] But the broad contours of an alternative model can be derived from the commitments to equality between the sexes and quality of life for children that we have identified.

Such an alternative model would require guidelines that take account of the full costs of child rearing and attempt to place children in at least as good a position as they would have been had the divorce not occurred. This approach would also require some effort to minimize disparities between custodial and noncustodial households, and would avoid subordinating claims of a first marriage to those of a second.

So too, the state should play a more active role in guaranteeing child support. Scandinavian policies, which experimental Wisconsin programs have replicated, offer a useful model. Under their approach, the government collects child support payments and provides supplemental subsidies where parental resources are insufficient.[68] A national strategy along these lines would both serve a public interest and meet a public responsibility. Failure to assist children jeopardizes not only their economic future but our own. The quality of life we can expect in our later years depends on the quality of life we provide now for the generation that will support us later.[69]

Expanding the Reform Agenda

Critics of divorce reform have long argued that a central problem arises from treating the issue as simply divorce, when in fact the issue is marriage and men's and women's roles within it.[70] We believe that in fact the issue is still broader. It implicates fundamental understandings of private relationships and public responsibilities. Those understandings should, in our view, build on the normative commitments noted earlier—commitments to substantive equality between sexes, to sharing principles in intimate relationships, and to policies that maximize children's interests. In these final paragraphs, we summarize certain policy implications of this normative vision.

First, and most fundamental, we do not believe that such policy initiatives should be limited to contexts involving divorce. Although this book directs our focus to issues of marital dissolution, the principles we identify have broader scope. A commitment to gender equality and sharing behavior calls for support of varied social arrangements; it would, for example, entail legal recognition for unmarried domestic partners.[71] Our point is not to privilege particular family forms but to support the cooperative caretaking behavior that a variety of intimate relationships makes possible.

To that end, we seek legal norms that neither presume a single model of behavior for all couples nor remain indifferent to the particular arrangements that couples fashion. Rather than trying to lump all divorces under one procedure, the state should create simplified administrative structures for parties with no children, no substantial property, and no legal disputes, and should establish clearer norms and more accessible procedures for couples with more complicated situations.[72]

Such an approach could leave room for private ordering by individuals who make antenuptial contracts under accepted principles of fair dealing and judicial safeguards against abuse.[73] For the remainder of couples, who will negotiate divorce settlements in the shadow of divorce law, the governing principles require redefinition.

Legal reforms should support sharing relationships by rewarding sharing behavior. Parties who have forgone opportunities in order to contribute to their family's care and to their spouse's work should receive a portion of past and future family resources that is commensurate with their contribution. The state should take affirmative steps to implement these distributional principles by establishing priorities or presumptions for allocation of marital property and spousal support, and by actively assisting enforcement.

Strategies for child support should reflect similar concerns. In order to further both gender equality and child welfare, support guidelines should take account of the full costs of child rearing and should seek to minimize disparities between custodial and noncustodial households. Such guidelines should also avoid encouraging parties to assume new family obligations that are inconsistent with those already incurred.

Our normative commitments imply an expanded concept of responsibility not only for divorcing spouses and parents but also for the state. Gender inequalities are in part attributable to public policies and warrant public intervention. We need both special programs for divorced parties and changes in broader welfare and employment policies that affect family life. To prevent family status from determining economic status, governmental welfare programs must not penalize either single-parent households or two-parent households in allocating assistance.[74] Expanded child-care and parental leave provisions, flexible workplace schedules, wider health and pension coverage, counseling services for single parents and children, retraining programs for displaced homemakers, and further social initiatives targeting minority and low-income groups are also crucial to any effective reform strategy.[75]

This is not a modest agenda, and we do not minimize the political obstacles to its adoption. Nor do we underestimate the complexity of distributional and incentive issues that it raises. But we also believe that these broader policy initiatives are the logical extension of ideals to which our society already pays allegiance. If we are serious about promoting gender equality in this generation and ensuring a decent start in life for the next, we need to translate our rhetorical commitments into social priorities.

Notes

1. Beyond No-Fault: New Directions in Divorce Reform

1 I have traced this history elsewhere. See Kay, "Equality and Difference: A Perspective on No-Fault Divorce and Its Aftermath," 56 *U. Cinn. L. Rev.* 1, 4–14, 26–55 (1987).

2 See, generally, M. Glendon, *Abortion and Divorce in Western Law* 64–81 (1987) (tracing this history and placing it in comparative context).

3 J. Madden, *Handbook of the Law of Persons and Domestic Relations* 256–61 (1931) (noting that Pennsylvania enacted its first complete divorce code in 1785).

4 *Id*. at 288.

5 *Id*. at 293 (quoting Ballinger's Ann. Wash. Codes & St. § 5716(7)). This provision was repealed in 1921. See Note, "Incompatibility of Parties as Ground for Divorce," 4 *Wash. L. Rev.* 83, 84 (1929).

6 J. Madden, *supra* note 3 at 291.

7 M. Rheinstein, *Marriage Stability, Divorce, and the Law,* 313–16 (1972).

8 *Id*. at 7–105.

9 Report of a Group Appointed by the Archbishop of Canterbury in January 1964, *Putting Asunder: A Divorce Law for Contemporary Society* (1966).

10 Law Commission, *Reform of the Grounds of Divorce: The Field of Choice* (1966).

11 *Report of the Governor's Commission on the Family* (1966).

12 Uniform Marriage and Divorce Act (1970) (amended 1971 and 1973); see also R. Levy, *Uniform Marriage and Divorce Legislation: A Preliminary Analysis* (1969) (internal document prepared by Reporter Levy for the Special Committee on Divorce of the National Conference of Commissioners on Uniform State Laws) (copy on file in Kay's office).

13 The Law Commission proposed a standard resting *either* on marriage breakdown without judicial inquest, to be presumed after six months separation, *or,* if that were not politically feasible, a separation ground to be added to the existing fault-based grounds. *Law Commission, supra* note 10 at 54–55.

14 Elizabeth II, 1969 c. 55 (22 October 1969).

15 Family Law Act of 1969, ch. 1608, 1969 Cal. Stat. 3312, 3314–51 (codified as amended at Cal. Civ. Code §§ 4000–5138 (West 1983 and Supp. 1989).

16 Uniform Marriage and Divorce Act, 9A U.L.A. 156 (1987).

17 For a comparison of the original proposals and the final product, see B. Lee, *Divorce Law Reform in England* (1974); Kay, *supra* note 1 at 41–44 (California law), 48–51 (Uniform Act).

18 As I have shown elsewhere, fifteen states have "pure no-fault" divorce laws in the sense that they have abolished all fault-based grounds for divorce and established instead the principle of marriage breakdown as the exclusive basis for dissolution; twenty-one states have added a no-fault provision of the marriage-

breakdown variety to their existing fault grounds; and fourteen states and the District of Columbia have combined fault grounds with a no-fault provision based on voluntary separation or incompatibility. See Kay, *supra* note 1 at 5–6 (listing the three groups of states in footnotes 19, 20, and 22, respectively).

19 See Friedman, "Rights of Passage: Divorce Law in Historical Perspective," 63 *Oreg. L. Rev.* 649 (1984).

20 Utah added "irreconcilable differences" to its list of fault-based grounds in 1987. Act Relating to Domestic Law, ch. 106, 1987 Utah Laws 645, 646 (amending Utah Code Ann. § 30-3-1(3)(a) (1989).

21 See Kay, *supra* note 1 at 7–14.

22 Friedman, *supra* note 19 at 664.

23 See, generally, Mnookin and Kornhauser, "Bargaining in the Shadow of the Law: The Case of Divorce," 88 *Yale L.J.* 950 (1979).

24 I have elaborated this point elsewhere. See Kay, *supra* note 1 at 42–44 (California law), 46–51 (Uniform Act).

25 Glendon, *supra* note 2 at 86–92.

26 L. Weitzman, *The Divorce Revolution: The Unexpected Social and Economic Consequences for Women and Children in America* 184–214, 323–56 (1985). Weitzman's book received the prestigious American Sociological Association Award for a Distinguished Contribution to Scholarship in 1986 and the Book Award of the A.S.A. Family Section in 1988. Weitzman was also a corecipient of the C. Wright Mills Award.

27 Glendon, *supra* note 2 at 105. While Glendon surveys the laws of twenty Western countries, she focuses her discussion of divorce law on England, France, West Germany, Sweden, and the United States. *Id.* at 64.

28 Freed and Walker, "Family Law in the Fifty States: An Overview," 22 *Fam. L.Q.* 367, 408–09 (Table V) (1989).

29 *Id.* at 472–73 (Table VI). In practice, this latter rule would appear to function to make some women worse off than they would have been if fault were ignored.

30 Freed and Walker, "Family Law in the Fifty States: An Overview," 21 *Fam. L.Q.* 417, 508 (1988).

31 Freed and Walker report that thirty-six states have some form of joint custody. Freed and Walker, *supra* note 28 at 467 (Table IX).

32 Weitzman, *supra* note 26 at 366–67.

33 *Id.* at 373–74.

34 Some of these recommendations are discussed *infra* in the text accompanying notes 107–63.

35 Weitzman, *supra* note 26 at 184–214.

36 Kay, *supra* note 1 at 77–89.

37 Waldron, "When Justice Replaces Affection: The Need for Rights," 11 *Harv. J.L. & Pub. Pol'y* 625, 628 (1988).

38 See Friedman, "The Necessity for State Recognition of Same-Sex Marriage: Constitutional Requirements and Evolving Notions of Family," 3 *Berkeley Women's L.J.* 134 (1987–88).

39 Even if the movement to legalize same-sex marriage does not achieve its goal, the possibility of co-adoption of children by a same-sex couple, or second-parent

adoption, may provide some security for the parent-child relationships in such households. See Patt, "Second Parent Adoption: When Crossing the Marital Barrier Is in a Child's Best Interests," 3 *Berkeley Women's L.J.* 96 (1987–88).

40 Levy, *supra* note 12 append. B at B-1 to B-18. Twenty years later, Levy introduced a Symposium on Property Distribution at Dissolution by identifying the four basic questions that structure the topic: "(1) Is it in fact 'property' (the identification question)? (2) Is it marital or nonmarital (the characterization question)? (3) How much is it worth (the valuation question)? (4) How much of it does each spouse get (the distribution question)?" Levy, "An Introduction to Divorce-Property Issues," 23 *Fam. L.Q.* 147 (1989).

41 Freed and Walker, *supra* note 28 at 393–94 (Table IV).

42 See "Equal versus Equitable," 5 *Equitable Distrib. J.* 73 (1988).

43 Cohen and Hillman, "Analysis of Seventy Select Decisions after Trial under New York's Equitable Distribution Law, from January 1981 through October 1984, Analyzed November 1, 1984," at 5 (unpublished manuscript) (copy on file in Kay's office). See, for a penetrating account of the New York reform effort, Marcus, "Locked In and Locked Out: Reflections on the History of Divorce Law Reform in New York State," 37 *Buffalo L. Rev.* 375 (1989).

44 Weitzman, *supra* note 26 at 104–09.

45 Glendon, *supra* note 2 at 91–94.

46 Reynolds, "The Relationship of Property Division and Alimony: The Division of Property to Address Need," 56 *Fordham L. Rev.* 827, 837–41, 866–71 (1988). Reynolds concludes, after an analysis of cases in six states that incorporate need factors into their property division statutes, that Montana has best achieved the UMDA goal of expressly preferring property division to alimony as a means of addressing need. *Id.* at 888.

47 Mitchelson v. Mitchelson, 86 N.M. 107, 110, 520 P.2d 263, 266 (1974); Cal. Civ. Code § 4800(a) (West Supp. 1989); La. Civ. Code Ann. art. 155 (West Supp. 1989).

48 Pangburn v. Pangburn, 152 Ariz. 227, 230, 731 P.2d 122, 125 (Ariz. Ct. App. 1986) ("Where an absence of sound reasons in the record would justify contrary results, apportionment of community assets upon dissolution must be substantially equal"); Welch v. Welch, 694 S.W.2d 374, 376 (Tex. Ct. App.–Houston [14th Dist.] 1985) ("While it is not required that the property be divided equally, the trial court must divide the estate in an equitable manner [cite omitted]. Such discretion is not unlimited, however, and there must be some reasonable basis for an unequal division of the property"); Idaho Code § 32-712(1) (1983).

49 Blumberg, "Marital Property Treatment of Pensions, Disability Pay, Workers' Compensation, and Other Wage Substitutes: An Insurance, or Replacement, Analysis," 33 *U.C.L.A. L. Rev.* 1250, 1251 and note 4 (1986). See also "Equal versus Equitable," *supra* note 42 at 73 (noting that while most states require only an equitable award at divorce, "in practice, however, equal division is frequently used as a starting point for settlement negotiations, and an equal division is often the expected outcome after long marriages").

50 9A U.L.A. 103 (1987); see also Krauskopf and Thomas, "Partnership Marriage:

The Solution to an Ineffective and Inequitable Law of Support," 35 *Ohio St. L.J.* 558, 586–91 (1974) (proposing a partnership family model effective during marriage). The UMPA provides a sharing principle operative at the inception of the marriage to characterize the spouses' relationship toward their property. In 1984, Wisconsin became the first common law state to adopt a version of the UMPA, thus increasing the number of community property states to nine. Act of April 4, 1984, ch. 186 § 47, 1983 Wis. Laws 1153, 1163–75 (codified at Wis. Stat. Ann. §§ 766.001–766.97 (West Supp. 1988)). See, generally, Weisberger, "The Wisconsin Marital Property Act: Highlights of the Wisconsin Experience in Developing a Model for Comprehensive Common Law Property Reform," 1 *Wis. Women's L.J.* 5 (1985).

51 Joan Krauskopf was the first legal commentator to propose that the economic theory of investment in human capital might be adapted to recognize a wife's investment in her husband's professional development upon divorce. See Krauskopf, "Recompense for Financing Spouse's Education: Legal Protection for the Marital Investor in Human Capital," 28 *U. Kan. L. Rev.* 379, 381–88 (1980).

52 Weitzman, *supra* note 26 at 388 (emphasis omitted). Weitzman defines career assets as "the tangible and intangible assets that are acquired in the course of a marriage as part of either spouse's career or career potential—pensions and retirement benefits, a professional education, license to practice a profession or trade, enhanced earning capacity, the goodwill value of a business or profession, medical and hospital insurance, and other benefits and entitlements." *Id.* at 387–88. Her fuller discussion of career assets is found *id.* at 110–42.

53 Blumberg, *supra* note 49 at 1260. She goes on to point out that a majority of jurisdictions treat all pensions, whether vested or nonvested, as property for the purpose of division on divorce; only two states restrict recognition to vested pensions; and several other states refuse to accord marital property status to pension interests when the employee-spouse is not entitled even to a cash-out value at job termination prior to retirement. *Id.* at 1260–64.

54 H. Clark, *The Law of Domestic Relations in the United States* 606 (Student ed. 1988); see also Comment, "Hanson v. Hanson, Mitchell v. Mitchell: The Division of Professional Goodwill upon Marital Dissolution," 11 *Harv. Women's L.J.* 147 (1988) (arguing that the distinction between personal and commercial goodwill drawn by some courts should be abolished and a broad definition of goodwill accepted).

55 Clark, *supra* note 54 at 606–08.

56 Blumberg, *supra* note 49 at 1279–98.

57 Freed and Walker count thirty-eight states and the District of Columbia that have addressed this issue either by case discussion or by statute. Freed and Walker, *supra* note 28 at 419 (Table VI).

58 See Kay, *supra* note 1 at 74 note 368 (citing cases from twenty-four states). More recently, the Supreme Court of Iowa has clarified its position by holding that, while the advanced degree or professional license *"in and of itself* is not an asset for property division purposes . . . , nevertheless, the future earning capacity flowing from an advanced degree or professional license is a factor to be consid-

ered in the division of property and the award of alimony." *In re* Marriage of Francis, 442 N.W.2d 59, 62 (Iowa 1989) (emphasis in original).

Two panels of the Michigan Court of Appeals are in disagreement over whether a professional degree is a marital asset. Compare Olah v. Olah, 135 Mich. App. 404, 410, 354 N.W.2d 359, 361 (1984) ("we do not adhere to the proposition that a degree is property and therefore a marital asset"), with Woodworth v. Woodworth, 126 Mich. App. 258, 260, 337 N.W.2d 332, 333–34 (1983) ("The basic issue in this case is whether or not plaintiff's law degree is marital property subject to distribution. The trial court held that it was. . . . Plaintiff contends that his law degree is not such a marital asset. We disagree").

Several other states as well have refused to characterize professional degrees or licenses as marital property. See Hoak v. Hoak, 370 S.E.2d 473, 476–77 (W. Va. 1988); Geer v. Geer, 84 N.C. App. 471, 353 S.E.2d 427 (1987); Petersen v. Petersen, 737 P.2d 237 (Utah Ct. App. 1987); Hodge v. Hodge, 513 Pa. 264, 520 A.2d 15 (1986); Helm v. Helm, 289 S.C. 169, 345 S.E.2d 720 (1986); Beeler v. Beeler, 715 S.W.2d 625 (Tenn. Ct. App. 1986); Jones v. Jones, 454 So. 2d 1006 (Ala. Civ. App. 1984). The question is currently pending before the Utah Supreme Court in the case of Martinez v. Martinez, opinion below reported at 754 P.2d 69 (Utah Ct. App. 1988), cert. granted 765 P.2d 1277 (Utah 1988).

59   *In re* Marriage of Graham, 194 Colo. 429, 432, 574 P.2d 75, 77 (1978). The Supreme Court of Colorado recently reaffirmed Graham on this point. See *In re* Marriage of Olar, 747 P.2d 676, 680 (Colo. 1987).

60   66 N.Y.2d 576, 489 N.E.2d 712, 498 N.Y.S.2d 743 (1985).

61   *Id.* 66 N.Y.2d at 583, 489 N.E.2d at 715, 498 N.Y.S.2d at 746.

62   See, e.g., Hoak v. Hoak, 370 S.E.2d 473, 476–77 (W. Va. 1988); *In re* Marriage of Olar, 747 P.2d 676, 679 n.2 (Colo. 1987); Drapek v. Drapek, 399 Mass. 240, 244–45, 503 N.E.2d 946, 949 (1987); Petersen v. Petersen, 737 P.2d 237, 241 (Utah Ct. App. 1987).

63   Kay, "An Appraisal of California's No-Fault Divorce Law," 75 *Cal. L. Rev.* 291, 314–16 (1987) ("Rather than focus on the gain enjoyed by the student spouse and attempt to enable the supporting spouse to participate in that gain as a co-owner, I suggest that we emphasize instead the loss incurred by the supporting spouse and devise rules that require the student spouse to make up that loss") (footnote omitted).

64   See *infra* text accompanying notes 205–10.

65   See Vernier and Hurlbut, "The Historical Background of Alimony Law and Its Present Statutory Structure," 6 *Law & Contemp. Probs.* 197 (1939).

66   Ellman, "The Theory of Alimony," 77 *Cal. L. Rev.* 1, 7 (1989). Some of Ellman's proposals for dealing with this "sea-change" are discussed *infra* in the text accompanying 211–16.

67   *Id.* at 7–8 (footnotes omitted). Ellman notes that while the constitution requires alimony laws to be gender-neutral, the social and economic realities are such that "alimony claims are in fact overwhelmingly brought by women against men." *Id.* at 4 note 2.

68   See e.g., *In re* Marriage of Morrison, 20 Cal. 3d 437, 573 P.2d 41, 143 Cal.

Rptr. 139 (1978) (reversing trial court's award of $400 per month for eight years, $1.00 per year for three years, then to terminate absolutely for a fifty-four-year-old wife with minimal work experience after a twenty-eight-year marriage). See, generally, Weitzman, *supra* note 26 at 164–67 (reporting her finding of a shift from permanent to transitional awards in the wake of no-fault divorce).

69   See, e.g., Lash v. Lash, 307 So. 2d 241 (Fla. Dist. Ct. App. 1975) (reversing award of nine months of rehabilitative alimony to a displaced homemaker after a twenty-six-year marriage); Comment, "Alimony in Florida: No-Fault Stops at the Courthouse Door," 28 *U. Fla. L. Rev.* 521 (1976) (arguing that retention of fault as a factor in determining the spousal support award is inconsistent with no-fault divorce grounds and should be abolished).

70   See Weitzman, *supra* note 26 at 169.

71   See cases cited in notes 68–69, *supra;* additional cases are collected in Kay, *supra* note 1 at 72 note 363. Joan Krauskopf reported in 1988 that the appellate courts had succeeded in "curbing the excesses of rehabilitative alimony" and had established a "new trend turning the course of a brutal war." Krauskopf, "Rehabilitative Alimony: Uses and Abuses of Limited Duration Alimony," 21 *Fam. L.Q.* 573 (1988).

72   Clark, *supra* note 54 at 799.

73   *Id.* at 799. Frances Olsen has traced the rise and fall of this so-called tender years presumption which favored mothers over fathers as caretakers of young children. She demonstrates that women were advantaged and disadvantaged both theoretically and practically by the creation of this presumption as well as by its demise. Olsen, "The Politics of Family Law," 2 *Law & Ineq.* 1, 12–19 (1984).

74   See Clark, *supra* note 54 at 799–800; Freed and Walker, *supra* note 30 at 522 ("the tender years doctrine has lost ground and is rejected or relegated to a role of 'tie-breaker' in most states").

75   Compare Comment, "The Tender Years Presumption: Is It Presumably Unconstitutional?" 21 *San Diego L. Rev.* 861 (1984) (unconstitutional), with Klaff, "The Tender Years Doctrine: A Defense," 70 *Cal. L. Rev.* 335 (1982) (constitutional).

76   Compare Chambers, "Rethinking the Substantive Rules for Custody Disputes in Divorce," 83 *Mich. L. Rev.* 477, 515–24 (1984) (hereafter "Rethinking") (concluding, after reviewing empirical evidence favoring mothers as custodians because they are women, that "the inclination toward a maternal preference should probably be resisted"), with Fineman and Opie, "The Use of Social Science Data in Legal Policymaking: Custody Determinations at Divorce," 1987 *Wis. L. Rev.* 107, 123 (defending mother custody in general as a "proper result, supported by the real life choices and preferences of the vast number of people" and criticizing Chambers's position as "pro-father"—a charge he vehemently denies. See Chambers, "The Abuses of Social Science: A Response to Fineman and Opie," 1987 *Wis. L. Rev.* 159, 160–61).

77   See, e.g., Uniform Marriage and Divorce Act § 402 (1973). Freed and Walker report that thirty-one states and the District of Columbia have statutory custody guidelines. See Freed and Walker, *supra* note 28 at 467 (Table IX).

78   Mnookin, "Child-Custody Adjudication: Judicial Functions in the Face of In-

determinacy," 39 *Law & Contemp. Probs.* 226, 255–62 (Summer 1975). Others agree. See Elster, "Solomonic Judgments: Against the Best Interest of the Child," 54 *U. Chi. L. Rev.* 1, 11–28 (1987); Chambers, "Rethinking," *supra* note 76 at 480–86.

79   J. Goldstein, A. Freud, and A. Solnit, *Beyond the Best Interests of the Child* 53 (1973) ("The least detrimental alternative . . . is that specific placement and procedure for placement which maximizes, in accord with the child's sense of time and on the basis of short-term predictions given the limitations of knowledge, his or her opportunity for being wanted and for maintaining on a continuous basis a relationship with at least one adult who is or will become his psychological parent"). Mnookin agrees that a court should prefer a psychological parent over any claimant (including a natural parent) who is a stranger to the child. Mnookin, *supra* note 78 at 282. He doubts, however, that this test is preferable to the best interests standard, because he does not think that "existing psychological theories provide the basis to choose generally between two adults where the child has some relationship and psychological attachment to each." *Id.* at 286–87.

80   See Neely, "The Primary Caretaker Parent Rule: Child Custody and the Dynamics of Greed," 3 *Yale L. & Pol'y Rev.* 168 (1984). Chief Justice Neely authored the opinion for the West Virginia Court of Appeals that first adopted the primary caretaker rule; Garska v. McCoy, 278 S.E.2d 357 (W. Va. 1981). The rule has since been adopted in Minnesota, see Pikula v. Pikula, 374 N.W.2d 705 (Minn. 1985), and rejected over a dissent in North Dakota, see Gravning v. Gravning, 389 N.W.2d 621 (N.D. 1986). Gravning is discussed in O'Kelly, "Blessing the Tie That Binds: Preference for the Primary Caretaker as Custodian," 63 *N.D. L. Rev.* 481 (1987) (recommending at 533–54 that North Dakota adopt a "weak" version of the primary caretaker rule: a weighted preference for the primary caretaker as custodian). Other states consider the primary caretaker's relationship with the child as one factor in the custody decision. See, e.g., Tuttle and Tuttle, 62 Or. App. 281, 285–86, 660 P.2d 196, 199 (1983) (identity of the primary parent is a relevant and important, but not dispositive, consideration in custody decisions); *In re* Maxwell, 8 Ohio App. 3d 302, 306, 456 N.E.2d 1218, 1222 (1982) (while the Ohio statute precludes the court from according a "presumptive quality" to the primary caretaker rule, "it is a factor which must be given strong consideration as it bears on the child's interaction and interrelationship with his parents, as well as the child's adjustment to his home"). Chambers concludes, after reviewing the available empirical research, that there is no solid foundation for concluding that children, even young children, either will or will not be better off if placed with the primary caretaker. Chambers, "Rethinking," *supra* note 76 at 560–62. He nevertheless recommends legislative adoption of a preference for placing young children (roughly between six months and five years) with the primary caretaker, unless the other parent demonstrates by clear and convincing evidence that he or she is the more appropriate custodian. *Id.* at 563.

81   See Cook, "Joint Custody, Sole Custody: A New Statute Reflects a New Perspective," 18 *Conciliation Cts. Rev.* 31 (1980), reprinted in *Joint Custody and*

Shared Parenting 168 (J. Folberg ed. 1984) (discussing the California joint custody statute).

82   See *supra* note 31. The statutes vary enormously. See Folberg, "Issues and Trends in the Law of Joint Custody," in Folberg, ed., *supra* note 81 at 159.

83   Chambers supports joint physical custody arrangements that are based on mutual agreement of the parents, but he recommends that legislatures act to deprive courts of the power to impose joint custody over the objections of one or both parents. Chambers, "Rethinking," *supra* note 76 at 565–66.

84   See McKinnon and Wallerstein, "Joint Custody and the Preschool Child," 25 *Conciliation Cts. Rev.* 39 (December 1987); Steinman, "Joint Custody: What We Know, What We Have Yet to Learn, and the Judicial and Legislative Implications," 16 *U.C. Davis L. Rev.* 739 (1983).

85   Compare Bartlett and Stack, "Joint Custody, Feminism and the Dependency Dilemma," 2 *Berkeley Women's L.J.* 9 (1986), with Schulman and Pitt, "Second Thoughts on Joint Child Custody: Analysis of Legislation and Its Implications for Women and Children," 12 *Golden Gate U.L. Rev.* 539 (1982). See also Singer and Reynolds, "A Dissent on Joint Custody," 47 *Md. L. Rev.* 497 (1988).

86   Schepard, "Taking Children Seriously: Promoting Cooperative Custody after Divorce," 64 *Tex. L. Rev.* 687, 752 (1985).

87   Cal. Civ. Code § 4607 (West Supp. 1989).

88   Judge King reported San Francisco's experience prior to the enactment of mandatory mediation. See King, "Handling Custody and Visitation Disputes under the New Mandatory Mediation Law," 2 *Cal. Law.* 40, 41 (Jan. 1982) (noting that the San Francisco Superior Court routinely heard between five and fifteen contested custody/visitation cases on each calendar day for order to show cause hearings prior to February 1977, when the court began its program of mandatory mediation; after that date, the number of contested cases declined dramatically, with only five contested cases heard in 1980 and three through November 1981). More recent self-reported data from the California conciliation courts indicate that partial or full agreement is reached in 62% of the matters referred to mandatory mediation: Los Angeles County reports a reduction from 11% to 2% in the number of contested custody trials during the last three months of 1982. See *Report of the Advisory Panel on the Child Oriented Divorce Act of 1987,* at 26 (Special Report on California's Mandatory Divorce Mediation Program Submitted to Senator Alan Robbins, April 1987) (hereafter *Report on Child Oriented Divorce Act*).

89   Bruch, "And How Are the Children? The Effects of Ideology and Mediation on Child Custody Law and Children's Well-Being in the United States," 2 *Int'l J.L. & Fam.* 106, 116–21 (1988).

90   *Id.* at 121.

91   An unrelated but contemporaneous legal reform, however, reduced the duration of child support awards in many states. In 1971, the states ratified the Twenty-sixth Amendment to the U.S. Constitution, which lowered the voting age to eighteen. Influenced by this change, most states reduced the age of majority from twenty-one to eighteen, a development that resulted in the termination of support for many college-age children whose parents were divorced.

Judith Wallerstein and Shauna Corbin have reported that even affluent fathers fully capable of continuing to support their college-age children after majority refrain from doing so, in the belief that they have satisfied their legal obligations to their children by paying the full amount of court-ordered support. Wallerstein and Corbin, "Father-Child Relationships after Divorce: Child Support and Educational Opportunity," 20 *Fam. L.Q.* 109, 118–21 (1986). Efforts to restore the age of support to twenty-one for educational purposes have proved controversial; see also Moore, "Parents' Support Obligations to Their Adult Children," 19 *Akron L. Rev.* 183 (1985) (arguing that laws extending a support obligation only to divorced parents are unfair); Comment, "In Support of Education: An Examination of the Parental Obligation to Provide Postsecondary Education in California," 18 *Pac, L.J.* 377 (1987).

92   Child Support Enforcement Amendments of 1984, Pub. L. 98-378, 98 Stat. 1305 (amending tit. 4, pt. D of the Social Security Act, codified at 42 U.S.C. §§ 651–667 (1982 and Supp. IV 1986)).

93   45 C.F.R. § 302.56(c) (1988). The regulations were issued by the Federal Office of Child Support Enforcement. Diane Dodson has described the major types of support guidelines that have been adopted pursuant to this mandate. Dodson, "A Guide to the Guidelines," 10 *Fam. Advoc.* 4 (Spring 1988). These include the equal living standards model, which is designed to ensure the achievement of an equal standard of living between the custodial and non-custodial households; the income shares model, which is based on an economic analysis of the amount spent on children by parents in intact families, varied by income level; and several influential models developed by the states of Wisconsin, Massachusetts, and Delaware.

94   The Family Support Act of 1988, tit. 1, § 103, Pub. L. 100–485, 102 Stat. 2343, 2346 (amending 42 U.S.C. § 667).

95   Bruch, "Problems Inherent in Designing Child Support Guidelines," in *Essentials of Child Support Guidelines Development: Economic Issues and Policy Considerations* (Office of Child Support Enforcement, May 1987) (Proceedings of the Women's Legal Defense Fund National Conference on the Development of Child Support Guidelines, Queenstown, Maryland, September 1986). Bruch's evaluation is an important theoretical and practical contribution to the current debate over child support guidelines.

96   Weitzman, *supra* note 26 at 262; see also Bruch and Wikler, "The Economic Consequences," 36 *Juv. & Fam. Ct. J.* 5 (Fall 1985) (Special Issue on Child Support Enforcement).

97   See *supra* note 92.

98   See, generally, Clark, *supra* note 54 at 735–39.

99   The Family Support Act, *supra* note 94 (amending 42 U.S.C. § 666). This provision is subject to a contrary agreement between the spouses.

100 Weitzman, *supra* note 26.

101 See, e.g., Friedan, "How to Get the Women's Movement Moving Again," *New York Times Magazine,* November 3, 1985, at 26.

102 Melli, "Constructing a Social Problem: The Post-Divorce Plight of Women and Children," 1986 *Am. B. Found. Res. J.* 759, 761 and note 4. She observes

that Weitzman's successful transformation of data documenting the traditional and continued inadequacy of financial awards at divorce into a major social problem illustrates the proposition that destructive social conditions become social problems because they reinforce the ideology of some substantial part of the population.

103   Cal. S. Res. 28, 1985–86 Reg. Sess. § 4.

104   Herbert Jacob has identified the process that enabled the California no-fault divorce law to make its way through the legislature in the late 1960s with little public notice or debate. He theorizes that this process represents a distinctive form of policy-making, which he calls "routine" policy processes, and he believes that it explains the rapid spread of the no-fault concept across the country during the last twenty years. H. Jacob, *Silent Revolution: The Transformation of Divorce Law in the United States* 11–15, 43–61, 80–103 (1988). As Jacob predicted, *id.* at 164–65, however, it is unlikely that the California legislature will enjoy similar anonymity while responding to Weitzman's findings, given the focused public attention discussed *supra* in the text at notes 101–02.

105   *Final Report of the Senate Task Force on Family Equity,* at P-2 (June 1, 1987) (hereafter *Family Equity Report*).

106   *Id.* at P-3. The Task Force suggested, however, that the legislature might wish to consider these propositions at a future time "if legislation aimed at correcting the inequities of the current system does not prove effective."

107   Other commentators have undertaken this task. See, e.g., Jacob, *supra* note 104 at 159–64; Jacob, "Another Look at No-Fault Divorce and the Post-Divorce Finances of Women," 23 *L. & Soc'ty Rev.* 95 (1989); Singer, "Divorce Reform and Gender Justice," 67 *No. Car. L. Rev.* 1103 (1989); Melli, *supra* note 102 at 768–70.

108   The Task Force held one public hearing on October 16, 1986, received oral and written testimony from respondents across California, and reviewed reports, studies, legislation, and recommendations from family law experts in California and elsewhere.

109   *Family Equity Report, supra* note 105 at P-3.

110   Lauerman, Book Review, 2 *Berkeley Women's L.J.* 246, 250 (1986).

111   Weitzman, *supra* note 26 at 395–98. As I have noted elsewhere, this recommendation is consistent with the 1966 proposal of the California Governor's Commission on the Family for the creation of a family court. See Kay, *supra* note 63 at 310, note 155.

112   *Family Equity Report, supra* note 105 at II-4.

113   S.B. 1209 (Roberti), 1987–88 reg. ess., 1987 Cal. Stat. ch. 1134 (codified at Cal. Gov't Code § 68553 (West Supp. 1989)). Section 1 of chapter 1134, which is not codified, indicates the legislature's intent that the training program for judges be at least thirty hours per year. Other Task Force recommendations—such as improving working conditions for family law judges, providing additional resources for family courts, a uniform state-administered court personnel system, and the collection of family law statistics—have not yet been implemented.

114   See *Family Equity Report, supra* note 105 at III-3. Weitzman's proposal is
      discussed *supra* in the text accompanying note 52.
115   Pensions, goodwill, and other retirement benefits are recognized as communi-
      ty property if acquired after marriage. See Kay, *supra* note 63 at 305.
116   *Family Equity Report, supra* note 105 at III-2 to III-9.
117   66 N.Y.2d 576, 489 N.E.2d 712, 498 N.Y.S.2d 743 (1985). O'Brien is dis-
      cussed *supra* in the text at notes 60–62.
118   *Family Equity Report, supra* note 105 at III-9. As the Task Force recognized, the
      implementation of these recommendations would require the legislature to
      repeal Cal. Civ. Code § 4800.3 (West Supp. 1989), enacted in 1984, which
      requires only that the community be reimbursed for community expenditures
      toward a spouse's education and training under certain circumstances.
119   See text at note 62, *supra*. A Canadian writer reports that the Supreme Court
      of Ontario cited O'Brien favorably in a 1987 decision awarding a wife $30,000
      for her contribution to her husband's dental practice. Bissett-Johnson and
      Newell, "Professional Degrees in Marital Property: Canadian Developments,"
      15 *Community Prop. J.* 63, 76 (1988) (discussing the unreported case of Car-
      atun v. Caratun).
120   See, e.g., Batts, "Remedy Refocus: In Search of Equity in 'Enhanced
      Spouse/Other Spouse' Divorces," 63 *N.Y.U.L. Rev.* 751 (1988) (concluding
      that, while enhanced earning capacity is a marital asset subject to distribution
      upon divorce, the enhanced spouse should compensate the other spouse for his
      or her contribution, but thereafter should realize any excess postdivorce gain
      resulting from the enhancement); Schuleter and Gott, "The 'Diploma Dilem-
      ma': Whether a Professional Degree or License Should Be Treated as a Marital
      Asset on Divorce," 15 *Community Prop. J.* 28, 43–46 (1988) (arguing that a
      professional degree or license should be treated as property, and proposing a
      model statute that allocates educational debts to the degreed spouse; returns
      out-of-pocket contributions, plus adjustments for interest and inflation, to the
      supporting spouse; and provides for an award to the supporting spouse of up
      to 50% of the degreed spouse's expected incremental earnings under certain
      circumstances); Ellman, *supra* note 66 at 65–71 (rejecting a property charac-
      terization and instead proposing a reformulation of alimony that would permit
      some, but not all, claims by supporting spouses); Kay, *supra* note 63 at 311–15
      (rejecting property characterization in favor of rule designed to require stu-
      dent spouse to make up the loss suffered by the supporting spouse).
121   Weitzman, *supra* note 26 at 84. She found that the "number of cases in which
      there was an explicit order to sell the home rose from about one in ten in 1968,
      to about *one in three* in 1977." *Id.* at 78.
122   *Id.* at 83 (discussing cases).
123   The first case so holding was *In re* Marriage of Boseman, 31 Cal. App. 3d 372,
      107 Cal. Rptr. 232 (1973) (affirming order authorizing wife to live with the
      children in the family home until the youngest child reached majority in a case
      where the home was the only asset of the community). The Boseman court
      relied on a California legislative report, written two months after the no-fault

divorce law became effective, which indicated that the legislative intent expressed in Cal. Civ. Code § 4800(b)(1) (West 1970) authorized deferral of a sale of the family home if an immediate sale would be "unnecessarily destructive of the economic and social circumstances of the parties and their children." Cal. Assembly Comm. on Judiciary, Report on A.B. 530 and S.B. 252 (the Family Law Act), 1 Assembly J. 785, 787 (1970). Subsequent cases further developed this practice, and ultimately the court in *In re* Marriage of Duke, 101 Cal. App. 3d 152, 155, 161 Cal. Rptr. 444, 446 (1980), prescribed the following balancing test for determining when sale of the family home should be deferred: "Where adverse economic, emotional and social impacts on minor children and the custodial parent which would result from an immediate loss of a long established family home are not outweighed by economic detriment to the noncustodial party, the court shall, upon request, reserve jurisdiction and defer sale on appropriate conditions." The Duke court rejected the limitation imposed by earlier cases that deferral of the sale should be based solely on an economic support basis and instead broadened the scope of the award to include the listed noneconomic factors.

124   Act Relating to Family Law, ch. 463, 1984 Cal. Stat. 1927 (formerly codified at Cal. Civ. Code § 4800.7), repealed by Act Relating to Family Law, ch. 730, § 2, 1988 Cal. Legis. Serv. 1661, 1663 (West).

125   *Family Equity Report, supra* note 105 at IV-4.

126   S.B. 1341 (Hart and Watson), 1987–88 reg. sess., 1988 Cal. Stat. 1661, (West) 1662 ch. 729, § 1 (codified at Cal. Civ. Code § 4700.10 (West Supp. 1989)). Economic feasibility refers to the ability "to maintain the payments of any note secured by a deed of trust, property taxes, insurance for the home during the period the sale of the home is deferred" and to maintain "the condition of the home comparable to that at the time of trial." In making this determination, the trial court is required to consider "the resident parent's income, the availability of spousal support, child support, or both spousal and child support, and any other sources of funds available to make those payments." The legislature declared that its intent in setting these guidelines was "to avoid the likelihood of possible defaults on the payments of notes and resulting foreclosures, to avoid inadequate insurance coverage, to prevent deterioration of the condition of the family home, and to prevent any other circumstance which would jeopardize both parents' equity in the home."

127   The ten factors listed in Cal. Civ. Code § 4700.10(b) (West Supp. 1989) are:

(1) The length of time the child has resided in the home.

(2) The child's placement or grade in school.

(3) The accessibility and convenience of the home to the child's school and other services or facilities used by and available to the child, including child care.

(4) Whether the home has been adapted or modified to accommodate any physical disabilities of a child or a resident parent in a manner such that a change in residence may adversely affect the ability of the resident parent to meet the needs of the child.

(5) The emotional detriment to the child associated with a change in residence.

(6) The extent to which the location of the home permits the resident parent to continue his or her employment.

(7) The financial ability of each parent to obtain suitable housing.

(8) The tax consequences to the parents.

(9) The economic detriment to the nonresident parent in the event of a deferred sale of home order.

(10) Any other factors the court deems just and equitable.

128 Cal. Civ. Code § 4700.10(e)(2) (West Supp. 1989).

129 Weitzman, *supra* note 26 at 381.

130 *Family Equity Report, supra* note 105 at IV-9.

131 Cal. S.B. 1750, 1985–86 Reg. Sess. S.B. 1750 failed passage in the Senate Judiciary Committee. See Cal. Sen. Daily J. 5564 (1985–86); see also *infra* note 134.

132 *Family Equity Report, supra* note 105 at IV-8.

133 See *supra* text accompanying notes 125–28.

134 Weitzman, *supra* note 26 at 387.

135 See Family Law Act of 1969, ch. 1608, tit. 6, 1969 Cal. Stat. 3312, 3333; current version at Cal. Civ. Code § 4801(a) (West Supp. 1989).

136 Weitzman, *supra* note 26 at 213; see also *supra* text accompanying notes 70–71, discussing Weitzman's findings documenting the shift from permanent to temporary awards.

137 *Family Equity Report, supra* note 131 at V-8.

138 *Id.*

139 Weitzman, *supra* note 26 at 339 (reporting that one year after divorce men's postdivorce standard of living has increased by 42% while that of women has declined by 73%). The accuracy of the magnitude of the postdivorce change Weitzman reports has been disputed. See Hoffman and Duncan, "What Are the Economic Consequences of Divorce?" 25 *Demography* 641 (1988).

140 *Family Equity Report, supra* note 105 at V-8.

141 *Id.*

142 *Id.* at V-9 to V-10. The report cites *In re* Marriage of Brantner, 67 Cal. App. 3d 416, 420, 136 Cal. Rptr. 635, 637 (1977), which had pointedly informed trial court judges that "the husband simply has to face up to the fact that his support responsibilities are going to be of extended duration—perhaps for life." The Brantners had been married for twenty-five years.

143 *Family Equity Report, supra* note 105 at V-10 to V-12.

144 *Id.* at V-12 to V-14. See also *infra* note 151.

145 *Id.* at V-14 to V-15.

146 *Id.* This recommendation was not embodied in a bill. See *infra* note 152.

147 *Family Equity Report, supra* note 105 at V-15 to V-16.

148 S.B. 1296 (Hart), 1987–88 reg. sess., 1988 Cal. Stat. ch. 407 (amending Cal. Civ. Code § 4801 (West Supp. 1989)). Senator Hart inserted a letter of intent into the Senate Journal indicating that "SB 1296 does not, and is not,

intended to establish the marital standard of living as a mandatory 'floor' or 'ceiling' for a spousal support award." Cal. Sen. Daily J. 7791 (daily ed. August 24, 1988). The bill also changes existing law by requiring the court to take account of the "extent to which the supported spouse contributed to the attainment of an education, training, a career position, or a license by the other spouse" in determining whether a spousal support award should be granted rather than merely in determining the supported spouse's capacity for self-support. Cal. Civ. Code § 4801 (West Supp. 1989).

149   S.B. 907 (Lockyer), 1987–88 reg. sess., § 2, 1987 Cal. Stat. ch. 1086 (amending Cal. Civ. Code § 4801(d) (West Supp. 1989)). The provision quoted in the text applies except upon written agreement by the parties to the contrary,

150   *Id.* The statutory presumption is qualified by the following three sentences: "However, the court may consider periods of separation during the marriage in determining whether the marriage is in fact of long duration. Nothing in this section precludes a court from determining that a marriage of less than 10 years is a marriage of long duration. Nothing in this section limits the court's discretion to terminate spousal support in subsequent proceedings upon a showing of changed circumstances." *Id.* In view of these qualifications, the Task Force recommendation that the length of a marriage of long duration be left to court interpretation may have been substantially preserved.

151   S.B. 1615 (Marks), 1987–88 reg. sess. (vetoed September 30, 1988). The governor's veto message indicated his concern "that this legislation is ambiguous and lacks definition in many important areas. Among the unanswered questions arising from this measure are what is intended by the phrase 'commensurate with . . . age and standard of living,' whether the spouse would be required to seek some level of employment if none commensurate with the prior standard of living is available, and what is meant by a party's 'ability to find' employment." Messages from the Governor, Cal. Sen. Daily J. 8416 (daily ed. October 5, 1988).

152   S.B. 1614 (Marks), 1987–88 reg. sess., 1988 Cal. Legis. Serv. 2237 (West) Cal. Stat., ch. 969, (codified as amending Cal. Civ. Code § 4801.6 (West Supp. 1989) and Cal. Civ. Pro. Code § 1218 (West Supp. 1989)). This measure contains a provision inserted at the request of the Association of District Attorneys making clear that no additional enforcement or collection duties are imposed upon district attorneys. This proviso undercuts the Task Force recommendation expanding the enforcement responsibility of district attorneys in the area of spousal support. See also text at note 146, *supra.*

153   Weitzman, *supra* note 26 at 262–322.

154   *Id.* at 391–93.

155   See *Family Equity Report, supra* note 105 at VI-1 to VI-5.

156   Cal. Civ. Code §§ 4720–4732 (West Supp. 1989).

157   Cal. Civ. Code § 4701 (West Supp. 1989).

158   *Family Equity Report, supra* note 105 at VI-2.

159   *Id.* at VI-4 to VI-5 (noting that delinquent child support payments in California at the end of 1986 totaled $1.25 billion, a figure that includes only cases on file with district attorneys' offices).

160   *Id.* at VI-6 to VI-9. The report stresses that this recommendation would not affect the legal rights of young adults between eighteen and twenty-one since its proposal is limited to increasing the age of support. The report does, however, state that in order to be entitled to support, a person between eighteen and twenty-one "must also submit to parental control and custody." *Id.* at VI-9.

161   Cal. S.B. 215 (Watson and Marks) 1987–88 reg. sess.

162   A.B. 2840 (Harris), 1987–88 reg. sess. § 2, 1988 Cal. 1988 Cal. Legis. Serv. 473, 474 (West) Stat., ch. 153, codified at Cal. Civ. Code § 4704.5 (West Supp. 1989). Compare Cal. Civ. Code § 196.5 (West Supp. 1989).

163   The Task Force recommended that the treatment of expenses and support for children of first and second families be equalized. *Family Equity Report, supra* note 105 at VI-10 to VI-14. The legislature responded to this proposal by enacting S.B. 1588 (Hart), 1987–88 reg. sess., 1987 Cal. Stat. ch. 964 (amending Cal. Civ. Code §§ 4721, 4725 (West Supp. 1989)); A.B. 2840 (Harris), 1957–88 reg. sess. §§ 2, 3, 1988 Cal. Stat. ch. 153 (adding Cal. Civ. Code § 4705.5 (West Supp. 1989) and amending Cal. Civ. Code § 4721 (West Supp. 1989); S.B. 2573 (Hart), 1987–88 reg. sess. § 1, 1988 Cal. Stat. ch. 1295 (amending Cal. Civ. Code § 4725 (West Supp. 1989)).

164   The legislature implemented Task Force recommendations concerning review of an official booklet regarding the collection of child and spousal support; see S.B. 907 (Lockyer), 1987–88 reg. sess. § 4, 1987 Cal. Stat. ch. 1086 (amending Cal. Welf. & Inst. Code § 11475.5 (West Supp. 1989)), and mandatory security deposits for child support payments in cases where the obligor was not subject to an enforceable wage assignment order; see S.B. 906 (Lockyer), 1987–88 reg. sess., 1987 Cal. Stat. ch. 1389 (codified at Cal. Civ. Code § 4701.1 (West Supp. 1989)). No legislation has yet been introduced to implement two other Task Force recommendations, one designed to clarify that the simplified 10% modification procedure contained in Cal. Civ. Code § 4700.1 (West Supp. 1989) applies only to increases and not to decreases; see *Family Equity Report, supra* note 105 at VI-16 to VI-19, the second dealing with joint custody, see *id.* at VI-22 to VI-27.

165   Weitzman, *supra* note 26 at 225.

166   Act Relating to Child Custody, 1979 Cal. Stat. ch. 915 (codified as amended at Cal. Civ. Code §§ 4600, 4600.5 (West Supp. 1989)).

167   Weitzman, *supra* note 26 at 250.

168   *Id.* at 257–58.

169   *Id.* at 394.

170   *Family Equity Report, supra* note 105 at VII-3 to VII-7.

171   Cal. S.B. 2047 (Marks), 1985–86 reg. sess.

172   *Family Equity Report, supra* note 105 at VII-6.

173   *Id.* at VII-5 (citing oral testimony of Nancy Lemon, Esq., and written testimony of Del Martin); see also Germane, Johnson, and Lemon, "Mandatory Custody Mediation and Joint Custody Orders in California: The Dangers for Victims of Domestic Violence," 1 *Berkeley Women's L.J.* 175, 195–98 (1985).

174   *Id.* at VII-6.

175   Cal. S.B. 377 (McCorquodale), 1987–88 reg. sess., failed passage in the

Assembly Judiciary Committee. Cal. Civ. Code § 4608 (West Supp. 1989) contains a similar independent corroboration requirement for allegations of child abuse.

176 *Family Equity Report, supra* note 105 at VII-7.

177 *Id.* at VII-10.

178 S.B. 1306 (Morgan and Seymour), 1987–88 reg. sess., 1988 Cal. Stat. ch. 1442 (codified at Cal. Code § 4600(d) (West Supp. 1989)).

179 See *Family Equity Report, supra* note 105 at VII-8 to VII-9.

180 *Family Equity Report, supra* note 105 at VII-14. The report notes that one Task Force member, Judith Wallerstein, believed such a presumption should apply only to infants aged two years or younger. Her view is consistent with her research. See McKinnon and Wallerstein, *supra* note 84 at 46 (noting that "one of the most surprising findings in this study [a longitudinal study of twenty-five families with children aged fourteen months to five years] was that the *children below the age of 3* seemed well able to handle the many transitions of the joint custody arrangement, whereas the *3, 5 year olds seemed to have more difficulty*").

181 The Task Force identified a need for research to evaluate the impact on children of court-imposed and mediation-influenced joint custody arrangements. *Family Equity Report, supra* note 105 at VII-14 to VII-16. Wallerstein formulated several questions that such a study might address. These are included in Appendix B of the report. A well-designed study of these matters would indeed be useful.

182 Cal. Civ. Code § 4607(a) (West Supp. 1989).

183 *Family Equity Report, supra* note 105 at VII-16 to VII-17 (quoting the *Report on Child Oriented Divorce Act, supra* note 88).

184 S.B. 2510 (Robbins), 1987–88 reg. sess. § 6, 1988 Cal. Stat. ch. 1550 (amending Cal. Civ. Code § 4607(a) (West Supp. 1989)).

185 *Family Equity Report, supra* note 105 at VII-18 to VII-23.

186 Cal. S.B. 2513 (Robbins) 1987–88 reg. sess. (vetoed September 26, 1988; veto message at Cal. Sen. Daily J. 8382 (daily ed. October 5, 1988). Other recommended safeguards included an exemption from mediation for cases involving a history of spouse or child abuse, and a provision designed to reduce the influence of mediator bias by allowing a party to challenge a mediator without cause or prejudice and continue mediation with another mediator. Senator Robbins's bill, S.B. 2511, 1987–88 reg. sess., would have provided special training for mediators relevant in cases involving domestic violence and would have required the Judicial Council to develop written guidelines and a definition of the term *history* for purposes of determining a history of domestic violence. S.B. 2511 was enacted, but vetoed by the governor on September 13, 1988, for budgetary reasons. See Cal. Sen. Daily J. 8335 (daily ed. September 16, 1988) (governor's veto message).

187 *Family Equity Report, supra* note 105 at VII-17 to VII-18. This recommendation was implemented by S.B. 907 (Lockyer), 1987–88 reg. sess. § 1, 1987 Cal. Stat. ch. 1086 (codified at Cal. Civ. Code § 4607(a) (West Supp. 1989)).

188 J. Wallerstein and S. Blakeslee, *Second Chances: Men, Women and Children a Decade after Divorce* xi (1989).

189 Ira Ellman has proposed the expansion of tort doctrine to permit a wider range of claims by former spouses against each other for harm inflicted during the marriage. Such claims would not lie to assess blame for marital failure, but rather would permit recovery under circumstances enabling strangers to sue each other. Ellman reasons that an overt recognition that a tort recovery may be appropriate might reduce the tendency of judges to take such harm into account in dividing property or awarding support in the divorce proceeding. Ellman, "Implementing the Theory of Alimony: Of Presumptions, Fault, and Tort Claims" (unpublished manuscript on file in Kay's office). I think Ellman's idea is promising, but I suggest that the tort action not be joined with the divorce proceeding. Consolidation of the two claims might defeat Ellman's purpose in eliminating the last vestiges of marital fault from the financial calculus he refers to as alimony. See Ellman, *supra* note 66. See, generally, "Tort Claims against Spouses," 6 *Eq. Distrib. J.* 37 (April 1989).

190 Marcus, "Locked In and Locked Out: Reflections on the History of Divorce Law Reform in New York State," 37 *Buf. L. Rev.* 375 (1989).

191 J. Bernard, *The Future of Marriage* 3–53 (1972).

192 The emergence of the modern women's movement occurred roughly with the publication of Betty Friedan's book, *The Feminine Mystique,* in 1963. See M. Carden, *The New Feminist Movement* 154 (1974).

193 See B. Friedan, *The Second Stage* 15–41 (1981); C. Orsborn, *Enough Is Enough: Exploding the Myth of Having It All* (1986).

194 See, generally, S. Hewlett, *A Lesser Life: The Myth of Women's Liberation in America* (1986).

195 See Taub, "From Parental Leaves to Nurturing Leaves," 13 *N.Y.U. Rev. L. & Soc. Change* 381 (1984–85); Note, "H.R. 4300, The Family and Medical Leave Act of 1986: Congress' Response to the Changing American Family," 35 *Clev. St. L. Rev.* 455 (1987).

196 See *supra* note 139.

197 One writer argues that women tend to lose value on the marriage market more rapidly than men, with increased age, loss of attractiveness, and presence of children counting as negative factors. See Cohen, "Marriage, Divorce, and Quasi-Rents: Or, 'I Gave Him the Best Years of My Life,'" 16 *J. Legal Stud.* 267, 278–87 (1987). If this observation is accurate, remarriage may be difficult for many women.

198 Cronan, "Marriage," in *Notes from the Third Year: Women's Liberation* 62, 65 (1971).

199 See, e.g., *Rethinking the Family: Some Feminist Questions* (B. Thorne and M. Yalom eds. 1982); Kay, *supra* note 1 at 80–89; Olsen, "The Family and the Market: A Study of Ideology and Legal Reform," 96 *Harv. L. Rev.* 1497 (1983).

200 Judith Wallerstein, in her ten-year follow-up study of divorcing couples in Marin County, California, reports, "Divorce is deceptive. Legally it is a single event, but psychologically it is a chain—sometimes a never-ending chain—of

events, relocations, and radically shifting relationships strung through time, a process that forever changes the lives of the people involved." Wallerstein and Blakeslee, *supra* note 188 at xii; see also *id.* at 277–94 (outlining the psychological tasks of divorce).

201   R. Bellah, R. Madsen, W. Sullivan, A. Swidler, and S. Tipton, *Habits of the Heart: Individualism and Commitment in American Life* 90–93 (1985) (noting that Americans believe in love as the basis for enduring commitments in marriage, and observing that this belief creates a dilemma for Americans who perceive a tension between the desire for sharing with a loved one and the felt need for individual freedom).

202   Compare Prager, "Sharing Principles and the Future of Marital Property Law," 25 *U.C.L.A. L. Rev.* 1, 11–14 (1977). See also Waldron, *supra* note 37 at 647 (pointing out that "having something to fall back on if an attachment fails may be a *condition* of being able to identify intensely with one's attachments, rather than something which derogates from that intensity").

203   See *supra* text accompanying note 50.

204   See, generally, Bruch, "The Definition and Division of Marital Property in California: Towards Parity and Simplicity," 33 *Hastings L.J.* 769 (1982) (discussing this and other reforms).

205   See *supra* note 63.

206   I read Deborah Batts's recent proposal as consistent with my approach. See Batts, *supra* note 120 at 784–97.

207   See *supra* text accompanying notes 57–62.

208   Joan Krauskopf has proposed the use of a nonmodifiable monetary award, such as in gross maintenance, as "the most justifiable way in which to recompense a spouse who has contributed to the other spouse's increased earning capacity." Krauskopf, *supra* note 51 at 401. As indicated in the text, I am working along the same general lines, but I differ from Krauskopf in believing that we will gain flexibility by retaining the modifiability characteristic of traditional alimony while eliminating its termination dates.

209   See Mahoney v. Mahoney, 91 N.J. 488, 502–03, 453 A.2d 527, 535 (1982) (creating "reimbursement alimony" to reimburse one spouse for monetary contributions to the other spouse's professional education when the contributions were made "with the mutual and shared expectation that both parties to the marriage will derive increased income and material benefits" as a result of the professional practice). More recently, a lower New Jersey court has indicated that since reimbursement alimony, unlike traditional alimony, looks to the past contributions of a spouse rather than to future needs, it normally should not terminate on remarriage. Reiss v. Reiss, 200 N.J. Super. 122, 490 A.2d 378 (N.J. Super. Ct. Ch. Div. 1984) (denying husband's motion to terminate former wife's reimbursement alimony when she remarried after having received only two monthly payments of $1,500 each toward a total award of $46,706.50), *aff'd in part and rev'd in part on other grounds,* 205 N.J. Super. 41, 500 A.2d 24 (N.J. Super. Ct. App. Div. 1985).

210   See Ellman, *supra* note 66.

211   *Id.* at 53–71. Ellman's theory also permits a homemaker spouse to claim half

the value of her lost earning capacity, even though it exceeds the market value of her domestic services, when these services included primary responsibility for the care of children. *Id.* at 71–73.

212 *Id.* at 65.

213 Ellman argues that such a limitation on recovery will eliminate otherwise distorting market pressures. He reasons, "some spouses would invest in their partner when they should instead invest in themselves because the investment in their partner would be risk-free. After the fact, when the investment has soured, the existence of a claim would encourage divorce, because the spouse could then recover her loss, while, if she remained married, she could not." *Id.* at 68. This limitation is itself qualified by Ellman's recognition that any recovery is necessarily subject to the husband's ability to pay. But if the investment has really soured, that qualification might reduce the divorce incentive to the vanishing point.

214 Ellman, *supra* note 66 at 69; see also *supra* note 211.

215 Ellman, *supra* note 66 at 70.

216 *Id.* at 70.

217 See *supra* text accompanying notes 177–78.

218 See Kay, *supra* note 1 at 80–89.

219 Fineman, "Dominant Discourse, Professional Language, and Legal Change in Child Custody Decisionmaking," 101 *Harv. L. Rev.* 727 (1988).

220 See *id.* at 736–37.

221 See *id.* at 769.

222 See Kay, *supra* note 1 at 35–37. In recommending that courts and lawyers regain control of the custody decision from social workers practicing mandatory mediation, Fineman at one point seems to defend the adversary system of divorce litigation as preferable to the therapeutic model. Fineman, *supra* note 219 at 769–70. A few pages further on, however, she supports her endorsement of the primary caretaker rule by noting that its predictability "reduces the need for litigation." *Id.* at 772. Surely we need not resort to the adversary system to perform the fact-finding function of identifying the parent primarily responsible for the day-to-day care of children. Nor should we be optimistic about the ability of parents who are recent adversaries to "work out arrangements concerning their children" (*id.* at 774), following the initial contested judicial decision unaided either by the legal system or by therapists sensitive to the dynamics of family interaction.

223 Fineman, *supra* note 219 at 770.

224 See Kay, "A Family Court: The California Proposal," 56 *Cal. L. Rev.* 1205 (1968). Compare Wallerstein and Blakeslee, *supra* note 188, at 278–79, observing, "The first task of divorce . . . is to bring the marriage to an end in as civilized a manner as possible, without one partner guiltily giving away his or her rights, taking flight just to get it over with, playing saint or sinner, sadist or masochist, or being controlled by the wish to inflict pain or get revenge. . . . Although it is extraordinarily difficult, adults must negotiate and conclude financial and child custody arrangements with as much reality, morality, emotional stability, and enlightened self-interest as they can muster. This demands

the near impossible at the time of greatest stress. The adults need to set aside intense, competing passions, realistically assess the children's needs as separate from their own, and strike the best and fairest overall deal. When well done, this task has the potential to ease future years for adults and children. Done poorly, it can set the stage for years of continued anger, deprivation, and suffering for everyone involved." In my view, a family court, staffed and supervised as the text describes, can help the divorcing parties and their lawyers perform this task well.

225   At Senator Lockyer's request, the California Senate has created a Senate Task Force on Family Relations Court to consider, among other matters, the proposal of the California Child Victim Witness Judicial Advisory Committee to require the consolidation of all family relations civil actions in one division of the Superior Court. *Final Report of the California Child Victim Witness Judicial Advisory Committee* 9 (October 1988). Cal. S. Res. 7, 1989–90 reg. sess. The Task Force should be able to consider, among other questions, the matters raised in the text.

226   A proposed model agreement that enables parties contemplating marriage to reimpose fault as the basis for divorce and penalizes one spouse for obtaining a unilateral no-fault divorce may be subject to similar criticisms. See Haas, "The Rationality and Enforceability of Contractual Restrictions on Divorce," 66 *N.C.L. Rev.* 879 (1988).

2. Private Ordering Revisited: What Custodial Arrangements Are Parents Negotiating?

1   See Kay, chap. 1, this volume.

2   See Mnookin, "Child-Custody Adjudication: Judicial Functions in the Face of Indeterminacy," 39 *L. & Contemp. Prob.* (No. 3) 226, 235–37 (1975).

3   See Kay; Freed and Walker, "Family Law in the Fifty States: An overview," 18 *Fam. L.Q.* 369–471 (1985).

4   Mnookin and Kornhauser, "Bargaining in the Shadow of the Law," 88 *Yale L.J.* 950, 952–58 (1979).

5   See R. Levy, *Uniform Marriage and Divorce Legislation: A Preliminary Analysis* (1968); Mnookin, *supra* note 2.

6   See Mnookin and Kornhauser, *supra* note 4 at 951, note 2. Since the publication of that article there have been few others that claim to know what proportion of custody cases are adjudicated. Most did not involve empirical research, and those that did are subject to methodological questions. See McIsaac, "Court-connected Mediation," 21 (2) *Conciliation Cts. Rev.* 49–59 (1983); Weitzman and Dixon, "Child Custody Awards: Legal Standards and Empirical Patterns for Child Custody," 12 *U.C. Davis L. Rev.* 473–521 (1979); Graham, "Dispute Resolution in Dissolution Cases: A Marion County Profile," 21 *Willamette L. Rev.* 551–68 (1985).

7   Polikoff, "Why Are Mothers Losing: A Brief Analysis of Criteria Used in Child Custody Determinations," 7 *Women's Rights L. Rep.* 235–43 (1982).

8 Neely, "The Primary Caretaker Role: Child Custody and the Dynamics of Greed," 3 *Yale L. & Pub. Pol'y Rev.* 168 (1984); L. Weitzman, *The Divorce Revolution: The Unexpected Social and Economic Consequences for Women and Children in America* 243 (1985).

9 M. Roman and W. Haddad, *The Disposable Parent: The Case for Joint Custody* (1978).

10 See Bartlett and Stack, "Joint Custody, Feminism and the Dependency Dilemma," 2 *Berkeley Women's L.J.* 9–41 (1986); Scott and Derdyn, "Rethinking Joint Custody," 45 *Ohio St. L.J.* 455–98 (1984); Weitzman, *supra* note 8.

11 See Bartlett and Stack, *supra* note 10.

12 See J. Wallerstein and J. Kelly, *Surviving the Breakup: How Children and Parents Cope with Divorce* (1980).

13 See Weitzman, *supra* note 8.

14 See Scott and Derdyn, *supra* note 10.

15 See Cal. Civ. Code § 4600.5.

16 Cal. Civ. Code § 4600, 4600.5 (emphasis added).

17 *Id.*

18 The statute makes clear, however, that when parents have joint legal custody, either parent acting alone has the power to consent to medical treatment when the child is with that parent.

19 Because the father has physical custody in comparatively few families and because the combination of father physical–father legal custody is quite rare, for some of our analysis we combined the last two categories.

20 Cal. Civ. Code § 4600.5. Effective January 1, 1989, this section was amended to make plain that the mediator was to use his or her best efforts to bring about a settlement "that is in the best interests of the child or children," and deleted the language suggesting that the resolution should necessarily ensure contact with both parents. The 1989 legislation also added a new provision that stated that the existing custody standard "established neither a preference nor a presumption for or against joint legal custody, joint physical custody, or sole custody, but allows the court and the family the widest discretion to choose a parenting plan which is in the best interest of the children." S.B. 2510 (Robbins) enacted by 1988 Cal. Stat. 1550, codified at Cal. Civ. Code at § 4607 (West Supp. 1987).

21 A mediator helps parents clarify and discuss the issues in their conflict in order to reach an agreement. The mediator also serves as a resource, providing information about the various custodial arrangements available to the family. In contrast, evaluators are professionals appointed to determine, using interviews and observation of parent-child interactions, the best possible custody arrangement in order to make a recommendation to the judge. Often mediators and evaluators are part of a separate department attached to the court, such as Family Court Services in San Mateo and Santa Clara counties. It is the county's local option whether one person can be both mediator and evaluator for a family.

22 Even though they are unable to agree before the trial, parents may come to an agreement during the trial owing to the advice of their lawyer or an informal conference in the judge's chambers in which the judge indicates he intends to

follow the guidelines set forth in the evaluator's report should he have to decide custody.

23   Our larger study also includes an additional 196 families for whom the court record did not reveal the final custodial outcome. These 196 families are not included in the analysis here. "Status only" divorces, in which no determination with respect to custody was made, and cases with no final judgment account for 124 of these cases. An additional 60 families reported that they had reconciled at our Time 2 data collection. For 12 families, the court records were unavailable owing to dismissals, changes of venue, or missing files. Finally, for 20 cases with final judgments, the court record did not indicate the custody award.

24   We secured first-round interviews from one or both parents in 1,124 families. If we were able to contact an individual by phone, nearly all agreed to be interviewed. However, a valid telephone number was found for at least one of the parents in only 1,327 families, and in some of these we were never able to contact the parent. The most important reason for nonresponse was an inability to reach a parent by phone after repeated calls. Less than 2% of families where one or both parents were reached by phone declined to participate.

25   We classified as uncontested any divorce in which (1) there was a default judgment secured; or (2) where a response was filed, but a final judgment secured on an uncontested basis where there had been *no* intervening motions for orders to show cause or any other evidence of legal conflict. All other cases were categorized as not uncontested, even though most of these showed no evidence of a contested judicial hearing.

26   For a fuller description of our sampling procedures and interviewing methods, see E. E. Maccoby, C. E. Depner, and R. H. Mnookin, "Custody of Children Following Divorce," in *Impact of Divorce, Single Parenting, and Stepparenting on Children* (E. M. Hetherington and J. D. Arasteh eds. 1988).

27   For those families in which the parents reported that the last two weeks were typical, we used the diary for that period to determine residence. If the family indicated that the last two weeks were not typical, but that there was a regular pattern, we instead used the parents' report of the regular pattern. For those few families who said the last two weeks were not typical and there was no regular pattern, we used the actual time spent during the last two weeks to categorize the family. When both parents were interviewed, there was slightly more discrepancy in reports concerning the last two weeks than in reports about the regular or usual pattern—an understandable finding in view of the fact that the two parents were almost never reporting about the same two-week period. For this reason, we have chosen the number of overnights spent with each parent in a usual or regular two-week period as the best index of de facto residence and averaged the reports of the two parents to make the determination.

28   We classified de facto residence as "split" in any family where one child resided with one parent and some other child resided with the other parent. For children who resided with some other relative or were away at boarding school, their residential pattern was classified as "other."

29 The scale was constructed as follows: In the Time 3 interview, each parent was asked to rate on a 10-point scale "how much conflict there was up to the time of the divorce judgment" about the arrangements for visitation and custody, "where 1 means no disagreements" and "10 means brutal courtroom battling." The parents gave separate ratings for custody and visitation, but because analyses indicated that these measures were highly correlated, we concluded that they were measuring the same issue. We constructed a mean score between the parents for both custody and visitation, and we chose whichever score was greater for that family in the construction of our conflict scale. For those families for which only one parent was interviewed, that parent's score became the family score. The scores for parents in families where we interviewed only one spouse did not significantly differ from the scores of parents in families where both spouses were interviewed. We used the 10-point family score together with information from the court records to create our four-level conflict scale by partitioning the 10-point scale to make a preliminary assignment among our four levels, and then using court record information to make the final assignments. The cut-off scores for the preliminary assignments were Level I ("negligible"), 1.0–3.5; Level II ("mild"), 4.0–5.0; Level III ("substantial"), 5.5–7.0; and Level IV ("intense"), 7.5–10.0. These points were chosen to match the distribution of the preliminary scale. Four decision rules were used to make the final assignments.

(1) We left in Level I only cases in which the family level interview score was 3.5 or below *and* the court record showed the divorce was uncontested. Families with a low interview conflict score and a court record indicating the case was *not* uncontested were moved up to Level II.

(2) Cases in Level III or IV, which the court records showed to be uncontested, were moved down one level. Thus, if the parents' interview rating was a 6, which would have otherwise put the family in Level III, the case would be reclassified into Level II if the court records indicated that the divorce was uncontested. Similarly, a family that otherwise would have fallen into Level IV was reclassified as Level III if the divorce was uncontested.

(3) If a case was preliminarily assigned to Level I or II, but the court record showed the family had been sent to court-annexed mediation, the case was reassigned to Level III. Where the parents' subjective conflict rating placed them in the "Substantial" or "Intense" level, and they had seen a court-appointed mediator, no adjustment was made.

(4) Any case preliminarily assigned to Levels I, II, or III, where the court record indicated that the case had been referred for a custody evaluation, or where there was a sealed packet in the file that appeared to contain such an evaluation, was reassigned to Level IV. We reassigned 127 cases using Rule 1, 58 using Rule 2, 29 using Rule 3, and 33 using Rule 4.

30 The form of the question was slightly different for those respondents who did not participate in a telephone interview, but instead filled out a written questionnaire. For the small fraction of cases for which we had responses to both versions of this question, the versions were highly correlated: mothers ($N = 76$), $R = .86$, fathers ($N = 56$), $R = .91$.

31   If every father for whom we had no information had desired mother custody, then 58% of all fathers would have wanted mother custody.

32   In 1979, 21.2% of the final decrees provided for mother physical custody and joint legal custody; 4.4% provided for joint physical custody, which necessarily includes joint legal custody.

33   In 1981, 23.9% of the final decrees provided for mother physical custody and joint legal custody; 13% provided for joint physical and legal custody.

34   The characteristics of parents without joint legal custody are not the same as those with such custody, so it is not easy to hold constant other factors. For further analysis, see Albiston, Jaccoby, and Mnookin, "Does Joint Legal Custody Matter?" 2 *Stanford L. Policy Rev.* 167–79 (1990).

35   Because of the large number of fathers failing to make a specific request, this relationship is significant for mothers only.

36   We determined residence for the period concurrent with (or if that datum was missing, subsequent to) the time of the divorce decree. The interview responses of the two parents were averaged in cases where the categorization would have been inconsistent had we relied on one or the other.

37   There were an additional two Level IV families that went as far as a contested trial *without* completing an evaluation.

38   Of our 908 cases, we were able to construct the conflict scale for the 781 families where at least one parent was interviewed at Time 3. Of those 127 families without Time 3 interviews, 3 had custody evaluation and thus would have been classified as Level IV, and 1 case went to a contested trial. None of these 127 cases was decided by the judge. Therefore, out of our 908 families, in only 13 cases was custody decided by the judge.

39   This mean is significantly different from the mean for mother physical custody cases but is not significantly different from the mean for father physical custody cases.

40   Of the ninety-four families who went to court-annexed mediation and were in Level IV, 42% ($N = 39$) resulted in joint physical custody.

3. The Economics of Divorce: Changing Rules, Changing Results

1   For the history of the movement to no-fault divorce in the United States, see H. Jacobs, *Silent Revolution: The Transformation of Divorce Law in the United States* (1988); Friedman, "Rights of Passage: Divorce Law in Historical Perspective," 63 *Ore. L. Rev.* 649 (1984). For a comparative examination of no-fault divorce rules in the United States and Western Europe, see M. Glendon, *Abortion and Divorce in Western Law* 63–111 (1987).

2   L. Weitzman, *The Divorce Revolution: The Unexpected Social and Economic Consequences for Women and Children in America* xiv (1985).

3   H. Carter and P. Glick, *Marriage and Divorce: A Social and Economic Study* 394 (rev. ed. 1976).

4   In two decades, families maintained by women alone increased from 36 to 50% of all poor families. Of the net increase of 129,000 poor families in 1983, 95%

were headed by women. U.S. Bureau of the Census, *Money Income and Poverty Status of Families and Persons in the United States: 1983* (1984).

5   See D. Chambers, *Making Fathers Pay: The Enforcement of Child Support* 45–50 (1979) (97% of divorced mothers and children in their custody would fall below lower standard budget income as compared to 10% of divorced fathers, if fathers paid court-ordered support and mother tried to live on support only); Weitzman, *supra* note 2 at 337–43 (one year after divorce, men experienced a 42% improvement in their standard of living while women experienced a 73% decline); Hoffman and Duncan, "What Are the Economic Consequences of Divorce?" 25 *Demography* 641 (1988) (recalculation of Weitzman's data suggests that women experienced only a 33% decline in their standard of living); Duncan and Hoffman, "A Reconsideration of the Economic Consequences of Divorce," 22 *Demography* 495 (1985) (in the first year after divorce, the economic status of women fell an average of about 30%); Weiss, "The Impact of Marital Dissolution on Income and Consumption in Single-Parent Households," 46 *J. Marriage & Fam.* 115 (1984) (same); Hampton, "Marital Disruption: Some Social and Economic Consequences, in *Five Thousand American Families: Patterns of Economic Progress* 171–74 (1975) (47% of divorced husbands were in the top three deciles of income as compared to only 20% of divorced wives).

6   See G. Sterin and J. Davis, *Divorce Awards and Outcomes: A Study of Pattern and Change in Cuyahoga County, Ohio 1965–1978* (1981); Weitzman, *supra* note 2 (Los Angeles and San Francisco, Calif.); McGraw, and Sterin, Davis, "A Case Study in Divorce Law Reform and Its Aftermath, 20 *J. Fam. L.* 443 (1981–82) (Cuyahoga County, Ohio); McLindon, "Separate but Unequal: The Economic Disaster of Divorce for Women and Children," 21 *Fam. L.Q.* 351 (1987) (New Haven, Conn.); Welch and Price-Bonham, "A Decade of No-Fault Divorce Revisited: California, Georgia, and Washington," 45 *J. Marriage & Fam.* 411 (1983) (Clark County, Ga., and Spokane County, Wash.); Seal, "A Decade of No-Fault Divorce: What It Has Meant Financially for Women in California," 1 *Fam. Adv.* 10 (1979) (San Diego, Calif.). See also Peters, "Marriage and Divorce: Informational Constraints and Private Contracting, 76 *Am. Econ. Rev.* 437 (1986) (comparing alimony and property awards in states with unilateral no-fault divorce to these in states without unilateral no-fault).

7   Some commentators have questioned the significance of the changes. See, e.g., Sugarman, chap. 5, this book; Melli, "Constructing a Social Problem: The Post-Divorce Plight of Women and Children," 1986 *A.B.F. Res. J.* 759, 769–70 (1986). While I agree with these commentators that it is a mistake to characterize the fault regime as "the good old days," I disagree with the proposition that the changes researchers have noted are insignificant. Although it is true that some of the observed changes—for example, the number of alimony awards—are relatively modest when measured in terms of absolute difference, in percentage terms the change is substantial. See note 8, *infra* (declines in the number of alimony awards ranging from 25% to 55%). In my view, the change is akin to the rise in the divorce rate that occurred during the 1970s, the significance of which few would question. This change, similarly, was quite small in terms of absolute difference (4.7% in 1970, 9% in 1978) but quite dramatic as a percent-

age change (91%). See S. Levitan and R. Belous, *What's Happening to the American Family* 29 (1981).

8   See McGraw, Sterin, and Davis, *supra* note 6 at 473 (from 26% in 1972 to 18% in 1978 in Cuyahoga County, Ohio); McLindon, *supra* note 6 at 362 (from 59% in 1970–71 to 30% in early eighties in New Haven, Conn.); Seal, *supra* note 6 at 12 (from 66% in 1968 to 30% in 1976 in San Diego, Calif.); Welch and Price-Bonham, *supra* note 6 at 415 (from 15.4% in 1970 to 10.9% in 1980 in Clark County, Ga.; from 9.7% in 1970 to 7.0% in 1980 in Spokane County, Wash.); Weitzman, *supra* note 2 at 167 (from 20% in 1968 to 15% in 1972 in Los Angeles and San Francisco, Calif.).

9   McGraw, Sterin, and Davis, *supra* note 6 at 474–75 (permanent awards decreased from 60% of total to 30% after introduction of no-fault in Cuyahoga County, Ohio); McLindon, *supra* note 6 at 364 (all but one woman received permanent award before no-fault as compared to 60% after no-fault in New Haven, Conn.); Seal, *supra* note 6 at 12 (permanent awards decreased from 46% of total to 37% after introduction of no-fault in San Diego, Calif.); Weitzman, *supra* note 2 at 164 (in Los Angeles, Calif., permanent awards decreased from 62% of total to 32% after no-fault). But see Welch and Price-Bonham, *supra* note 6 at 415 (in Clark County, Ga., permanent awards increased from 51.4% to 59.3% of the total after introduction of no-fault; in Spokane County, Wash., permanent awards increased from 37.9% to 40% of the total after introduction of no-fault).

10 McLindon, *supra* note 6 at 375 (in three of four income categories wives received an average of 84% of property before no-fault and 57% after no-fault in New Haven, Conn.); Seal, *supra* note 6 at 12 (24% fewer wives received marital home, 30% fewer received furniture, 10% fewer received automobile, 27% fewer were exclusively awarded other assets after no-fault in San Diego, Calif.); Welch and Price-Bonham, *supra* note 6 at 416 (wives received smaller share of assets in Spokane County, Wash., after introduction of no-fault divorce); Weitzman, *supra* note 2 at 74 (in 86% of cases in San Francisco and 58% in Los Angeles, wives received majority of property before no-fault; in 34% of cases in San Francisco and 35% in Los Angeles, wives received majority of property after no-fault); Sterin and Davis, *supra* note 6 at 112 (Table 6.2) (Cuyahoga County, Ohio, wives received less property after introduction of no-fault divorce when divorce granted on no-fault ground of mutual agreement between spouses, but not when divorce was granted on fault grounds or on no-fault ground of two years separation). But see Welch and Price-Bonham, *supra* note 6 at 416 (wives were not more likely to receive a smaller share of property after introduction of no-fault divorce in Clark County, Ga.).

11 Seal, *supra* note 6 at 12 (70% of husbands were assigned joint debts before no-fault divorce as compared to 42% after no-fault in San Diego, Calif.); Welch and Price Bonham, *supra* note 6 at 416 (wives received larger share of debts after introduction of no-fault in Spokane County, Wash.); Weitzman, *supra* note 2 at 102 (husbands assumed majority of family debts in 88% of cases before no-fault, as compared to 58% of cases after no-fault in Los Angeles and San Francisco, Calif.). But see McLindon, *supra* note 6 at 379 (husbands' average share of

family debts was 78% before no-fault as compared to 84% after no-fault in New Haven, Conn.); Welch and Price-Bonham, *supra* note 6 at 416 (wives received larger share of joint debts but smaller share of other liabilities after introduction of no-fault divorce in Clark County, Ga.).

12   For example, the Uniform Marriage and Divorce Act, the leading model no-fault divorce law, provides that the court "may grant a maintenance order . . . only if it finds that the spouse seeking maintenance: (1) lacks sufficient property to provide for his reasonable needs; and (2) is unable to support himself through appropriate employment or is the custodian of a child whose condition or circumstances make it appropriate that the custodian not be required to seek employment outside the home." Uniform Marriage and Divorce Act § 308(a) (1973). A recent divorce law survey reports that, as of 1987, alimony "awards are increasingly no-fault oriented. . . . The emphasis is on the actual need of the recipient and the ability of the other spouse to pay." Freed and Walker, "Family Law in the Fifty States: An Overview," 21 *Fam. L.Q.* 417, 472 (1988).

13   Between 1970 and 1978 the labor force participation rate of married women rose from 40.8% to 47.6%. U.S. Bureau of the Census, *American Families and Living Arrangements* 12 (Charts 18–19) (Current Population Reports Special Studies Series P-23, No. 104, May 1980). For married women with preschool-age children the labor force participation rate rose from 30.3% to 41.6% between 1970 and 1978; comparable increases occurred from 1960 to 1970 when the rate for married women with preschool-age children rose from 18.6% to 30.3%. *Id.*

14   Between 1970 and 1980 the divorce rate rose from 47 to 90 per 1,000 married persons. See S. Levitan and R. Belous, *What's Happening to the American Family?* 29 (1981).

15   See Weitzman, *supra* note 2 at 350–63. The trend appears to be even more pronounced among the young. In one readers' poll of young American women, 69% said that husbands should be required to pay alimony only until a woman is self-supporting. Only 7% thought that alimony should be paid "all the time." *Glamour,* July 1981 at 21.

16   Weitzman, *supra* note 2 at 186 (under the fault law, 19.7% of wives with children under six were awarded alimony, as compared to 12.8% under the no-fault law).

17   Although the law did make it harder for employed wives and those who could readily enter the labor market to obtain alimony, courts were directed to consider the ability of the supported spouse to engage in gainful employment "without interfering with the interest of dependent children in his or her care." California Family Law Act, § 8, 1969 Cal. Stat. 3333, codified at Cal. Civ. Code § 4801(a)(5) (West 1983). See also note 13, *supra* and accompanying text.

18   Under the old law, a wife was eligible to receive alimony only if she was an "innocent" spouse who had established that her husband was guilty of marital misconduct sufficient to establish grounds for a divorce. See Cal. Civ. Code § 146 (West 1954) (repealed 1969).

19   See, e.g., Weitzman, *supra* note 2 at 26–28; Fineman, "Implementing Equality: Ideology, Contradiction and Social Change: A Study in Rhetoric and Results in the Regulation of the Consequences of Divorce, 1983 *Wis. L. Rev.* 789, 802

(1983); Mnookin and Kornhauser, "Bargaining in the Shadow of the Law: The Case of Divorce," 88 *Yale L.J.* 950, 950–54, 968–69 (1979); Seal, *supra* note 6 at 11–12.

20 See, e.g., Rios v. Rios, 34 A.D.2d 325, 311 N.Y.S.2d 664, aff'd 29 N.Y.2d 840, 327 N.Y.S.2d 853, 277 N.E.2D 786 (1971).

21 In states that enacted no-fault options that were not unilateral or that were coupled with lengthy waiting periods, wives' bargaining power was, of course, preserved. See notes 39–42, *infra* and accompanying text.

22 See, e.g., Weitzman, *supra* note 2 at 363–66; Fineman, *supra* note 19 at 875–86; Lauerman, Book Review, 2 *Berkeley Women's L.J.* 246, 250 (1986). As judges decide very few divorce cases, their decisions can affect the typical divorce case only by establishing expectations about likely outcomes, which, once again, affect the bargaining positions of the parties. Lawyer and litigant expectations about judicial decision making may or may not be accurate, a factor that further complicates the causation issue. On the role of divorce rules in determining bargaining positions generally, see Mnookin and Kornhauser, *supra* note 19.

23 See Weitzman, *supra* note 2 at 363–66; Fineman, *supra* note 19 at 875–86.

24 The fact that legislatures had directed judicial attention to factors like need and employability at the same time that they eliminated fault requirements (see note 12 *supra* and accompanying text) would, of course, enhance this possibility.

25 See, e.g., Weitzman, *supra* note 2 at 384 (urging retention of equal property division rule).

26 *Id.* at 75.

27 *Id.* at 98.

28 Weitzman, for example, reports that wives "are, in fact, likely to fare better under rules that guarantee them an equal share of the marital property," although the only evidence to support this conclusion is two anecdotal reviews of New York appellate cases and a compilation of comments at public hearings in New Jersey. *Id.* at 106–07. The lack of empirical evidence on economic outcomes in equitable distribution states has sometimes led women's advocates to take contrary positions on the merits of the two systems. For example, in New York and Wisconsin, women's groups lobbied for equal distribution, whereas in Pennsylvania they lobbied for equitable distribution. See Foster, "Commentary on Equitable Distribution," 26 *N.Y.L.S. L. Rev.* 1, 31 (1981); Fineman, *supra* note 19 at 843–71.

29 McLindon, *supra* note 6 at 373. An earlier report from Cuyahoga County, Ohio, provides less detailed data but also concludes that wives typically received more than half of the marital property following no-fault reforms. See Sterin and Davis, *supra* note 6 at 112.

30 Compare McLindon, *supra* note 6 at 362 (59% of New Haven women received alimony in 1970s; 30% did in 1980s) with U.S. Bureau of the Census, *Child Support and Alimony, 1981,* 2 (Table A) (Current Population Reports Series P-23, no. 124) May 1982 (14% of U.S. divorced wives received alimony in 1978). A statewide survey of divorce in Connecticut also reported a lower alimony rate than McLindon does. Permanent Commission on the Status of Women, *Marital Dissolution: The Economic Impact on Connecticut Men and Wom-*

en, 25 (1979) (19% of surveyed divorced wives were awarded alimony in 1978).

31 For a similar view, see Jacobs, *supra* note 1 at 163–64.

32 N.Y. Dom. Rel. L. § 170 (McKinney's 1988). See also Arkansas Stat. Annot. § 34-1202 (voluntary separation for three years required); Miss. Code Annot. § 93-5-2 (joint petition with separation agreement required); Tenn. Code Annot. § 36-4-101(12) (requiring separation agreement if couple has minor children).

33 Arkansas, Pennsylvania, and Tennessee require three years; Illinois and Maryland require two years; Connecticut and New Jersey require eighteen months; and North Carolina, Ohio, South Carolina, Virginia, and West Virginia require one year. Some others require a six-months separation. See Fam. L. Rep. Ref. File (BNA) 400-01.

34 Peters, *supra* note 6.

35 The waiting periods range from six months to three years. Compare Peters, *supra* note 6 at 446, with Fam. L. Rep. Ref. File (BNA) 400-01.

36 According to Peters's analysis, unilateral divorce reduced alimony by $186 per year, child support by $462 per year, and property settlements by $137. Peters, *supra* note 6 at 449.

37 The results were significant at the .10 confidence level. *Id.*

38 Another researcher, using a different data set, has recently compared the salary/wage income, likelihood of receiving child support, and home ownership patterns among women divorced on fault and no-fault grounds and concluded that no-fault divorce produced no adverse effects on these variables. See Jacobs, "Another Look at No-Fault Divorce and the Post-Divorce Finances of Women," 23 *Law & Soc. Rev.* 96 (1989).

39 Sterin and Davis, *supra* note 6; Weitzman, *supra* note 2; McGraw, Sterin, and Davis, *supra* note 6; McLindon, *supra* note 6; Seal *supra* note 6; Welch and Price-Bonham, *supra* note 6. Other reports describe outcomes under no-fault without comparing them with those in the fault era. See Wishik, "The Economics of Divorce: An Exploratory Study," 20 *Fam. L.Q.* 79 (1986); Connecticut Permanent Commission on the Status of Women, *supra* note 30; B. Baker, *Family Equity at Issue: A Study of the Economic Consequences of Divorce on Women and Children* (1987).

40 See Kay, chap. 1.

41 In Connecticut, an eighteen-month separation was required. See Conn. Gen. Stat. Annot. § 46b-40 (West 1986). In Ohio, a two-year separation was required. Ohio Divorce Reform Act of 1974, codified at Ohio Rev. Code Annot. § 3105.01(k) (Baldwinn 1976). The Ohio statute has since been amended to require only a one-year separation as an antecedent to a divorce. Ohio Rev. Code Annot. sec. 3105.01(k) (Baldwinn 1989).

42 For a description of the property rules in Ohio before and after no-fault, see McGraw, Sterin, and Davis, *supra* note 6 at 446–50. For a description of the property rules in Connecticut before and after no-fault, see McLindon, *supra* note 6 at 372, note 122. The addition of property division criteria to the Connecticut law was apparently intended by the legislature to increase awards to divorced wives. *Id.*

43   The research was aimed at determining the impact of New York's equitable
     distribution law on postdivorce economic outcomes, as well as providing data
     to assess the pros and cons of equal as opposed to equitable property distribu-
     tion; this chapter will not address these issues or fully report on the research.
44   1966 N.Y. Laws, ch. 254 codified at N.Y. Dom. Rel. L. § 170 (McKinney's
     1988) (divorce obtainable without a showing of marital fault only when the
     couple has entered into a separation agreement and lived separate and apart for
     one year).
45   Equitable distribution was not adopted until 1980. 1980 N.Y. Laws, ch. 281
     codified at N.Y. Dom. Rel. L. § 236 B (McKinney's 1986).
46   Fault was explicitly eliminated as a basis for denying alimony. Compare former
     N.Y. Dom. Rel. L. § 236 (McKinney's 1977) and N.Y. Dom. Rel. L. § 236B(6)
     (McKinney's 1986).
47   See notes 57–59 *infra* and accompanying text.
48   In 1978 New York was one of six states (Florida, Mississippi, New York, South
     Carolina, Virginia, and West Virginia) that awarded property to the titleholder.
     See Foster and Freed, "Divorce in the Fifty States: An Overview as of 1978,"
     13 *Fam. L.Q.* 105 (1979).
49   Under the former law, a wife who was guilty of misconduct sufficient to justify a
     divorce was not entitled to either an alimony award or to exclusive occupancy of
     the marital residence. See former N.Y. Dom. Rel. L. § 236 (McKinney's 1977).
     As of 1987, marital misconduct is a bar to alimony in only eight states. See
     Freed and Walker, "Family Law in the Fifty States: An Overview," 21 *Fam. L.Q.*
     417, 473 (Table VI) (1988).
50   See N.Y. Dom. Rel. L. § 236B(1) (d) (McKinney's 1986). For a comparison
     with other state rules on equitable distribution, see Fam. L. Rep. Ref. File
     (BNA) 400-52.
51   At the time the statute was enacted, the court was directed to consider:

         1) the income and property of each party at the time of marriage and
     at the time of commencement of the action;
         2) the duration of the marriage and the age and health of both parties;
         3) the need of a custodial parent to occupy or own the marital resi-
     dence and to use or own its household effects;
         4) the loss of inheritance and pension rights upon dissolution of the
     marriage as of the date of dissolution;
         5) any award of maintenance under subdivision six of this part;
         6) any equitable claim to, interest in, or direct or indirect contribution
     made to the acquisition of such marital property by the party not having
     title, including joint efforts or expenditures and contributions and ser-
     vices as a spouse, parent, wage earner and homemaker, and to the career
     or career potential of the other party;
         7) the liquid or non-liquid character of all marital property;
         8) the probable future financial circumstances of each party;
         9) the impossibility or difficulty of evaluating any component asset or
     any interest in a business, corporation, or profession, and the economic

desirability of retaining such asset or interest intact and free from any claim or interference by the other party.

N.Y. Dom. Rel. L. § 236B(5) (McKinney's 1986). Since the enactment of the statute three additional factors (tax consequences, wasteful dissipation of assets by a spouse, and transfer or encumbrance of a marital action made in contemplation of a divorce) have been added. N.Y. Dom. Rel. L. § 236B(5) (McKinney's 1986). For a comparison with other state standards on equitable distribution, see Fam. L. Rep. Ref. File (BNA) 401-502.

52   N.Y. Dom. Rel. L. § 236B(5) (d) (1) (McKinney's 1986).
53   Blickstein v. Blickstein, 99 A.D. 287, 472 N.Y.S.2d 110 (2d Dept. 1984); O'Brien v. O'Brien, 66 N.Y.2d 576, 589–90, 498 N.Y.S.2d 743, 750, 489 N.E.2d 712, 719 (1985).
54   N.Y. Dom. Rel. L. § 236B(5) (d) (5) (McKinney's 1986).
55   N.Y. Dom. Rel. L. § 236B(6) (1) (McKinney's 1986).
56   N.Y. Dom. Rel. L. § 236B(6) (McKinney's 1986).
57   "Memorandum of Assemblyman Gordon W. Burrows," in *1980 New York State Legislative Annual* 130 (1980).
58   *Id.*
59   *Id.*
60   O'Brien v. O'Brien, 66 N.Y.2d 576, 585, 498 N.Y.S.2d 743, 747, 489 N.E.2d 712, 716 (1985).
61   In order to examine judicial decision making under the new law, data were also drawn from all reported trial-level decisions on equitable distribution and from the records on appeal in all reported appellate cases on equitable distribution through December 1986.
62   A divorce was considered contested if it was initiated on fault grounds (N.Y. Dom. Rel. L. § 170 (1–4) (McKinney's 1988)) and the defendant answered the complaint. The vast majority of "contested" cases are ultimately settled.
63   A divorce was considered consensual when sought on the basis of a written separation agreement between the parties or judgment of separation coupled with a one-year's separation. N.Y. Dom. Rel. L. § 170(5–6) (McKinney's 1988).
64   A divorce was considered to be granted on default when initiated on fault grounds (N.Y. Dom. Rel. L. § 170(1-4) (McKinney's 1988)) and the defendant failed to answer.
65   New York's financial reporting requirement applies only to contested divorce actions. See N.Y. Dom. Rel. L. § 236A(2) (McKinney's 1986) (actions filed prior to July 1980); N.Y. Dom. Rel. L. § 236B(4) (McKinney's 1986 and Supp. 1989).
66   Because contested, consensual, and default cases are not evenly represented among the divorce population as they were in my sample, the sample average is not an accurate representation of the true average marital duration for divorcing couples in the three surveyed counties. The categories were appropriately weighted to create percentages applicable to the total divorce population. The weighted average marital duration was 11.1 years in 1978 and 10.2 years in 1984.

67   Seal, *supra* note 6 at 11–12 (reporting average marital duration of 6.1 years for San Diego, Calif., sample).

68   McLindon, *supra* note 6 at 357 (reporting average marital duration for New Haven sample of 11.8 years); Wishik, *supra* note 39 at 83 (reporting average marital duration for Vermont sample of 10.6 years).

69   See McLindon, *supra* note 6 at 357 (reporting that 76% of New Haven sample in 1982–83 had children; of those with children, average number was 1.79); Wishik, *supra* note 39 at 83 (reporting that 61% of Vermont sample in 1982–83 had children).

70   The weighted averages were 1.4 children in 1978 and 1.1 in 1984.

71   Both income figures are in 1984 dollars.

72   U.S. Bureau of the Census, *City and County Data Book* 390 (10th ed. 1983) (reporting median family income in 1979 of $16,326 [$23,346 in $1984] in New York County, $21,222 [$30,347 in $1984] in Onondaga County, and $27,278 [$39,008 in $1984] in Westchester County).

73   Because our sample is not an accurate representation of the total population of divorcing couples, the percentages of alimony for each case category within each county were appropriately weighted to create percentages applicable to the total population.
      The likelihood of obtaining an alimony award varied dramatically by case category. In 1978, 45% of contested, 38% of consensual, and only 9% of default cases resulted in alimony awards. In 1984, the proportions were similarly skewed; 30% of contested, 23% of consensual, and 6% of default cases contained provisions for alimony.

74   The 1978 alimony award rate is higher than the national rate for that year reported in census data (14.3%), while the 1984 rate is lower than the national rate reported in census data (13.9%, 1983; 14.6%, 1985). U.S. Bureau of the Census, *Child Support and Alimony, 1985,* 6 (Current Population Reports Special Studies series P-23 no. 154, April 1989).

75   The average duration of nonpermanent awards did not vary substantially over the survey period. In 1978, the average was 4.5 years; in 1984 it was 4.7 years. The averages did vary substantially by county and case category. In Onondaga County, for example, during both survey years the average duration of a time-limited alimony award was much higher in consensual (8.1 years, 1978; 7.7 years, 1984) than in contested cases (3.8 years, 1978; 3.8 years, 1984). By contrast, in New York County, awards in consensual cases averaged 2.8 years in 1978 and 5.9 years in 1984; contested cases averaged 5.0 years in 1978 and 3.8 years in 1984. In Westchester, awards in consensual cases averaged 6.7 years in 1978 and 5.7 years in 1984; awards in contested cases averaged 5.3 years in 1978 and 5.4 years in 1984.

76   In the contested category, permanent awards declined from 75% of the total to 31%. In the consensual category, they declined from 81% of the total to 44%; in the default category, they declined from 82% of the total to 41%.

77   In New York County, permanent awards declined from 72% to 38% of the total. In Westchester County, permanent awards declined from 78% to 40% of the

total. In Onondaga County, permanent awards declined from 88% to 44% of the total.

78   The decreased tendency for longer-married wives to receive alimony was present in all case categories, although it was greatest in the contested group. Here, 70% of wives married twenty or more years received alimony in 1978, as compared to only 36% in 1984. The change was also constant across all surveyed counties.

79   In 1978, for wives with available employment information, 37% of those employed (63/169) and 64% of those unemployed (61/95) received alimony, or 47% (124/264) of the total. If the same percentages applied in 1984 one would anticipate that 37% of those employed (77/208) and 64% of those unemployed (51/79) would receive alimony, for an overall alimony receipt rate of 44% (128/287).

80   All income and award figures are in constant 1984 dollars. Conversion was accomplished by dividing the consumer price for 1978 by the consumer price index for 1984. Consumer price index figures were obtained from U.S. Department of Commerce, Bureau of the Census, *Statistical Abstract of the United States* 444 (Table 729) (1987). Although the income data apply only to the contested cases, there is no reason to presume that much larger changes took place within the other case categories.

81   In 1978, the average alimony award was $922 for the contested category, $741 for the consensual category, and $685 for the default category. In 1984, the average award was $785 for the contested category, $986 for the consensual category, and $641 for the defaults.

82   In 1978, the average alimony award for the divorce population was $821 in Westchester County and $483 in Onondaga County. In 1984, the average alimony for the divorce population was $768 in Westchester County and $446 for Onondaga County. A N.Y. County average could not be computed due to the frequency of defaults and scarcity of alimony awards in this group.

83   In both years awards for contested and consensual groups were quite similar, and awards in default cases were considerably lower. The default cases also evidenced the greatest erosion in the level of child support (38% per minor child).

84   The inclusion of implicit child support in the averages did not appreciably raise the level of support in either time period. With such implicit child support included, the overall averages were $562 in 1978 and $450 in 1984. Payments denominated as spousal maintenance were considered to be implicit child support whenever their termination was explicitly tied to an emancipation event, such as reaching the age of majority. Pursuant to the Supreme Court's decision in Commissioner v. Lester, 366 U.S. 299 (1961), spouses could denominate payments intended for the benefit of children as alimony and claim the alimony deduction. The Lester principle created a tax incentive, particularly for obligors in upper-income brackets, to identify child support payments as alimony in order to obtain the benefit of the deduction. For an example of tax-planning strategy under the Lester principle, see J. Areen, *Cases and Materials on Family Law* 689 (1978). The Lester decision was overturned by Congress in the domes-

tic relations tax reform provisions of the Deficit Reduction Act of 1984, codified at I.R.C. § 71(a) (2) (A) (1988). This may have reduced the incentive to
mislabel in some of the 1984 cases.

85 In New York County it was impossible to calculate an average for the total 1984
population, owing to the high proportion of default cases and large amount of
missing data on child support in the default files during that year. Most of the
default cases involving minor children during that year contained no information on child support. It was impossible to determine whether there was an
existing child support order or whether the lack of data indicated a zero award.

86 The overall shifts in physical custody arrangements were nonetheless significant
at the .05 confidence level.

87 The percentages are for the consensual and contested cases only. Because of the
large amount of missing data in the default files, the proportion of home owners
could not be firmly determined for this group.

88 Equity could not be determined for the consensual or default cases.

89 The average masks substantial differences between counties. For both years
equities were lowest in Onondaga County ($35,198 in 1978, $26,346 in 1984)
and highest in New York County ($135,768 in 1978, $223,420 in 1984).

90 These overall results mask some considerable disparities between counties and
between case categories. In 1984, for example, the likelihood of a wife receiving
a rented home ranged from 69% in the Westchester contested sample to 36% in
the Onondaga consensual sample. Overall, the likelihood of an award of a rental
home to a wife declined in consensual cases (56%, 1978; 48%, 1984) and
increased in contested cases (46%, 1978; 64%, 1984). Awards to husbands
(29%, 1978; 18%, 1984) and the vacancy rate (25%, 1978; 18%, 1984) correspondingly declined in contested cases and increased in consensual cases (husbands: 29%, 1978 and 33%, 1984; vacancy rate: 15%, 1978 and 19%, 1984).

91 Occupancy of the marital home includes situations in which a spouse obtains
sole title, with or without paying a cash/settlement to the other spouse, and
situations in which ownership remains constant and a spouse is granted the
right to live in the marital home until some future contingency (e.g., the emancipation of the children) occurs.

92 The overall changes in ownership and occupancy patterns were not completely
consistent across case categories, however. Although the probability of husbands receiving ownership or occupancy increased across all categories, the
probability of wives receiving ownership was not constant. In the contested
cases wives were actually more likely to receive outright ownership in 1984 than
in 1978 (30%, 1978; 36%, 1984). The reason for this difference is that the
decline in occupancy awards was much more dramatic in the contested (21% to
8%) than in the consensual (16% to 14%) cases, and within the contested
category wives as well as husbands benefited from the shift.

93 Although sales did increase in the default category (from 18% to 27%), the
number of cases is too small to make overall assessments of trends.

94 The percentages do not add to 100 because, in one case, sale proceeds went to
the couple's children.

95 Sales declined by 3%, vacancy of rental units increased by 4% for this group.

96   In contested cases, the likelihood of wives married ten or more years obtaining the home declined from 61% to 56%. In the consensual category it declined from 61% to 47%, and among defaults it declined from 65% to 42%. Given the relatively small number of default cases with complete information on disposition of the marital home and marital duration ($N = 40$, 1978; $N = 32$, 1984), the default data do not permit definitive conclusions.

97   Overall, wives with custody of minor children obtained the marital home (rented or owned) 62% of the time in 1978 as compared to 35% for wives without custody. Wives without custody of minor children obtained the home 60% of the time in 1984 as compared to 36% for wives without custody.

98   In the contested and consensual cases, in 1978, wives with custody obtained ownership (with or without offsetting payment) of the marital home in 36% of the cases as compared to wives without custody, who obtained ownership in only 7% of the cases; in 1984 wives with custody obtained ownership in 44% of the cases, as compared to wives without custody, who obtained ownership in 12% of the cases. Sales were no less likely in this situation (28%, 1978; 27%, 1984) than they were for the overall case sample, however.

99   The exception is Washington, where the permanency of awards did not decline, as noted above. For an explanation of the Washington outcome, see note 100 and accompanying text.

100 The Ohio waiting period at the time of the research was two years (Ohio Rev. Code § 3105.01(k) (Baldwinn 1976)); the Connecticut waiting period is eighteen months (Conn. Stat. Annot. § 46b-40 (West 1986).

101 Weitzman, *supra* note 2 at 164, 167 (alimony awards declined by 25%; permanent awards decreased from 62% to 32%).

102 McGraw, Sterin, and Davis, *supra* note 6 at 473, 475 (alimony awards increased from 1966 to 1972 by 6%; 60% of awards were permanent in both years).

103 See *id.* at 473–77 (alimony).

104 In Ohio, the decline in permanent alimony awards was also greatest in the no-fault-era cases brought on no-fault (i.e., a two-year separation or a spousal agreement) grounds; indeed wives' property awards did not decline at all in post-no-fault divorces brought on fault grounds.

105 See Weitzman, *supra* note 2 at 31–32. See also note 12, *supra* and accompanying text.

106 Uniform Marriage and Divorce Act § 308 (1973) (court may grant maintenance only if it finds that spouse lacks sufficient property to provide for reasonable needs and is unable to support himself through appropriate employment or is custodian of a child whose condition or circumstances make it appropriate that the custodian not be required to seek outside employment). See also R. Levy, *Uniform Marriage and Divorce Legislation: A Preliminary Analysis* 144–47 (1969) (urging abolition of alimony except in exceptional circumstances).

107 Dakin v. Dakin, 62 Wash.2d 408, 121 P.2d 962 (1963). See also McKendry v. McKendry, 2 Wash. App. 882, 472 P.2d 569 (1970) (permanent alimony not favored). Morgan v. Morgan, 59 Wash.2d 639, 369 P.2d 516 (1962) (same); Murray v. Murray, 26 Wash.2d 370, 174 p.2d 296 (1946) (forty-six-year-old,

able-bodied, childless wife who had good education and business training and considerable business experience would be granted $50 monthly alimony for only six months in order to encourage her to seek employment).

108   Weitzman, *supra* note 2 at 193–94.

109   This is particularly interesting given the absence of any property distribution scheme in New York prior to the equitable distribution law. The extremely high rate of joint home ownership, coupled with the absence of legislative norms, appears to have made possible the development of a sharing norm.

110   Weitzman, *supra* note 2 at 79. Weitzman is unclear about whether custody did make a difference before the introduction of no-fault.

111   McLindon, *supra* note 6 at 376. McLindon does not provide data on wives with custody versus wives without it.

112   Sterin and Davis, *supra* note 6 at 114. Custodial mothers received custody 76% of the time before no-fault, as compared to 48% of wives without custody. Although the researchers do not provide comparative percentages for the surveyed population after no-fault, they indicate that "the difference between custodial mothers and other wives had almost evaporated." *Id.*

113   See Weitzman, *supra* note 2 at 78.

114   See, e.g., McLindon, *supra* note 6 (one hundred cases in each of two years).

115   Sterin and Davis, *supra* note 6; McGraw, Sterin, and Davis, *supra* note 6; McLindon, *supra* note 6; Wishik, *supra* note 39.

116   The one exception is the research done in Cuyahoga County, Ohio (Sterin and Davis, *supra* note 6; McGraw, Sterin, and Davis, *supra* note 6), in which the researchers also examined outcomes in 1965, several years before no-fault divorce was introduced.

117   See text at note 105 *supra*.

4. Stepparents, Biological Parents, and the Law's Perceptions of "Family" after Divorce

1   "Family Relations Six Years after Divorce," in *Remarriage and Stepparenting: Current Research and Theory* 185, 186 (Pasley and Ihinger-Tallman eds. 1987).

2   "Parenting in the Binuclear Family: Relationships between Biological and Stepparents," in *id.* at 225, 232–33. At three years after divorce, 35% of women had remarried and 23% more had "cohabitors"; at the same point, 55% of men had remarried and 21% had cohabitors.

3   "The New Extended Family: The Experience of Parents and Children after Remarriage," in Pasley and Ihinger-Tallman, *supra* note 1 at 42, 44 (1987). The same calculation has been made by the demographer Paul Glick. See "80's Stepfamilies: Forming New Ties," *New York Times*, September 24, 1987, at 21, 22.

4   "80's Stepfamilies," *supra* note 3.

5   The valuable new volume of essays cited *supra* note 1 includes summaries from several perspectives of the research on stepparents, as well as reports from a few of the principal researchers themselves on the current stage of their research. In

it, Constance Ahrons and Lynn Wallish, Frank Furstenberg, Mavis Hetherington, and John Santrock and Karen Sitterle report on their own research. In a chapter reviewing the literature, Ganong and Coleman identify about fifty-seven empirical studies of the stepparent relation conducted between the early 1950s and 1985. Of these, all but eleven were published in the decade between 1976 and 1985 (*id.* at 138–40). Additional research on the stepparent relationship, not reported by Ganong and Coleman or included in the Pasley and Ihinger-Tallman volume, is being conducted by James Peterson and Nicholas Zill (see, e.g., "Marital Disruption, Parent-Child Relationships, and Behavior Problems in Children," 48 *J. Marriage & Fam.* 295 [1986]). New research by Zill and others is also reported in *Impact of Divorce, Single Parenting and Stepparenting on Children* (E. Hetherington and J. Arasteh eds. 1988). Judith Wallerstein has recently published the ten-year follow-up of her study of mothers with custody of their children. See J. Wallerstein and S. Blakeslee, *Second Chances: Men, Women, and Children a Decade after Divorce* (1989). See also the review of research in F. Furstenberg and G. Spanier, *Recycling the Family: Remarriage after Divorce* (1984).

6   The most notable recent work is by Bartlett, "Rethinking Parenthood as an Exclusive Status: The Need for Alternatives When the Premise of the Nuclear Family Has Failed," 70 *Va. L. Rev.* 879 (1984) (discussing stepparents as well as other caretakers of children other than a biologic parent); Ramsey and Masson, "Stepparent Support of Stepchildren: A Comparative Analysis of Policies and Problems in the American and British Experience," 36 *Syr. L. Rev.* 659 (1985); Mahoney, "Support and Custody Aspects of the Stepparent-Child Relationship," 70 *Cornell L. Rev.* 38 (1984) (hereafter "Support and Custody Aspects"); and Mahoney, "Stepfamilies in the Federal Law," 48 *U. Pitt. L. Rev.* 491 (1987) (hereafter "Stepfamilies").

7   I will not be discussing unmarried partners of a divorced biologic parent. I will also have little to say about married partners of a biologic parent whose children from a prior relationship were born outside of marriage, even though the states (and the U.S. Supreme Court) have been wrestling with the rights of never-married biologic fathers when the child lives with the mother and a stepfather. See the chain of cases that began with Quilloin v. Wolcott, 434 U.S. 246 (1978) and includes, most recently, Michael H. v. Gerald D., — U.S. —, 105 L.Ed2d 91 (1989).

8   Blackstone, 1 *Commentaries* 447.

9   Ahrons and Wallish, in Pasley and Ihinger-Tallman, eds., *supra* note 1.

10 *Id.* at 228; Cherlin, "Remarriage as an Incomplete Institution," 84 *Am. J. of Soc.* 634 (1978). Within couples one or both of whom have been previously married with children, the partners often disagree about who counts as part of the family. Pasley, "Family Boundary Ambiguity," in Pasley and Ihinger-Tallman, eds., *supra* note 1 at 206.

11 Comment at Conference, Berkeley, Calif., November 1988.

12 Coleman and Ganong, "The Cultural Stereotyping of Stepfamilies," in Pasley and Ihinger-Tallman, eds., *supra* note 1 at 19, 29–30.

13 *Id.* at 33.

14   See L. Duberman, *The Reconstituted Family: A Study of Reconstituted Couples and Their Children* 128–29 (1975).

15   See, e.g., Zill and Rogers, "Recent Trends in the Wellbeing of Children in the United States and Their Implications for Public Policy, in *The Changing American Family and Public Policy* 31 (Cherlin ed. 1988).

16   "The New Extended Family: The Experience of Parents and Children after Remarriage," in Pasley and Ihinger-Tallman, eds., *supra* note 1 at 42.

17   In addition to Furstenberg, see Hetherington, in Pasley and Ihinger-Tallman, eds., *supra* note 1 at 195–96.

18   Cherlin, *supra* note 10 at 634. Furstenberg questions Cherlin's conclusion on the basis of his own research that found that remarried couples living with stepchildren experienced marital difficulties no more frequently than remarried couples with no stepchildren. Furstenberg and Spanier, *supra* note 5 at 188. See also response by Cherlin, "Dix ans apres 'le mariage comme' institution incomplete," 97 *Dialogue* 65 (1987).

19   Hetherington, in Pasley and Ihinger-Tallman, eds., *supra* note 1 at 198, 204.

20   See Ganong and Coleman, "Effects of Parental Remarriage on Children: An Updated Comparison of Theories, Methods and Findings from Clinical and Empirical Research," in Pasley and Ihinger-Tallman, eds., *supra* note 1 at 94.

21   Bartlett, *supra* note 6.

22   Of course, as the critical legal literature aptly points out, any time the law stays its hand and appears to adopt a stance of neutrality, it in fact ratifies existing power relationships that could not survive but for the force of law. In the context of stepparents, the "neutrality" I refer to here is, as ever, not truly neutral, for each biologic parent has certain rights and responsibilities given or imposed by the state that prevent a truly neutral environment from existing, even if one were possible to imagine.

23   Even Margaret Mead, in deploring the absence of a well-developed incest taboo in the stepparent relation, did not place blame on the law. See Mead, "Anomalies in American Post-Divorce Relationships," in *Divorce and After* 107 (P. Bohannon ed. 1970).

24   See A. Larson, *The Law of Workmen's Compensation* § 62.10 (1983).

25   See 42 U.S.C. §§ 401–33. For a thorough discussion of the Social Security provisions bearing on stepchildren, see Mahoney, "Stepfamilies," *supra* note 6 at 491, 496–514. Since 1960, stepchildren living with a stepparent have also been covered upon the stepparents becoming disabled.

26   Controversy can occur under Social Security in cases in which a fixed sum of money has to be divided among relatives, some of whom claim that they deserve the money more than the stepchildren. See Mahoney, "Stepfamilies," *supra* note 6 at 491, 501–04.

27   Of course, payments out of the Social Security fund are based on contributions and in some slight way, everyone's Social Security tax is a tiny bit higher because of the coverage of stepchildren, but to any given worker at any point, the coverage of stepchildren comes without any new cost that the worker experiences paying.

28   There is an organization known as the Stepfamily Association of America that,

among many things, monitors legal developments affecting stepparents, but, to date, its lobbying efforts have been limited.

29 A line stolen from George S. Kaufman and Edna Ferber's *The Royal Family* (1927), a play about a theatrical family closely resembling the Barrymores.

30 I have stated the effects of the AFDC child support provisions in the way least flattering to the government. Put more charitably, the government does bear the burden of an absent parent's nonpayment. In some states, in the past, the welfare grant for a family was reduced by the amount that a noncustodial parent was under an order to pay, whether or not he paid it. Under the current federal welfare legislation, the custodial parents assign to the government their rights to the receipt of the child support and receive the same grant each month that they would receive if there was no child support order in effect.

31 Under the 1988 amendments, all states must participate in the so-called AFDC-U program, which makes eligible for welfare benefits children living with both parents so long as one of the parents is unemployed but has had a recent substantial connection with the labor force. The federal welfare legislation still does not cover the "working poor" two-parent family.

32 42 U.S.C. § 602(a)(31).

33 Even when a state is taking into account the income of a stepparent, it excludes from the stepparent's income any amounts the stepparent is paying for the support of biologic children from a prior relationship.

34 But see Harris, "Stepparent Deeming and the Tax Intercept," *Clearinghouse Rev.,* August–September 1985.

35 I can find no research comparing the durability of nomarital and marital relationships, whether for all groups or for low-income groups in particular.

36 See chap. 6 by Krause and chap. 7 by Rhode and Minow in this volume.

37 A few cases impose some obligations on stepparents during the course of a marriage if they have accepted the child into their home and acted in loco parentis. See Mahoney, "Support and Custody Aspects," *supra* note 6 at 38, 41–43.

38 Furstenberg discusses men's loss of allegiance to biologic children with whom they cease to live and their comparatively high attentiveness to stepchildren with whom they later live. See "Good Dads—Bad Dads: Two Faces of Fatherhood," in Cherlin, ed., *supra* note 15 at 193, 202–04.

39 See Women's Legal Defense Fund, *Compilation of Child Support Guidelines* (1988). See also the unusual decision in Logan v. Logan, 120 N.H. 839, 424 A.2d 403 (1980).

40 Weise v. Weise, 699 P.2d 700 (Utah 1985).

41 See, e.g., Miller v. Miller, 478 A.2d 351 (N.J. 1984).

42 See *id*.

43 See helpful discussion in Ramsey and Masson, *supra* note 6.

44 *Id*. at 691.

45 Snow v. Snow (1971) 3 All E.R. 833 (Div. Ct.).

46 See Ramsey and Masson, *supra* note 6 at 690.

47 The father in the British case reported *supra* note 45 plainly did not accept the

notion, as indicated not only by his appeal but also by the fact that he published a book about the injustice he felt.

48   See Furstenberg and Spanier, *supra* note 5 at 94.; Furstenberg, "Child Care after Divorce and Remarriage," in Hetherington and Arasteh, eds., *supra* note 5 at 245.

49   See J. Hollinger et al., *Adoption Law and Practice* § 2.10(3) (1988).

50   *Id.* at § 6(a)(2).

51   See statutes cited in *id.* at § 2.10(3), note 90.

52   The only study I can find is Wolf and Mast's interview-based study of fifty-five families in one white, prosperous Pennsylvania county. Wolf and Mast, "Counselling Issues in Adoptions by Stepparents," 32 *Social Work* 69 (1987). See also Masson, "Stepparent Adoptions," in *Adoption* 146 (J. Masson ed. 1984).

53   England keeps nationwide statistics on adoption. One British scholar has calculated that fewer than 20% of stepparents adopt the children with whom they live. Masson, *supra* note 52 at 149–50.

54   See Furstenberg, "Child Care after Divorce and Remarriage," *supra* note 48.

55   At the same time, as child support enforcement becomes more effective, more uninvolved noncustodial parents may be willing to consent to adoption in order to escape liability. As an extreme example, in a study I conducted of the use of jail as a technique for enforcing child support, I found some men who were released from jail when they signed forms consenting to the adoption of their children by their children's new stepfather. D. Chambers, *Making Fathers Pay: The Enforcement of Child Support* (1979).

56   In their recent review of research on stepparent-child relationships, Ganong and Coleman listed research questions they found largely or totally unaddressed in the literature. One of the questions was, "What effect does stepparent adoption have on stepchildren?" Ganong and Coleman, *supra* note 20 at 94, 110.

57   I can find no legislative histories of the expanded statutes that reveal the considerations their drafters had in mind for permitting adoptions in a wider range of circumstances. Even the comments accompanying the Uniform Adoption Act are unilluminating.

58   One extreme case is Mann v. Garrette, 556 P.2d 1003 (Okla. 1976), in which the Oklahoma Supreme Court held that a single support payment made at the suggestion of counsel during the statutory period precluded the adoption from going forward over the father's objection.

59   See *In re* Adoption of Ruckus, unpublished slip opinion, Ohio Ct. App. (1987) (payments were obtained through the IRS intercept program, which permits the IRS to deduct delinquent payments out of refunds owed to a taxpayer). See this and other cases discussed in Hollinger, *supra* note 49, § 2.10(3), at notes 78–82.

60   See Boyd v. Harvey, 327 S.E.2d 55 (Ga. Ct. App. 1985).

61   Wolf and Mast, *supra* note 52 at 71 (reporting on the reasons the adoptive parents gave to the agency that writes a report to the court prior to the adoption).

62   J. Bernard, *Remarried: A Study of Marriage* (2d ed. 1971).

63   In Wolf and Mast's study of stepparent adoption, the most frequently stated single reason given by the mother and adopting stepfather for wanting the

adoption was to permit a name change. The largest grouping of children being adopted were between five and seven, which the authors read as consistent with the desires of many adopters to "have the child's name changed prior to school enrollment." Providing access to benefits and insurance was another, occasionally stated reason. Wolf and Mast, *supra* note 52, at 70.

64 Wolf and Mast reported that in most cases the custodial parent and adopting stepparent expected their child to have no further contact with the relinquishing parent. In only about a quarter of the cases the custodial parent and stepparent did not rule out the possibility of future contact with the relinquishing parent. *Id.* at 71.

65 See Hollinger, *supra* note 49, § 13.8.3.5 (1988).

66 *Id.*

67 See Masson, *supra* note 52 at 150–51.

68 See *id.* at 154.

69 See Masson, "Old Families into New: A Status for Stepparents," in *The State, the Law and the Family: Critical Perspectives* 234–35 (Freeman ed. 1984).

70 For recent figures in California, see Mnookin, chap. 2, this volume.

71 Many of the cases are reviewed in Bartlett, *supra* note 6, and Mahoney, "Support and Custody Aspects," *supra* note 6. See also H. Clark, *The Law of Domestic Relations in the United States* 826 note 55 (2d ed. 1988).

72 Oreg. Rev. Stat. § 109.119.

73 See Colo. Rev. Stat. § 14-10-1236.

74 See cases in Mahoney, "Support and Custody Aspects," *supra* note 6 at 38, 62–65. Some trial courts have bent their divorce statutes to treat a stepchild as a "child of the marriage" for purposes of custody, but such adventurous interpretations have generally been rejected on appeal. *Id.* A few have held that they had no authority to grant custody but found some sort of authority to award continuing visitation by the stepparent.

75 Consider, e.g., a Washington case in which the court found that a dedicated and loving stepmother had devoted herself to a deaf child while the biologic father stood at the sidelines "apathetic and fatalistic." The court had to cope with the fact that its divorce statute, based on the Uniform Act, seemed to provide no standing for stepparents. In seeming desperation, the court grasped onto another, purely procedural statute directing that the petition for dissolution must list "the names, ages, and addresses of any child dependent upon either or both spouses" as a reed strong enough to give it jurisdiction to determine custody. *In re* Marriage of Allen, 626 P.2d 16 (1981). See also *In re* Carey, 16 *Fam. L. Rep.* 1028 (Ill. Ct. App. 1989) (compare majority and dissenting opinions).

76 162 Mich. App. 248, 412 N.W.2d 702 (1987).

77 E.g., *In re* Custody of N.M.O., 399 N.W.2d 700, 703 (Minn. App. 1987).

78 Doe v. Doe, 399 N.Y.S.2d 977 (1977); Root v. Allen, 151 Colo. 311, 377 P.2d 177 (1962); Patrick v. Byerly, 325 S.E.2d 99 (Va. 1985); Bailes v. Sourts, 340 S.E.2d 824 (Va. 1986).

79 Stanley D. v. Deborah D., 467 A.2d 249 (N.H. 1983); *In re* Custody of N.M.O., *supra* note 77; Gorman v. Gorman, 400 So. 2d 75 (Fla. Ct. App. 1981). See Painter v. Bannister, 258 Iowa 1390, 140 N.W.2d 152 (1966). Ironically,

because of the statutes under which the cases arise, it may be easier for a step-parent to obtain custody in a divorce proceeding (even though the biologic parent has also been living with the child) than it is in a dispute with an absent parent at the time of a custodial parent's death (even though the absent parent may have lived apart from the child for many years). In the divorce case, the court is accustomed to applying a simple "best interests" test, without a presumption for either "parent."

80   See *In re* Custody of Krause, 111 Ill. App.3d 604, 444 N.E.2d 644 (1982).

81   See the appellate decisions in Henrikson, *supra* note 76, or in Pape v. Pape, 444 So.2d 1058 (Fla. App. 1984). See also the reported behaviors of the trial judges in *In re* Custody of N.M.O., *supra* note 77, in Zuziak v. Zuziak, 426 N.W.2d 761 (Mich. App. 1988), and in La Croix v. Deyo, 452 N.Y.S.2d 726 (App. Div. 1982).

82   Patrick v. Byerly, *supra* note 78.

83   *In re* Custody of N.M.O., *supra* note 77.

84   Doe v. Doe, *supra* note 78.

85   See, e.g., *In re* Marriage of Allen; *supra* note 75; Doe v. Doe, *supra* note 78; Root v. Allen, *supra* note 78.

86   B. Maddox, *The Halfparent* 20 (1975), quoted in Bartlett, *supra* note 6 at 912.

87   Bartlett, *supra* note 6 at 879.

88   Cebryzynski v. Cebryzynski, 63 Ill. App. 637, 379 N.E.2d 713 (1978).

89   I say "almost" because in the few states that treat a stepparent as a parent for determining a child's eligibility for AFDC benefits, the parentlike status is imposed on a stepparent.

90   See, e.g., Bartlett, *supra* note 6; Chambers, "Rethinking the Substantive Rules for Custody Disputes in Divorce," 83 *Mich. L. Rev.* 477 (1984); Garrison, "Why Terminate Parental Rights?" 35 *Stan. L. Rev.* 423 (1983).

91   See *supra* text at notes 67–69, and Bartlett, *supra* note 6.

92   See Schephard, "Taking Children Seriously: Promoting Cooperative Custody after Divorce," 64 *Tex. L. Rev.* 687 (1985).

93   My reasons for preferring primary caretakers are explained in Chambers, *supra* note 90. The case will be rare in which a stepparent has, for several years, been the primary caretaker of a child who is still of preschool age at the time of the divorce of the stepparent and the custodial parent.

94   I offer this suggestion hesitantly. The cases in which a child has lived for many years with an active residential stepparent but has also visited regularly with a noncustodial parent are particularly painful. See, e.g., *In re* Custody of Krause, *supra* note 80.

5. Dividing Financial Interests on Divorce

1   Ira Ellman, Carl Schneider, and Michael Wald provided especially helpful comments on this chapter and shared with me unpublished manuscripts of theirs that helped shape some of the points I make. Laura Fashing and Laura Fremont provided considerable editorial assistance to this project.

2   Although no-fault sought to treat men and women equally in many respects, plainly, no-fault advocates did not promise women postdivorce financial equality. Nor do no-fault statutes themselves make such promises. Finally, there is nothing in the "no-fault" label itself that suggests such an outcome. No-fault divorce and no-fault auto insurance were being promoted at the same time, and the no-fault label in the auto accident field stands, broadly speaking, for quite a different norm. Whereas under the old fault regime the auto victim who was wronged sought compensation from the other party (this is parallel to the old fault-based divorce regime), under auto no-fault people involved in auto accidents are responsible for their own losses. To be sure, auto no-fault reform centrally included a first-party insurance mechanism that permits victims to spread their losses. But it would hardly analogously follow that the wealthier of the parties to the divorce was intended, under no-fault divorce, to play the role of the auto insurer. See, generally, H. Jacob, *Silent Revolution: The Transformation of Divorce Law in the United States* (1988), Kay, "An Appraisal of California's No-Fault Divorce Law," 75 *Cal. L. Rev.* 291 (1987), and Kay, "Equality and Difference: A Perspective on No-Fault Divorce and Its Aftermath," 56 *U. Cin. L. Rev.* 1 (1987). As Martha Minow and Deborah Rhode point out in chap. 7 feminists were not importantly involved in the original no-fault debate.

3   One has to be a bit careful, however, about too quickly accepting the blanket assertion that such an outcome would be unintended. As I read the record, a certain few "undeserving" women were indeed meant to be made worse off by no-fault. This is by no means to suggest that every woman who previously obtained alimony was thought to be an "alimony drone," but rather that a perceived small number of women were seen as unfairly exploiting the fault system. Ending that exploitation, to the extent it existed, was, I suggest, a goal of no-fault divorce. Nonetheless, I agree that the no-fault reform certainly was not expected to make most (or even a substantial portion of) divorced women worse off than they would have been had the prior regime continued, and it would have met with considerable resistance in its adopted form were such a result clearly projected.

4   I do not consider the claims of minor children, and hence I ignore entirely the issue of child support and any other financial adjustment that might be made where minor children are involved. This topic is addressed in other chapters. Remember also that two in five divorces do not involve couples with minor children.

5   For some important critiques of Weitzman's book, see Jacob, "Another Look at No-Fault Divorce and the Post-Divorce Finances of Women," 23 *Law & Soc'y Rev.* 95 (1989) (hereafter "Another Look"); Jacob, "Faulting No-Fault," *Am. B. Found. Res. J.* 773 (1986); and Melli, "Constructing a Social Problem: The Post-Divorce Plight of Women and Children," *Am. B. Found. Res. J.* 759 (1986). For a response, see Weitzman, "Bringing the Law Back In," *Am. B. Found. Res. J.* 791 (1986). As Herbert Jacob has recently put it, "Divorce per se has enormously adverse economic consequences for many women. . . . no-fault proceedings have left the adverse effects of divorce largely unimpaired." 23 *Law & Soc'y Rev.* 113.

6 Since future earnings are, generally speaking, the product of human capital, and since the value of property (i.e., other capital) lies, broadly speaking, in its ability to produce future income, one could instead think of divorce as allocating one thing—the capital of all sorts—that the couple has. On this view, what has traditionally been called alimony, and more lately spousal support, can be characterized as a method of implementing the allocation of some of the human capital of one spouse (typically the husband) to the other.

One advantage of this view is that it avoids the step of first having to decide very thorny questions about what is "property." It could also lead to the adoption of a single principle for the allocation of all capital. This could be particularly useful now that it is widely recognized that some people have various kinds of valuable financial interests that generate future income but which are not traditional "property." These include items such as pension rights, professional licenses and business good will that are neither tangible property (houses and other real or personal property) nor conventional intangible interests like bank accounts, stocks and bonds. As Herma Hill Kay has noted in Chap. 1, this volume, whether or not these items should be considered, on the one hand, "property" to be divided on divorce along with, and pursuant to the rules governing, other property or, on the other, a potential source of future spousal support payments, and covered by the rules relevant to future earnings, has become a highly controversial matter.

7 L. Weitzman, *The Divorce Revolution: The Unexpected Social and Economic Consequences for Women and Children in America* 56, 62–63 (1985). In 1978, 58% of divorcing couples had a net worth of less than $20,000; only 20% had a net worth in excess of $50,000.

8 In her table 5 at 62, Weitzman shows that 46% of divorcing couples owned a home in 1978. In her table 6 at 63 she shows that couples itemized a family home in their divorce records 6% more often in 1977 than in 1968, a change that Weitzman believes to reflect a "real increase in home ownership" at 64. Based on this information, my table 5.1 assumes that 40% of divorcing couples owned a home in 1968 and 46% in 1977. These numbers are combined with those reported in Weitzman's table 10 at 78 to produce my table 5.1. To the extent that men fared slightly better under the new regime, perhaps this was not because no-fault is unfair to women as a group but because the few women who were thought to benefit unfairly under the old system no longer do.

9 Weitzman, *supra* note 7 at 144, 167–69.

10 See *id.,* table 13 at 169.

11 My table 5.3 is constructed from Weitzman's table 13 at 169.

12 Weitzman, *supra* note 7 at 145.

13 *Id.* at 171.

14 *Id.* at 164.

15 I am also skeptical that even the small changes noted from one period to the other were actually caused by the adoption of the no-fault system. As we have seen, Weitzman, *id.,* explored the impact of no-fault by examining actual case records in divorces resolved under the old regime (in 1968) and under the new regime (in 1972 and 1977). Data from the first two of these periods gave her

measuring points close to the effective date of the statutory change (1970), but seemingly safely on either side of it so that people would not say that the results on the first date were already importantly contaminated by the forthcoming legal change or that the results on the second date were too new to capture the impact of the change. For this reason, choosing the years she did rather than, say, the six-month period on either side of the new law's going into effect makes a lot of sense to me.

Still, four years passed between these two samples, and nine between 1968 and 1977, her third period of observation. In measuring the impact of the adoption of no-fault, the question is whether other things changed during these years that would have led to different results even under the old regime. If so, we run the risk of attributing to no-fault things that were otherwise caused.

Thinking back to that period, it strikes me that in many ways our nation was a different place in 1968 than it was in 1972 and 1977, and, most important for us here, during that period there was considerable flux in features of American life that are divorce-relevant. For example, a great deal was going on in the women's movement, female labor force participation rates continued to grow, and attitudes toward marriage were shifting. As a result, these forces could have led to different divorce outcomes for men and women by 1972 and 1977 even if the fault system had remained in place. For example, as Weitzman's data in table 15 at 177 show, women were more likely to obtain alimony if they were housewives at the time of divorce than if they were employed in the paid labor force; hence as more women enter the paid labor force, that alone would be expected to lead to fewer women receiving alimony.

Weitzman might have tried to contend with this causal conundrum by simultaneously examining for 1968 and 1972/1977 not just California but also states that did not enact no-fault divorce laws in that period. Or she might have examined some pre-1968 data to see if there was a pre-no-fault trend afoot that should be taken into account. Or she might have employed complex multiple regression analysis that sought to exclude the possible effects of these other variables. But since she did none of these things, I draw the following conclusion. If the change between 1968 and 1972/1977 in how women and men fare financially on divorce had been quite large, then perhaps one could confidently conclude that changes in divorce law were importantly responsible for at least part of the financial change. But since there was no large financial change, one must be extremely cautious about attributing any impact to no-fault.

16 Weitzman, *id.*, bases her conclusions in part on other data she has gathered that I ignore here—primarily interviews with judges and lawyers in the divorce process to whom hypothetical divorce cases were put. Given her findings from real cases, I am doubtful that the answers she received to the hypotheticals reflect the changing treatment of women in fact.

17 What are we to make of the primary theory underpinning Weitzman's analysis (*id.*) that in the old system the woman had bargaining chips, but that in the era of unilateral no-fault divorce she does not? As Marsha Garrison has pointed out, this theory is one that focuses on the change in the "grounds" of divorce. Garrison, chap. 3, this volume. Garrison further argues in her chapter that the

data from several studies, importantly including her new New York data, factually discredit this theory. I explore here briefly why the bargaining power theory is incomplete and probably unpromising in the first place.

It is easiest to envision the role of bargaining power in the stereotypical case of the forty-or-fifty-year-old husband who has fallen in love with another woman and now badly wants out of his marriage. The idea is that under the fault system his innocent and wronged wife was able to extract something from him in return for his release from their marriage—leverage that is destroyed by the adoption of unilateral no-fault divorce. But even here, the point should not be overblown. Even prior to no-fault, if the wife was uncooperative and sought to take advantage of her ability to prevent the divorce, the husband could simply move out and move in with his new lover without marrying her. That option was hardly out of the question in the late 1960s, and it would be even more plausible today.

Anyway, even if this represents a good example of where the wife might exercise her bargaining power, what proportion of all divorces are like this? After all, some wives seek to divorce their husbands for other men; some couples mutually decide their marriage is not working and should be brought to an end; some women conclude they are tired of their current marriage and want out; others want out because their husbands are beating them or cheating on them. In all these examples, however, the wife had no bargaining leverage under the old system; indeed, where she was the moving party, his power presumably was greater than hers. Consider further those cases where the man just split and the woman sought a divorce on desertion grounds; she could hardly be expected to have exercised bargaining leverage when there was no one to bargain with.

Possibly a very large proportion of divorces is caused by the man who wants out. But so far as I can tell, we do not have solid data on the question. If, as I suspect, it turns out that our stereotypical man seeking to escape his current legal ties is only one of many common reasons for divorce, this suggests that, overall, women's bargaining power was not a terribly important source of economic reward that the no-fault system took away.

Also note that this model assumes that no-fault ends the wife's bargaining power. Although I agree it is, in principle, diminished in the case where the man wants out, it should not be assumed that the wife has no bargaining power to exercise against such a husband under no-fault even in California. This is because of her ability to threaten delay in the proceedings by dragging out their negotiations over their property settlement, something he is likely to want resolved before entering into another marriage. Moreover, in some states, where no-fault divorce is still not available absent mutual consent, or where unilateral no-fault divorce requires a considerable waiting period, I agree with Garrison that the wife's bargaining power remains very much like what it was under the fault system.

Even if bargaining power was important for some women under the old system, to reiterate the point that Garrison makes, any changes that have been made in the underlying substantive rights of domestic relations law must be considered in predicting or explaining the "impact" of no-fault. Another possibly important consideration for any theory, as Weitzman well recognizes, is whether the exercise of judicial discretion has changed under no-fault. For example, since under the fault system men were, by convention, almost always treated as the guilty parties (regardless of the actual facts), this meant, one could argue, that men were formerly punished by having to pay a lot. By contrast, since under the no-fault regime there is no one to punish, one might predict that men's obligations would diminish. Alternatively, or additionally, women might be worse off (or better off) under the new regime if the enforcement of men's obligations were less (or more) effective.

Were the outcomes under fault and no-fault dramatically different, it would be considerably more important to try to disentangle which, or which combination, of these factors (and perhaps others) best explained the results.

18 Some economists, however, have suggested that the elimination of fault, or at least the elimination of contract breach considerations, in determining the parties' financial rights and duties on divorce can contribute to economically inefficient marital arrangements. See, e.g., Landes, "Economics of Alimony," 7 *J. Legal Stud.* 35 (1978), and Oster, "A Note on the Determinants of Alimony," 49 *J. Marriage & Fam.* 81 (1987).

19 See, generally, Love, "Punishment and Deterrence: A Comparative Study of Tort Liability for Punitive Damages under No-Fault Compensation Legislation," 16 *U.C.D. L. Rev.* 231 (1983).

20 Some states today seem to have adopted just this view. See, e.g., Garrison's discussion of the New York rule in chap. 3, this volume.

21 See, generally, F. Harper, F. James, and O. Gray, *The Law of Torts* (2d ed. 1986) at § 8.10, and Ward, "Tort Claims in Divorce Litigation," *Trial*, November 1988, at 63.

22 Ira Ellman addresses the same models considered here and in the next section and comes to the same general conclusions, but for somewhat different reasons. Ellman, "The Theory of Alimony," 77 *Calif. L. Rev.* 1, 13–40 (1989).

23 See M. Glendon, *Abortion and Divorce in Western Law* 105 (1987).

24 Of course, excluding this aspect of partnership law already weakens the usefulness of the analogy.

25 On the dissolution of their partnership, financial partners ordinarily are repaid their original capital contributions before any net accumulated profits of the partnership are shared between them.

26 Tobin, Book Review, 20 *Loyola L.A. L. Rev.* 1641 (1987).

27 Landes, *supra* note 18.

28 See, e.g., Cohen, "Marriage, Divorce and Quasi Rents; Or, 'I Gave Him the Best Years of My Life,'" 16 *J. Legal Stud.* 267 (1987); Ellman, *supra* note 22; and Oster, *supra* note 18.

29 See Scott, "Rational Decisionmaking about Marriage and Divorce" (1989) (unpublished manuscript).

30 This is the theme emphasized by Lloyd Cohen, *supra* note 28. In an earlier pioneering work, Gary Becker and his colleagues drew on Becker's general "human capital" theory to offer a broad theory about matrimonial dissolution (one that is, however, largely unconcerned about the role that legal rules govern-

ing the division of financial interests on divorce might play). To oversimplify their argument, the Becker team predicts that divorce will occur when its economic benefits (including the potential benefits of remarriage) outweigh its losses. See, Becker, Landes, and Michael, "An Economic Analysis of Marital Instability," 85 *J. Polit. Econ.* 1141 (1977). The point I am emphasizing in the text is that spousal support rules might affect that calculus in ways that are thought socially desirable.

31 Jacob reports several studies concluding that no-fault itself is not responsible for the large increase in the divorce rate that has occurred since the adoption of no-fault. See Jacob, "Another Look," *supra* note 5 at 99.

32 This effect could be blunted by having the divorce "tax" paid to the state rather than to the other spouse.

33 Along these lines, Sharon Oster, *supra* note 18, found (with an admittedly weak data set) that wives who contest divorce petitions filed by their husbands wind up with significantly increased spousal support awards.

34 As Frank Furstenberg has recently pointed out, although mothers are likely to be more hostile to the participation in the family of absent fathers who do not provide economic support to the mother and child, the increased participation of fathers who have been coerced to make financial contributions might diminish rather than promote family harmony. Moreover, Furstenberg notes that though it is widely believed that voluntary participation in the family by absent fathers is good for children, the empirical proof that the father can help the children other than through financial contributions is surprisingly weak. See Furstenberg, "Supporting Fathers: Implications of the Family Support Act for Men" (1989) (unpublished manuscript).

35 For lists of other principles for dividing financial interests, see, e.g., J. Areen, *Cases and Materials on Family Law* 591–95 (1985), and J. Eekelaar and M. MacLean, *Maintenance after Divorce* 33–58 (1986).

36 I assume that pension rights, e.g., are part of marital property. See, generally, Blumberg, "Marital Property Treatment of Pensions, Disability Pay, Workers' Compensation, and Other Wage Substitutes: An Insurance, or Replacement, Analysis," 33 *U.C.L.A. L. Rev.* 1250 (1986). I put aside the possibility that special adjustments might be thought to be required owing to the presence of minor children, such as the delayed sale of the family home.

37 I do not address the question of transitional fairness—that is, the rights of parties who married under the fault regime expecting to be governed by its rules and who now find themselves subject to no-fault.

38 Weitzman, *supra* note 7 at xii; see also 323, 337–39.

39 Hoffman and Duncan, "What Are the Economic Consequences of Divorce?" 25 *Demography* 641 (1988).

40 It must be appreciated that even if former spouses were to enjoy equal living standards after divorce, many would expect to suffer a decline simply because of the loss of economies of scale that occurs when one household is broken up into two. Of course, that loss might be offset by efforts of the parties or governmental assistance to bring new income into their households. Indeed, Weitzman found

that "the combined post-divorce income of the two former spouses is often greater than the family income at the time of divorce," *supra* note 7 at 325.

41 Weitzman (*id.*) interviewed people who, in 1978, had been divorced for about one year.

42 Weitzman's data show that to the limited extent that there has been remarriage by one year after divorce, it is much more common among men. *Id.* at 327.

43 Data from the late 1970s showed that 70% of divorced women who received alimony were in the paid labor force or looking for paid work, although the labor force participation rates among this group dropped sharply for those over forty-five. Three-quarters of mothers receiving child support were in the work force, 84% of that group on a full-time basis. See Grossman and Hayghe, "Labor Force Activity of Women Receiving Child Support or Alimony," 103 *Monthly Lab. Rev.,* November 1982 at 39, 41.

44 She also employed some measurement procedures favorable to men that are worth noting. First, she assumed that men paid all the child and spousal support ordered. Second, she ignored any additional income that might have become available to a spouse as a result of remarriage.

45 It is the reported result of this procedure that Hoffman and Duncan criticize, *supra* note 39.

46 Mnookin's data (chap. 2, this volume) show that though fathers ask for substantial physical custody less often than they say they want it, they still ask for it with some substantial regularity.

47 For direct support of this position, see Goldfarb, "Marital Partnership and the Case for Permanent Alimony," in *Alimony: New Strategies for Pursuit and Defense* (Section of Family Law of the American Bar Ass'n) 45 (1988).

48 See Jacob, "Another Look," *supra* note 5 at 104, where Jacob also notes that in 1975 nearly two-thirds of all divorced women were under age thirty.

49 See, e.g., Uniform Marriage and Divorce Act, § 308, 9A U.L.A. (1973).

50 See J. Rawls, *A Theory of Justice* (1971).

51 Depue v. Flatau, 100 Minn. 299, 111 N.W. 1 (1907).

52 Ploof v. Putnam, 81 Vt. 471, 71 A. 188 (1908).

53 See J. Fishkin, *The Limits of Obligation* (1982).

54 Garrison (chap. 3, this volume) reports what one magazine reader's poll found young women in the 1980s think about alimony.

55 See, e.g., Batts, "Remedy Refocus: In Search of Equity in 'Enhanced Spouse/ Other Spouse' Divorces," 63 *N.Y.U. L. Rev.* 751 (1988). See also Landes, *supra* note 18.

56 I thank Weitzman for privately making this intriguing suggestion to me.

57 Discussions with Michael Wald contributed importantly to my thinking about this issue.

58 George Norton has proposed a spousal support formula that could be viewed as falling between, or combining, these two models. A transfer of 33–40% of the higher earner's income minus 50% of the lower earner's income would be made for a period no longer than the length of the marriage. See Norton, "The Future of Alimony: A Proposal for Guidelines," in *Alimony, supra* note 47 at 176, 184.

6. Child Support Reassessed: Limits of
Private Responsibility and the Public Interest

1   See H. Krause, *Child Support in America: The Legal Perspective* (1981) (hereafter *Child Support*); H. Krause, *Illegitimacy: Law and Social Policy* (1971) (hereafter *Illegitimacy*); Krause, "Equal Protection for the Illegitimate," 65 *Mich. L. Rev.* 477 (1967) (hereafter "Equal Protection"); Krause, "Bringing the Bastard into the Great Society: A Proposed Uniform Act on Legitimacy," 44 *Tex. L. Rev.* 829 (1966) (hereafter "Uniform Act").

2   President Ronald Reagan issued an executive order to assess the impact of federal activity on the family. Exec. Order No. 12,606, 3 C.F.R. 241 (1987 comp.), reprinted in 5 U.S.C. § 601 note at 139–40 (Supp. V 1987) (hereafter Exec. Order). The order asked:

> (a) Does this action by government strengthen or erode the stability of the family and, particularly, the marital commitment?
>
> (b) Does this action strengthen or erode the authority and rights of parents in the education, nurture, and supervision of their children?
>
> (c) Does this action help the family perform its functions, or does it substitute governmental activity for the function?
>
> (d) Does this action by government increase or decrease family earnings? Do the proposed benefits of this action justify the impact on the family budget?
>
> (e) Can this activity be carried out by a lower level of government or by the family itself?
>
> (f) What message, intended or otherwise, does this program send to the public concerning the status of the family?
>
> (g) What message does it send to young people concerning the relationship between their behavior, their personal responsibility, and the norms of our society?

3   In the fall of 1988, presidential candidates competed hotly on family issues, such as day care. All but forgotten presidential aspirants called for an increase in the American birthrate, e.g., *New York Times,* October 24, 1987, at 9, col. 1 (Rev. Pat Robertson), and pregnancy leave (Representative Pat Schroeder's proposal is still pending in Congress). Senator Pat Moynihan's 1988 welfare reform shows a family and child support enforcement focus. See, e.g., *Welfare: Reform or Replacement? (Child Support Enforcement—II): Hearings before the Subcomm. on Social Security and Family Policy of the Senate Comm. on Finance,* 100th Cong., 1st Sess. (1987). The party platforms reflected different approaches to the problem of child care. *New York Times* August 17, 1988, at A20, col. 1. The Republicans: "In returning to our traditional commitment to children, the Republican Party proposes a radically different approach: establish a toddler tax credit for preschool children as proposed by Vice President Bush, available to all families of modest means, to help them support and care for their children in a manner best suited to their families' values and traditions." *Id.* The Democrats: "We believe that Government should set the standard in recognizing that worker productivi-

ty is enhanced . . . by major increases in assistance making child care more available and affordable to low and middle income families, helping states build a strong child care infrastructure, setting minimum standards for health, safety and quality." *Id.* at A20, col. 2; See also "Governor Michael Dukakis on Family Policy," *Am. Fam.,* October 1988, at 5; Moritz, "Family Policy in the 1988 Campaign: More Than Patronage and Promise?" *Am. Fam.,* October 1988, at 3; Rovner, "Democrats Lining Up behind 'Family' Banner," 46 *Cong. Q. Weekly Rep.* 183 (1988); "Vice President George Bush on Family Policy," *Am. Fam.,* October 1988, at 4.

4   Consider "82 Key Statistics on Work and Family Issues," *Nat'l Rep. on Work & Fam.* (BNA) Spec. Rep. No. 9 (September 1988).

5   See, e.g., S. Rep. No. 447, 100th Cong., 2d Sess. (1988). Compare the minority view of Senator Dan Quayle in the same report at 64–69. See "Parental Leave Bill Put on Fast Track in Congress by House and Senate Sponsors," 2 *Nat'l Rep. on Work and Fam.* (BNA) No. 5, at 1 (February 17, 1989); Rovner, "Child-Care Debate Intensifies As ABC Bill Is Approved," 47 *Cong. Q. Weekly Rep.* 585 (1989).

6   See, e.g., Besharov and Tramontozzi, "The Costs of Federal Child Care Assistance," *Am. Fam.,* September 1988, at 10; "Bush Calls for $330 Million Package of Child Care Initiatives and Tax Credits," 2 *Nat'l Rep. on Work & Fam.* (BNA) No. 5, at 1 (February 17, 1989). Proposals remain active: Rovner, "Partisan Bidding War Erupts over Aid to Poor Children," 47 *Cong. Q. Weekly Rep.* 653 (1989); Rovner, "Senate's Child-Care Measure Would Broaden U.S. Role," 47 *Cong. Q. Weekly Rep.* 1543 (1989).

7   See, e.g., Working Group on the Family, "The Family: Preserving America's Future" (November 1986) (unpublished report transmitted with letter dated December 2, 1986, from Gary L. Bauer, under secretary of the U.S. Department of Education, to President Reagan; copy on file in the offices of the *University of Illinois Law Review*); cf. Exec. Order, *supra* note 2.

8   See, e.g., Chambers, "The 'Legalization' of the Family: Toward a Policy of Supportive Neutrality," 18 *J.L. Reform* 805 (1985). But see Burt, "Coercive Freedom: A Response to Professor Chambers," 18 *J.L. Reform* 829 (1985).

9   See, generally, M. Rheinstein, *Marriage Stability, Divorce, and the Law* chap. 4 (1972).

10   See *U.S. Department of Commerce, Bureau of the Census, Current Population Reports, Population Characteristics, Series P-20, No. 433, Marital Status and Living Arrangements: March 1988* (1989).

11   E.g., Krause, "Legal Position: Unmarried Couples," 34 *Am. J. Comp. L.* 533 (Supp. 1986).

12   For example, is marital community property an idea that came one hundred years too late? See Glendon, "Is There a Future for Separate Property?" 8 *Fam. L.Q.* 315, 322–25 (1974).

13   The federal child support enforcement legislation is discussed *infra,* text at notes 24–40.

14   See *infra,* text at notes 24–26.

15   *Restatement of Conflict of Laws* § 458 comment a, at 548 (1934).

16 *Illegitimacy, supra* note 1 at 106–08.

17 See Stack and Semmel, "The Concept of Family in the Poor Black Communi-
ty," in Staff of Subcomm. on Fiscal Policy of the Joint Economic Comm., 93d
Cong., 1st Sess., *Studies in Public Welfare, Paper No. 12, The Family, Poverty, and
Welfare Programs: Household Patterns and Government Policies,* pt. II, at 275
(Comm. Print 1973) (R. Lerman ed.) (hereafter *Studies in Public Welfare*). Cf.
G. Cooper and P. Dodyk, *Income Maintenance* 285 (1973):

> Though consanguinity has been traditionally recognized as an acceptable basis
> for the allocation of support costs, that criterion is markedly discordant
> with the ability-to-pay notions which determine so much of the modern alloca-
> tion of public costs. Particularly where an extended net of liable relatives is
> recognized under state law, the wisdom of departing from the normal general-
> revenue tax base may be questioned. Indeed, even where one is dealing with
> the relation of father to son, one finds the reports replete with cases in which
> the biological nexus is paralleled by no ties of familiarity, affection or support,
> —cases which raise grave doubt as to the ultimate significance of simple-blood
> relationship for the problems at hand. Moreover, whatever the conclusions one
> may reach on such matters, one must contend with the fact that reluctance to
> precipitate enforcement of support obligations causes many applicants to re-
> frain from seeking public assistance. The aversion to trenching upon the al-
> ready stretched resources of another household has caused many, particularly
> among the elderly, to prefer private penury to public assistance. Whatever the
> gain derived from reliance upon support obligations, its cost is some degree of
> frustration of the central purpose of public assistance.

18 Sugarman, "*Roe v. Norton:* Coerced Maternal Cooperation," in R. Mnookin, *In
the Interest of Children: Advocacy, Law Reform, and Public Policy* 365, 415–417
(1985).

19 See Stack and Semmel in *Studies in Public Welfare, supra* note 17.

20 *Child Support, supra* note 1 at 285–306.

21 Congress added 42 U.S.C. § 602(a)(11) (requiring notice to state child support
collection agency of AFDC benefits) in 1950.

22 Greenspan v. Slate, 12 N.J. 426, 437, 97 A.2d 390, 395 (1953).

23 Blackstone, 1 *Commentaries,* vol. 1, *447–48 (1765).

24 "Twelfth Annual Report Released to Congress," *Child Support Rep.,* August
1988, at 3 hereafter "Report").

25 See *Child Support, supra* note 1 at 323–30, discussing the drawn-out controversy over the non-AFDC support collection feature of the enforcement legislation.
It is well worth emphasizing the significance of the extension of the federal
support enforcement legislation beyond the welfare context. The provisions
concerning non-AFDC support enforcement alleviate the all too common lot of
the abandoned mother who has sufficient productive capacity and pride to keep
herself and her children above the welfare eligibility line, but whose earning
capacity may have been impaired by a role-divided marriage and now is restricted by the custodial services she renders her children. While the typical
father's earnings enable him to make a reasonable contribution to child support,

he does not earn enough to do that without pain. Thus, unless seriously encouraged, many fathers are unwilling to make their proper contributions. These contributions, though significant in terms of their children's needs, too often are not large enough to make it economical to involve lawyers in repeated enforcement forays under the cumbersome and correspondingly expensive traditional child support enforcement procedures.

26 U.S. Department of Health and Human Services, Office of Child Support Enforcement, *Twelfth Annual Report to Congress for the Period Ending September 30, 1987* vol. 1, 7 (1988) (hereafter *Report to Congress*), *id.,* vol. 2, tables 3, 5.

27 The federal enforcement legislation is codified at 42 U.S.C. §§ 651–65 (1982). The text following this note briefly summarizes the federal enforcement process. For more detailed explanations, see *Child Support, supra* note 1, at 307–87; M. Henry and V. Schwartz, *Essentials for Attorneys in Child Support Enforcement* (M. Reynolds ed. 1986); M. Henry and V. Schwartz, *A Guide for Judges in Child Support Enforcement* (M. Reynolds 2d ed. 1987).

28 Child Support Enforcement Amendments of 1984, Pub. L. No. 98-378, 98 Stat. 1305 (codified as amended in scattered sections of 47 U.S.C.) (hereafter 1984 amendments). See also H.R. Rep. No. 527, 98th Cong., 1st Sess. (1983). The text following this note summarizes important provisions of the 1984 amendments.

29 See *infra,* text at notes 39–40.

30 "States Report Child Support Debts to Credit Bureaus," *Child Support Rep.,* August 1988, at 1.

31 Clark v. Jeter, 108 S.Ct. 1910 (1988); Paulussen v. Herion, 475 U.S. 557 (1986); Pickett v. Brown, 462 U.S. 1 (1983); Mills v. Habluetzel, 456 U.S. 91 (1982).

32 D. Chambers, *Making Fathers Pay: The Enforcement of Child Support* (1979).

33 1984 amendments, *supra* note 28, § 17, 98 Stat. at 1321–22 (codified as amended at 42 U.S.C.A. § 667 (West Supp. 1989)).

34 H.R. Rep. No. 527, 98th Cong., 1st Sess. 48 (1983):

> The Committee recommends that the report include a full and complete summary of the opinions and recommendations of an advisory panel to be comprised of at least one person who is representative of parents entitled to receive child support on behalf of their children, at least one person who is representative of absent parents obligated to pay child support, and at least two people with professional expertise in child support issues in the fields of law and economics, at least one person who is a member of the judiciary, at least one person who is a member of a State legislature, and at least one person with expertise in the administration of child support enforcement programs.

35 U.S. Department of Health and Human Services, Office of Child Support Enforcement, *Development of Guidelines for Child Support Orders: Final Report* I-4 (1987).

36 See Brackney, "Recent Development—Battling Inconsistency and Inadequacy: Child Support Guidelines in the States," 11 *Harv. Women's L.J.* 197 (1988);

Dodson, "A Guide to the Guidelines: New Child Support Rules Are Helping Custodial Parents Bridge the Financial Gap," *Fam. Advoc.,* Spring 1988, at 4; Rhode and Minow, chap. 7, text at notes 59–69.

37   1984 amendments, *supra* note 28, § 23(b)(1), 98 Stat. at 1330.

38   *Id.* § 23, 98 Stat. at 1329–30.

39   Family Support Act of 1988, Pub. L. No. 102-485, 100 Stat. 2343 (to be codified in scattered sections of 42 U.S.C.). For a summary and text of the 1988 amendments, see 15 *Fam. L. Rep.* (BNA) 1047–48, 2001–08 (1988). The text following this note briefly summarizes important provisions of those amendments.

40   This paternity establishment provision comes fifteen years after it was proposed to the Senate Finance Committee. See *Illegitimacy, supra* note 1, at 133–37; H. Krause, *Family Law: Cases, Comments and Questions* 875–76 (2d ed. 1983). Then, the proposal was enacted by the Senate, but not by the House, and dropped in conference.

41   See *Report to Congress,* vol. 2, *supra* note 26, tables 58–71.

42   "Report," *supra* note 24 at 3 (quoting Director Stanton).

43   L. Weitzman, *The Divorce Revolution: The Unexpected Social and Economic Consequences for Women and Children in America* (1985); see "Review Symposium on Weitzman's *Divorce Revolution,*" 1986 *Am. B. Found. Res. J.* 757 (hereinafter "Review Symposium").

44   Bruch and Wikler, "The Economic Consequences," *Juv. & Fam. Ct. J.,* Fall 1985, at 5.

45   *Report to Congress,* vol. 1, *supra* note 26 at 5.

46   *Child Support, supra* note 1 at 431.

47   See *U.S. Department of Commerce, Bureau of the Census, Current Population Reports, Household Economic Studies, Series P-70, No. 13, Who's Helping Out? Support Networks among American Families* (1988).

48   "The study shows that half of the teen fathers lived with their child at least for some time after the baby's birth. However, only one third of the fathers married the mother of the baby within twelve months of conception. The study also shows that teenage fathers who were married prior to conception were the least likely to have completed high school: 62 percent of those fathers dropped out of school compared to about 37 percent of those whose first birth was conceived outside of marriage whether they subsequently married or not." "Teenage Fatherhood," *Am. Fam.,* March 1988, at 19; see, generally, J. Smollar and T. Ooms, *Young Unwed Fathers: Research Review, Policy Dilemmas and Options* 52–53 (1987).

49   Chambers, *supra* note 32 at 3–9, 253. Senator Daniel Moynihan has a more "optimistic" perception of the situation:

This is a matter to be pressed *to* the point of punitiveness. . . . Hunt, hound, harass: the absent father is rarely really absent, especially the teenage father, but merely unwilling or not required to acknowledge his children's presence. The Child Support Enforcement program has the great virtue of paying for itself as well as having the inestimable advantage of linking the issue of welfare dependency to the more general issue of women's entitlements. . . . And for the too-much-pitied unemployed teenage male there would be nothing wrong with a federal work program—compulsory when a court has previously ordered him to support his children—with the wages shared between father and mother. This latter is not likely to get started or to work very well if it does. The disorder of the times would likely enough defeat it. But it does make a statement about legitimacy: there must be an acknowledged providing male. (D. Moynihan, *Family and Nation* 180–81 [1986]).

50 *Report to Congress,* vol. 2, *supra* note 26, table 49; see also L. Loyacono and S. Smith, *State Budget Implications: Child Support Enforcement* appends. B and C (1988). Below "par" AFDC cost-effectiveness ratios for 1987 are reported for New Hampshire (.83), Delaware (.92), Maryland (.96), New York (.74), Nebraska (.85), Florida (.81), Kentucky (.93), Louisiana (.90), Tennessee (.97), Virginia (.59), Arizona (.53), New Mexico (.95), Oklahoma (.97), Texas (0.84), Colorado (.94), Alaska (.75), Nevada (.62), the District of Columbia (.53), Guam (.73), Puerto Rico (.52), and the Virgin Islands (.28). *Id.* In assessing the true meaning of "cost-benefit effectiveness," many caveats are in order. See *Child Support, supra* note 1, at 422–31, 446–55.

51 Krause, "Reflections on Child Support," 1983 *U. Ill. L. Rev.* 99, 106–11.

52 Krause, *supra* note 40 at 897–99, quoting Krause, "Automatic Adjustment Clauses in Support Agreements or Decrees," *Fair Share,* (April 1981) at 3–4.)

53 *Child Support Enforcement Program Reform Proposals: Hearings before the Senate Comm. on Finance,* 98th Cong., 2d Sess. 454, 458, 460 (1984) (hereafter *Hearings*) (statement of Harry D. Krause). Compare Bruch, "Developing Standards for Child Support Payments: A Critique of Current Practice," 16 *U.C. Davis L. Rev.* 49, 62 (1982).

54 See *supra* text accompanying note 35.

55 We could debate at length the relative effectiveness of specific enforcement techniques, from wage withholding to extradition and imprisonment. See Chambers, *supra* note 32; *Child Support, supra* note 1 at 81–84. We could discuss the U.S. Supreme Court's recent struggle with contempt sanctions, civil or criminal, in Hicks *ex rel.* Feiock v. Feiock, 108 S.Ct. 1423 (1988). But I think that the "better enforcement" debate is all but over. With mandated, formula-based setting of support obligations, with payroll deduction of support owed, and with computer-provided nationwide access to support-owing parents, the law now provides an effective arsenal for imposing the obligation as well as collecting child support. Continuing complaints that child support collections remain inadequate can no longer expect much response from better enforcement law, although there is always room for improvement.

56 And 42.7% of black children under the age of eighteen were poor. *Champaign-Urbana News-Gazette,* August 31, 1988, at 1, col. 1. See also, *New York Times,* September 3, 1988, at 22, col. 1.

57 *New York Times,* April 12, 1987, at E5, col. 2, lists maximum fiscal 1987 monthly benefits for a family of four as of January 1987. The highest paying states were as follows (given in parentheses are the figures as a percent of

estimated median monthly income for a family of four): Alaska: $833 (23%); California: $734 (26%); New York: $706 (26%); Connecticut: $688 (21%); Wisconsin: $649 (25%). The lowest paying states were Mississippi: $144 (7.3%): Alabama: $147 (6.6%); Tennessee: $189 (8.5%); Texas: $221 (8.5%); Arkansas: $224 (11.6%).

58 *Hearings, supra* note 53 at 454, 464–66 (statement of Harry D. Krause); see also *Child Support, supra* note 1 at 456–65.

59 For more detail, see Disregard of Child Support Payments, 53 Fed. Reg. 21,642 (1988) (codified in scattered sections of 45 C.F.R. pts. 302 and 303).

60 Even this small step has proved to be expensive. The $50 disregard reduced the overall savings to the taxpayer from a high near $250 million in 1984 to less than $25 million in 1987, and more than tripled the federal program deficit to about $300 million in the same period. *Report to Congress,* vol. 1, *supra* note 26, at 12.

61 Cf. Bowen v. Gilliard, 483 U.S. 587 (1987) AFDC provision that attributes child support benefits to the family unit is not unconstitutional).

62 Moynihan, *supra* note 49 at 147.

63 E.g., Gray, Book Review, 46 *N.Y.U. L. Rev.* 1228, 1233 (1971) (reviewing *Illegitimacy, supra* note 1): "Professor Krause . . . errs in suggesting that poor illegitimate children can be benefited by a systematic effort to force their fathers to pay support. . . . First, such a program would not create more stable families. Rather, the effect would be to encourage fathers to desert their illegitimate children entirely. Second, many children would not benefit financially even if fathers did pay, since the support payments would be deducted from any welfare benefits."

64 Glendon, "Modern Marriage Law and Its Underlying Assumptions: The New Marriage and the New Property," 13 *Fam. L.Q.* 441 (1980).

65 Minow, "The Properties of Family and the Families of Property," Book Review, 92 *Yale L.J.* 376, 379–81 (1982) (reviewing M. Glendon, *The New Family and the New Property* (1981)).

66 Jacob, "The Changing Landscape of Family Policy and Law," Book Review, 21 *L. & Soc'y Rev.* 744 (1988).

67 Blackstone, *supra* note 23, at *447–48.

68 See J. Beckstrom, *Evolutionary Jurisprudence: Prospects and Limitations on the Use of Modern Darwinism throughout the Legal Process* 50–53 (1989); J. Beckstrom, *Sociobiology and the Law: The Biology of Altruism in the Courtroom of the Future* (1985).

69 Blackstone, *supra* note 23, at *453.

70 An Act for the Relief of the Poor, 43 Eliz., ch. 2, § VII (1601); Blackstone, *supra* note 23, at *453–54; cf. Swoap v. Superior Court, 10 Cal. 3d 490, 516 P.2d 840, 111 Cal. Rptr. 136 (1973) (statute requiring children to reimburse state for aid paid to parents is not unconstitutional); see also Garrett, "Filial Responsibility Laws," 18 *J. Fam. L.* 793 (1979–80).

71 See e.g., Cannon v. Juras, 15 Or. App. 265, 515 P.2d 428 (Ct. App. 1973) (facts did not establish abandonment which would absolve son from support of his mother).

72 Blackstone, *supra* note 23, at *449 (footnotes omitted).

73   The *New York Times* reports: "A middle-income couple with two children will
      face total costs of about $130,000 per child in 1988 dollars by the time both
      children are 18 years old, said Thomas Espenshade, a senior fellow at the Urban
      Institute, a research organization in Washington, D.C. If the children go to
      college, the costs will significantly increase. 'Most prospective parents grossly
      underestimate the financial obligations of parenthood,' Mr. Epenshade said.
      Planners advise parents to begin saving for a child's college education as soon as
      possible. For a child born in 1988, four years at a public university might cost
      about $120,000 in tuition and other expenses." *New York Times,* February 20,
      1988, at A34, col. 1. "A study by the College Board indicates that from 1981 to
      1987, the cost of attending a private university increased 81 percent, while
      median family income rose 40 percent." *New York Times,* March 23, 1988, at
      B18, col. 1.

74   The traditional presumption that favors giving custody to the mother is dying a
      very slow death. The great majority of custody dispositions still go to the
      mother. Krause, *supra* note 40, at 727–35.

75   Even in trend-setting California, the flirtation with joint custody seems to be
      ebbing. On September 27, 1988, Governor George Deukmejian signed a law
      that declares California has "neither a preference nor a presumption for or
      against joint legal custody, joint physical custody, or sole custody, but allows the
      court and the family the widest discretion to choose a parenting plan which is in
      the best interests of the child or children." Sherman, "Doubts Grow on Joint
      Custody," *Nat'l L.J.,* October 24, 1988, at 3, col. 1 (quoting California law).

76   Rawles v. Hartman, 172 Ill. App. 3d 931, 527 N.E.2d 680 (App. Ct. 1988),
      leave to appeal denied, 123 Ill.2d 566, 535 N.E.2d 410 (1989).

77   See Kujawinski v. Kujawinski, 71 Ill. 2d 563, 578–80, 376 N.E.2d 1382,
      1389–90 (1978); see, generally, Moore, "Parents' Support Obligations to
      Their Adult Children, 19 *Akron L. Rev.* 183 (1985).

78   E.g., Doe v. Duling, 603 F. Supp. 960 (E. D. Va. 1985). (Virginia fornication
      and cohabitation statutes declared unconstitutional).

79   See, "Equal Protection," *supra* note 1 at 504–06; *Uniform Act, supra* note 1 at
      859.

80   Lehr v. Robertson, 463 U.S. 248, 261 (1983) and, very recently, consider
      Michael H. v. Gerald D., 109 S.Ct. 2333 (1989). In Lehr, the Court elaborated:

> The intangible fibers that connect parent and child have infinite vari-
> ety. They are woven throughout the fabric of our society, providing it
> with strength, beauty, and flexibility. It is self-evident that they are suffi-
> ciently vital to merit constitutional protection in appropriate cases. In
> deciding whether this is such a case, however, we must consider the broad
> framework that has traditionally been used to resolve the legal problems
> arising from the parent-child relationship. . . .
>
> The difference between the developed parent-child relationship that
> was implicated in *Stanley* and *Caban,* and the potential relationship in-
> volved in *Quilloin* and this case, is both clear and significant. When an
> unwed father demonstrates a full commitment to the responsibilities of

parenthood by "com[ing] forward to participate in the rearing of his child," his interest in personal contact with his child acquires substantial protection under the Due Process Clause. At that point it may be said that he "act[s] as a father toward his children." *But the mere existence of a biological link does not merit equivalent constitutional protection.* The actions of judges neither create nor sever genetic bonds. "[T]he importance of the familial relationship, to the individuals involved and to the society, stems from the emotional attachments that derive from the intimacy of daily association, and from the role it plays in 'promot[ing] a way of life' through the instruction of children as well as from the fact of blood relationship."

The significance of the biological connection is that it offers the natural father an opportunity that no other male possesses to develop a relationship with his offspring. If he grasps that opportunity and *accepts some measure of responsibility for the child's future,* he may enjoy the blessings of the parent-child relationship and make uniquely valuable contributions to the child's development. If he fails to do so, the Federal Constitution will not automatically compel a State to listen to his opinion of where the child's best interests lie. (*Id.* at 256, 261–62 [citations omitted and emphasis added])

81 For the Court's most recent opinion on related issues, see Michael H. v. Gerald D., 109 S.Ct. 2333 (1989).

82 Chambers, chap. 4, this volume.

83 See Ramsey and Masson, "Stepparent Support of Stepchildren: A Comparative Analysis of Policies and Problems in the American and English Experience," 36 *Syracuse L. Rev.* 659 (1985).

84 See Wallerstein and Corbin, "Father-Child Relationships After Divorce: Child Support and Educational Opportunity, 20 *Fam. L.Q.* 109, 115 (1986); see also Pearson and Thoennes, "Supporting Children after Divorce: The Influence of Custody on Support Levels and Payments," 22 *Fam. L.Q.* 319 (1988).

85 See Weitzman, *supra* note 43; Abraham, "*The Divorce Revolution Revisited:* A Counter-Revolutionary Critique," 3 *Am. J. Fam. L,* 87 (1989).

86 See, e.g., "Review Symposium," *supra* note 43.

87 See, e.g., Hunter, "Child Support Law and Policy: The Systematic Imposition of Costs on Women," 6 *Harv. Women's L.J.* 1 (1983).

88 See, e.g., Moss, "No-Fault Divorce Hurts," *A.B.A. J.,* December 1986, at 36.

89 Weitzman, *supra* note 43 at 337–43.

90 1984 amendments, *supra* note 28, § 23, 98 Stat. at 1329–30.

91 Horowitz and Dodson, "Child Support, Custody and Visitation: A Report to State Child Support Commissions" (July 1985) (unpublished paper prepared for the American Bar Association National Legal Resource Center for Child Advocacy and Protection, Child Support Project; copy on file in the offices of the *University of Illinois Law Review*).

92 See *Child Support, supra* note 1 at 58, 67.

93 See *In re* Marriage of Boudreaux, 201 Cal. App. 3d 477, 247 Cal. Rptr. 234 (Ct.

App. 1988) (where visitation rights are intentionally sabotaged, noncustodial parent may seek modification of original child support to enforce visitation); *Washington ex rel.* Burton v. Leyser, 196 Cal. App. 3d 451, 241 Cal. Rptr. 812 (Ct. App. 1987) (custodial parent who concealed herself and her children from noncustodial parent could not recover child support arrearages for period of concealment); Biamby v. Biamby, 114 A.D.2d 830, 494 N.Y.S.2d 741 (App. Div. 1985) (trial court erroneously granted unpaid child support in light of interference with visitation rights); Hoyle v. Wilson, 746 S.W.2d 665 (Tenn.) (custodial spouse denied child support payments for period she disappeared with the children), *reh'g denied,* 14 *Fam. L. Rep.* 1259 (Tenn. 1988); Rohr v. Rohr, 709 P.2d 382 (Utah 1985) (willful failure to pay child support justified lower court's refusal to modify custody and visitation rights).

94   Mo. Am. Stat. § 452.340.6 (Vernon Supp. 1989): "A court may abate, in whole or in part, any future obligation of support or may transfer the custody of one or more children if it finds:

> (1) That a custodial parent has, without good cause, failed to provide visitation or temporary custody to the noncustodial parent pursuant to the terms of a decree of dissolution, legal separation or modifications thereof; and
> (2) That the noncustodial parent is current in payment of all support obligations pursuant to the terms of or decree of dissolution, legal separation or modifications thereof. The court may also award reasonable attorney fees to the prevailing party.

95   "Report," *supra* note 24 at 3 (quoting Secretary Bowen).

96   Except for vestigial mention in relative responsibility laws (see Schneider, "Moral Discourse and the Transformation of American Family Law," 83 *Mich. L. Rev.* 1803 and note 31 [1985]), scattered attempts to resuscitate such laws, (see Byrd, "Relative Responsibility Extended: Requirement of Adult Children to Pay for Their Indigent Parent's Medical Needs, 22 *Fam. L.Q.* 87 [1988]; Garrett, *supra* note 70), a successful movement to allow grandparents visitation with their grandchildren (see Krause, *supra* note 40 at 792–98, 1149–50), and one attempt to impose support liability on grandparents (Wis. Stat. Ann. § 49.90 (lm)(a)1(West 1987) (effective January 1, 1990), the law has all but excised the elderly from the family.

97   Life is not all roses for all elderly persons. Lawrence Swedley of the National Council of Senior Citizens provides the following data:

> Fewer than half of all older people receive private or public pensions. For men, the median private pension is $3,190 a year; for women, it's $1,940. Social Security is the major source of income for the elderly, making up 38 percent on average. It is all that stands between nearly one-third of the elderly and poverty. The median annual benefit is $6,150. While 67 percent of retirees have income from assets, that constitutes just 26 percent of aggregate income. Median income for households headed by a person older than 65 is $14,334 (1987 Census). For single individuals, median income is $8,205. Lastly, even with the added protection Medi-

care will now provide against "catastrophic" costs, in 1989 beneficiaries will spend about $1,525 out of their own pockets on health care. For an average retiree, that doesn't leave too much for basic needs—let alone bonbons. (Letter to the Editor, *New York Times,* November 2, 1988, at A26, col. 4)

98 *New York Times,* April 23, 1987, at C1, col. 5.

99 *New York Times,* January 24, 1987, at 1, col. 1; see also Moynihan, *supra* note 49 at 94–96; Chakravarty and Weisman, "Consuming Our Children?" *Forbes,* November 14, 1988, at 222.

100 Rhode and Minow, chap. 7, text at note 53.

101 *Child Support, supra* note 1 at 299; see Chambers, "Comment—The Coming Curtailment of Compulsory Child Support," 80 *Mich. L. Rev.* 1614 (1982).

102 See A. Kahn and S. Kamerman, *Income Transfers for Families with Children: An Eight-Country Study* (1983); Kamerman and Kahn, "What Europe Does for Single-Parent Families," *Pub. Interest,* Fall 1988, at 70; Kamerman and Kahn, "Family Policy: Has the U.S. Learned From Europe?" (April 28, 1986) (unpublished paper prepared for the Ford Foundation Seminar on Comparative Social Policy, Columbia University, April 9, 1986; copy on file in offices of the *University of Illinois Law Review*); see also "Family Allowances," 12 *Ann. Rev. of Population L.* 1985 § 420 (1988). Despite budget woes, the debate in Britain is over *raising* child benefits. See "The Aid of the Family," *Economist,* October 22, 1988, at 19.

103 Cf. Rheinstein, *supra* note 9, at 425 (footnote omitted):

> The impact of social welfare measures upon family stability is potentially enormous. Through well-considered use they could constitute an effective device of rational family policy and prove much more effective than manipulation of the laws on divorce. But much research is needed to render these tools more effective and to avoid adverse consequences.
>
> So far little is known either about the effects upon family stability of those legislative and other measures which have been taken in numerous foreign countries but for which the United States does not, or not yet, have exact counterparts. The most conspicuous of these devices is the system of family allowances, which in 1959 existed in no less than thirty-eight countries, among them Canada. Mostly such legislation has been motivated by a desire to reverse a declining trend in the birthrate or simply to encourage fertility. In the Federal Republic of Germany general considerations of social welfare have been emphasized.

104 Family policy and tax policy remain unreconciled, their interrelationship often unrecognized. For a summary review, see Krause, *supra* note 40, at 280–92. Detailed analysis of the problem is provided by Bittker, "Federal Income Taxation and the Family," 27 *Stan. L. Rev.* 1389 (1975); McIntyre and Oldman, "Taxation of the Family in a Comprehensive and Simplified Income Tax," 90 *Harv. L. Rev.* 1573 (1977); See also Staff of House Select Comm. on Children, Youth, and Families, 99th Cong., 1st Sess., *A Family Tax Report Card: Round II* (Comm. Print 1985).

105 This is not even a new idea. Plato, *Laws,* vol. 1, bk. IV, at 313 (R. Bury trans. 1926) (circa 347 B.C.) suggested: He "that disobeys and does not marry when thirty-five years old shall pay a yearly fine of such and such an amount, —lest he imagine that single life brings him gain and ease, —and he shall have no share in the honors which are paid from time to time by the younger men in the State to their seniors." And much later, "Hartford taxed 'lone-men' twenty shillings a week 'for the selfish luxury of solitary living.'" G. Howard, *A History of Matrimonial Institutions* 153 (1904) (quoting from A. Earle, *Customs and Fashions in Old New England* 37 (1893)).

106 Harvard's Joint Center for Housing Studies reports that "the median income of a single parent under 25 was $6,233 in 1988, down 15 percent in inflation-adjusted terms from 1974." *Champaign-Urbana News-Gazette,* June 22, 1989, at B9, col. 4.

107 *New York Times,* March 15, 1989, at 14, col. 4 (quoting the Family Support Administration of the Department of Health and Human Services).

108 See Whitman, "The Hollow Promise," *U.S. News and World Rep.,* November 7, 1988, at 41.

109 See Gray, *supra* note 63 at 1233–34:

> Professor Krause's naive view of the role of law in the lives of poor families is reflected in his argument that poor children could be helped by a stricter enforcement of child neglect and dependency laws. He is apparently aware that neglect laws are generally vague and irrationally punitive statutes which are often applied by biased and poorly trained judges who, in any event, lack any resources with which to actually help poor children. Nevertheless, the author suggests that increased state intrusion into the lives of poor families is needed to protect their children. . . . The validity of this conclusion is, to say the least, doubtful. . . . Rather, public interferences in the lives of poor families tends to destroy the very family structure (although not a white, middle class one) which Professor Krause is at pains to encourage.

110 Children living in one-parent households number 15.3 million and 1.9 million more live with neither parent. From 1980 to 1988, the proportion of white children in one-parent households rose from 15% to 19%; among blacks, from 46% to 54%; and among Hispanics, from 21% to 30%. *Washington Post,* February 16, 1989, at A7.

111 I am not alone. See "Bringing Children Out of the Shadows," Book Review, *Carnegie Q.,* Spring 1988, at 1, 7 (reviewing and quoting from L. Schorr, *Within Our Reach: Breaking the Cycle of Disadvantage* (1988)):

> Summarizing her arguments, Schorr presents "five pillars" on which, she believes, a "new national commitment of consequence" with "staying power" must stand:
> First, the public must accept the evidence that favorable outcomes among high-risk children can be achieved by systematic intervention early in life. Interventions, to be effective, must offer a "broad spectrum" of services and continuity of care to families and children in the context

of the community in which they live. These programs must have skilled staff that can develop "reciprocal" relationships of trust and respect.

Second, the public must understand that "intensive and sometimes costly" preventive care for vulnerable families and children represents a sound allocation of resources. Such assistance, she maintains, is cheaper by far than the price society already pays for neglected health, unemployment, and crime. Americans, in other words, must "recognize that investments to improve the futures of disadvantaged children represent a joining of compassion with long-term self-interest."

112   Cf. Sherman, "Keeping Baby Safe from Mom," *Nat'l L.J.*, October 3, 1988, at 1, col. 1 (making pregnant women legally responsible for their fetuses); Garrison, "Why Terminate Parental Rights?" 35 *Stan. L. Rev.* 423, 436–37 (1983) (parental visitation rights for children in foster care).

113   For medical studies of such phenomena, see Chasnoff, Griffith, MacGregor, Dirkes, and Burns, "Temporal Patterns of Cocaine Use in Pregnancy," 261 *J. A.M.A.* 1741 (1989); Novick, Berns, Stricof, Stevens, Pass, and Wethers, "HIV Seroprevalence in Newborns in New York State," 261 *J. A.M.A.* 1745 (1989).

114   "A report by the National Academy of Sciences called the growing number of homeless children a 'national disgrace.'" *New York Times,* September 20, 1988, at A1, col. 1. "The report estimates that on any given night families with 100,000 children are homeless. . . . The report itself was written in the bland, moderate style typical of the academy, a private organization that advises the Government on policy issues in science and health. It analyzed the causes of homelessness and the health problems associated with it, and it recommended Federal action to improve health services, housing and income levels to reduce homelessness. But a more strongly worded supplementary statement, endorsed by 10 of the 13 experts on the panel that wrote the report complained that the report was 'too limited' in its language and approach." *Id.*

115   "Lost Generation in Welfare Hotels: Growing Up with Drugs and Despair," *New York Times,* February 22, 1988, at 1, col. 1. A New York City plan calls for the closing of welfare hotels sheltering homeless families. As a result, "since Aug. 1, [1988,] city officials said, 702 families have been moved out of welfare homes; 2,586 families remain in 41 welfare hotels." *New York Times,* March 3, 1989, at B3, col. 1.

116   Cf. Shapiro v. Thompson, 394 U.S. 618 (1969) (statute denying welfare benefits to residents of state for less than one year declared unconstitutional).

117   There is a delicate balance to be struck between the reproductive rights and lifestyle of the mother and the fundamental rights of the child. The choice is between education and coercion. At a November 1988 health law conference in Boston, I heard Professor Martha Field eloquently rejecting coercion in favor of education. I would much prefer that route myself, but education has been tried. It is not working. See Field, "Controlling the Woman to Protect the Fetus," 17 *Law Med. & Health Care* 114 (1989). A summary of recent fetal

abuse cases and controversy is presented by Jost, "Mother versus Child," *A.B.A. J.,* April 1989, at 84. See also Sherman, *supra* note 112.

118   See Krause, "Child Welfare, Parental Responsibility, and the State," in *Studies in Public Welfare, supra* note 17, pt. II, at 255, 266–73.

119   See *supra* note 104.

120   J. Cribbett and C. Johnson, *Principles of the Law of Property* 96–97 (3d ed. 1989).

121   An early analysis and history of the marriage penalty are in *American Families: Trends and Pressures, 1973: Hearings before the Subcomm. on Children and Youth of the Senate Comm. on Labor and Public Welfare,* 93d Cong., 1st Sess. 204, 204–11 (1973) (statement of Dr. Harvey E. Brazer, professor of economics and research associate, Institute of Policy Studies, University of Michigan).

122   I.R.C. § 221(a)–(b) (1982) (repealed 1986).

123   See McIntyre, "Rosen's Marriage Tax Computations: What Do They Mean?" 41 *Nat'l Tax J.* 257 (1988); Rosen, "The Marriage Tax Is Down but Not Out, 40 *Nat'l Tax J.* 567 (1987).

124   See Druker v. Commissioner, 697 F.2d 46 (2d Cir. 1982) (marriage penalty is not unconstitutional); Barter v. United States, 550 F.2d 1239 (7th Cir. 1977) (same), *cert. denied,* 434 U.S. 1012 (1978).

125   Senator Moynihan summarizes the figures:

> The current [Social Security] reserve is approaching $100 billion. Between now and the year 2000 it will grow to $1.4 trillion. (As of 1987, the entire assets of private pension funds were about $1.49 billion.) This revenue stream must be deposited with the Treasury. If at the end of the day the Treasury has more money on hand than it needs, it simply retires privately held debt. . . . The national debt begins to shrink. Our present deficit "path" takes us, in theory at least, to a zero deficit by 1993. If that happens, the revenue stream from Social Security will be sufficient to begin retiring debt by 1994. As public debt declines, private savings increase. By 2010 the Social Security reserve is projected to be nearly $4.5 trillion ($4,600,000,000!). If we wanted to go all the way, we could probably have zero national debt by that time. (*New York Times,* May 23, 1988, at A19, col. 2)

126   "Interest on U.S. Debt to Top Budget's $150 Billion Deficit," *New York Times,* October 8, 1988, at 1, col. 4.

127   *Champaign-Urbana News-Gazette,* September 18, 1988, at B-1, col. 1.

128   "According to Agriculture Department finance officers, commodity price support operations rose to a record $25.8 billion in 1986." *Champaign-Urbana News-Gazette,* November 26, 1988, at 1 col. 3. Bovard, "Farm Policy Follies," *Pub. Interest,* Spring 1989, at 75, 75, calculates: "American consumers pay over $10 billion more for their food than they would in a free market. For the same aggregate cost, the government could give every full-time subsidized farmer two new Mercedes each year. With the $250 billion that government

and consumers have spent on farm subsidies since 1980, Uncle Sam could have bought every farm, barn, and tractor in thirty-four states."

129   "In 1983, the nation's 24,000 superfarms with over $500,000 in annual sales received an average of $26,805 in direct government payments, while the smallest farms averaged $1,211." "Should We Save the Family Farm?" *Rep. from Inst. for Phil. & Pub. Pol'y,* Summer 1988, at 1, 5 (quoting from W. Galston, *A Tough Row to Hoe: The 1985 Farm Bill and Beyond* (1985)). In an ironic foreign policy twist, we provide the Soviet economy a price for our food exports that is below our own production cost. This does major harm to unsubsidized farmers in friendly countries, for instance, Australia.

130   Bowen v. Gilliard, 483 U.S. 587, 632 (1987) (Brennan, J., dissenting) (citation omitted).

131   Cf. C. Murray, *Losing Ground: American Social Policy, 1950–1980* 227–28 (1984), advocating "scrapping the entire federal welfare and income-support structure for working-aged persons, including AFDC, Medicaid, Food Stamps, Unemployment Insurance, Worker's Compensation, subsidized housing, disability insurance, and the rest. It would leave the working-aged person with no recourse whatsoever except the job market, family members, friends, and public or private locally funded services. It is the Alexandrian solution: cut the knot, for there is no way to untie it."

Although pointing in the opposite political direction, Dr. Murray's medicine smacks of the infantile 1960s—if we trash what there is, the millennium will emerge. Senator Moynihan has explained what will emerge in twelve years. See *supra* text accompanying note 62.

132   *New York Times,* June 25, 1989, at 7, col. 3; *id.,* June 28, 1989, at B3, col. 1.

7. Reforming the Questions, Questioning the Reforms: Feminist Perspectives on Divorce Law

1   See, e.g., E. May, *Great Expectations* 2–3 (1980); R. Griswold, *Family and Divorce in California, 1850–1890: Victorian Illusions and Everyday Realities* (1982); W. O'Neill, *Divorce in the Progressive Era* (1969); R. Phillips, *Putting Asunder: A History of Divorce in Western Society* (1988).

2   For discussion of the marital rape exemption, see D. Russell, *Rape in Marriage* (1982); D. Finkelhor and K. Yllo, *License to Rape: Sexual Abuse of Wives* (1985); Freeman, "But if You Can't Rape Your Wife, Who[m] Can You Rape?: The Marital Rape Exemption Reexamined," 15 *Fam. L.Q.* 1 (1981). For spousal and child abuse, see E. Pleck, *Domestic Tyranny: The Making of American Social Policy against Family Violence from Colonial Times to the Present* 3–13, 80–94, 182–183 (1987); R. Gelles and M. Straus, *Intimate Violence: The Definitive Study of the Causes and Consequences of Abuse in the American Family* 20–32 (1988); L. Gordon, *Heroes of Their Own Lives: The History and Politics of Family Violence* (1988). For courts' refusal to enforce support obligations in the context of ongoing marriages, see McGuire v. Mcguire, 157 Neb. 226, 59 N.W.2d 336, 342 (1953); D. Rhode, *Justice and Gender* 141 (1989); Krauskopf, "Partnership

Marriage: Legal Reforms Needed," in *Women into Wives: The Legal and Economic Impact of Marriage* 39, 96 (J. Chapman and M. Gates eds. 1977).

3   For a fuller discussion of these themes, see M. Minow, *Making All the Difference* (forthcoming); Olsen, "The Myth of State Intervention in the Family," 18 *U. Mich. J.L. Ref.* 835 (1985); Olsen, "The Family and the Market: A Study of Ideology and Legal Reform," 96 *Harv. L. Rev.* 1497 (1983).

4   *Women's Work, Men's Work: Sex Segregation on the Job* (H. Hartmann and B. Reskin eds. 1986); *Gender in the Workplace* (C. Brown and J. Pechman eds. 1987).

5   Although younger couples tend toward somewhat more equal distributions of family responsibilities, wide disparities persist even within this group. For studies of women's disproportionate homemaking duties, see P. Roos, *Gender and Work: A Comparative Analysis of Industrial Societies* 16–29 (1985); G. Staines and J. Pleck, *The Impact of Work Schedules on the Family* 63 (1983); D. Rhode, *supra* note 2 at 172–75.

6   Estimates suggest that two-thirds of married women with children curtail or forgo paid work to pursue homemaking responsibilities. See *Final Report of the California Senate Task Force on Family Equity,* California State Senate, June 1, 1987, (hereafter *California Task Force Report*) reprinted in part in 1 *Hastings Women's L.J.* 9, 23 (1989). Women's disproportionate assumption of family obligations is encouraged by employment policies that make it especially difficult for men to exercise child-care responsibilities. For example, recent studies find that less than 2% of surveyed companies offer paternity leaves, few men take them, and far fewer do so for more than a very brief period. See sources cited in Rhode, *supra* note 2 at 355, note 25; Congressional Caucus for Women's Issues, *Fact Sheet on Parental Leave Legislation* (Washington, D.C., 1985); Catalyst, *Maternity/Parental Leaves* (1986).

7   In the late 1980s, female-male earnings ratio for full-time workers was 65% in annual wages and 70% in weekly wages. National Committee on Pay Equity, Briefing Paper no. 1, "The Wage Gap" (April 1989). For an overview of explanations for the gap, see, e.g., *Comparable Worth: New Directions for Research* (H. Hartmann ed. 1985); *Ingredients for Women's Employment Policy* (C. Bose and G. Spitz eds. 1987).

8   See S. Kamerman and A. Kahn, *The Responsive Workplace: Employers and a Changing Labor Force* (1987).

9   See, generally, *Women, Households, and Structural Transformation* (L. Beneria and C. Stimpson eds. 1987); R. Sidel, *Women and Children Last: The Plight of Poor Women in Affluent America* (1986); Marcus, "Reflections on the Significance of the Sex/Gender System: Divorce Law Reform in New York," 42 *U. Miami L. Rev.* 55 (1987).

10 See, generally, S. Okin, *Justice, Gender and the Family* (1989); Z. Eisenstein, *The Radical Future of Liberal Feminism* (1981): J. Elshtain, *Public Man, Private Woman: Women in Social and Political Thought* (1981); Law, "Women, Work, Welfare and the Preservation of Patriarchy," 131 *U. Penn. L. Rev.* 1251 (1983).

11 See, e.g., P. Giddings, *When and Where I Enter: The Impact of Black Women on Race and Sex in America* (1984); Collier and Yanagisako, "Feminism, Gender, and Kinship," in *Theoretical Perspectives on Sexual Difference* (D. Rhode ed.

1990); Ryan, "The Explosion of Family History," 10 *Rev. in Am. Hist.* 181 (1982).

12   See L. Weitzman, *The Divorce Revolution: The Unexpected Social and Economic Consequences for Women and Children in America* (1985); H. Jacob, *Silent Revolution: The Transformation of Divorce Law in the United States* (1988); Fineman, "Implementing Equality: Ideology, Contradiction and Social Change," 1983 *Wis. L. Rev.* 789; Friedman, "Rights of Passage: Divorce Law in Historical Perspective," 63 *Or. L. Rev.* 649 (1984); Kay, "Equality and Difference: A Perspective on No-Fault Divorce and Its Aftermath," 56 *U. Cin. L. Rev.* 1 (1987); Kay, "An Appraisal of California's No-Fault Divorce Law," 75 *Calif. L. Rev.* 291 (1987); and Marcus, *supra* note 9.

13   Even at the height of the fault era, alimony was awarded in less than a fifth of all cases, and noncompliance was pervasive. See Weitzman, *supra* note 12 at 17–18; Jacob, *supra* note 3; Goldfarb, "Rehabilitative Alimony, the Alimony Drone, and the Marital Partnership," in *National Symposium on Alimony and Child Support* (American Bar Association, Family Law Publication, 1987).

14   Herma Kay was one of the few women scholars who played a major role in formulating the first no-fault statute, and her account of its legislative history is especially instructive. See articles cited in *supra* note 12. See also *California Task Force on the Family* (1967).

15   These initiatives received firmer constitutional footing in 1979 when the Supreme Court invalidated an Alabama statute that made alimony available only to wives. Orr v. Orr, 440 U.S. 268 (1979). The new rules governing marital property also sought more fairly to reflect the contributions of both spouses to the relationship. These rules replaced the traditional practice in non–community property states that awarded property to the title holder, who was usually the husband.

16   Scholars have begun to redress the omissions of earlier reforms. For issues affecting low-income families, see J. Hecker, "An Examination of No-Fault Divorce: Has It Affected Minority Women to the Same Degree It Has Affected White Women?" (unpublished paper, Stanford Law School, 1987); H. Rodgers, *Poor Women, Poor Families: The Economic Plight of America's Female Headed Households* 39 (1986); G. Duncan, *Years of Poverty, Years of Plenty: The Changing Fortunes of American Workers and Families* 57 (1984); D. Ellwood, *Poor Support: Poverty in the American Family* (1988). For concerns of displaced home-makers, see notes 40–46 and accompanying text. For concerns of couples with no need for elaborate legal procedures, see Cavanagh and Rhode, "Project, The Unauthorized Practice of Law and Pro Se Divorce," 86 *Yale L.J.* 104 (1976); Rhode, "Policing the Professional Monopoly: A Constitutional and Empirical Analysis of Unauthorized Practice Prohibitions," 34 *Stan. L. Rev.* 1 (1981).

17   Some opponents of reform were concerned that divorce on demand would weaken the family, and some segments of the bar worried that no-fault procedures would reduce the role (and income) of lawyers. See Cavanagh and Rhode, *supra* note 16.

18   Commentators differ on the extent of this asymmetry but all agree on the general dynamic. Compare Weitzman, *supra* note 12, with Women's Research and Edu-

cation Institute, Congressional Caucus for Women, *The American Woman: A Report in Depth* 78–82 (1987) (citing surveys); McLindon, "Separate but Unequal: The Economic Disaster of Divorce for Women and Children," 21 *Fam. L.Q.* 351 (1987); Wishik, "Economics of Divorce: An Exploratory Study," 20 *Fam. L.Q.* 79 (1986).

19   See Kahn and Kamerman, "Child Support in the United States: The Problem," in *Child Support: From Debt Collection to Social Policy* (A. Kahn and S. Kamerman eds. 1988); Arendell, "Women and the Economies of Divorce in the Contemporary United States," 13 *Signs* 121 (1987).

20   In addition to Lenore Weitzman's influential work, see sources cited in note 12 and Rhode, *supra* note 2 at 146–53.

21   See Herma Kay's evaluation in chap. 1 of California reforms and her call for "nonpunitive, nonsexist, and nonpaternalistic framewords for marital dissolution." See also the discussions in Garrison, chap. 3, and Sugarman, chap. 5, on the role of no-fault legislation in causing women's postdivorce inequalities.

22   Compare Weitzman, *supra* note 12, with Fineman, "Illusive Equality: On Weitzman's Divorce Revolution," 1986 *Am. Bar Found. Res. J.* 781; Jacob, "Faulting No-Fault," 1986 *Am. Bar Found. Res. J.* 773. See also Garrison, chap. 3, and Sugarman, chap. 5. Similar causal disputes have centered on the extent to which escalating rates of marital breakdown are attributable to liberalization of legal rules. See, e.g., M. Rheinstein, *Marriage Stability, Divorce, and the Law* (1972): O'Neill, *supra* note 1.

23   See discussion in the first and final parts of this chapter.

24   *New York Times,* February 7, 1983, A1, A14.

25   See Prager, "Sharing Principles and the Future of Marital Property Law," 25 *U.C.L.A. L. Rev.* 1 (1977); Glendon, "Is There a Future for Separate Property?" 8 *Fam. L.Q.* 315 (1974).

26   See discussion in the first part of this chapter.

27   See U.S. Bureau of the Census, *Who's Minding the Kids?* (1987); U.S. Department of Labor, *Childcare: A Workforce Issue* (1988); Kamerman and Kahn, *supra* note 8; Rhode, "Occupational Inequality," 1988 *Duke L.J.* 1207; Taub, "From Parental Leaves to Nurturing Leaves," 13 *N.Y.U. Rev. L. & Soc. Change* 381 (1985); R. Spalter-Roth, *Unnecessary Losses: Costs to Americans of the Lack of Family and Medical Leave* (1988).

28   Only three states have fixed equal division requirements. Others have presumptions in varying forms. In some jurisdictions, rebuttable presumptions are applicable to all marriages or to lengthy marriages; in other states 50-50 formulas are a starting point against which other statutory factors such as relative need and relative contribution are to be applied. See Blumberg, "Marital Property Treatment of Pensions, Disability Pay, Workers Compensation, and Other Wage Substitutes: An Insurance, or Replacement, Analysis," 33 *U.C.L.A. L. Rev.* 1250, 1251–52, note 4 (1986). "Equal vs. Equitable," 5 *Equitable Dist. J.* 73 (July 1988).

29   See text accompanying notes 40–41 *infra*.

30   For discussion of the way women's employment choices are constrained by sex-

based stereotypes and family obligations, see Rhode, *supra* note 2 at 161–74, 179–81, and sources cited in *supra* notes 4 and 5.

31 See *California Task Force Report, supra* note 6.

32 *Id.* at 31; Weitzman, *supra* note 12 at 78.

33 See Fineman, *supra* note 12 at 866–87; *New Jersey Supreme Court Task Force on Women and the Courts* 60–80 (1984); Schafran, "Gender Bias in the Courts," in *Women as Single Parents: Confronting Institutional Barriers in the Courts, the Workplace, and the Housing Market* 45–47 (E. Mulroy ed. 1988); Weitzman, *supra* note 12.

34 Compare J. Golden, *Equitable Distribution of Property,* § 8.17 (1983), with Avner, "Using the Connecticut Equal Rights Amendment at Divorce to Protect Homemakers' Contributions to the Acquisition of Marital Property," 4 *Bridgeport L. Rev.* 265 (1983).

35 See cases discussed in Note, "Family Law: Professional Degrees in 1986—Family Sacrifice Equals Family Asset," 25 *Washburn L.J.* 276 (1986); *In Re Marriage of Sullivan,* 37 Cal. 3rd 762, 691 P. 2d 1020, 209 Cal. Rptr. 354 (1984): O'Brien v. O'Brien, 66 N.Y. 576, 498 N.Y.S. 2d 743, 489 N.E. 2d 712 (N.Y. 1985).

36 See Krauskopf, "Recompense for Financing Spouse's Education: Legal Protection for the Marital Investor in Human Capital," 28 *Kan. L. Rev.* 379 (1980); see also Cal. Code Ann. Civ. § 4800.3 (reimbursement for community contributions to education or training). For example, common economic techniques of assessing the replacement value of homemakers' nonmarket contributions to career assets ignore the societal devaluation of women's work and neglect less tangible forms of assistance. See Krauskopf, "Maintenance: A Decade of Development," 50 *Mo. L. Rev.* 259, 317 (1979).

37 For further discussion of these principles, see the discussion in the text accompanying notes 40–48. For arguments favoring compensation to spouses through spousal awards rather than "property" rights in professional degrees, see Ellman, "The Theory of Alimony," 77 *Cal. L. Rev.* (1989), and Kay, chap. 1, this volume.

38 *California Task Force Report, supra* note 6 at 30–33. For discussion of the recent California legislation regarding deferred sales of homes for custodians of minor children, see Kay, chap. 1. For comparable provisions in other states, see *California Task Force Report, supra* note 6 at 30–33, and Wash. Rev. Code § 26.09 080 (4).

39 Weitzman, *supra* note 12; McLindon, *supra* note 18; Peters, "Marriage and Divorce: Informational Constraints and Private Contracting," 76 *Am. Ec. Rev.* 437 (1986).

40 Weitzman, *supra* note 12; *Household Wealth and Asset Ownership 1984* (Current Population Reports, Series P-70 no 70, 1986); Fineman, *supra* note 12; *New Jersey Supreme Court Task Force, supra* note 33 at 60–80.

41 Weitzman, *supra* note 12, at 33–35, 265–272, 284; T. Arendell, *Mothers and Divorce: Legal, Economic, and Social Dilemmas* (1986); Displaced Homemakers Network, *A Status Report on Displaced Homemakers and Single Parents in the U.S.* (1987).

42 Weitzman, *supra* note 12 at 35.

43 See Schafran, *supra* note 33; *New Jersey Supreme Court Task Force, supra* note 33; Weitzman, *supra* note 12; Goldfarb, *supra* note 13; Displaced Homemaker's Network, *supra* note 41; *California Task Force Report,* supra note 6.

44 See Arendell, *supra* note 41; Rhode, *supra* note 2, and sources cited in note 33.

45 For discussion of judicial education, see, e.g., Weitzman, *supra* note 12, and J. Lieberman, *Child Support in America* (1986). For analysis of the need for greater consistency in judicial decision making, see, e.g., Krauskopf, "Maintenance," *supra* note 36 at 263, and Glendon, "Fixed Rules and Discretion in Contemporary Family Law and Succession Law," 60 *Tul. L. Rev.* 1165, 1170 (1986).

46 Thus, a standard that considered only career sacrifices in measuring spousal support might offer inadequate protection to parties who could not prove what opportunities they might have pursued had they not been primary homemakers. Cf. Ellman, *supra* note 37.

47 *California Task Force Report, supra* note 6 at 42–53. The California legislature enacted a provision specifying the "standard of living established in marriage" as the basis for support awards without the exception for longer marriages. See Kay, chap. 1, this volume. The Task Force also made recommendations designed to promote more realistic expert assessments of homemakers' vocational options and spousal subsidies for retraining. These were enacted by the legislature and vetoed by the governor. *Id.*

48 For discussion of special counseling, job training, and income and supplemental income programs for these groups see Arendell, *supra* note 41; Rhode, *supra* note 2; Sidel, *supra* note 9; and sources cited in note 41. See, generally, text accompanying notes 74–75 *infra.*

49 See Lieberman, *supra* note 45; Krause, chap. 6, this volume; Duncan, *supra* note 16; Rogers, *supra* note 16; M. Katz, *In the Shadow of the Poorhouse: A Social History of Welfare in America* (1986).

50 See, e.g., Weitzman, *supra* note 12; Mnookin, chap. 2, this volume.

51 See studies discussed in J. Wallerstein and S. Blakeslee, *Second Chances: Men, Women and Children a Decade after Divorce* (1989); Dornbusch et al., "Single Parents, Extended Households, and the Control of Adolescents," 56 *Child Devel.* 326 (1985).

52 See Jacob, *supra* note 12; Ellwood, *supra* note 16; Bane, "Politics and Policies of the Feminization of Poverty," in *The Politics of Social Policy in the United States* (M. Weir, A. Orloff, and T. Skocpol eds. 1988); Goodban, "The Psychological Impact of Being on Welfare," 59 *Soc. Serv. Rev.* 403 (1985).

53 See Minow, "Rights for the Next Generation: A Feminist Approach to Children's Rights," 9 *Harv. Women's L.J.* 1 (1986) (arguing that children's needs are public, not merely private concerns) and notes 64–69 and accompanying text infra.

54 According to most surveys, over half of divorced men have failed to meet their obligations, and arrearages have averaged between two-thirds and three-fourths of the amounts due. Weitzman, *supra* note 12 at 357–413: M. Glendon, *Abortion and Divorce in Western Law* 97–103 (1987); Cassetty, "Emerging Issues in Child Support Policy and Practice," in *The Parental Child Support Obli-*

gation 3, 4 (J. Cassetty ed. 1983); Ellwood, *supra* note 16 at 284. Most studies find that compliance rates are not significantly higher among noncustodial parents with the ability to pay. See Shafran, *supra* note 33 at 55; D. Chambers, *Making Fathers Pay: The Enforcement of Child Support* (1979) and Parnas and Cermak, "Rethinking Child Support," 22 *U.C. Davis L. Rev.* 759, 762–763 (1989).

55 See, e.g., Arendell, *supra* note 41; Hunter, "Child-Support Law and Policy: The Systemic Imposition of Costs on Women," 6 *Harv. Women's L.J.* 1, 2 (1983); Neely, "The Primary Caretaker Parent Rule: Child Custody and the Dynamics of Greed," 3 *Yale L. & Pol'y Rev.* 168 (1984);

56 Beginning in October 1989, the states' guidelines are to establish the amount of child support due unless the court makes a written finding that their application would be unjust or inappropriate. Guidelines must be reviewed once every four years. Wage withholding is automatic unless the court finds good cause or the parties have a written agreement providing for other arrangements.

57 See Schafran, *supra* note 33 at 54. For example, the U.S. Bureau of Labor Statistics estimates that when a noncustodial parent earns $2,000 a month and a custodial parent earns $1,000, the noncustodial parent would have to provide over 50% of his or her gross income in support to equalize the families' postdivorce standard of living. As Schafran notes, no current guidelines come close to that figure.

58 Cal. Civ. Code § 4720–4732 (West 1989).

59 See R. Williams, "Final Project Report," in *Development of Guidelines for Child Support Orders: Advisory Panel Recommendations and Final Report* (Office of Child Support Enforcement, U.S. Department of Health and Human Services) (1987). The key difference between the two variations of income sharing is that under the first approach, the percentage of parental income attributable to child support is either constant or increases with income; in the federal variation, the percentage decreases as income rises. Under either approach, income may be imputed to the custodial parent in order to preserve incentives to work.

60 We are indebted to the excellent background study by Janice Steinschneider, "Guiding Child Support: A Feminist Analysis of Child Support Guidelines" (Harvard Law School, unpublished paper, May 1987). For a further overview, see, e.g., *Proceedings of the Women's Legal Defense Fund's National Conference on the Development of Child Support Guidelines; Essentials of Child Support Guidelines Developments: Economic Issues and Policy Considerations* (1986).

61 See *Statement of NOW Legal Defense and Education Fund on the Status of the 1984 Child Support Enforcement Amendments before the Subcomm. on Public Assistance and Unemployment Compensation, Comm. on Ways and Means, U.S. House of Representatives, February 23, 1988* (S. Goldfarb and E. Moore); Johnson, "Do Minnesota Child Support Guidelines 'Support' Children?" 3 *Law & Ineq.* 343, 348 (1985). Wage withholding also does little to reach parental resources that come from irregular jobs, investments, or other sources of nonsalary income.

62 In jurisdictions that combine actual or imputed parental income before apportioning support obligations (see note 59), there is ambiguity over whether

custodial parents can be excused from seeking wages if they stay home to care for children. See Steinschneider, *supra* note 60; *Proceedings* supra note 60.

63   See Furstenberg, "Good Dads—Bad Dads: Two Faces of Fatherhood," in *The Changing American Family* (A. Cherlin ed. 1988); Furstenberg et al., "The Life Course of Children of Divorce: Marital Disruption and Parental Contact," 48 *Am. Soc. Rev.* 656 (1983). See also *California Task Force Report,* supra note 6 (criticizing the second-family hardship deductions for undermining prior obligations to the first family).

64   Even if every woman collected the full amount due, the U.S. Census Bureau estimates that the number of divorced women and children in poverty would fall by less than 5%. Amott, "Working for Less: Single Mothers in the Workplace," in Mulroy ed., *supra* note 33 at 108. Of course, greater progress would be possible if child support awards were higher, and some will be, once guidelines become mandatory. Even so, those most knowledgeable about federal legislative initiatives warn against viewing them as a solution to child support problems. See Krause, *supra* note 49. See also Pearson, Thoennes, and Jaden, "Legislating Adequacy: The Impact of Child Support Guidelines," *Law & Soc. Rev.* (forthcoming) (three-state study finding a 15% increase in child support awards after implementation of guidelines and attributing major limitations in impact to inadequate family resources).

65   See Ellwood, *supra* note 16; W. P. O'Hare, *America's Welfare Population: Who Gets What* 10 (Population Reference Bureau) (September 1987); Van DeVeer, "Adequacy of Current AFDC Need and Payment Standards," 21 *Clearinghouse Rev.* 141, 144, 145 (1987).

66   According to a federal advisory panel on child support, a primary objective of the proposed federal guidelines is to avoid "extraneous negative effects on the major life decisions of either parent. In particular, the guidelines should avoid creating economic disincentives for remarriage or labor force participation." A further concern, noted in Part I, is to reduce the public costs of welfare assistance to divorced families. Measured even by these limited goals, current guidelines fall short. Their insensitivity to gender inequalities makes welfare assistance essential and restricts custodial parents' ability to choose between full-time work and providing in-home child care. R. G. Williams, *Final Project Report in Development of Guidelines for Child Support Orders: Advisory Panel Recommendations and Final Report* I-4 (Office of Child Support Enforcement, U.S. Department of Health and Human Services) (1987).

67   These issues must be addressed in the context of fundamental changes in work, welfare, and family policy, changes that are essential to any effective divorce reform strategy. See text accompanying notes 70–75 *infra*.

68   See Glendon, *supra* note 54 at 82–95; Doffell, "Child Support in Europe: A Comparative Overview," in Kamerman and Kahn, *supra* note 8; Chambers, "The Federal Government and a Program of 'Advance Maintenance' in the United States," in *id.* at 343; Garfinkel and Uhr, "A New Approach to Child Support," 75 *Pub. Interest* 111 (Spring 1984).

69   See Krause, *supra* note 49.

70   Llewellyn, "Behind the Law of Divorce: II," 33 *Col. L. Rev.* 249, 262 (1933), quoted in Kay, chap. 1, this volume.

71   See M. Freeman, *Cohabitation an Alternative to Marriage?* (1983); Blumberg, "Cohabitation without Marriage: A Different Perspective," 28 *U.C.L.A. L. Rev.* 1125 (1981); Friedman, "The Necessity for State Recognition of Same-Sex Marriage: Constitutional Requirements and Evolving Notions of Family," 3 *Berkeley Women's L.J.* 134 (1988); Note, "The Legality of Homosexual Marriage," 82 *Yale L.J.* 573 (1973). We do not mean to imply that all unmarried couples will necessarily be treated the same as married couples, but rather that the same principles should be applicable. Thus cohabitants who have engaged in substantial sharing behavior should have rights and responsibilities similar to those of spouses who have engaged in such behavior. See Rhode, *supra* note 2 at 134–41. See, generally, Breech, "Cohabitation in the Common Law Countries a Decade after *Marvin:* Settled in or Moving Ahead?" 22 *U.C. Davis L. Rev.* 717 (1989).

72   Some states have implemented such structures. See, e.g., Fla. Stat. Ann. § 61-052 (West 1985) and Cal. Civ. Code § 4512 (West 1983).

73   We do not underestimate the difficulties of preventing coercive settlements in contexts where the parties' resources are unevenly distributed. But neither do we believe that couples should be deterred from marriage by economic concerns that could be addressed through antenuptial contracts, as long as those contracts meet basic standards of fairness (e.g., full disclosure, conscionable terms, etc.). See, e.g., *In re* Marriage of Dawley, 17 C.3d 342, 349–58 (1976). See, generally, L. Weitzman, *The Marriage Contract* (1981).

74   Although rates of poverty and persistent poverty are exceptionally high among single-parent families, half of all poor children live in two-parent families. As David Ellwood notes, it would not only be "uncaring but counterproductive" to exclude these households from assistance. Ellwood, *supra* note 16 at 85. See also Arendell, *supra* note 41; Duncan, *supra* note 16; Mulroy, ed., *supra* note 33; Rogers, *supra* note 16.

75   For a representative overview of such strategies, see Ellwood, *supra* note 16; M. Glendon, *The New Family and the New Property* (1981); Rhode, *supra* note 2; Kamerman and Kahn *supra* note 8; Bane, *supra* note 52; I. Garfinkel and S. McLanahan, *Single Mothers and Their Children: A New American Dilemma* (1987).

Index